Alphabet Juice

The Energies, Gists, and Spirits of Letters, Words, and

Combinations Thereof; Their Roots, Bones, Innards, Piths,

Pips, and Secret Parts, Tinctures, Tonics, and Essences;

With Examples of Their Usage Foul and Savory

Alphabet Juice

Roy Blount Jr.

Sarah Crichton Books
Farrar, Straus and Giroux
New York

Sarah Crichton Books
Farrar, Straus and Giroux
18 West 18th Street, New York 10011

Distributed in Canada by Douglas & McIntyre Ltd.
Printed in the United States of America
First edition, 2008

Library of Congress Cataloging-in-Publication Data
Blount, Roy.
    Alphabet juice : the energies, gists, and spirits of letters, words, and combinations
    thereof : their roots, bones, innards, piths, pips, and secret parts, tinctures, tonics, and
    essences: with examples of their usage foul and savory / by Roy Blount. —1st ed.
       p.   cm.
    "Sarah Crichton Books."
    ISBN-13: 978-0-374-10369-9 (hardcover : alk. paper)
    ISBN-10: 0-374-10369-0 (hardcover : alk. paper)
    1. Vocabulary—Humor.   2. English language—Dictionaries—Humor.   I. Title.

PN6231.W64B48 2008
818'.5407—dc22

                    2008008918

Designed by Ralph Fowler / rlf design

www.fsgbooks.com

10 9 8 7 6 5 4 3

For Jon Swan, a word man

Ali G:

How many words does you know?

Noam Chomsky:

Normally, humans, by maturity, have tens of thousands of them.

Ali G:

What is some of 'em?

—Da Ali G Show

Alphabet
Juice

*A*ccording to scholars of linguistics, the relation between a word and its meaning is **arbitrary**. In proof, they point to pigs. Steven Pinker, in *Words and Rules*, observes that pigs go *oink oink* in English, *nøff nøff* in Norwegian, and in Russian *chrjo chrjo*. That may *look* arbitrary. As if it went something like this:

ENGLISH COMMITTEE MEMBER #1
What'll we put down for pig noise?

MEMBER #2
(*whose motives are unclear*)
Let's name it for my uncle Oink.

MEMBER #3
No, we need to capture more of that *grunh*, *grunh* . . .

Weary groan arises.

MEMBER #4
In Russia . . .

He or she is shouted down.

COMMITTEE CHAIRMAN
People. We have to move on.

Have you ever tried to spell any of the various sounds that pigs make? It isn't easy. It's damn well worth trying, but eventually you have to settle on something close. (Chickens being more articulate, you'll find their noises to be pretty similar the world round. Baby chicks go *peep peep* in English, *pío pío* in Spanish, *piyo piyo* in Japanese.)

And I'm not sure Pinker is playing fair with that *chrjo*. It's not Russian letters. How am I supposed to know how Russian people or pigs pronounce it? Fortunately, by Googling "Russian pigs go," I have obtained the input of an online chatperson (at ask.metafilter.com) named "MrAnonymous," who sounds like he knows what he is talking about:

> In Russian, pigs go *hroo*, *hroo*. Note that these are rolled *r*'s and the *h* is more of a *hk* sound, like when you try to build a loogie. (Don't try and pronounce the *K*, just flem up the *H*.)

That, although it should be "try *to* pronounce" and **phlegm**, is not bad. Over the years and around the world, generation building upon generation, people have put much mimetic effort into the spelling of pig utterance.

For that matter, *grunt* works for me, and I resent any insinuation that I have been programmed by random convention. Dictionaries in their grudging way call *grunt* "probably imitative." The word is a distinct refinement, or counterrefinement, of the Old English *grunettan*, and although the parallel Greek *gry*, in comparison, looks less than fully swinish, you can see the resemblance. The French for "to grunt" is *grogner*. You know what the French for the growl of a car is? *Vroum!*

That car is running on alphabet juice. So, less obviously, are *spice* and *tang* and *strength* (do you think that word fits its meaning no better than would, say, *delicacy*?) and, excuse me, *sphincter*, which shares a root, incidentally, with the Sphinx.

Marshall McLuhan, whom we celebrate for coming up with such **meme**s as "the global village" and "the medium is the message," played fast and loose with the roots of words, according to his biographer, Philip Marchand: he "pored over etymologies in the OED as if they were mystic runes," and irritated colleagues at Cambridge by making up fanciful derivations to support his theories. I prefer a firmer grip on etymology—"the wheel-ruts of modern English," as etymonline.com puts it.

So I am not going to think of the mysterious statue and say *sph-* is soft (face of a woman, and we may think of sphagnum moss), the middle part is retentive-sounding, and the *x* is for unknown. I am going to consult several reliable lexicographical sources, and report to you that the original Sphinx, the monster whose riddle Oedipus solved, was named by the

Greeks from their verb *sphingein*, to squeeze, because she strangled her victims. Pronouncing *sphincter*, or *squeeze*, constricts the throat.

Oddly enough, McLuhan did his Ph.D. dissertation on Thomas Nashe, who described a comely maid as "fat and plum every part of her as a plover, a skin as slick and soft as the back of a swan, it doth me good when I remember her. Like a birde she tript on the ground, and bare out her belly as majestical as an Estrich." (In one or two places I have slightly modernized Nashe's Elizabethan spelling, but I wouldn't touch *Estrich*. Another old version of *ostrich* was *Austridge*. The roots go back, via the Latin *avis struthio*, to the Greek *strouthokamelos*, camel-sparrow.)

I say "oddly enough" because McLuhan, according to Marchand, "was never interested in the 'music of words.'" In *Understanding Media*, McLuhan maintained that the phonetic alphabet—"in which semantically meaningless letters are used to correspond to semantically meaningless sounds"—had alienated people from the body. The ink had hardly dried on that notion when the Free Speech Movement broke out at Berkeley, and pretty soon people were running naked and letting their hair grow wild.

Maybe many of them were trying to break away from the alphabet, but I wasn't. To me, letters have always been a robust medium of sublimation. I don't remember what I was like before I learned my ABC's, but for as long as I can remember I have made them with my fingers and felt them in my bones. Where are we, at the moment? We're in the midst of a bunch of letters, and if you're like me, you feel like a pig in mud.

What a great word *mud* is. And *muddle*, and *muffle*, and *mumble* . . .

You know the expression "Mum's the word." The word *mum* is a representation of lips pressed together. Since it's not merely a sound, *mmmm*, but a word, to say it we have to move our lips. For the separator we choose that utterly unintellectual (though it's what we say when trying to think) vowel sound *uh*, which thrusts at the heart of *push* and *shove* and *grunt* and *love*.

The great majority of languages start the word for "mother" with an *m* sound. The word *mammal* comes from the *mammary* gland. Which comes from baby talk: *mama*. To sound like a grownup, we refine *mama* into *mother*; the Romans made it *mater*, from which: *matter*. And *matrix*. Our word for the kind of animal we are, and our word for the stuff that everything is made of, and our word for a big cult movie all derive from baby talk.

What are we saying when we say *mmmm*? We are saying *yummy*. In the pronunciation of which we move our lips the way nursing babies move theirs. The fact that we can *spell* something that fundamental, and connect it however tenuously to *mellifluous* and *manna* and *milk* and *me* (see **M**), strikes me as marvelous. You know the expression "a magic spell"—

Here the scholar cries, *Aha!* (See **H**.)

And the scholar has a point. I'm not here to play tricks (see **abracadabra**), but to find traction. I am saying arbitrary, schmabitrary.

Linguisticians will concede me **onomatopoeia**: *snap*, *crackle*, *pop*, and so on. But they marginalize these words by throwing up the inconstancy of pig sounds, and then they get on with their theories. Steven Pinker does allow that some people might channel their magical thinking into "sound symbolism (words such as *sneer*, *cantankerous*, and *mellifluous* that naturally call to mind the things they mean)."

As it happens, scrutiny of the term **symbolic** in that sense has led me to find a discrepancy in the greatest lexicographical work in English, the *Oxford English Dictionary*, but I won't dwell on that (see **wh-**). I will say that theorizing stands and falls on its examples. Here is Pinker:

> Sound symbolism, for its part, was no friend of the American woman in the throes of labor who overheard what struck her as the most beautiful word in the English language and named her newborn daughter *Meconium*, the medical word for fetal excrement.

This has the ring of an urban legend, a tendentious one, like Ronald Reagan's mink-coated woman stepping from a limousine to claim her welfare check. If there was a woman who gave her baby girl such a name, she had a highly idiosyncratic ear. (Of the thousand most common female names according to the 1990 census, Miriam was the only one ending in *m*, and it was 285th.) Salmonella, maybe, or Campho-Phenique, but Meconium? No. This mother—I will stop short of saying that linguisticians conjured her up, consciously or unconsciously, to reinforce their denial of so much evidence of the senses, but I will say that this mother is not, in this respect, a good example.

The Japanese, I am told, have two different words for two different kinds of imitative language: *giseigo*, mimic-voice-language, for instance *potsu-potsu*, rainfall of medium force; and *gitiago*, mimic-condition-language, for instance *pittari*, to fit exactly. Neither of those examples may seem intuitive to English speakers, but every language has its deep aesthetic network of sonic correspondences. The very consistency of English is inconsistent—don't expect *remember* to be the opposite of *dismember*, or *pitch*, because its vowel sound is like the first one in *sphincter*, to betoken a withered peach. But all language, at some level, is body language. (Or anyway, all English is body English. See the quote from Allen Tate at **spin**.) Who wants a tongue to be cut-and-dried?

It beats me why any writer would *want* to minimize the connection between high-fiber words (*squelch*, for instance, or *wobble* or *sniffle* [see **-le**], or the **flinch** and **wince** family, or the *-udge*'s, or *prestidigitation*) and the bodily maneuvers from which they emanate and those they evoke. But I don't claim to be a scientist. Science naturally abhors what it can't universalize. For many years, the dominant theory in the science of linguistics has been Noam Chomsky's, that all human language is made possible by a universal, recursive (that is to say, allowing of insertions such as this one) grammar, hardwired in our genes.

Now *hardwired*, objectively, refers to metal drawn out into threads. (*Hard* has a harder sound than *soft*, and what a fine word *wire* is: thin—wiry—and sonically drawn out, like its French counterpart, *fil*. The German *Draht* is more broadly evocative of the drawing out.) But okay, chromosomes are threads. (And what a kinesthetic word *thread* is. It's one of several palpably transmissive *thr-* words: **through**, *thorough*, *thrill*, *throat*, *throw*, *thrum*, and *throb*.) Chromosomes are not exactly laid end to end, as I understand them, but never mind, mental activity is demonstrably electric (see **electricity/chewing tobacco**). But what travels through the wires? What force through the green fuse?

Alphabet juice. The quirky but venerable squiggles which through centuries of knockabout breeding and intimate contact with the human body have absorbed the uncanny power to carry the ring of **truth**.

If you handle them right. The fact that I have made a living for forty years selling combinations of letters on the open market, in every medium, print or electronic, except greeting cards, does not entitle me to tell you how to write or talk. I do hope you realize that every time you use *disinterested* to mean *uninterested*, an angel dies, and every time you write *very unique*, or "We will hire whomever is more qualified," thousands of

literate people lose yet another little smidgen of hope. And please promise me you will never lose your grip on the subjunctive to the extent that
someone did in this sentence from *USA Today*: "If Ramirez stayed in
Cleveland, the Indians may not be seven victories shy of their first World
Series title since 1948."

"If Ramirez *had* stayed," I cry aloud. "The Indians *might* not be! Damn!
Damn! Damn!"

I hope this book will be useful to anyone who wants to write better, including me. I have written some of the clumsiest, most clogged-yet-
vagrant, hobbledehoyish, hitch-slipping sentences ever conceived by the
human mind. On the radio I can sometimes talk spontaneously to tolera-
ble effect, with the help of voice tone and adrenaline; but almost nothing that pops into my head flows when I set it down in letters. (That's
about the ninth time I have written *that* unremarkable sentence, a simple
statement of fact, and even now I'm not sure that there is anything to be
said for the kind of semi-sprung rhythm that has arisen in "head flows.")
Fortunately, I enjoy fooling with letters, moving them around, going back
over them, over and over, screaming . . . The terrible thing about writing
is also the great thing about it: you can keep on changing it. "We say that
we perfect diction," wrote Wallace Stevens. "We simply grow tired." (See
simply.) But it's a good tired. That's an interesting expression: *a good tired*.
Do we adapt any other past participle to such purpose? I'm stumped. But
it's a good stumped.

The franchise I claim is not prescriptive, but over the counter. Quality
over the counter. People who mistreat English, or who, with no doubt the
purest intentions, discount *Sprachgefühl* (see **kinesthesia**), are messing
with the *stuff* I trade in. If the ABC's lose their savor, I will be hard-
pressed to pass along, not to mention get paid for passing along, such an
intimate pleasure as I felt while listening to NPR's *Fresh Air* not long ago.
The country singer Don Walser, now deceased, was being interviewed by
Terry Gross. She asked him about his yodeling.

He said he did two different yodels, a cowboy yodel and a swish yodel.

A what? Walser was a big hearty Texan who didn't seem like the sort of
performer who would get off on mocking sissy airs. Anyway, yodeling very
nearly transcends gender. Even if you wanted to, how would you make a
yodel sound nelly?

Then I realized: *"Swiss* yodel." When the soft *s* and the *y*-as-in-*yummy* glide together they make the sound that for some reason we spell *sh*-:

> Oh how I wish you
> Would wish I would kiss you.

I would be the last person to argue that the sounds of our letters are thoroughly explicable. (Did you know that Hells Angels refer to themselves as "AJ" because it sounds so much like "HA"?) They are a wonder on the tongue. And a tongue—although Robert Benchley called it "that awful-looking thing right back of your teeth"—is what a language is.

No doubt it would be superficial to liken the universal grammar theory to a virtual program wherein all the steps of Ginger Rogers and Fred Astaire are reduced to a flow chart, with no attention to Fred's ears or the ineffable things Ginger does with her shoulders. But I get no kick from genetics. For depth I prefer digging back to eldritch-grungy roots, Proto-Indo-European (**PIE**) or Semitic: *wegh*-, to go; *reub*-, to snatch; *hsp*, to be insolent.

In this I am motivated by a distant ancestor. In 1656, Thomas Blount produced the first English dictionary to go into the origins of words: *Glossographia, or, a dictionary interpreting all such hard words, of whatsoever language, now used in our refined English tongue.* In the New York Public Library I have turned the actual uncrumbling seventeenth-century pages of the fifth edition of Blount's *Glossographia*:

> Coffa or Cauphe, a kind of drink among the Turks and Persians (and
> of late introduced among us) which is black, thick and bitter,
> destrained from berries of that nature, and name, thought good and
> very wholesom: they say it expels melancholy, purges choler . . .

Alphabet Juice is my glossographia. Juice as in *au jus*, juju, power, liquor, electricity. (Loose words and clauses left lying around are like loose live wires—they'll short-circuit, burn out, disempower your lights.) As in influence; as in squeezin's; as in, the other day I saw a woman walking down the street wearing some highly low-cut shorts. On her hourglass figure, the top of those shorts was at about, I would say (not a snap judgment), twenty minutes. Just below that part of the back where some people—she, for instance—have dimples was where her waistband cut across; and just below the waistband, in two-inch letters, was an inspired, if vulgar, brand name: *Juicy*. (See **zaftig**.)

Note: When a word or phrase appears in boldface, it is the subject of a separate alphabetical entry, which you might want to check out. (In bold-face italic, it is under consideration qua word or phrase as opposed to topic.) If you read this book the way I would read it and the way I've written it, you will wear it out, thumbing back and forth, without ever being sure you've read it all.

Abbreviations of reference books frequently cited:

AHD:	*American Heritage Dictionary of the English Language*
Chambers:	*Chambers Dictionary of Etymology*
OAD:	*New Oxford American Dictionary*
OED:	*Oxford English Dictionary*
RHU:	*Random House Webster's Unabridged Dictionary*
WIII:	*Webster's Third New International Dictionary, Unabridged*

a · A · a

Jerry Clower once said that the football coach at Mississippi State was making progress on keeping his players in school: "He's got those boys making straight A's! Some of their B's are still a little crooked, but . . ."

A stands for *answer*, *across* (in crossword puzzles), *adultery*, highest grade . . . No, I don't mean the highest grade of adultery, but I'll say this: In my experience, the highest grade of adultery in the movies—I don't recommend it elsewhere—involves Diane Lane.

In *Lane* the *a* is long, open-mouthed, with a touch of consonantal *y* at the end. Not to say there's a universal value in that sound, but in English people do like to holler *yay*, *hooray*, *hey*, *okay*, *fuckin-A*, *anchors aweigh*, *U!S!A!* (in better times), and *up*, *up and away*. In Lewis Carroll's "Jabberwocky," what did someone "chortle in his joy"? "Callooh! Callay!" Inspired nonsense gets down into a language's jelly.

Donkeys bray, hounds bay, boys stray.

On the other hand there's *oy vey*—Yiddish for "oh, woe." But the Spanish *ay-ay-ay*, expressing frustration, is pronounced more or less like i-yi-yi.

Denotative upbeat long-*a* words include *May*, *lei*, *play*, *gravy*, *pay* (assuming you're receiving), *gay*, *way* (as opposed to *no way*, and as in "Where there's a way, there's a will"), and *ray* (of hope, of light, of sun, of Charles).

There are some unjolly *ay*'s: *nay* (begins on a negative note), *stay* (as it must sound to a dog), *slay*, *flay*, *fray*, and *gray*. But whaddya say, *bébé*? And maybe the long *a*'s in *hate* and *pain*, abruptly brought down by *t* or *n*, contribute to the hurt conveyed by those words. Consider the disappointment if someone hailed you with "Hey! . . . *not*."

➤ *a*

WIII devotes forty-nine lines of tiny type to this minimal wordlet, which has two distinct pronunciations: a clipped *ay* when emphasized, as in "You have a nerve," and a brief *uh* when not, as in "Can I have a dollar?" The **PIE** root of *a* is longer than *a* itself: *oin-o* or *oinos*. From that root we also get *one*, *alone*, *any*, *inch*, and part of *eleven*, whose various constituents—how cool is this—amount to "one left over after ten."

At first English had no *a* or *an* as we know them. Their purpose was served by an early form of *one*: *an*, rhyming with *pain*. Unstressed, this became more or less our *an*. Eventually the clumsiness of *an* before a consonant ("An snake! Get an gun!") gave birth to *a*.

The most inspired use, though strictly speaking incorrect, of this *a* is in *Oliver Twist*. "The law," a solicitor informs the spouse-abused Mr. Bumble, "supposes that your wife acts under your direction."

"If the law supposes that," replies Bumble, "the law is a ass—a idiot." Not only funnier than "an ass, an idiot," but more convincing.

To learn how greatly the word *a* loomed as a factor when I wrote a story in tandem, so to speak, with a giant who claimed to have had sex with twenty thousand women, see **Wilt: A Tall Tale**.

➤ *aa*

If the lexicographers aren't pulling our leg, *aa* is a two-syllable Hawaiian word, pronounced ah-ah, for *lava* with a rough surface. As opposed to *pahoehoe*, which is lava with a smooth surface. At first glance, *aa* may look smoother than *pahoehoe*, but sound it out: there's a hiccup between the *ah*'s not unsimilar to those in Tarzan's *ah-ahhh-ahhh* yodel.

➤ *aah*

After *a* and *aa*, this is the first word in AHD and RHU. A sigh of satisfaction.

"Bit premature, isn't it?" mutters *aardvark*, sulking in the wings.

➤ *aardvark*

Obsolete Afrikaans for "earth pig." I have long thought of this as the first word in the dictionary. Now that we know it is not, let's get some sense of the animal.

Though plumpish, flat-snouted, and near-hairless, it is related to the golden mole and the elephant, not the pig. It is nocturnal and can't see well, so this, according to the African Wildlife Foundation, is how an aardvark leaves its burrow: "It comes to the entrance and stands there motionless for several minutes. Then it suddenly leaps out in powerful jumps. At about thirty feet out it stops, raises up on its legs, perks up its ears and turns its head in all directions. If there are no sounds, it makes a few more leaps and finally moves at a slow trot to look for food."

Okay! Let's get jumping.

➤ *abracadabra*

I thought I had found a flaw in AHD, where it says *abracadabra* originally "was a magic word, the letters of which were arranged in an inverted pyramid and worn as an amulet around the neck . . . One fewer letter appeared in each line of the pyramid, until only *a* remained to form the vertex of the triangle." That doesn't work, I exclaimed:

abra
cad
ab
ra

abra
cad
ab
r
a

I had leapt to a conclusion. WIII includes a visual representation of the amulet, which goes:

abracadabra
abracadabr
abracadab
abracada
abracad
abraca
abrac
abra
abr
ab
a

Am I relieved that this book didn't turn, just **now**, into a flock of pigeons.

➤ *absolutely*

Is heard more and more often in conversation as truth gets more and more relative, whether we like it or not. We need a good solid thumping way of saying yes when, as Alessandra Stanley puts it in *The New York Times*, "practically every . . . drama in prime time is a spooky mystery in which things are never as they seem and nobody can be trusted." Cf. *amen*.

➤ Addison, Joseph

Dr. Samuel Johnson wrote that Addison "never deviates from his track to snatch a grace; he seeks no ambitious ornaments, and tries no hazardous innovations." Serious prose tends to be like that today, and good for it. Good verb there, *snatch*. Grace is not to be snatched. But I miss rambunctiousness, brio. Writers today may have one eye on foreign rights, unlike Walt Whitman, who prided himself on being "untranslatable; I sound my barbaric yawp over the roofs of the world."

➤ adjective

Modifies a noun or pronoun. From the Latin meaning, literally, "to throw at." Not "to strew about." Nora Ephron on Sheilah Graham's memoir, *A State of Heat*: "She uses adjectives like raisins, sprinkling them here and there: 'I was cool but automatically charming to this fat, bewitched man.'"

➤ *admittedly*

James Beard: "I have eaten Underwood's Deviled Ham ever since I can remember. At one time I thought it was a great treat, nowadays I think it is anything but. Admittedly, it is not made with smoked ham, but with fresh ham and flavoring, and the texture is almost a puree, with a greasy consistency." Does he mean that *he* concedes it to be fresh ham with flavoring, or that Underwood does? Beginning a sentence with an adverb followed by a **comma** is a handy way to vary *rhythm*, but it often leads to ambiguity. Cf. **hopefully**. See **arguably**.

➤ adverb

Modifies a verb, an adjective, or another adverb. From the Latin meaning, roughly, "added-on word." Writing teachers will tell you: Rely on strong nouns and verbs, not layers and layers of adjectives and adverbs. This advice is so very thoroughly, almost invariably, sound, generally speaking, that to take exception to it, briefly, can't hurt.

Mark Twain wrote, "I am dead to adverbs. They cannot excite me." And yet he wrote this, too: "A powerful agent is the right word . . . Whenever we come upon one of these intensely right words in a book or newspaper the resulting effect is physical as well as spiritual, and electrically prompt."

Intensely is an adverb, and so is *electrically*. Connect the latter (which has a lickety-split sound) to an intensely right (and sudden-sounding) adjective—*electrically prompt*—and you have captured something that's still wiggling. If on the other hand you cook up something that promptly congeals into last week's lasagna, don't try to perk it up with adverbs. Go for a metaphor, such as *last week's lasagna*. Or better, leave it at *congeals*. *Always* eschew that stock-humorous *promptly*, as in "He strode into the drawing room and promptly lost his breakfast."

William Faulkner: "The aim of every artist is to arrest motion, which is life, by artificial means and hold it fixed so that a hundred years later, when a stranger looks at it, it moves again since it is life." Only two adverbs in that—*later* and *again*—and they are structural.

See **very**.

➤ adverbial or adjectival drift

What is adverbial drift? Gary Herwitz, an accountant convicted of insider trading, told the Brooklyn federal court judge Nicholas Garaufis on June 8, 2006, according to the *New York Post*: "I stand before you today because I unequivocally made the biggest mistake of my life."

What he meant was, "I tell you unequivocally that I stand before you today because I made the biggest mistake of my life." His *unequivocally* had got loose and attached itself to "made the biggest mistake." Unless he meant to say that he made the mistake wholeheartedly and without quibbling, which seems unlikely.

What is adjectival drift? The same accountant's lawyer was quoted as saying, "The reason Gary Herwitz broke the law is simply inexplicable."

His *reason* was inexplicable? Perhaps what he *did* was beyond explanation, although judging from the news story, there were grounds to assume (since we don't know him personally) that what he did, his lawbreaking, was prima facie explicable: if he'd gotten away with it, he would have made $20,000 in a few days.

Perhaps the judge would have made this point, if the lawyer had expressed herself more clearly. At any rate she, the lawyer, can't mean that Herwitz's *reason* for doing what he did was inexplicable, because she professedly can't imagine what the reason was. Her adjective, *inexplicable*, has lost its mooring and snagged itself on *reason*.

See **sexism and pronouns**.

➤ *advice*

A root of the *vice* part, according to AHD, is the Latin *visum*, what seems (good). Note, *seems*. The essential advice is "If I were you, I'd listen to me."

Any given generation gives the next generation advice that the given generation should have been given by the previous generation but now it's too late.

However, I do have this bit of advice for young writers. As Wynonie Harris sang, "Keep on churning till the butter comes." See **sentence fragment**.

➤ *agenda*

Why is this a pejorative term? What's wrong with having an agenda? I wish to hell I had more of one. (Is that good English? "More of one"? I think it is, but it doesn't look printworthy.) Politicians play on the word's sounding sort of dirty, like . . . *pudenda*?

It comes from the Latin plural for "things to be done," but in English it's singular.

➤ *aight*

This lackadaisical morpheme, a staple of webchat, is an inspired folk spelling of a popular oral contraction (influenced, no doubt, by what used to be called ebonics) of *all right*, gutted of its *l*'s and *r*'s. A more writerly version, *a'ight*, would show where letters are missing, evoke the faint inter-**vowel** jump between *ah* and *ite*, and avoid the appearance of rhyming with *straight*. But that would be too fussy for electronic communication, particularly among the young, and in this case less meticulous is more poetic.

If *all right* were one word (if *alright* weren't wrong), *aight* would be called a *syncope*: a word with sounds omitted from the middle, as in **probably** pronounced to rhyme with *wobbly*, or *forecastle* contracted to *fo'c's'le*, which is the only three-apostrophe word I can think of.

> You fo'c's'le folks'll be happy to know
> The cook is now forty-six fathoms below.
> That ratatouille (p'tooey!) of his'll be
> Something something something visibly.

The word *syncope*—three syllables, accent on the first—is from the Greek for "together" and "cut." "How do you think this will cut together?" people say about film footage. In medicine the word retains its original meaning: a swoon, which is caused by a brief cutback in blood pressure.

Swoon, from the Anglo-Saxon, is more expressive than *syncope*, but there's something catchy about *syncopation*, which, in dance music or verse, puts the stress on normally unaccented beats. (But don't pronounce it sin-*co*-pa-shun.) You might say that *syncopatin'* (as when Bessie Smith in "Cakewalkin' Babies" sings, "Here they come, look at 'em demonstratin', / Goin' strong, ain't they syncopatin'") is inherently syncopated in that the stress falls on the one and the three rather than the two or the four, but that **of course** depends on context. The word could be tucked away in stodgy iambic regularity:

"If no one's *regu*latin'—well, we cannot all be syncopatin' all the time."

Not so stodgy at that. On the page, there's no accompanist laying down a regular beat for us—writer and reader—to skate back and forth across, but there are implicit rhythms and infinite variations thereupon.

The *syn*-central word *idiosyncrasy*, meaning a behavioral **quirk** characteristic of a particular person, is also from the Greek: *idio* for "individual," *syn* for "together," and *crasy* for "mix." Sounds like a party.

➤ *ain't*

Too bad this tangy, useful verb, which was standard in the eighteenth century, has been so stigmatized since the nineteenth.

Just as **y'all**, as a plural of *you*, fills a gap in English, so does *ain't* as a contraction of *am not*. Anyone attempting to pronounce *amn't* may attract a crowd of well-wishers admiring his or her pluck, but whatever other words the speaker surrounds it with will be lost. And compare:

(*a*) "I'm not going."
(*b*) "I ain't going."

Which one of the two do you think is a lot more likely to be going?

Now you may protest that *ain't* is promiscuous, that it's also used to mean (*a*) *aren't*, (*b*) *isn't*, (*c*) *hasn't*, and (*d*) *haven't*.

(a) "We ain't going."

(b) "He ain't going."

(c) "He ain't got any intention of going."

(d) "You ain't got any shot at going."

I don't think any of them are going.

And where would American song lyrics be without *ain't*?

"I Haven't Got Nobody"

"There is no cure for the summertime blues."

"It Isn't Me, Babe"

"Isn't She Sweet?"

"I might not know what love is, / But I know what it isn't."

"Two Out of Three Isn't Bad"

"It Isn't Necessarily So"

"Amn't Misbehavin'"

➤ *algorithm*

Which ninth-century person would be proudest if he or she could come back today? My candidate is the Arab mathematician Muhammad ibn Musa. From his cognomen, al-Kwārizmī, the man of Kwarizm (now Khiva), we derive (via Latin and Old French) the word *algorithm*, a mathematical formula used in computer calculations, most notably in search engines. Algorithms are **Google**'s bread and butter.

The Arabic or decimal system of numbers, which the world uses today, used to be called *algorism*, also after al-Kwārizmī. And *algebra* comes from his book on the subject, *Kitab al-Jabr wal-Mugabala*, which Chambers translates as "Rules of Reintegration and Reduction." (The *al-Jabr* part means literally "the bone-setting.")

➤ *algolagnia/algology*

Don't confuse 'em. The first is sadomasochism, the second, the study of algae. See **names, famous, whose correct pronunciation** . . .

➤ *alphabet*

Nice that *alpha* and *beta* work so well together. Is it accidental that they run one and two? They're pleasing to the lips and tongue, as are *aleph beth*, *Ali Baba*, *Alabama*, and *alabaster cities gleam*.

What if the first two Greek letters were, say, *mu* and *omega*? Now, class, let's recite the muomeg. You will be seated according to muomegical order.

And what if our name for the rack of English letters came from the first two of them? Now, class, let's recite the abie. Not so bad, at that. But the Old English word for the alphabet was *abecede*. The Middle English was *abece* or *abse*. As late as the seventeenth century, *alphabet*-resisters were trying to establish the term *Christ's crossrow*.

Here's to that which pleaseth lips and tongue.

➤ *although*

From the bio bit on IMDb.com about Jeffrey Wright: "Although he alters aspects of his physical appearance for each role, his voice is often unrecognizable from one role to the next." If *although* means "regardless of the fact that; even though," that just doesn't parse. We've got to rehabilitate *although*—it tends to get tossed in for **rhythm** regardless of meaning. See **conjunction dysfunction**.

➤ *amazing*

I am locked in a desperate struggle with myself to quit using this word as the highest possible all-purpose accolade.

"How was the beheading?"

"It was incredible, unbelievable, amazing."

Can't anybody say "wonderful" or "splendid" or even "far-out" anymore?

My friend Ann Lewis heard someone say, "I was amazed—and rightfully amazed."

One thing *amazed* has going for it is that hey-hey long **A**.

See **awesome**; **incredible**.

➤ *amen*

Here are a couple of strange rootfellows. Both *amen* and *Mammon* come from the Semitic root *'mn*, to be firm, confirmed, reliable, faithful, keep faith, believe.

A friend of mine says she was present when the ending of a family prayer, "Amen," was topped by the family's six-year-old: "Ah'm out."

See **word**.

➤ *American*

Canadians and Latin Americans resent that people of the United States of America presume to go by the name of, simply, Americans. But what are we going to do, call ourselves Statesians? Youessers?

The War for Statesian Independence?

The Youessian Civil Liberties Union?

When the nation was founded, there was considerable discussion of this issue. One proposal was that the nation be called Fredonia, and its citizens, Fredes.

In *Duck Soup*, the Marx Brothers' best movie, they take helter-skelter control of a country called Freedonia, two *e*'s. They lead it, "with a hey-nonny-nonny and a ha-cha-cha," to war. The opposing country's leader calls for peace, but Groucho says, "It's too late. I've already paid a month's rent on the battlefield." What if George W. Bush had been that straight with us in 2003?

➤ anglicization

Sleepy LaBeef, the rockabilly singer ("It Ain't What You Eat It's the Way How You Chew It"), told me once that his hometown, Smackover, Arkansas, is an anglicization of the French *sumac couvert*, covered with sumac. Is that not cool?

➤ *anxious*

Try not to say "I'm anxious to see you" if you mean "I'm eager to see you." *Anxious* properly means uneasy and apprehensive about something coming up. Like the German *Angst*, it comes from the Latin for "to choke." And sounds like it: try saying *nxsh* expansively.

On the other hand, the sound of *eager*, with its long *e* (as in *keen*) and hard *g* (as in *snag*), evokes desirous impatience, like a dog straining at a leash. The original meaning of *eager*, "tart or cutting," is obsolete—because, I would suggest, the sound didn't fit that sense. *Eager* shares a **PIE** root, *ak-*, with other words whose meanings entail sharpness (*acrid*, *acute*), but it lacks the sharp sound made by the flat *a* and hard *c*.

➤ apostrophe

We rightly shudder at promiscuous or misplaced apostrophization, for instance when a family named Bennett puts up a sign in front of their house that says *The Bennett's*, thereby suggesting that there is only one, self-aggrandizing Bennett. (*The Bennetts* or *The Bennetts'* would do.) But sometimes we hear that apostrophes should *never* be used in a plural. For instance in *The Alphabet Abcedarium*, by Richard A. Firmage: "For clarity I have occasionally inserted the mark (usually with vowels, *e.g.*, *O*'s) although my preference is to be technically correct and omit them." Hey, Richard, don't apologize. It's helpful to use an apostrophe in the plural of a letter or numeral: *T*'s, *w*'s, 9's. What is the reader to make of *T*s and *w*s or even 9s? That last looks like nine shillings, or a typo. If you were to write, "There are four *i*s in Mississippi," or for that matter, "four *s*s in Mississippi"—you see what I mean. "Four *i*'s and four *s*'s" is the only way to go.

➤ apothegm (or *apophthegm*)

Perhaps because words that come down to English from ancient Greece were transmitted by scholarly scribes rather than via oral, vernacular tradition, some of them sound highly unlike what they mean. This is a phonetically counterintuitive word for "a terse aphorism." But it comes from *apophthegma*, from *apophthengesthai*, to speak plainly. There would be only one way to pronounce such a word: carefully.

➤ *appreciate*

Means both to acknowledge the value of something, and for that value to go up. A judiciously, ungushily gracious word. Fan to Willie Nelson: "I bet you don't remember me." Willie's reply: "No, but I sure do appreciate you remembering me."

➤ *arbitrary*

Linguisticians assert that words are arbitrary symbols for the meanings they represent. Perhaps this enables language scientists (tongue depressors, I would call them, if I weren't above such a cheap shot) to reduce all words to phonemes and morphemes and so on, which I suppose is useful in the way (but surely not to the extent) that reducing people to various kinds of tissue is. But as a principle of English-language appreciation, at least, separation of sound from sense is audibly, utterly wrong.

Let's riffle through the dictionary: *shrivel, shove, scribble, scrawl, screwdriver, skimpy, silly, feeble, scoop, scramble, amble, scour, scraggly, rugged, stub, chewy, chunk, chock, contact, doughy, doughty, haughty, up, down, dour, frown, smile, arabesque, arc, imp, scoff, sarcastic, scold, sclerosis, schuss, through, thorough, touch, trench, gong, twist, grim, fierce, truculent, obelisk, obfuscate, queasy, magnet, flicker, flight, fling, flock, flinch, flex, flirtatious, fit, fixed, fizzle, dead, alive, deal, compulsive, chatter, chaste, button, frowzy, froth, moan, mope, mellow, neat, nebbish, needle, oleaginous, ululate, scrounge, prestidigitation*—if linguisticians can't hear any correspondence between sound and sense in those words, they aren't listening. Even when words aren't coined with sound and sense conjunctively in mind, the words that sound most like what they mean have a survival advantage. Obviously this is not true of all words, particularly ones that have been made up by scholars and technocrats, but could you switch *sniff* for *scratch* and *whiff* for *itch*? *Strict* might as well mean the same as *loose*? Are there not sonic as well as geographical grounds for calling a teeny beach outfit a *bikini* instead of a *smock*?

The meanings of words change to fit their sounds and other associations—word and meaning grow together after long association, each
changing a bit to fit the other, like people and their dogs, or married cou-
ples. For instance, *eager* (see **anxious**) and **demean**, which comes from the
same background as *demeanor*, and which purists insist should mean "to
conduct (oneself)," as in "Little Lucy demeaned herself quite well during
naptime." But that just doesn't sound right. Perhaps if the past tense of
demean had become *demeant*, as in *meant well* . . . But no, the tang of
mean meaning malicious or ignoble is unsuppressible in that context. So
demeaning has become more or less synonymous with *debasing* or *humbling*, as in "Little Lucy finds the whole concept of compulsory naptime
demeaning."

As proof that words are arbitrary, linguisticians cite *dog*, which refers
to roughly the same animal as *chien* or *Hund* or *perro*. But dogs are
the same only roughly. Doesn't *dog* sound like what the English expect
from a dog? Doesn't *chien* sound like one of those little French dogs,
Hund a heavier or anyway more strenuous German one, *perro* a bouncy
Spanish with growly r's? Scandinavian and Dutch dogs are *hunds* and
honds. You wouldn't call a chihuahua a *hund*. The Italian for dog is
cane, from the Latin. English puts a howl in *hund* by rounding it out to
hound.

How about something more uniform than a dog: a *dot*. In Swedish,
Danish, Norwegian, Dutch, German, Hungarian, Italian, Portuguese, and
Spanish, it's either *Punkt*, *punt*, *pont*, *punto*, or *ponto*, all close cousins of
the English *point*. (In Dutch a dot may also be a *stip* or a *spikkel*, which look
familiar, or an *oog*, which also means *eye*.) In Japanese it's *itten* or *dotto*. In
Russian, *tochka*. In Finnish, *piste*. Call me crazy, but I sense closely related
responses to "What shall we call this little thing?"

What does linguistics mean by *arbitrary*? Etymonline.com, a website
that does not choose words carelessly, uses *arbitrary* (I am tempted to say
"arbitrarily") in reference to words improvised from other-than-ancient
roots. Etymonline calls *flabbergast* "likely an arbitrary formation from
flabby or *flapper* and *aghast*" (quite likely indeed, I'd say, but arbitrary?)
and *rumbustious* "an arbitrary formation perhaps suggested by *rum* and
boisterous, *robustious*, *bumptious*, etc.," and says *sylph* "seems to be an arbitrary coinage, but perhaps it holds a suggestion of Latin *sylva* and Greek

nymph." Perhaps? Perhaps? *Perhaps* is a hybrid of the Latin for "for" and
the Old Norse meaning literally "by chance," but it doesn't suggest a roll
of the dice; it suggests grounds for belief.

Kleenex, says Etymonline, is "an arbitrary alteration of *clean* and
brand-name suffix *-ex.*" Well, sir. According to the Kleenex website, the
paper manufacturer Kimberly-Clark, after World War I, had a surplus of
"creped wadding," which it had been trying to develop into a gas-mask
filter. The wadding became the company's "first consumer product, Kotex.
At this time, marketing a product for the menstrual cycle proved rather
difficult." So someone came up with the idea of ironing the wadding down
flat to create "a disposable cleansing tissue . . . The tissues could be a
clean, convenient replacement for the unsightly 'cold cream towel' that
hung in many bathrooms . . . It is likely . . . the capital *K* and the *-ex* ending were adopted from *Kotex.*"

The Kotex website doesn't tell us where that word comes from, but we
may speculate. It rhymes (except for emphasis on the first syllable) with
protects. Why not Coatex? That might have evoked *coati,* an omnivorous
mammal related to the raccoon. But why *-ex*? Dictionaries define the prefix *ex-,* but not the suffix. A relatively early English *-ex* word was *latex,* not
branded as arbitrary by Etymonline because it goes back to 1662 in
English (meaning "body fluid"), and derives from Latin *latex* (liquid or
fluid), which in turn probably (but counterintuitively) comes from Greek
latax (dregs).

"Brand-name suffix" indeed: Windex, spandex, Sominex, NASONEX,
Purex, FedEx, cineplex, and, for that matter, Brand X.

Why so popular? Maybe a hint of mystery (the X-Files), and of *techni-
cal,* but there's something catchy about the sound *cks: folks, thanks, kicks,*
the famous *Variety* headline "Hicks Nix Sticks Flix," "How's tricks?" And
Jax, Ex Lax, Pentax, Filofax, Ajax, Cinemax, Betamax, Stax, borax, Fox,
Xerox, Botox, Clorox, Maalox, Red Sox, Jack in the Box, Trix, Weetabix,
Netflix, Publix, Lux, Electrolux.

Compare *sex.* And *text.* And, maybe, **kiss**.

Let's consider the word *arbitrary* itself. Linguistic doctrine uses it to
dismiss any organic or inherent connection between word and meaning
(generally speaking, allowing for obvious **onomatopoeia** such as in *whisper*
or *bang*). AHD gives us four definitions of *arbitrary*:

1. "Determined by chance, whim, or impulse, and not by necessity, reason, or principle." Does that fit any human production that survives for very long? We might say it was pure chance that inspired Lewis Carroll to write, "'Twas brillig, and the slithy toves . . . ," but it wasn't by chance that he let it stand. We might say it was impulse that inspired someone millennia ago to start a race with "Get ready . . . Get set . . . Go!" But it still works. If his or her impulse had been to say "Get ready . . . Get go . . . Set!" or "Get ready . . . Get set . . . Agglutination!" it would not have caught on. And what about *whim*! Is *whim* not a crackerjack word? Does *crackerjack* not satisfy the principle that the best words of commendation are words that are essentially pleasing to pronounce and to hear?

2. "Based on or subject to individual judgment or preference." It is my individual judgment that *judgment* ought to have an *e* between the *g* and the *m*, and in fact the entire United Kingdom agrees with me, but does that mean I could get away with it in a **spelling bee**?

3. "Established by a court or judge rather than by a specific law or statute." By an arbiter, in other words. *Arbitrary* comes from the Latin *arbiter*, one who goes somewhere (to settle a dispute), from *ad*, to, and *baetere*, to come or go. So *arbiter* was originally as elementally composed as *gofer* or *go-to guy* or *getaway driver* or a *goaway* bird (in Kenya: its cry is *Gawn, gawn!*) or a *wait-a-bit tree* (also in Kenya: it grabs ahold of you with tiny tenacious prickles). Is an arbiter arbitrary in the sense of impulsive or whimsical? Not one who deserves the title. We may think of Solomon, or of Petronius Arbiter, author of the *Satyricon*, of whom Tacitus wrote:

> His days were passed in sleep, his nights in social engagements and the pleasures of life. The fame which other men attain by diligence he won by indolence, and he was not considered a debauchee and a profligate, like others who exhaust their substance, but a man of refined luxury. His sayings and his acts, in proportion as they were free and ostentatious of recklessness, were so much the more gladly taken as a type of

simplicity. Yet as pro-consul of Bithynia and presently as consul, he showed himself as a vigorous and capable man of affairs. Then declining again upon vice, or aping vice, he was admitted by Nero among the select few of his friends—the arbiter of elegance, those things only appealing to the jaded emperor's eyes and other senses which the approval of Petronius commended to him.

Baseball umpires are sometimes called arbiters (largely for purposes of **elegant variation**), and it is true that the grand old umpire Bill Klem once said, of a ball or strike, "It isn't anything until I call it." But nobody ever called him random.

4. "Not limited by law; despotic." See **Tupou IV, King Taufa'ahau**. Not to say that language is never arbitrary.

➤ *arguably*

Margalit Fox, in the May 22, 2005, *New York Times*, missed a chance to clarify the vexed usage of this word—further muddling it, instead—when she wrote: "Eddie Barclay, who for three decades after World War II was arguably the most powerful music mogul in Europe and inarguably the most flamboyant, died on May 13 in Paris." What *Eddie was arguably the most powerful* means, and presumably is meant to mean here, is "a case [that is, an argument] can be made that Eddie was the most powerful." You can argue for a notion or against it, but if *demonstrably* means you can demonstrate that a notion is true, and *conceivably* that you can conceive it to be, then *arguably* means you can argue that it's true. Fine, so far. However, therefore, *inarguably the most flamboyant* must mean "no case can be made that Eddie was the most flamboyant," when the writer clearly wants to say, "no case can be made that he wasn't." Clarity would have been served nicely by "arguably the most powerful music mogul in Europe and *indisputably* the most flamboyant." *Dispute* means only to argue against.

➤ *artisanal*

Dictionaries want you to pronounce it *ar*-tis-in-al, instead of ar-*tis*-in-al. Give me a break. I applaud the artisanal production and marketing of, say, mesclun, and no doubt I would be a more holistic person if I bound my own books and sold them at the farmers' market. But I don't care how devoted to their craft the artisans of, say, sausage are, if they expect me to start holding my breath over three trailing syllables, they should not hold their breath.

Try singing this:

Shop ar-*tis*-in-al and you'll be glad!

Now try singing this:

Shop *ar*-tis-in-al and blehhh . . .

Ask me to accept *ar*-tis-in-al and I'm tempted to take in vain the name of the Egyptian patron deity of artisans (you could look it up): *Pteh*.

See **lamentable**; **Utopian**.

➤ arts, the

"Maybe it's true that artists adopt a flamboyant appearance," said Quentin Crisp, who did: vivid scarves, violet eye shadow, upswept hair under a black fedora. "But it's also true that people who look funny get stuck with the arts." (See **common** and **funny looks**.)

So let's not be over-reverent about art, but let's not sell it short, either.

"In a picture I want to say something comforting, as music is comforting. I want to paint men and women with that something of the eternal which the halo used to symbolize; and which we seek to convey by the actual radiance and vibration of our coloring." —Vincent van Gogh

➤ A's

The baseball team of Oakland, California. Formerly the Athletics, formerly of Kansas City and before that, Philadelphia. Baltimore's nine (see **elegant variation**) may be referred to as the O's for short, but they're still the Orioles. The A's are just the A's. I alphabetize them here, collectively, because I don't believe I have ever heard anyone referred to in the singular as an A. And what is the team's possessive? The A's', I suppose. Not pretty. People should consider what the possessive will be before they give something a name. As I write this, the Arkansas legislature is still arguing about what the possessive of Arkansas should be, Arkansas' or Arkansas's. Neither is pretty.

➤ as

Issues as to the correctness of *as*, such as *as* as opposed to *like* and *not so . . . as* as opposed to *not as . . . as*, have been thrashed out over the years. If anyone gets apoplectic anymore over the old slogan "Winston tastes good like a cigarette should," it's to do with cancer, not grammar. "Not so deep as a well" does please the tongue more than "not as deep as a well," but the latter is acceptable.

That little word *as*, however, can still get a writer in trouble—as, for instance, in the first sentence of the paragraph above. Too many *as*'s. Change it to "The issues of *as* versus *like* and *not so . . . as* versus *not as . . . as* have been thrashed out over the years." No one would be so clumsily lavish with *as* as I was on purpose above, but consider the following thought-provoking passage, regarding Tennessee Williams, by the excellent writer Daniel Mendelsohn in the scrupulously edited *New York Review of Books*:

> His dramatic preoccupation with suffering, with madness and
> desperation, can strike us, in the Prozac era, as excessive; even
> more, his vision of the feminine as pathetic—which is to say, as liable
> to pathos, as vulnerable, pitiable, as well as hopelessly striving—is
> likely to strike us, in the post-feminist era, as dated and perhaps
> embarrassing.

In the space of ten words, four *as*'s, one of which seems to shimmy back and forth, connectionwise, between *his vision* and *well as*. Why not go for the unchallenged record: "as liable to pathos, as vulnerable, as pitiable, as well as as hopelessly striving . . . ," or, better, "as well as as as hopefully striving as a kitten in a tree."

➤ *avant la lettre*

This is a cool expression that I have never quite had the nerve to use. Not because of anti-French sentiment, but because it never seems to look quite natural when I try it on. I decline, with regret, to wear a cowboy hat for the same reason.

But maybe you can make it—the expression—work for you. It means "before there was a name for [some quality or category]." As in, "My great-uncle Llewellyn was a flower child *avant la lettre*." "Robert E. Lee was passive-aggressive *avant la lettre*." Or, to be **really** literal, "Snakes were making the *s* sound *avant la lettre*."

➤ *average*

I am surprised to learn that this middling word, according to AHD, comes to us from the Middle English *averay*, charge above the cost of freight, from the Old French *averie*, from the Old Italian *averia*, duty, from the Arabic ʿ*awariya*, damaged goods, from *awar*, blemish. The Semitic root, even more surprisingly, is said to be ʿ*wr*, to be(come) blind.

> "As an average man," said Mr. Harcourt, "I found the whole thing quite above my head. I have no doubt that people do carry hobbies, such as badgers, to an extreme, but I'm not sure I want to *hear* about such people. Still, an average man is always proud to think that he has sat patiently through a lecture of which he has hardly understood a word."
>
> —*Cards of Identity*, Nigel Dennis

➤ *avocado*

For some time I labored under the delusion that this was Spanish for "lawyer." Made sense, being so close to *advocate*. But I wondered, often aloud and in company: What is it about the nice soft yellow-green chunks in my salad that suggests an attorney?

Then someone took me aside and informed me that the Spanish for "lawyer" is *abogado*.

Okay, okay, but hold on.

The first known word for the fruit was *ahuacatl*, which in the Aztec language, Nahuatl, also means "testicle." I suppose an avocado is shaped sort of like a testicle. (WIII says the Aztecs used the avocado as an aphrodisiac. I don't know.) The Spanish rendered *ahuacatl* as *aguacate*. It's from that *huac/guac* that we get *guacamole*.

So what about the legal aspect? According to AHD, some Spanish speakers rejected *aguacate* in favor of the familiar *avocado*, which was indeed at that time Spanish for "lawyer." Why was it changed to *abogado*? Maybe because lawyers didn't want to be associated with those nice soft chunks.

If Spaniards couldn't be bothered to pronounce *ahuacatl*, you know English speakers couldn't—they picked up the lawyer-resembling version. So did the French: *avocat du diable* means "devil's advocate," but it could also mean "devil's avocado." And I'll bet a lot of Francophones have wondered, down through the years, what those *morceaux verts*, *gentils et mous* have to do with *les hommes de loi*.

Another French word for the fruit is *poire d'alligator*. In English, by roughly the same token, the fruit is sometimes called "alligator pear." AHD says this derives from the notion that avocado trees grow in places infested by alligators. Doesn't it seem more likely that the leathery green rind of the avocado fruit makes it look like a pear—or, all right, a testicle— in alligator clothing?

I don't suppose I have to tell you that *alligator* comes from the Spanish *el lagarto*, the lizard. In English it was *alligarta* or *alligarto*—ending in a vowel—until the First Folio version of *Romeo and Juliet*, where it swims into our ken spelled *Alligater*. (Romeo tells Juliet he knows where he can get some poison: from an apothecary whose shop is decorated with a stuffed alligator "and other skins of ill-shaped fishes.") This was like *potato* becoming *tater*; *hollow*, *holler*; and *fellow*, *feller*. But I guess it looked literary, at least once -*er* became -*or*, because even the French picked it up.

However (according to *Harrap's Slang Dictionary, English-French/French-English*), the French do not toss around "See you later, alligator" in literal translation. It's "*À tout à l'heure, voltigeur*." (As of 1984.) A *voltigeur* is an acrobat.

➢ *awesome*

This word has been used so loosely (and increasingly pronounced to **rhyme** with ***possum***, hence with even more awe leached from it), that even *totally awesome* has about the same force as *cool*.

In an age of postmodern detachment and therapy-happy ameliorism, nothing evokes old-school awe, which AHD defines as "a mixed emotion of reverence, respect, dread, and wonder inspired by authority, genius, great beauty, sublimity, or might." Maybe something cozier:

> "I hold you in awe."
> "Awww."

Someone on **Urbandictionary.com** reports that *awesome* has been trimmed to *awes*, "cos shortening words is totally coo." Oh, plea.

See *incredible*; *amazing*.

b · **B** · b

B sort of looks like two lips pressed together, waiting for a vowel to give them voice, and that is bilabial *b* all over. It's basic, *b* is. We make *boo-boo* sounds to babies. A hurt or a mistake is a *boo-boo*. *Bubuleh, baby, bimbo, bum, banana, burp, basic, bah, bug, Bobo, bone, bingo, bye-bye, baa baa* (actually more like *mehhh) black sheep, Babar, boy, bubble, Betty Boop. Boobs, bosom. Bobble. Thingamabob. Beavis and Butthead.*

It can be *brutal: bonk, boff, break, bang, biff, batter, bong. Blitz.*

At any rate, *brusque: Bah! Boo! Bummer! Back off!*

➢ *babble/babel*

It's hard to believe that these two words, whose meanings are so close, have no etymological connection. But they don't, say the scholars: *babble* is from baby talk and *babel* from the Bible. I don't know. Spooky. *Babble* is the precursor to speech, *babel* the collapse of it. Full circle.

The Phoenician alphabet, by the way, was the first phonetic one. No connection there either. WIII connects *phonetic* to *ban* and *Phoenician* to the Greek *phoinos*, bloodred, and *phonos*, murder.

Sometimes, late at night, I suspect that someone once discovered that *babble* and *babel* sprouted from one bud, and *Phoenician* and *phonetic* from another; and he or she had to be killed.

➢ baseballese

Players' language—"sitting dead on cheese," for instance—can be gnomically economical. Bill Murray, who played minor-league ball and is a part-owner of minor-league teams, is adept at picking this up. He sees a batter fail to swing at a pitch right down the middle and says, "*I take that yard*," which means "Even I could have hit that one out of the park." Or maybe it's a form of **subjunctive**: "Even if I were the batter . . ."

Players' language can be disarmingly pithy. Willie Mays in his last season: "It's good to have people love you all over the world, but it boils down to 'Can you play?'"

That same year Mays was asked by a fifth-grade student, "When did you first know you were good?" He answered, "Every time the ball went up in the air, I felt I could catch it."

Ernie Banks: "Baseball is a game of relaxed skills, but you have to have a certain amount of hate to do well."

The language of old-school baseball *writing* is more expansive. In a piece for *The Atlantic*, "Diamond Nuggets," I undertook to roll a lot of this language into a ball and take it yard. Here is one nugget:

> Looks like, barring tragic injury, The Force will be with us for a while. Eyeing the arc of Rollie Wilt's 3—0 cripple picked on by slugging phenom Wilton "The Force" Coursey, a press-box wag shook his head over the mammoth smash and wondered aloud, "Ruth? Aaron?"
>
> Came back the quip, "People to compare him to, or books in the Bible?"
>
> To which was rejoined, "Aaron's not a book, he's Moses' brother."
>
> "We will be too, by the time that clout comes down," was the re-rejoinder. Speaking of biblical Aaron, he turned rod into serpent and caused it to bud, blossom, and bear almonds—everything but make contact with horsehide. That's about what Tintin Coates did to Dodger lumber in a 2—0 whitewash Wednesday. "He threw us more knucklers than we could shake a stick at," sighed L.A.'s Bobby "Chef" Boyardy. But they tried.

See **interviewese; sayings from sports**.

➤ *beg the question*

What a great shame that the original meaning of this expression is pretty much lost. In argument people so often do "assume as proven what is to be proven," as in "Have you stopped beating your wife?" But today *begs the question* is most often used to mean "unavoidably raises the question." The phrase no longer skewers a fallacy. So what are you going to say when someone asks you whether you've stopped beating your wife? "You're assuming as proven what is to be proven," I guess. This way of putting it— aside from its allowing the inference that someone might very well prove that you did formerly, at least, beat your wife—lacks *begging the question*'s bite. It was so gratifying, back in the day, to call someone a beggar over a flaw in logic.

These days—say you're on one of those TV shows where people shout at each other over current issues. If you accuse your opponent of begging the question—in the venerable sense, which held up for centuries—most of your audience and quite likely your opponent will think you're giving him credit for forcefully bringing something up. If you use the term in its more recent sense, some of your audience (let us hope) will think you are an ignoramus. So don't use it. Just discard that arrow from your quiver. Once the classic meaning of a phrase begins losing ground to a less useful but more apparent one, it's time to tell it goodbye. (Another example may be *busybody*, which for centuries meant someone with his or her nose in other people's business, but which I frequently hear being used by young people to mean someone who keeps very busy, physically. Also *bushwhack*, which used to mean ambush—to attack from the bush—but now generally means to make one's way forcefully through brush, off-trail.)

Begged questions (in the venerable sense) may be effective, because they have a near-epigrammatic (perhaps Berraistic) snap: "You can't believe anything politicians say, because they lack credibility." Compare that to an actual epigram: "Politicians are pragmatic people. If telling the truth worked, they'd have tried it by now." That isn't circular, but it is bent. Except perhaps in mathematics, there is no such thing as entirely straightforward, assumption-free reasoning. Language is always to some extent tendentious. This is what we have to work with. Think of words in terms of foodstuffs: whatever we cook up won't be composed of pure nutrients; it will derive from odd life-forms that breathe underwater or grow in the ground. But we can use fresh, organic ingredients, we can wash contaminants off them, and we can avoid globbing them up with heavy batter and frying them in oils that clog our arteries. Actually it's a lot harder to do that with words than with trout or carrots, but it's the goal for an honest writer to aspire to.

➤ *belly*

I am pleased to report that my grandchildren are growing up using this word instead of *stomach* or its twee baby-talk variant, *tummy*. *Stomach*, with its initial hiss and terminal *k* sound, is from the Greek and works well in *stomach pump* and as a synonym for *appetite* in a negative context: "He has no stomach for navel piercing." *Belly*, with its boomy *b* and flowing *l*, is from the Old English *belg*, bag, and before that the **PIE** root *bhelgh-*, to swell, which has also generated *bellow*, *billow*, *bolster*, *bulge*, and *budget* and is an extension of *bhel-²*, whence *bloom*, *bowl*, somehow *flower*, and perhaps *blood*. *Bellyache* sounds heartier, more bearable, than *stomachache*, and in its verb form *bellyache* is a resounding if pejorative synonym for the milder Latinate *complain*. (Another Old English synonym is *gripe*, which is sharper.) You would not want to substitute *stomach* for *belly* in oomphy words like *belly dance*, *belly flop*, *bellyful*, *belly laugh*, and *belly up*.

Nor would you want to say *gut dance*, but the deeper, brusquer sound of *gut* (from Old English) works well in *gut check* and *gut feeling*. I am also glad when doctors use the viscerally pronounced *gut* instead of the more abstract *abdomen*, from Latin.

See **body**.

➤ Berraisms

For a network TV special that was to come out during the World Series of 2001, I was asked in August of that year to compare the malapropisms of Yogi Berra with those of George W. Bush. The events of September 11 put the **kibosh** on that little feature, but I recall making the point that while neither man was one you would expect to be the leader of the Free World, the quotations of Yogi were charming in a Zen sort of way, as when he said, while watching an old Steve McQueen movie on television, "He must have made that before he died," or when, after buying an enormous Tudor house for his family, he said proudly, "It's nothing but rooms!" When asked what he would do if he found a million dollars, he replied, "If the guy was real poor, I'd give it back to him."

As opposed to **Bushisms**.

➤ *bestiality*

Come on, y'all. Let's look at the letters. It's not *beast-i-ality*. This, like *zo-ology*, is a word that is coming loose from its phonetic moorings. If you want it to be pronounced beastiality, then spell it that way. And then spell *festive* and *festival* that way—*feastive* and *feastival*—and pronounce them that way. And turn *incessant* into *incease-ant*, and pronounce *pleasant* pleezunt.

➤ *bit much*

You need never concede ignorance, lack an insight into anything, nor brook disagreement, if you keep this expression handy.

"What do you think of Antonin Scalia?"

"Bit much, isn't he?"

"I'll say! How do you like this wine?"

"Bit much, isn't it?"

"Hm? Think so? Oh . . . I see what you mean, the notes of cinnamon and leather. Hey—catch the Yankee game last night?"

"Bit much, wasn't it?"

"Well, one to nothing . . . Oh, A-Rod punching the mascot?"

"Mmm."

➤ Blanc, Mel

He created Woody Woodpecker's laugh and the voices of Bugs Bunny and all sorts of characters on Jack Benny's radio show. He would ride in the family car when he was a child, he once said, "and look at animals and wonder, how would that kitten sound if it could talk. And I'd tighten up my throat and make a very small voice. I never realized I was rehearsing.

Jack's writers used to try to throw me—give me things I couldn't do. One fellow wrote in, 'Mel does sigh of goldfish.' I went up to the mike and pursed my lips, that's all."

After a car wreck, Blanc was in a coma for three weeks. "This brain specialist came in every day. 'How you feeling today, Mel?' he says. I didn't answer him. One day he came in—and my wife and son were in the room, so I know it's true—and he said, 'Hey, Bugs Bunny, how are you?' and I answered him, in Bugs's voice, 'Just fine, doc.' I was dead, but my characters were still alive."

➤ *blend*

The proper linguistic term, I take it, for **portmanteau word**. As such it has the virtue of **brevity**, even precision, but it isn't much fun. Its root—*bhel-*[1], to shine, flash, burn—is quite a blend, however. Various extensions of it have given us *blue, bleach, blond, blind, blanket, black, flagrant, flamingo,* and *phlox.* (Sometimes I wonder about these roots. If only I could read **Pokorny** in the original.)

Smog (smoke plus fog) is an example of a blend.

➤ blurbs

When the One Great Scorer runs the numbers on what I have done for other people compared to what they've done for me, I hope I will get some credit for the fact that books with my blurbs on them almost invariably sell much better than my books. In his book-talk blog on nytimes.com, Dwight Garner actually gave one of my old blurbs, for Pete Dexter's *Paris Trout*, a rave: "I'm not sure I've ever seen words of praise as insanely great as . . . 'I put it down once to wipe off the sweat.' Do they give awards for this kind of thing?" No, they don't. If I do say so myself, that was one of my best, but I'm partial to this one, which I was proud to give to a collection of sketches by the sublime Bob & Ray: "Bob and Ray are funnier than anybody, even each other."

None of which is to be construed as a solicitation of more blurbing opportunities. They arrive weekly as it is. Sometimes I eventually get around to reading such a book too late to respond to it, and it's good, and I feel guilty. (For instance, *Confederacy of Silence*, by Richard Rubin. There, I feel better.) But even if I just skimmed all the bound galleys and type-scripts that come in the mail, I wouldn't have time to bathe myself, much less write my own books. And then, hey, a blurb for the ages isn't com-posed in a day. Clive Cussler once sent a new novelist, with whom he had evidently had previous dealings, a letter in which he provided a whacking good blurb and added, in closing, "Consider yourself lucky. I paid $7000 to have you edit a manuscript. I did this for free and my time is worth a hell of a lot more than yours."

In 1990, when I was forty-nine, Twayne published a critical biography of me, by Jerry Elijah Brown. The book was undoubtedly a more thor-oughgoing appreciation than I warranted, but my reaction at the time was *Wait a minute wait a minute I haven't even gotten cranked up good yet—have I? Mother of God, can this be the height of my powers?* When asked to give the book a blurb, I declined. Now I see a missed opportunity. I could have said, "This is the life!" But that would have been tantamount to what Hemingway's Catherine Barkley says about the rain, "I see myself dead in it." Maybe I could have said, "This is the life (in progress)!" Now, seven-teen years later, my arc may have run its course. After you do a book on words, what is left? Maybe someone will publish a collection of my great-est blurbs, and I can write an introduction. "'Insanely great' —*The New York Times*" would look good on the cover.

The word *blurb* was coined by the early-twentieth-century humorist and illustrator Gelett Burgess, who was quite a **meme**ster: he also wrote, "I never saw a purple cow, / I never hope to see one. / But I can tell you all right now, / I'd rather see than be one." His heritage endures more vividly than those of most American presidents.

Burgess also coined *bromide*. And many other words that have died de-servedly, for instance *oofle*, for a person whose name you can't remember, and *floogijab*, for something that "sounds like a compliment but has a sting in the tail." In 1910 *The Architectural Record* published his article about go-ing to Paris to see the new art and to interview Fauves. Picasso, he re-ported, "is a devil. I use the term in the most complimentary sense, for he's young, fresh, olive-skinned, black eyes and black hair, a Spanish type, with an exuberant, superfluous ounce of blood in him. I thought of a Yale sopho-more who had been out stealing signs, and was on the point of expulsion."

Dylan Thomas wrote the best blurb ever, for Flann O'Brien's *At Swim-Two-Birds*: "This is just the book to give your sister if she's a loud, dirty, boozy girl."

➤ body

One of the notions recorded in Flaubert's *Dictionary of Accepted Ideas* (Jacques Barzun translation): "If we knew how our body is made, we wouldn't dare move." Is this any way to think about our language (not to mention our ideas)? I don't think so. I think we want to know as much about our **vowels** as about our bowels. Which is to say, not too much, but it is interesting to note that *vowel* comes from the Old French *vouel*, which comes from the Latin *littera vocalis*, voiced letter; and *bowel* comes from the Latin for "sausage," *botulus*, hence the severe food poisoning named *Botulismus* by the Germans, who know sausage, all of which raises (no, it does not **beg**) this question: Is it such a great idea, after all, to avoid knowing how sausage is made?

➤ *book*

As of April 2008, the number-one definition of this term at **Urbandictionary.com** was "an object used as a coaster, increase the height of small children, or increase the stability of poorly built furniture: 'Where do you want me to put your drink?' 'Oh, just leave it on top of that book.'" In favor, 349 votes; against, 137.

The second most approved-of was "verb meaning to run or leave in a hurry," which is African-American slang of (I was going to say "**ironically enough**," but not really) long standing. Up, 244; down, 70.

Number three was "cool: the first option given when trying to type 'cool' in a text message using t9." Up, 172; down, 70. (In the more expansive definition number five, *t9* was identified as "predictive text on cell phones," in which "the numbers 2665 spell both *book* and *cool*, but *book* is the first word to display. To save time, it is left and understood to mean 'cool.'"

Number four was "1. A source of information. 2. A source of entertainment. 3. A tool barely used by todays societies, because it is not 'cool' to read a book." (Maybe that *is* ironic enough. Let us leave ironic enough alone.) In a footnote, the definer adds, "Which is a shame, really, because once upon a time (and today, in countries with little money) a book was a precious commodity." Up, 156; down, 85.

Number twelve began promisingly, but degenerated: "A collection of paper strips, usually bound together and labeled on the cover or binding. The strips, or pages, contain various sections, or chapters, which relate facts or a story. Generally, all topics discussed in the book relate to each other and form a point, which is the main theme of the book. Many books relate stories, whether funny, action-packed, romantic, horrible, dramatic, etc. Some books are very evil and discuss topics boring and very fact-based. These are called School books, and should be burned." Up, 15; down, 13.

"Bring a book!" was defined as "[a] command that follows a description of something to indicate that it's boring. 'No hitting, alcoholism, or passive-aggressive behavior between you two? You call that a relationship? Bring a book!'" Up, 68; down, 20.

Franz Kafka, for his part, said (as translated, *of course*, from the German), "A book ought to be an icepick [or ax] to break up the frozen sea within us."

⇒ Bossom/Bottum

Winston Churchill is said to have met a man whose name, Bossom, put him off. "It's neither one thing nor the other," he said.

In 1999 *The New York Observer* reported that Joseph Bottum, books and arts editor for *The Weekly Standard*, had addressed his fellow staffers in a memo, stating that he was tired of having his last name misspelled. He demanded that the magazine "enact a strict rule from now on . . . On everything that leaves this office, my last name must always be double-checked to make sure it is spelled with a *u* instead of an *o* . . . On our masthead or as a byline for something I've written, it should be 'J. Bottum.' On all other occasions when my name is written down, it should be 'Joseph Bottum.' When we set up radio or TV programs, or think-tank debates, it should be 'Joseph' for lowbrow stuff and 'Dr. Bottum' for highbrow stuff." When reached by *The Observer*, Bottum (a Ph.D. in medieval philosophy) said, "I think it happens more often now because people use spell-checkers."

➤ *bow-wow*

An antiquated theory of the origin of language is the "bow-wow theory," that words evolved from imitations of animals. I'd say there is some juice in that theory (see **hmmmmm**), but *bow-wow* is indeed an **arbitrary** representation of how a dog goes. I don't think a dog can make a *b* sound. Maybe a little *buffe*, like the sound French people make to be dismissive, but surely from a dog it would be more of an *uffe*, to which *woof* is close enough.

However, *bow-wow* is one of many useful **conventions** of dictionary and tradition. It's how grownups tell you a dog goes, and they mean well, so you accept it. You need to know it. It's coin of the realm. You honor it up to a point. But you need to find a better way to spell how a dog goes, not to mention how childhood goes.

➤ *bread*

> Eaters of Wonder Bread
> Must be underbred.
> So little *to* eat.
> Where's the wheat?

In fact I know from my youth that for sopping up barbecue sauce, or for retaining, at least temporarily, the juices of sliced tomatoes and mayonnaise, there is nothing like soft spongy white bread. But sometimes we must stray from the candidly lyrical voice, in order to raise an interesting point—in this case, what *bread* and *breed* have in common.

With each other, and with *barmy*, *fervid*, and *imbroglio*.

Give up?

It's their **PIE** root: *bhreu-*, meaning "to boil, bubble, effervesce, burn; with derivations referring to cooking and brewing" (AHD).

Can't you picture it, all the disparate descendants of *bhreu-* getting together at a family reunion?

Bread: So, now, you'd be my third, fourth . . . ?

Breed: Cousin twice removed, mm-hm.

Bread: I see the resemblance, of course, but . . . your grandmother . . . ?

Breed: Was a Yeast, but see, she married a Brew, and so on one side you've got the—well, we're not related to the Beers, directly, but of course the foam that comes up in fermenting—

Bread: That's Barm, yes, I know. Hence Great-uncle Barmy.

Breed: Talking to Bratwurst, right over there—*don't* make eye contact. Anyway bubbling, offspring: Breed.

Bread: Uh-*huh.* Now Effervesce, how does she—?

Breed: Bit of a stretch, but she's a Fervid, basically. Fervid, Ferment— you know how the Romans were about changing *b* words to *f* words.

Bread: Speaking of Fervids, keep them away from Imbroglio.

Breed: I know. I heard.

➤ brevity

The soul of making a point. *Automobile accident* may sound refined, but *car wreck* is more essential. My favorite sentence in Strunk and White's *Elements of Style* is "Use no unnecessary words." Nor syllables: I still remember how bracing it was back in the eighties when someone at *The Atlantic*, **probably** Bill Whitworth, pointed out how much my reminiscence of living in a trailer would improve if we changed "watched it lengthening" (a reference to the stream from my burst water pipe) to "watched it lengthen."

A counternotion, to be sure, is that in order to register anything on anybody's mind today you have to tell them what you're going to tell them, then tell it to them, then tell them what you told them. In 2007 *The Atlantic* printed this from Michael Hirschorn:

"I still believe that a lot of the 'Web 2.0' hype is just that—hype."

But there is only so much room, or ROM, available in any reader's mind; it's not an attic you can shove sloppily stuffed trunks into. In the

2004 U.S. presidential election, one of the reasons John Kerry didn't beat Bush was that he beat around it. Advance excerpts of a speech Kerry was to deliver in the heat of the campaign included these forty-nine words:

> You deserve a president who will not play politics with national security, who will not ignore his own intelligence while living in a fantasy world of spin, and who will give the American people the truth about the challenge our brave men and women face on the front lines.

In the event, Kerry did deliver these seventy-five:

> I believe you deserve a president who isn't going to gild that truth, or gild our national security with politics, who is not going to ignore his own intelligence, who isn't going to live in a different world of spin, who will give the American people the truth, not a fantasy world of spin, but a world where we challenge our brave men and women to be able to meet the test of our time.

I guess you could call that a Kerryism. **Bushisms** carried the day.

You caught my misquote up there, didn't you? I *thought* I didn't have my favorite Strunk and White sentence quite right, so I checked. (Would that more people would check before they quote me. To borrow a **Berraism**, "Half the things I said, I didn't say.")

It's "Omit needless words."

One of the **great three-word sentences**. Tighten it a notch or two? "Cut extra words"? No, brevity isn't everything; there's also tone.

See **redundancy**.

➤ *brick-and-mortar*

A condescending term for actual, like, "banks" that exist in, like, "building" form on a particular "street" in a "town." The equivalent with regard to reading material is, perhaps, *paper-and-ink*. There are advantages to brick-and-mortar institutions, and to paper-and-ink ones. Actually holding a double handful of a substance made from trees . . . is handy. It gets your whole hands involved. Reading from a monitor, instead of a book, is like playing videogame football instead of tossing a football around.

See **meatspace**.

➤ *bug*

Lexicographers have found no evidence that *bug* in its unscientific but familiar meaning of insect (generally something beetleish) derives from an earlier meaning of *bug* or *bugge*: hobgoblin, object of terror. OED will tell you this: that when *bug* came to mean a small, corporeal creepy crawly, the spooky meaning fell into disuse. (It lurks today in *bugaboo*, *bugbear*, *bogeyman*, and the bugs that infect computers.) The first appearance in print (in 1642) of the new *bug*, according to OED: "Gods rare workmanship in the Ant, the poorest bugge that creeps." There's something nice about that, isn't there?—that a tiny real thing well constructed (that is to say, enduringly evolved) pushed aside a big vague supernatural horror.

➤ *bullshit*

Having written the foreword to an exhaustive little glossary entitled *The F Word*, and furthermore having been scrupulous over the years in rendering the language of, for instance, professional athletes as it is spoken, I am not one to condemn "dirty words." It is tacky to replace, in print, some letters with asterisks (though *f*rt* does have an expressive look to it, and see *F*) or with a **dash**, or, per letter, with **hyphens**, which must cause children to ask, "Mommy, what does *'s* minus minus *t'* spell?"

But swears, as children call cusswords, remain a problem for mainstream print periodicals. "My slider had turned to shit," a ballplayer told me back in the late seventies, with regard to a breaking pitch of his that had temporarily crapped out, so to speak. Knowing that *Sports Illustrated* wouldn't print *shit*, I changed it to *crap*. Editing alchemized the man's slider further into *baloney*.

Two decades later, however—well, this was a special case. When I was a boy, Bob Feller—the fireballing Cleveland Indian known in the press as "Rapid Robert"—was one of my heroes. Little did I know that some fifty years later I would interview him, on a cruise ship, and he would say of a book he had put out, "You won't find a single four-letter word in there. I don't go for that bullshit." And I would quote it, and *SI* would publish it.

A number of words for blankety-blank language started out as anything but. *Swear*, for instance, like *answer*, comes from the root *swer-*, to speak, talk. In English *swear* meaning "to make a solemn declaration or statement with an appeal to God . . . or some sacred object in confirmation" (OED) goes back to AD 900; it didn't come to mean blaspheme—without some such modifier as "lowly"—until 1430.

In 1969 *The New York Times*, rather than quote defendants in the Chicago Seven trial in their frequent use of *bullshit*, alluded to the term as "a barnyard epithet." Let us note that if *bullshit* were, in fact, a term tossed about by cows and chickens, it wouldn't necessarily be an insulting one. Originally, an epithet was any descriptive term for somebody, as in "Rapid Robert." Let's say a given rooster—to use a euphemism for *cock* that is hearty enough in its own right—is regarded, all along the roost he rules, as the best there ever was at getting everything edible out of a cow-patty. He might be called "The Bullshit King."

The trouble with *bullshit* is that it drives out a number of vivid words—call them euphemisms, but they are inventive—like *bushwah*, *buncombe*, *balderdash*, *codswallop* (about which dictionaries say "origin obscure," but it looks to me like an obvious reference to whacking off), *hogwash*, *tommyrot*, *mumbo jumbo*, *flapdoodle*, *bilge*, *blather* (lots of juice still left in that, if you have an Irish accent), *bunk*, and, yes, *baloney*. Here is a word for an unnecessarily coarse synonym: *dysphemism*.

Bullshit does have a rich and complex pedigree. Its first syllable comes from the **PIE** root *bhel-*[2], says AHD: to blow, swell; with derivatives referring to various round objects and to the notion of tumescent masculinity." (The notion of it?) Some of those derivatives are *boulevard*, *balloon*, *ballot*, and *fool*. The second syllable's root is *skei-*, to cut or split, whose root-relatives include *science*. To defecate is to separate a bit of something from oneself. *Science* is from the Latin *scire*, to discern, originally (AHD) "to separate one thing from another." So "cut the shit" is redundant. But I will make every effort, in this book, to keep the bullshit quotient down.

➤ Bushisms

The notable quotations of George W. Bush derive from inner conflict. For instance:

"You know, when I campaigned in 2000 [he must have meant 2004], I said I want to be a war president. No one wants to be a war president, but I am one."

"I think—tide turning—see, as I remember—I was raised in the desert, but tides kind of—it's easy to see a tide turn."

Or from a denial of outer conflict, for instance this, which he said when success in Iraq was nowhere in sight:

"I thought we would succeed quicker than we did."

Berraisms are different. Once Yogi was playing in a scramble golf tournament, in which all players in a foursome tee off but thereafter take turns playing only the ball closest to the hole. Berra hit a nice drive up the middle. One of his partners followed with one just a bit better. Yogi lingered next to the ball he'd hit so well. "If I was playing alone," he said wistfully, "I'd play mine." Most people would have had the same feeling, but they would have stopped themselves before saying that. They would have reflected, "I'm not playing alone, though, so . . ." Then they would have said either nothing or something less memorable than what Berra said. Berra reacts more quickly and on two planes of possibility at once.

Which doesn't mean he lacks prudence: "You got to be careful if you don't know where you're going," he said once, "because you might not get there."

Here is Bush in prophetic mode, in New Orleans on the first anniversary of Hurricane Katrina: "There will be a momentum, momentum will be gathered. Houses will begat jobs, jobs will begat houses."

Shouldn't a daily Bible reader know that *begat* is past tense?

Bush's way with the word *momentum* here is peculiarly passive and unurgent: There will be rosebuds, rosebuds will be gathered. Maybe the disastrous momentum gathering dynamically in Iraq, as he spoke, was giving him pause at some level. Or maybe he didn't care what happened to New Orleans. His schedule, on this occasion, had him departing that precarious city at five; he left at two. A man who would leave New Orleans

three hours *earlier* than he's supposed to—and I mean, two *p.m.*!—has a
sense of momentum that is **different from/than** mine.

See **Goldwynisms; spoonerisms**.

➤ *bust*

Say you went into business selling busts of, say, Pamela Anderson, showing her bust busting out—that would be no bust, if you busted your butt,
but if you didn't get permission you might get busted.

How can this word have acquired so many different meanings, you may
have wondered. So did I, till I looked it up in several dictionaries. Nothing
much there by way of explanation, really. Maybe it all comes down to
bust's being fun to say, like, say, ***stuff***.

c · C · c

Hard or soft, this is a letter that may seem needless. Wouldn't *civic* just as well be *sivik*? Yes, if you want it to look like Croatian. And could you relax with a kup of hot khokolate? *Amerika* is Kafka or sixties, *bakon* is chemical or Japanese. If you dropped the *c* from *ck*, you'd have *baking* for *backing*, *biker* for *bicker*, and *took a liking* for *took a licking*. As it is, we have *such a stomachache*. Isn't that enough confusion?

Richard A. Firmage, in *The Alphabet Abecedarium*, presents T. H. White's paraphrase of a story of *C* told by Marie de France. She, I have just learned by Googling her, was a mysterious twelfth-century Anglo-Norman poet who wrote in French. Her "Bisclavret" is the story of a corker of a man who turns into a beast when he takes off his clothes and runs in the woods, and then his wife—but I'm not going to spoil it for you; it's on the Web in lucid translation. The *C* story is something else. Here is my paraphrase of White's:

It seems there was a wolf who heard that people in monasteries could get in out of the weather, didn't have to hunt, and yet frequently ate lamb. So he resolved to become a monk. You can't do that, he was told, unless you get some education, so he went to the abbey schoolmaster, who undertook, with some reluctance, to teach him the alphabet. Letters didn't come naturally to the wolf. When the schoolmaster showed him an *A*, he had no idea how to connect with this pointy abstraction, but finally the tutor pounded it into him. *B* took even longer. By the time the wolf *sort of* got *B*, he was panting and slack-jawed and about to jump out of his pelt. "Okay," said the schoolmaster, "here's the third one. What does this stand for?" He showed him a *C*.

"Lamb!" cried the wolf, so he flunked.

See also *K*.

➤ *cancan/Cancún/cooncan*

I got to wondering whether these words had anything in common, so I went to Google. Believe it or not, it would appear that the three of them have not appeared together in one text, except for lists of every word there is, until now.

Cooncan is a game—a forerunner of rummy—for two players using forty cards. People **probably** play it in Cancún, because they do around the world. An Iraqi blogger reported in 2004 that the most popular game in Baghdad, after cooncan, was "Who can squash the most mosquitoes wins." In the 1990s Benetton asked a hundred Turkish men what were the characteristics of a "modern woman." Answers included "does not use all of her jewellery at one time," "instead of trying to lose weight with popular methods can nourish right," "does not need feminism for equality," and "does not make cooncan a lifestyle." Cooncan pops up in oral-tradition African-American poetry. In China a similar game is called kon khin. *Cooncan* is believed to be an alteration of the Mexican Spanish *con-quián*, itself an alteration of the Spanish *con quién*, meaning "with whom?," the issue of the game being whom the cards wind up with.

People in Cancún, a touristy Mexican island resort, will tell you that the name comes from the Mayan for "pit of snakes," but according to long-time resident Jules Siegel, author of the *Cancun User's Guide*, that is modern folklore. One interpretation is that it means "seat of the Great Kan," a reference to Kukulcán, or Quetzalcoatl, the plumed serpent god.

The retro-*louche* French dance, the cancan, in which women lift their skirts and wave them, may get its name from a French word for "scandal," or from a French child's word for "canard"—on the assumption that the rumpy side-to-side movements of the dance are comparable to the gait of a duck.

The late George Plimpton left a request that any memorial celebration for him feature cancan dancers without panties. He got the dancers, but (at least at the gala version I went to) he also got panties. Understandable—but here's something bordering on scandalous: Googling Cancan + "no panties" produces zilch. Nothing. This search engine has a long way to go, to encompass all of human knowledge.

➤ *cantankerous*

RHU sees this as "reflecting *contentious, rancorous*." Makes sense to me. *Contentious* cries out for a *k* to reinforce its effect. *Rancorous* (cognate of *rancid*) needs another syllable and a prefix close to *con-* (with) to make it not just bitter but argumentative, to give its bite something to chew on.

Or you could say that people, trying to come up with the right-sounding word to fit their various **agenda**s, pulled this word together. That might be people-centric, as opposed to **logocentric**, but hey, we're people, let's say it.

➤ *cellulite*

Dictionaries prefer a long *i*, but I've only heard people say "celluleet," maybe because of the association with heavy, not light. Origin: 1960s, from the French *cellule*, small cell. Definition: "persistent subcutaneous fat causing dimpling of the skin, esp. on women's hips and thighs." In an ideal world, we could use it to power our cars.

➤ *cheese*

According to *A Brief History of the Smile*, by Angus Trumble, not every culture says "cheese" in order to smile for a photograph. In Spain it's *patata* (potato), in Denmark *appelsin* (orange), in Sweden *omelett* (omelet), in Finland *muikku* (a kind of fish), in Korea *kim chi* (cabbage), in Poland *dzem* (marmalade), in China *ch'ieh tzu* (eggplant), and "the letter *x*, pronounced *sheez*, much like *cheese*, though far softer, is used by Brazilian Portuguese-speakers." I'm taking bets that I can frown while saying any of these. What I want to know is, what makes the Danish confuse *appelsin* and oranges? Well, the Old French called oranges *pomme* (fruit or apple) *d'orenge* . . .

In the sense of "big cheese," RHU suggests derivation from the Urdu *chiz*, meaning "thing."

No doubt the cheese industry resents the use of *cheesy* to mean "chintzy," and the chintz industry feels the same way about the use of *chintzy* to mean "cheesy." The two industries should get together and mount an advertising campaign: "Cheese and Chintz, Partners in Progress."

➤ *cherry-picking*

As a widespread *subjective/objective* term for selecting only those facts that support one's position, and ignoring others, this is fairly recent. Neither WIII nor AHD has the verb *cherry-pick*, and other print dictionaries define it in terms of selectivity, though a pejorative tinge begins to show in OAD's example "the company should buy the whole airline and not just cherry-pick its best assets." The metaphor may derive originally from basketball (hanging around under the basket waiting for a pass and an easy basket, OAD) or from shopping (buying only items that are on sale, RHD), and from the portable crane known as a cherry-picker, which suggests the lengths people may go to, to find the bits they want.

It might just be a matter of selecting the best bits of fruit from the big bin at the market—but why cherries? Why not *plum-picking*? A plum is a different kind of prize—full-bodied (*plump*, *plumb*) and pendulous. You stick in your thumb and pull it out, or it falls to you (*plummet*, *plunge*) from politics. *Cherry* bears no etymological kinship to *cherish*, *chérie*, or *cherub*, but as Donald Barthelme has noted, "Words have halos, patinas, overhangs, echoes." *Cherry* has evolved from the Greek *kerasia* into the right name for something as special as virginity or as cheery as the choice red bit on top of a sundae. "We do not mistake the words *the taste of chocolate* for the taste of chocolate itself," Barthelme writes, "but neither do we miss the tease in *taste*, the shock in *chocolate*."

See **nitpicking**.

➤ *chic*

French, right? Well, yes, but oddly enough, French from German **probably**, according to AHD: the German word *Schick*, meaning "skill, fitness, elegance, from Middle High German (*sich*) *schicken*, to outfit (oneself), fit in."

AHD gives the comparative and superlative as *chicer* and *chicest*. I'm sorry, but those ought to **rhyme** with *nicer* and *nicest*, not with *bleaker* and *bleakest*. I would say "more chic," "most chic," or even *plus chic, le plus* *chic.* For all its collaborationist etymology, *chic*'s a fancy French word, so why not make the most of it. *Chichi*, *of course*, is too chic. It is also, according to my 1940 French dictionary, a "piece of false hair (in short curls)."

How would we make the adverbial form of *chic*? *Chicly*, I guess, which looks awful. The French sensibly make it *chiquement*. And *chiqué* means "sham, pretense."

And *chique* means either quid of tobacco or chigger. Whoa! Where did that come from? Well, *chiquer* means "to chew" (tobacco only), which is what you do to a quid and what a chigger more or less does to tiny amounts of you. Don't see the *chic* aspect there. I didn't even know the French had chiggers. Teensy little dogs, yes.

None of this, oddly enough, has anything to do with the etymology of Chiclets—those little mouth-pleasers derive from *chicle*, "the coagulated milky juice of the sapodilla, used as the principal ingredient of chewing gum," as AHD puts it nicely. *Chicle* comes from the even chewier Nahuatl word *chictli*. Chiclets meaning teeth, in particular knocked-out ones, comes from the physical resemblance.

See **mic**.

➢ *chicken*

As to the word *favorite*, see **interviewese**. But once when I was asked what my favorite word was, and I was on live radio so had to say something, I said "Chicken." It has a *k* in it, and . . .

And think of all the emotive and fundamental words that chicken has a part in.

Schmaltz is chicken fat.

Pool, as in "pool our resources" and also as in the game of billiards, without which *The Music Man* would be unimaginable, is from the French *poule*, stakes, literally "hen." (Do the French gamble for poultry?)

Here's a song title from World War I: "Would You Rather Be a Colonel with an Eagle on Your Shoulder, or a Private with a Chicken on Your Knee?"

Chickenskin is a term for goose pimples.

Many birds and reptiles have gizzards. But surely the chicken's is the one people think of, having seen it fried (if they grew up when and where fried chicken was for real) on their dinner table. "We had *gizzards*, man," the Pittsburgh Steelers' great defensive end Dwight White told me after his retirement from the game, looking back at the four-time Super Bowl champion team of which he was a vital part: they had guts, innards tough enough to grind up opponents. From the Latin *gizzeria*, **giblet**s, perhaps ultimately from the Iranian—compare the Persian *jigar*, liver (RHU).

And yet *chicken* is another word for coward. Chickens are also slurred by the expression "you dumb cluck."

The name of Poussin, the French artist, means, in French, "spring chicken." Poussin lived to be seventy-one. His paintings, on grand antiquarian themes, contain the odd dove and *putti* aplenty, but to my knowledge not one chicken. And Poussin's *putti* . . .

As I was trying to think what to say about Poussin's *putti*, serendipity led me to this passage in an essay entitled "Spring Chicken," by the early American food writer Elizabeth Robins Pennell:

"The gentle little spring chicken is sweet and adorable above all its kindred poultry. It is innocent and guileless as Bellini's angels, dreamlike and strange as Botticelli's."

I realize *putti* are not interchangeable with cherubs, but they overlap, and Poussin's, which have been described as "officious," look like porky old men. In his *Bacchanal of Putti*, they are winglessly guzzling wine, making out, and riding a goat. Without seeming to enjoy it.

Could it be—and this is just a straw in the wind—that Poussin was determined from an early age to be no spring chicken, and not to paint any either?

A *chicken-and-egg question* is, for instance (RHU), "whether matter or energy is the basis of the universe."

And yet chickens would seem to be off into their own private worlds. Once on a farm in Georgia I heard three visiting adults admonish a toddler as follows:

"Quit trying to kiss that chicken. That chicken has been pecking at horse manure all afternoon."

"Don't kiss a chicken anyway. It's silly."

"It don't mean anything to the chicken."

See **weevil**.

➤ children's classic, in verse, all I have so far

> One day lately, an elderly elf
> Quietly quoted himself to himself:
> "I always say," he said, said he,
> "No one's half as elfin as me."

➤ *chutzpah*

An example of *chutzpah*: employing the word itself too lightly around someone who knows Yiddish. "People using it in English tend to feel that it's got something to do with laudable audacity or apparent effrontery that actually conceals a brave and often new approach to a subject or endeavor," writes Michael Wex in his authoritative book on Yiddish, *Born to Kvetch*. In fact *khutspe*, to give it the proper Yiddish spelling, "is both stupid and mannerless, lacking in class and usually unpleasant— propositioning a woman at her husband's funeral, for instance."

➤ clarity

Gertrude Stein, in the course of writing about Henry James:

> Mr. Owen Young made a mistake, he said the only thing he wished his son to have was the power of clearly expressing his ideas. Not at all. It is not clarity that is desirable but force.
>
> Clarity is of no importance because nobody listens and nobody knows what you mean no matter what you mean, nor how clearly you mean what you mean. But if you have vitality enough of knowing enough of what you mean, somebody and sometime and sometimes a great many will have to realize that you know what you mean and so they will agree that you mean what you know, what you know you mean, which is as near as anybody can come to understanding anyone.

What I would say about that is, she has a point. If she made her points that clearly more often, I would say that Mr. Owen Young, whoever he was, should have encouraged his son to do likewise. But she doesn't. Does she ever not.

She believed in writing and thinking and feeling all at the same time, unself-consciously, in "the complete actual present," because "one has no identity . . . when one is in the act of doing anything":

> I am I because my little dog knows me but creatively speaking the
> little dog knowing that you are you and your recognizing that he
> knows, that is what destroys creation. That is what makes school.

There again, she has a point. And "I am I because my little dog knows me" is a pippin. But because she writes whatever pops into her head, as it is popping, her points and her felicities pop up rarely. "It is natural to suppose that a rose is a rose is a rose is a rose" is preceded by pages and pages of this sort of thing:

> It only goes to show that liking is the same as leaving and letting is
> the same as Indian. It only goes to show that if it is left to them to
> decide anything each time every time they will choose Wednesday
> that is to say if Wednesday is chosen Wednesday and choosing
> is made to have that in connecting connecting removing and
> dwindling. This introduces regularly and reconnoitering and if in
> demonstration and developing and leaving it out which is when it is
> bound to be left out left out and three ringing. Ring around the rosy
> this makes it louder.

Looking back over what you've written and changing it and changing it and changing it and changing it is a drag, but *it* (doing what I just said) makes *it* (the writing) more gracious and forceful. See **quick**.

➤ *cliché*

Past tense of the French verb to stereotype: *clicher*, which is "imitative of the sound made when the matrix is dropped into molten metal to make a stereotype plate" (AHD). Some clichés—"cut off your nose to spite your face," for instance—hold up forever. Others die fast. "Lying there like a beached whale" was striking the first couple of times someone said it; now it's overripe. Or maybe it was moribund to begin with: a beached whale is too poignant to serve simply as an image of lazy corpulence.

➤ *cliticize*

Relax. Doesn't mean anything you think it might. Has to do with phono-logical status. In the word *I'm*, *'m* is a clitic.

➤ *coax*

Some people will decline to do something, at first, because they enjoy be-ing coaxed into it. I hate being coaxed. The word comes from *cokes*, a sim-pleton or fool, perhaps influenced by *coxcomb*, a silly fop. (Now there's a word: *fop*. "Akin to *fob*," says RHD.) Nor do I like to be cajoled. RHD speculates that there was once a French word *cajole* meaning "birdcage"—at any rate *cajoler* in French means "to persuade by flattery or promises" or "to chatter like a bluejay." I never heard a bluejay flatter anybody. (Swear, yes. Use bad grammar, yes. See "Jim Baker's Bluejay Yarn," by Mark Twain.)

I hate being wheedled, too, but that is a good word for its bad self. Ori-gin obscure. Don't you think there might be some subliminal connection to *weasel*?

➤ *cog*

Now that is a good solid word. Metaphors involving it—a worker as a cog in (or, more strictly speaking, on) a wheel, making a mistake as slipping a cog—don't grow stale. Like so many good words, its origin is probably Germanic/Scandinavian.

Cognitive, *cognizance*, and so on are not related to *cog*. They come from *co-* and the Greco-Latin *gnoscere*, to know. But isn't it nice how that *g* gets hard when we need it?

➤ *colon*

Unless the Greek words *kólon*, large intestine, and *kôlon*, limb or part of a verse, are related, the following words have nothing etymologically in common:

colon, the large intestine

colon, the **punctuation** mark

colón, the paper monetary unit of El Salvador

colonel, the military officer (the *r* in its pronunciation is a holdover from the Middle French variation *coronel*)

colony

You'd think *kólon* and *kôlon* would be related, but I can't find a reference book that even seems to care. Are lexicographers afraid that if the large intestine and punctuation get connected, **fart jokes** would result? I cannot think that ill of lexicographers.

At any rate, nothing about the word's derivation helps us define it. So, here is my sense of *colon* as punctuation mark: an introductory gesture, on the order of "and now I give you"; not quite a *ta-daaa*.

See **semicolon** and **dash**.

➤ color

One of the hardest things to render *verbal*ly (that is to say, in words, spoken or written). Who knows that *crimson* is purplish red and *scarlet* inclines toward **orange**? Probably only a potter or collector of **porcelain**s knows that *celadon* is a pale grey-green. *Puce* comes from the French for "flea," but if you think flea-color, do you think "dark or brownish purple" (RHD) or "deep red to dark grayish purple" (AHD) or "dark red or purple-brown" (OAD) or "a dark red that is yellower and less strong than cranberry, paler and slightly yellower than average garnet, bluer, less strong and slightly lighter than pomegranate, and blue and paler than average wine" (WIII)? In an expression like "He turned puce with rage," I'll bet the plosive ooh-hiss sound of *puce* has more impact than the muddy visual connection.

Cerulean evokes an image in the reader's mind, sky blue. That is what *azure*, too, means to me (and to WIII and OAD), but AHD says azure is "a light purplish blue." RHD says "a clear and unclouded sky" *is* "a light, purplish shade of blue." *Azure* derives from the Arabic for lapis lazuli, which RHD calls "a deep blue mineral." (The pigment ultramarine, if it's the real thing, is made from powdered lapis lazuli.) AHD defines *cerulean* as "deep blue; sky blue; azure," but *cerulean blue* as "a light-blue to strong greenish-blue color." When it comes to *violet*, AHD leaves nothing to the imagination: "the hue of the short-wave end of the visible spectrum, evoked in the human observer by radiant energy with wavelengths of approximately 380 to 420 nanometers."

See *livid*.

➢ comma

There are, *of course*, rules, but my instinct is to use commas like musical notations, for *rhythm*, emphasis, and clarity. This sentence from *The New York Times* is grammatically correct, but it needs another comma:

"Mr. Dutchin had two bachelor's degrees, in math and physics, from the Massachusetts Institute of Technology and a once-promising Wall Street career."

First time through, you halfway get the impression that the man's degrees came in part from his Wall Street career. I would toss in a comma after *Technology*, to keep the reader from jumping the track.

But then I would look at that, and I would begin to doubt that I could justify that comma, structurally. After all I wouldn't write, ". . . had degrees from the Massachusetts Institute of Technology, and a once-promising Wall Street career."

Better might be ". . . had a once-promising Wall Street career and two bachelor's degrees, in math and physics, from the Massachusetts . . ." Except that's out of chronological order.

How about losing two of the commas:

"Mr. Dutchin had bachelor's degrees in math and physics from the Massachusetts Institute of Technology and a once-promising Wall Street career."

No, that's too much to cram into one breath. (In speech you could keep a rhythm going, because "Massachusetts Institute of Technology" would become "MIT.") And the two degrees still make you think for a moment that "Massachusetts Institute of Technology" is going to be followed by, say, "Carnegie Tech."

The challenge in straightforward reportorial writing is to get all the relevant information you can into as little space as possible, without causing the reader to stop, double-hitch, blink, and reread. Poetry, you want to read over and over, to get as much savor and meaning from it as you can. When you read newspaper reporting over and over it's usually because there's a snag in it somewhere.

And finally I have found it in the sentence about Mr. Dutchin. It's not a matter of too few commas, it's putting *had* to awkward double duty (an infelicitous **zeugma**). Here's what I think I would do: "Mr. Dutchin had earned two bachelor's degrees, in math and physics, from the Massachusetts Institute of Technology. He'd once had a promising Wall Street career."

An **Urbandictionary.com** definition of *comma*: "a very important grammar thang. without it, many sentences would be very different. *with comma: I helped my uncle, jack, off his horse. without comma: I helped my uncle jack off his horse.*"

But this is cheating—in writing, you'd capitalize *Jack* as well as *I*, and the sense would be clear enough without the commas. See **unscribable**; **Moebius statement**.

➤ *common*

People who used to call themselves liberals and now call themselves progressives tend to talk these days about "common ground." It's a hard thing to find when "the common man" is so outmoded, "common denominator" is associated with "lowest," and one person's "common sense" is another's insanity.

Since **special** and *species* have a common root, you'd think that being a part of humankind would be special enough (even speciesistic, if you ask a wolf), but *special* **probably** meant "uncommon" before the year 1200. Maybe humanity is the species in which everyone wants to be special. Today, especially (and what is more special than today?), I doubt that any politician would count on striking a common chord by saying what Lincoln said: "Common-looking people are the best in the world: that is the reason the Lord makes so many of them."

What the Lord has made lately is the evangelical community. And the holistic community. And the towing and recovery community. (In Chattanooga, Tennessee, you can visit the International Towing and Recovery Hall of Fame and Museum, if you want to see some beautiful antique tow trucks and a memorial, the Wall of the Fallen, to tow truck operators who have given their lives trying to get people out of ditches.) To each of these communities, each of the others is a "special interest." And not in a good way. No one who outspokenly identifies with any community today is also as willing as the late Quentin Crisp was to insist that his or her community is not as special, in a good way, as it likes to assume.

Crisp (see **arts, the**) faced up to assaults and derision by "making the existence of homosexuality abundantly clear to the world's aborigines" (to the homophobic community, that is), but he also said, "I don't know why gay people . . . want to be cut off from nine-tenths of the human race. 'I have nothing in common with them,' they say. Why, you have everything in common but the funny way in which you spend your evenings."

How about us? Reader and writer? What can we assume we have in common? You know the story about the man who called the house of a business associate. Had to talk to him; it was urgent. The phone was answered by a small child:

"H'lo."

"May I speak to your father?"

"He isn't here."

"Your mother?"

"Unh-unh."

"A babysitter?"

"I'm not a baby."

"No, of course not. Your older sister, or—"

"She said don't bother Duane and her."

"I see. But just for one moment, you could ask her—"

"*Noooo.*"

"All right. It's very, very important that I talk to your father. Do you understand?"

"Now?"

"'Now'? Now what? Just . . . , when he comes home, your father, please tell him, as *soon* as he gets home, to call me."

"Okay. Bye."

"No! Don't hang up! I'm Baxter Brisendine. Tell him to call Baxter Brisendine. Can you remember that?"

"I'm Ricky."

"Okay, Ricky. Maybe you'd better write my name down, Ricky. Do you have a pencil?"

"No."

"Pen, then, crayon, anything—something to write with."

"Mmm . . . okay."

"Tell him—"

"It's a crayon."

"Good, good, that will be fine, Richie. Tell him, tell your father—"

"Ricky."

"Ricky! I *meant* Ricky! Ricky, tell your father—"

"A blue one?"

"Fine, blue crayon, that's perfect."

"Okay."

"No! Don't hang up!"

"I better."

"No! Please! Why?"

"Not spose to talk to strangers."

"It's all right. On the phone, it's all right! Trust me!"

"One called and just breathed."

"That wasn't me! Believe me—listen, *please*, Ricky, tell your father to call Baxter . . ."

"How do you spell it?"

"I'm going to tell you, Ricky. That's *B* . . ."

"Wait."

"Hmm? *B* . . . Did you get that? *B* . . ."

"*BB*."

"No, just one *B*. Let's start over, Ricky: *B*. Have you got that?"

"Nunh-unh."

"Why not? Ricky, this is *important*! Why in the name of—why *not*?"

"How do you make a *B*?"

We, you and I, have in common (aside from the fact that we instinctively don't trust Duane) that we both know our letters. "What is a masterpiece," asked Jean Cocteau, "but the alphabet out of order?"

Or maybe he said "the dictionary out of order." Either way, he said it in French—*dérangée*, or something—and I don't even remember now where I saw it quoted, in translation, which—we don't have time to get into that (or the matter of three **dash**es in one sentence) right now. Bottom line: you have to start somewhere.

➤ computerese

On Amazon.com I was entreated to "Check Out Our Advertisers! Click Here!"

Trying to be polite, I clicked. Got this response:

"The HTTP request was in an invalid format or contained invalid data. Reason: Invalid cookie checksum. For further assistance contact the server administrator." I don't even know what a server administrator is, much less a "cookie checksum."

Here are some other rude messages I have been confronted with:

"Warning: You are about to download something that contains executable code."

"You don't have permission to modify this print job."

"This program has performed an illegal operation and will be shut down. If the problem persists, contact the program vendor."

"America Online was unable to initialize your modem." Would it kill AOL to come up with something closer to "Sorry, line's busy"?

➤ conjunction dysfunction

In *The Hot Kid*, Elmore Leonard, droll master of hard-bitten dialogue, frequently omits conjunctions, as when someone observes that coalmine mules "fart a gas can kill you you step too close." Newspaper writing today tends, on the other hand, to toss around too many conjunctions, indiscriminately.

The New York Times, May 3, 2007, regarding the nonappearance of Vice President Dick Cheney in the perjury trial of his aide I. Lewis "Scooter"

Libby: "Mr. Cheney . . . cooperated with the investigation and expressed a willingness to testify if called, though he never was. Yet he was a central figure throughout . . ." *If . . . though . . . yet*—my head is spinning.

The Times again, September 19, 2007, on the surprisingly high quality of a wine "from Uruguay, which is sort of the Toledo Mud Hens of the major winemaking leagues. But hold on. Uruguay may have a lot in common with Argentina, although its winemaking is not yet at Argentina's level. But Uruguay has not been at it as long. Nonetheless . . ."

Associated Press, January 9, 2007, on Florida's victory over Ohio State the day before: Colorado "stunned Oklahoma on the very same field in the Fiesta Bowl on New Year's Day, while Florida and [Ohio State] finished with identical 13–1 records." *While* doesn't always imply simultaneity, of course; it can be a more casual form of *whereas*. But you can't use *while* to connect something that happened on January 1 to something that happened on January 8.

➢ consonants

Fiddling with letters is pleasant to me, but the pleasure is not as pure as my father's in his basement workshop, scratching around in his store of nuts, bolts, tacks, nails, brads, woodscrews, lockwashers, sockets, grommets, early-American fasteners inherited from his father or his father's father, and other doodads conceivably functional enough, or curious enough, to be held on to. Unlike **Flaubert** racking his vocabulary for the one right word (the great novelist's agony the more intense because in comparison to messy, multitudinous English there are too few words in French), my father would be whistling, quietly, to no tune. He was a man of large, stressful business and civic affairs, but I like to think of him rattling small hardware bits in the bowels of our home, the way a less reliable man might jingle his pocket change as he sets out on the town. No jingle to this rattling, though. The dominant sound was clickety, rackety: consonantal. When **vowels** get involved, then you got problems.

The word *consonant* is disappointingly drony, nasal. It should have more **crunch**. If it were Anglo-Saxon, it would. What if you were asked to define *consonant*? I wouldn't know where to begin. "Uh . . . , like, a *p*. Or an *f* . . ." Here's a definition, from RHU, to which I tip my hat:

1. *Phonet.* (in English articulation) a speech sound produced by occluding with or without releasing (p, b; t, d; k, g), diverting (m, n, ng), or obstructing (f, v; s, z, etc.) the flow of air from the lungs (opposed to *vowel*).

Can you imagine how sweaty but proud the lexicographer was when that was done? The punctuation alone must have involved hours of meticulous stitching. "People," that lexicographer's supervisor must have announced over the intercom, "we are knocking off for champagne. Loretta has nailed *consonant*."

Compare the AOD version: "a basic speech sound in which the breath is at least partly obstructed and which can be combined with a vowel to form a syllable." Simpler, easier to take onboard, but it doesn't kick off its shoes and dig its toenails into the matter. Doesn't even give any examples! Not even, "Take a deep breath and see if you can pick the consonants out of this definition."

Consonants are the yin, maybe, to **vowels**' yang, but I can never keep those Chinese *y*-words straight. Sometimes in word books you see *consonant* explained as "with-sonant," that is to say, "representing a sound that cannot be pronounced by itself, needing to be combined with a vowel to be clearly articulated" (Richard A. Firmage in his valuable *Alphabet Abecedarium*). But that doesn't apply to *s* or *z*. Do you think snakes and bees need vowels?

At any rate you'd think that the counterpart to *consonant* would be *sonant*. But that term, though it does pretty much boil down to the same thing as *vowel*, appears in dictionaries as the thing opposed to **surd**, which focuses on vocal-cord vibes rather than breath.

Absurd is from the Latin for "out of tune." In song, vowels carry the melody, the air. Consonants—separated in time to some extent by the vowels but also taking various amounts of time themselves—are the **rhythm** section; they provide the beat.

For my money, WIII's most telling contribution to the definition of *consonant* comes in its definiton of *vowel*: "one of a class of speech sounds (as of the *o* of English *hot* . . .) in the articulation of which the oral part of the breath channel is not blocked and is not constricted enough to cause audible friction."

Audible friction. Is that not the essence of a consonant? You're a prelingual person, groping to convey something . . . something scrapy, bumpy, raspy . . . You're going to be groping primarily for consonant sounds, with vowels in there to keep them apart, or to join them together—or maybe to convey a sense of how the friction made you feel. Maybe you're trying to convey how your leg got so inflamed and swollen: it bent, there was a shuddery moment like when a person is cold . . . you registered surprise and dismay . . . and *crack*:

"Brrrr . . . *oh* . . . ke."

And your spouse gives you a sympathetic look, and sort of coos—accent on the vowel, framed by softly, pettingly frictional sounds: *poor yooo*.

See **hmmmmm**, **sonicky**, and each consonantal letter in its turn.

➤ conventions

"By convention there is color, by convention sweetness, by convention bitterness, but in reality there are atoms and space." —Democritus, fourth century BCE.

Yes, and every letter and every word is a convention, stretched across the void. But how do conventions arise, and what makes them catch on and last? They have to appeal to people. *Convention* comes from the Latin for "coming together." A convention has to be something that more than one person is moved to take hold of. It's a convention to call your sweetheart "dumplin'" or "honeybun." It would also be a convention to call her "gulag," if she would stand for it, which she won't, and why would you want to be around someone who would?

Gulag is atoms and space and so is *dumplin'*, but *gulag* is not going to sound sweet to anyone whose perception we need concern ourselves with here. *Dumplin'* won't sound sweet to someone who connects it with *dump* or with a fatty thing to eat, but otherwise it can be a sexy thing to say and hear. Tone of voice, **of course**, means a great deal, but *gulag* won't fit a sweet tone of voice. *Dumplin'* will.

See **arbitrary**.

➤ corrections

Here is my favorite correction run—it appeared on December 6, 2003—by *The New York Times*:

> A sports article on Wednesday about Sylvester Croom, the new
> football coach for Mississippi State in the Southeastern Conference,
> rendered his comment to reporters incorrectly. He said, "I am the
> first African-American coach in the S.E.C., but there ain't but one
> color that matters here, and that color is maroon." [Maroon being
> Mississippi State's color.] He did not say, "There is only one color
> that matters here."

I love it because *The Times* thought it ought to clean up a Southerner's talk, and presumably the Southerner said, Leave my talk alone, I talk like this on purpose.

I am reminded of the story about the lady from Iowa who moved to New York and found herself at a high-toned society do. A socialite matron asked her where she was from. Iowa, she said. The matron smiled and drew her aside.

"My dear," she said kindly, "here we pronounce it 'Ohio.'"

➤ *could care less*

Is illogical. "Couldn't care less" sounds prissy. Neither sounds quite convincing.

➤ *cowlick*

There's a good word. Even if a cow has never licked your hair. *Lick* of course is **sonicky**. And nobody ever said *cow* wasn't a good word for a cow. You wouldn't call a cow a weasel.

➤ *crotch*

A good, vivid word with respect to a tree or a person, and there's no reason to let it in through the back door, so to speak, as in this letter to *The New*

York Times Magazine: "Great music, timeless music, is something that affects heart, mind, soul and, yes, the crotch too." There is much to be said,
though, for what might be regarded as a euphemism for *crotch*. I remember
when, under my mother's eye, an Atlanta haberdasher was making chalk
marks on my first suit. "We'll take it up a bit in the *stride*," he said. Are
there comparable active verbs we might convert into procedural synonyms
for the heart (the *beat* doesn't quite get it all), mind, or soul?

See **groin**.

➤ *crunch*

OAD: "Origin early 19th cent. (as a verb): variant of 17th-cent. *cranch*
(**probably** imitative), by association with *crush* and *munch*."

I like it: The Cranch family of chewing noises, in association with
Crush Development and Munch Productions, presents a whole new concept in breakfast-time sound.

After so much mocking of liberal positions in terms of softness, it's re-
freshing that environmentalist concerns have come to be called *crunchy*—
from the sound of raw vegetables and granola attacked with relish by well-
kept teeth.

➤ *cush-footed*

OAD says the word *cushy* (soft, easy, comfortable, as in a cushy job or
couch) comes from the Urdu *kushi*, pleasure. Two words later (after *cusk*,
"another term for TORSK," and *cusk-eel*), OAD says *cushion* derives ultimately (by way of the Old French word for "cushion for the hip," which I
assume means "cushion to place under the hip," not "cushion for people
who are hip") from the Latin *coxa*, hip, thigh.

RHU and AHD agree (with each other, and with me) that the Urdu (or
Hindi, as they have it) connection is far-fetched—that "*cushy* is a shortening of *cushion* with the *-y* suffix."

Cush-footed is a term used by the legendary pro football scout Lloyd
Wells. "Cush-footed, walks on his heels," he said of a prospect he had no
use for. I took this—along with Wells's accompanying body English—to
mean tender-footed, soft-footed. *Dictionary of American Regional English*

defines *cush foot* (preceded by a mark indicating "a word or sense of questionable genuineness") as "unusually big and clumsy feet," or "flat feet," perhaps from *cush*, meaning a hornless cow. From Wells I got a sense of cushiony feet—maybe they flatten out into big floppy flat ones.

Cush, according to Roy Wilder Jr. in *You All Spoken Here*, is "eggs, water, leftover cornbread, and diced onions, mixed with bacon grease, stirred in a frying pan, and cooked to the consistency of oatmeal." Wilder cites Dr. M. M. Mathews, in *Some Sources of Southernisms*, as saying that *cush* is an Arabic word brought from Nigeria and Angola by slaves. A substitute for couscous, then.

A cushaw, according to the *Dictionary of Smoky Mountain English*, is a large crookneck squash. A quote from 1924: "When I asked an old man why he preferred 'cushaws' . . . to pumpkins, he spat reflectively and answered: 'If we growed punkins up in yan cove, they'd break loose and roll down and kill somebody.'"

A musician, Richard "Kush" Griffith, is called Cushfoot back home in Louisville.

A song lyric sent to a chat group by somebody in Virginia:

> Well they call my baby "Cushfoot"
> 'Cause her ankles drag the ground.
> But, I'll tell you one more thing:
> They don't call her that when she's around.

And how about the Hindu Kush? What's soft about that? Nothing. No connection.

d · D · d

As a letter it's pronounced like *Sandra Dee* and *yes indeedy*, but it's a lot less perky as a sound: *duh*. If, as Chambers suggests, *mute* derives from "imitation of a dull sound made with tight-pressed lips," then *dumb* is an even duller sound to begin with, followed by a bit of slack-jaw in *uh* and ending in the tight-pressed lip sound with that subaural *b* (as in *butt* or *booboo*) for good measure. Backward, forgetting the *b*, would be *mud*. Can we imagine that, or *thud* or *clod*, ending in any other letter?

Do I mean to say that every word ending in *d* is pejorative? Good God, no. Consider *bed*, *wood*, *bud*, and *food*. And *d* begins *dear*, *darling*, *dove*, and *daddy*. But you know how well *s* works in *suspicious* and *l* in *lullaby*? That's how effective *d* is in heavy downer words: *dull*, *drugged*, *drudgery*, *dunce*, *dump*, *dunk*, *duffer*, *dust*, *dud*, *dolt*, *doddering*, *dowdy*, *doleful*, *dunderhead*, *dung*, *doo-doo*, *damn*, *doldrums*, *dead*.

And Homer Simpson's ejaculatory contribution to common parlance and the online OED, which spells it *doh*. I prefer the official *Simpsons* spelling, *D'oh*. It should always be capitalized, since it always stands alone, a complete sentence fragment sufficient to the moment, the oral equivalent of slapping oneself on the head. And there is considerable juice in that apostrophe, which captures the fleeting vocal jolt with which the definitive dumb dad of our time shifts from density to woe. When the stock market took a plunge in the summer of 2007, the *New York Post*'s banner headline was "D'ow!"

According to the OED, the first *D'oh* on *The Simpsons* appeared in 1988. The script called for an "annoyed grunt." Dan Castellaneta, who does Homer's voice, has said that the character's trademark exclamation was inspired by the *d'ohhhh* that James Finlayson, who frequently played a faux-mustachioed foil to Stan Laurel and Oliver Hardy, would emit in moments of extreme frustration. (Ollie approximates *d'ohhhh* himself occasionally, for instance when he is covered with both soot and flour in *Night Owls*. A good 30 percent, I would estimate, of the dialogue in Laurel and Hardy talkies is *oh* in various forms: *ohhhhh-woo*, *oh goshamighty ohhh*, *g'oh-oh-ho-ooo*, and so on. See *H*.) Finlayson's extraordinarily vigorous double takes (he is said to have literally knocked himself out doing one) were his version of "the slow burn," a term of art more often associated with Edgar Kennedy, another fuming antagonist for Stan and Ollie. Kennedy also worked with the Marx Brothers in *Duck Soup*. Playing a lemonade vendor, he does a distinct *d'ohhhh!* in the course of a long, inevitably asymmetrical exchange of indignities with Harpo.

Now the man who first got Laurel and Hardy together, in a silent short also entitled *Duck Soup*, was Leo McCarey, who went on to supervise most of their subsequent movies. McCarey has never received the recognition that other great directors of film comedy have, perhaps because he was so eclectic. Between 1933 and 1937 he directed three classic comedies (the Marx Brothers at their best in *Duck Soup*, Charles Laughton at his most appealing in *Ruggles of Red Gap*, and Cary Grant and Irene Dunne at their fizziest in *The Awful Truth*); another really good comedy (W. C. Fields and Burns and Allen in *Six of a Kind*); and three others I haven't seen starring, separately, Eddie Cantor, Mae West, and Harold Lloyd. Earlier McCarey did comedy with Charley Chase, and later, with Paul Newman. The one thread that runs through all his best work, writes David Thomson, is his use of the slow burn: "the deliciously delayed reaction to disaster on the part of a clown. It works because the audience responds to this superb intellectual disdain of the quantity of custard hanging from the comic's face." By the way, I've been unable to catch Kennedy doing a *d'oh* in a Laurel and Hardy movie. An *ohhh-fmph'v* and a long, drawn-out *ooooooooh* after his wife crowns him with an urn, but no *d'oh*. The one he does in *Duck Soup* may be as conscious an homage to Finlayson as Castellaneta's.

So Homer's *D'oh* comes from a long line of screen comedy. But it's also a new development. Whereas Laurel and Hardy can spend ten minutes and lots of Hardy *oooooh*'s trying to get one of Stan's boots off Ollie's foot, Homer's attention span (not unlike his audience's) is so brief and his self-awareness so limited that he does a *fast* burn. And the person who frustrates him is himself. Finlayson's *d'ohhhh* comes in the course of, for instance, a protracted sequence that begins with the boys' trying to sell him a Christmas tree and ends in their destruction of his house (and, to be fair, his demolition of their car). Kennedy's *d'ohhhh* is part of a long tit-for-tat culminating in Harpo dancing barefoot in the vendor's vat of lemonade. Homer's *D'oh* is an exclamation of fleeting self-reproach, or dismay, anyway, over a stupid move of his own that even he can't help noticing for a moment. He is the Marxes or Stan and Ollie and their victims rolled into one.

See **Tupou IV, King Taufa'ahau**.

➤ dactyl

A metrical foot from the Greek for "finger." A finger has three joints, one long and two short. A dactyl goes *dum*-da-da.

A double dactyl is a verse form invented by Anthony Hecht and Paul Pascal and often used by John Hollander: two four-line stanzas, each line consisting of two dactyls, except for the fourth, which lacks the last two syllables. In the first stanza, the first line is a bit of nonsense (frequently "higgledy-piggledy") and the second line is, in its entirety, the name of a well-known person. In the second stanza, the second or third line is a single word. Here is an example, by me:

> Hippety-hoppety,
> Hopalong Cassidy
> Hopped on old Topper and
> Brought down the horse.
>
> Since then, a life-change: he's
> Lost lots of weight, what with
> Polyunsaturates,
> Walks, and remorse.

➤ darlings

In his book *On the Art of Writing* (1916), Sir Arthur Quiller-Couch, an eminent critic, anthologist, and adventure novelist, handed down a guideline for writers that people are still handing down. Usually people attribute it to Mark Twain, William Faulkner, Ernest Hemingway, F. Scott Fitzgerald, George Orwell, Noël Coward, W. H. Auden, Oscar Wilde, or someone else whose fame has lasted longer than Sir Arthur's. Here is that guideline in its original form: "Whenever you feel an impulse to perpetrate a piece of exceptionally fine writing, obey it—whole-heartedly—and delete it before sending your manuscript to press: *Murder your darlings*."

Or, as Stephen King has put it, "Kill your darlings, kill your darlings, even when it breaks your egocentric little scribbler's heart, kill your darlings."

Some context: Before he lays the *darling* line on us, Quiller-Couch cites a "Persian lover" who "sought a professional letter writer and purchased a vocabulary charged with ornament, wherewith to attract the fair one as with a basket of jewels." That sort of thing, "extraneous, professional, purchased ornamentation," is not style, says Quiller-Couch. Nobody's going to argue with that. Purging those elements from your writing would be murdering somebody else's darlings.

What generations have taken from his admonition, though, is that we writers should root out our own self-indulgent bits, the vivid turns of phrase that call attention to themselves instead of advancing the narrative for . . . you. The reader. Who, like the Persian lover's fair one, is the darling who matters.

Yes, well. Sir Arthur's pen name was Q. Some frills trimmed there. But don't you suspect that after rejecting *Kill your pets* as too mean and *Eliminate your sweeties* as ambiguous, and then hitting, bingo, upon *Murder your darlings*—don't you suspect that he thought to himself, Q, you are cooking? He probably didn't think, I have just written the one thing that anybody will remember about me, if I'm lucky, ninety years from now. He probably thought he was on a roll. His next words are these:

> Is it possible, Gentlemen, that you can have read one, two, three or
> more of the acknowledged masterpieces of literature without having
> it borne in on you that they are great because they are alive, and
> traffic not with cold celestial certainties, but with men's hopes,
> aspirations, doubts, loves, hates, breakings of the heart; the glory
> and vanity of human endeavor, the transience of beauty, the
> capricious uncertain lease on which you and I hold life, the dark
> coast to which we inevitably steer, all that amuses or vexes, all that

gladdens, saddens, maddens us men and women on this brief and mutable traject which yet must be home for a while, the anchorage of our hearts?

No darlings there?

Neither the 1980 nor the 1992 edition of *Bartlett's Quotations* includes Q's *darling* quote. Both of them include one from *Othello*, a reference to "wealthy curled darlings." *Bartlett's* is full of darlings, and we would all love for ours to be there. Let's not forget that Othello murdered his, on bad advice.

➤ dash

I don't like a dash that seems to be saying "ta-daaa" or "get a load of this." For instance, from *Newsweek*: "A stunning best seller about WW II—by a writer who didn't survive it." That is far-too-common punctuational hype. A comma, or no punctuation at all, would suffice.

➤ death, coolest euphemism for

"Copping that eternal nod." —Louis Jordan.

➤ *deity*

Properly pronounced to **rhyme** with *velleity*, not with *gaiety*, as seems to be trendy on American television and radio now. Was Thomas Jefferson a day-ist? Similarly *spontaneity*, whose antepenultimate syllable is originally and preferably a long *e*, is perhaps most often pronounced spon-ta-nay-ity. Perhaps there is more of a kick to *nay* than *nee*, and pronouncers want to hold on to the *ay* in *spontaneous*; but it's *nee* in that word and should be in *spontaneity*. And day-ity, I don't know, where'd that come from? Did someone write a ditty that rhymed it with *laity*?

➤ *demean*

Crustier books on usage will forbid you from using this word to mean, roughly, *degrade*, because its original meaning was to conduct oneself in a certain way, hence *demeanor*. I'm not going to do that, because you wouldn't listen, and why should you: nobody uses *demean* in the original sense anymore, there are plenty of other words that serve that meaning perfectly well, and people have been using *demean* meaning "to lower" since at least 1601. (See, though this is a stretch, **fart jokes**.)

What I will do is quote Bob DiBiasio, the Cleveland Indians' vice president of public relations, who, when asked whether the Indians' nickname and logo were demeaning to American Indians, said it was a matter of "individual perception . . . *The Wall Street Journal* did an op-ed piece, and they asked the question, 'If something is not meant to demean, can it be demeaning?'"

And I will answer the topic question of whoever that columnist was: Yes, dumbass. *Of course* it can.

I would be sorry, personally, to see the logo's savvy-looking Chief Wahoo go. He looks like he is thoroughly in on whatever historical ironies the team's name might imply. But I can't say whether he is an insult to Navajos or Ojibwes or Sioux. I can say this: If someone offends you on purpose, you can fight back. It is much more offensive to be offended by someone whose sole and unsoul-searched excuse is that he or she doesn't mean to be offensive, which means that he or she doesn't care, and isn't about to care, whether you are offended or not.

See *nosism*.

➤ *diaphragm*

This fleshy-fibrous wall between the chest and the belly is the principal muscle of breathing, and, next to the lungs, the largest organ of speech.

A frog—perhaps the first animal to have a voice, unless you count rubbing legs together—has no diaphragm. It respirates by filling its mouth with air, closing its nostrils, forcing the air into its lungs by means of a swallowing movement, then opening its mouth so that the stretched lungs collapse and let out the air. A frog has primitive vocal cords (and in some cases a vocal sac below the mouth that fills with air and vibrates). To attract a mate or signal distress it can only croak, ribbet, or peep the same belched note repeatedly, sometimes at varying intervals—no pitch, only rhythm.

Mammals have diaphragms, which arch upward into the chest cavity, expanding the rib cage and with it the chest cavity and the lungs: inspiration. Plenty of air to play out over the strings-and-vibe section—the *glottis* (which includes the *larynx*, which contains the vocal cords), the *pharynx*, and the *uvula*—as the lips, tongue, and teeth click and fret and do their dances.

Pharynx and *larynx* are related to the Greek for, respectively, "chasm or cleft" and "gulf of the sea, the deep" (Chambers), and *uvula* is Latin for "little grape," but the word *diaphragm* has less resonance than the organ deserves. The silent *g* is a holdover from the Greek *diaphragma*, barrier, partition.

➤ dictionaries, gender-skewing

You have your archaic laddy-buck type dictionary: the *Dictionary of the Vulgar Tongue: A Dictionary of Buckish Slang, University Wit, and Pickpocket Eloquence* (1811), whose entries include:

> *Granny*. An abbreviation of grandmother; also the name of an idiot, famous for licking her eye, who died Nov. 14, 1719.

> *Green sickness*. The disease of maids occasioned by celibacy.

> *Hop-o-my-thumb*: A diminutive person, man or woman. She was such a hop-o-my-thumb, that a pigeon, sitting on her shoulder, might pick a pea out of her a-se.

> *Monosyllable*: A woman's commodity.

> *Tartar*: To catch a Tartar; to attack one of superior strength or abilities. This saying originated from a story of an Irish soldier in the Imperial service, who, in a battle against the Turks, called out to his comrade that he had caught a Tartar. "Bring him along then," said he. "He won't come," answered Paddy. "Then come along yourself," replied his comrade. "Arrah," said he, "but he won't let me."

> *Whiffles*: A relaxation of the scrotum.

Then there's *Webster's First New Intergalactic Wickedary* (1987), which I think it is fair to say would be opposed to any relaxation of the scrotum, and whose entries include:

> *Prudish Prudence*: practical wisdom of Prudes; Volcanic Virtue enabling Shrewd Shrews to question taken-for-granted, traditionally implanted ends-purposes and to ask Wild Whys in the light of which radically Other ways and means can be considered.

> *Nag*: a Scold with Horse Sense; a Biting Critic of cockocracy; one who has acquired the Virtue of Nagging. See *Horsey*.

> *fashion*: a primary means by which phallocratic fixers fix, tame and train women for their own designs; the bad magic by which fakers attempt to destroy female consciousness, embedding contagious anxieties and cravings, trying to trap women in houses of correction/houses of mirrors. *Cockaludicrous Comment*: "My desire is to save them [women] from nature."—Christian Dior.

> *O-logy*: holistic process of knowing that encircles all of the *-ologies*, Spinning around and through them, unmasking their emptiness, reducing their pretentious facades to Zero, freeing the flow of their "courses" through Spiraling creation: Gyn/Ecology.

> *flying fetuses*: astronauts in spaceships; technological offspring of male monogender mating; tube-fed orbiters who are mothered/monitored by ground controllers and their computers. *Cockaludicrous Comment*: SPACE FLIGHT ABORTED IN LAST SECONDS —headline, *The New York Times*.

➤ dictionary, rhyming

X. J. Kennedy once discouraged consultation of a rhyming dictionary, which "might suggest something that would stick out like a buzzard in a row of wrens." But a buzzard in a row of wrens—or more to the point, a bustard in a row of *blustered clustered custard lustered mustard flustered*— is only the mildest of the nonsensical delights afforded by the *New*

Rhyming Dictionary and Poets' Handbook (1931), by Burges Johnson, whose own verse includes "Alack the Yak," and who states in his introduction: "This is a dictionary which brings words together in groups because they 'rhyme,' and for no other reason." Some of those groups:

> EENY fantoccini, genie, greeny, queeny, sheeny, teeny, tweeny, weeny, visne.
>
> EGGLESS, EGLESS legless (etc.), *see* EG
>
> ELFLESS selfless (etc.), *see* ELF
>
> EESELESS cheeseless (etc.), see EASE
>
> ERSIONIST excursionist, immersionist, versionist.

What is a versionist? Turns out it's one who "engages in the manipulation of a fetus in the uterus to bring it into a favorable position for delivery." A job to be proud of.

> Something was bothering May.
> What it was, she couldn't say.
> She saw an immersionist,
> Who dipped her,
> An excursionist,
> Who tripped her,
> And, at last, a versionist,
> Who tipped her
> Son Ralph in such a way
> That that is why he's here today.

The first triolet I ever wrote:

> "Disinfectant (etc.) *see* ECT,"
> A line that occurred on its own—
> So terse yet it flows so unchecked,
> "Disinfectant (etc.) *see* ECT."

Expect no neater effect
Than this one, unsung and low-flown:
"Disinfectant (etc.) *see* ECT,"
A line that occurred on its own.

See **rhyme**.

➤ *different from/than*

I have long staunchly agreed with prescriptivists that *different from* is to be preferred over . . . Hell, I'm just going to say it: *Different from* is better than *different than*. What's the point in saying "My dog's different than your dog"? Of course he or she is. No two dogs are identical. If you're going to use *than*, which suggests that one thing is more something than the other, then be specific: "My dog's prettier than yours," and take the consequences.

However, you have perhaps noticed that under **tmesis**, I resort to *different than*: "Arthur Quinn's *Figures of Speech* comes from a different era than Wikipedia." In that case, *from* wouldn't work. Maybe I should have come up with a sentence completely different from that one.

At any rate, I am not going to fight you on this. As AHD says descriptively, *different than* "is well attested in the works of reputable writers." AHD does say that "where the comparison is drawn directly between two persons or things, *from* is the safer choice." But I hate to see it put in terms of safety. I prefer to put it in terms of standing up for your damn dog, as above.

The AHD usage note at *different* also explains (better than I could, and no differently from how I would) why I used *than* under **tmesis**.

➤ *dirty tricks*

Too bad this expression gained such a bad name under Richard Nixon, because it derived from *funny* pranks pulled against Nixon, over a period of twenty years, by the Democratic campaign worker Dick Tuck.

Tuck hired several pregnant women to show up at Nixon rallies waving signs saying NIXON'S THE ONE. At other Republican rallies, Tuck informed bandleaders that Nixon liked to be brought out onto a platform to the tune of "Mack the Knife." In the midst of a Nixon speech from the rear platform of a train, Tuck, dressed as a conductor, signaled the train to pull out of the station.

Trouble was, Nixon was so impressed by these tactics that he hired Donald Segretti to develop "a Dick Tuck capability." The Nixonian version— as even Nixon conceded, on tape—lacked *humor*. It evolved into the scandal that brought the Nixon presidency down. In June 1973, as a Senate committee was holding public hearings into the Watergate burglary that was eventually tied to Segretti and Nixon, Tuck ran into Harry Robbins Haldeman. Haldeman had been Nixon's chief of staff until recently, when Nixon, hoping to save himself from impeachment, had directed him to resign.

According to Tuck, Haldeman forced a smile and said, "You know, you started all this, Dick."

"But you guys," Tuck replied, "have certainly run it into the ground."

➤ *disgruntled*

Illogically, given its negational force in most compound words, the prefix *dis-* is sometimes, as here, regarded as an intensifier. To gruntle, colloquially, was to grumble, or as OAD puts it, to "utter little grunts."

As for *grunt*, that word, the dictionaries will all tell you, is, *duh*, "***probably*** originally imitative."

➤ *divisive*

There are two kinds of people: people who say "di-vice-ive" and people who say "di-viss-ive." The first kind is (are) right.

➤ *dollar*

The almighty dollar, we used to say, when a popular travel book could tell you how to do *Europe on five dollars a day*. The word's roots are European: the Germanic *taler* or *thaler*, a silver coin (for instance the Maria Theresa thaler, which is said to have been the only coin Arabic traders trusted), was in circulation in the American colonies, and around the world, long before there was a U.S.A. So was the Spanish eight-reales piece (which could be cut up into bits, hence "pieces of eight"), called in Britain and America "the Spanish dollar."

The dollar was made the official unit of U.S. currency in 1785, before the Constitution was worked out. *Buck* (already an informal term for the dollar, from *buckskin*, a fur-trade reference) would have been more indigenous, but too slangy I guess, and Harry Truman's Oval Office motto, "The buck stops here," might have suggested graft instead of acceptance of ultimate responsibility. (*Buck* in that expression, and in "pass the buck," is short for a buckhorn knife, often used in frontier poker games to mark the dealer.)

Where did *taler* or *thaler* come from? Joachimsthal, a town in Bohemia with a big silver mine and a mint.

In London in 2007 two American friends of mine went to a movie and paid the equivalent of $54 for admission and two candy bars.

➤ *donkey*

Donkey, a word that dates back only to the late eighteenth century, may (though evidence is faint) have derived from the name *Duncan*, or the color *dun*. At any rate it originally rhymed with *monkey*, and some people still pronounce it that way, notably Eddie Murphy as the voice of the donkey in the animated film *Shrek*. Presumably *donk-* came to rhyme with *honk* under the influence of a real donkey's voice. (*Honk* may come from the Amerindian word *cohonk*, for the Canada goose, which makes that sound.)

➤ *don't*

Doesn't "Don't the moon look lonesome?" have far more force and feeling than "Doesn't the moon look lonesome?" Seems so to me, and the same goes for "Don't he look natural, though" and "It just don't seem right to me."

And we're not necessarily talking *enallage*, which according to Arthur Quinn is "the rhetorical name for an effective grammatical mistake," as in "We was robbed." (He might also have cited "I should've stood in bed.") We're talking venerability: according to RHU, *don't* "remained the standard contraction for *does not* in both speech and writing through the Eighteenth century."

➤ *dot*

I'm sorry to have to tell you, especially if your name is Dorothy, that *dot* comes from the Old English *dott*, meaning "head of a boil."

Forget that, though—*dot* is a **pip** of a word.

There are three-dot columns. For example, Les Matthews's "Mr. 1-2-5 Street" column, in the *Amsterdam News* of Upper Manhattan, began one day in 1973 as follows:

> Janice Morgan looked like chop meat before the cops got to Tully Lionell in their Hotel Cecil room . . . Alvin Rose became so wrapped up in James Brown's music that he toppled out of the first balcony and fell on Hyla Hill, Terry Winston and Marty Hill, 7, 8 and 5 years old respectively. No serious injury . . . Ike and Tina Turner failed to keep Apollo engagement . . .

Maybe I should find a more cheerful example.

Then there are three-dot words, that is, words with three dots together: *Fiji*, *hijinks*, *Beijing*, *gaijin*. And *Pompeiiicist*, if there is such a thing as a scholar whose field is that ancient volcano-impacted city, Pompeii. Near misses: *jiu-jitsu* (from the Japanese for "soft arts") and the town, in Minnesota, of Bemidji (from the Ojibwe word *Bay-may-ji-ga-maug*, meaning "lake with cross waters," a reference to the nearby Mississippi River).

This just in: a four-dot word, from Thoreau's *The Maine Woods*: Ambejijis Lake.

And another: Ujiji, the town on Lake Tanganyika where Henry Stanley found Dr. Livingstone, he presumed.

Five dots together in a sentence (involving phonetic spelling of the way *idiot* is sometimes pronounced) would occur in this exchange:

"Uhhhh, whut's the name of that place where they have, like, Hono-
lulu?"

"Hawaii, ijit."

➤ *double entendre*

Not necessarily naughty. I remember when, in childhood, I first picked
up on the double meaning of Bon Ami cleansing powder's logo: a freshly
hatched baby chick over the words "Hasn't scratched yet." Nice. See *pun*.

➤ double negative

A no-no, according to strict grammarians. Descriptivists point out that
great writers through the ages have used intensive (or mayhap inatten-
tive) double negatives, and in congenial company there's nothing wrong
with "Ain't nothing wrong with that."

But in a letter to the editor of *The New York Times Book Review*, Susan J.
Behrens, identified as a college teacher of linguistics, maintains with regard to prescriptive grammar:

> Of course it's about class . . . Those not already credentialed are
> taken to intelligence task for using double negatives ("He didn't do
> nothing"). The political speechwriter or academic can use a double
> negative ("It is not without regret that I fire you") and be perceived
> as good with words.

The two examples are, *of course*, different. The first one literally says
the opposite of what is meant, without any gain in emphasis. It comes
off as sullen and unconvincing. The second one is off-putting to be sure
(too prissy to have come from a political speechwriter), but it's also an in-
tentional modification of "It is with regret," two negatives yielding
a hedgy but logically unimpeachable positive. That sort of double negative needn't even be mealymouthed. "It's not unusual to be loved by anyone," whatever else you may think of the song in question, is more
precise as well as more resounding and metrical than "It's usual." The
anyone there would be odd coming from anyone but Tom Jones, but so

would "taken to intelligence-task" from anyone who doesn't teach linguistics.

➤ *drawl*

"Probably from Low German *druelen*, to loiter, delay," says AHD, and other dictionaries agree, but WIII goes with frequentative (see *-le*) of *draw*, and provides the most drawn-out definition: "to speak slowly esp. as a matter of habit with vowels greatly prolonged so that vowels monophthongal in other styles of speech are often diphthongized (as in *bin*, *web*, *bad*, *knob*, *talk*, *good*)."

Let me loiter (no, not loiter, linger) for a moment to observe that I *leuh*-uhv that word *monophthongal*. Mm-m. Hey—I believe I just diphthongized a consonant. I don't like *diphthongized* (see **onomatopoeia**), though. *Diphthongalized* would have more swing to it, and I believe could be justified along the lines of *nasalized*.

People often tell me I have a Southern drawl. Occasionally someone tells me I pronounce *oil* and *all* the same. There he or she is wrong. It's true that Southerners flatten *oil* considerably, but when one Southerner says to another that he or she is low on oil, the listener doesn't think it's about a washday product. *All* is *awl*; *oil* is *aw'l*. You've got to have the ear for it. (See *y'all*.)

Once Stephen Colbert (see **truthiness**) and I were on a panel discussing humor, and he said he got rid of his Southern accent because people told him it made him sound stupid. I'm still kicking myself for not coming up with a rejoinder along the lines of "And that would have been a problem, in your work?" But I am glad that the thickheaded character he does so well on *The Colbert Report* doesn't have a Southern accent. And I'm glad I do. If you grew up monophthongalizing **pie**, would you want to turn it into the diphthongal *pi-ee* in hopes that people would think you were smart?

AHD's example of a drawl, "'We-e-elll,' the clerk drawled," is an example of how tricky it can be to render phonetics in English. *We-e* alone evokes a pig's squeal. A drawled *well* might better be spelled *wehhhhl*, but that looks funny. A diphthongized *well* may be more like *way-ul*, but that looks exaggerated.

I don't know how to spell the monophthongal *pie*. Maybe a cross between *pah* and the French *pin*.

A drawl is "a slow, lazy way of speaking," says OAD. I don't like that
"lazy."

➤ *duck*

Ever wonder which came first, the verb or the bird?

The verb.

See *cancan/Cancún/cooncan*.

➤ *dyslexic*

When I started first grade I was already hyperlexic, having learned to read
at my mother's knee. "Sound out the words," she would say, and in the
face of English's myriad phonetic inconsistencies, that is still my policy.

But I remember, or remember remembering, that I wrote letters backward—*S*'s and *Z*'s, and others. My teacher, Miss Connie Carswell, model
of kindness though she was, asked my mother whether I might be showing off in this way, but it wasn't like playing the guitar behind my back. I
couldn't remember which way an *S* went, and even now, well, dammit, it
seems counterintuitive, doesn't it, to make such a common letter as *S*
by starting on the right (assuming you start at the top) and winding up on
the left? That's backward. It's not the way the Phoenicians or the early
Greeks made precursors of *S*. Maybe I was *right* about *S*. Or maybe my
brain had a dyslexic or dysgraphic glitch. If so, my neurons found a route
around it, for Miss Connie's sake—in the process **perhaps** giving my ver-
bality an extra bit of torque, as pigeon toes can do for a runner. If the rest
of the world ever gets turned around on *S*, though, we may all feel more
natural.

According to the dyslexia page on the website of the Region XIII Education Service Center in Texas, any number of great achievers have been
dyslexic, including Gustave **Flaubert** (listed among "artists") and "Thomas
Thoreau" (listed among "writers and poets"). I don't know about those
guys, but it might help explain why Flaubert thrashed around so, trying to

come up with just the right brushstroke. I do know that W. B. Yeats, hands-down the greatest modern poet, was a terrible speller who since his death has been speculatively diagnosed as dyslexic. Yeats pursued mystic notions involving spirals. I wonder how he made his S's.

See ***hoo-hoos***.

e · **E** · e

The most frequent letter in English and in most other languages in which it appears. It has been said to be the first vowel sound uttered by an infant. Therein, to people other than the infant's parents at two in the morning, may lie its appeal. *Whee, yippee, free, see me.* (See Y.) If a writer can look at blank pages as clean sheets, maybe he or she can get going in the morning. On the other hand there's the generally far less enthusiastic short *e*, as in *wet, regret, fret,* and *bleh.* There's *heh-heh,* of course, which may be preferable to *hee-hee* in some circumstances but is less gleeful.

Originally, *e* was the Semitic *he,* representing a breathing sound (see *H*). Then it split into the Greek *epsilon,* which had the sound of *e* in *bet,* and *eta,* which had the sound of *e* in *be.* The Romans got along with just the one *e* for both sounds, and so does English. That's one reason we use so many *e*'s. We often use two of them to make the long *e* sound, as in *wee.* A lot of *e*'s get used in the representation of screams (*eeeek*) and high thin whines (*eeeee*). Also, *e* can stand for various other sounds, for instance the *e* in *the* when pronounced, as it usually is at least before consonants, as *thuh* or even *th'.* We have, for some reason, a word for this neutral-to-nearly-nonexistent vowel: *schwa.* From the Hebrew *shewa,* emptiness.

From time to time, just to show it can be done, someone will write a whole story or even a book without using the letter *e.*

Eh.

➢ editing

William Butler Yeats was a visionary who knew the value of revision. In an early draft of his poem "Adam's Curse," he wrote:

> I said, "A line will take us hours maybe
> And yet must seem a momentary thought
> Or all that stitching and unstitching's naught."

His friend Lady Gregory, without necessarily implying that he had dropped a stitch, suggested a change:

> Yet if it does not seem a moment's thought
> Our stitching and unstitching has been naught.

In her version the first line is calmer, more like natural conversation. The second line moves more like steady determination, and it's set appropriately in the present perfect. Yeats approved, and that's how it stands: the last word on sweating over copy. Lady Gregory also found something lacking in this line, of a poem Yeats never published:

> Although it is gentle and young and low

Her uninspired suggestion:

> And yet it's young and smooth and gentle and low

That, Yeats ignored. Nearly everything anyone puts on paper can be improved, and most things, through several drafts, desperately need to be. No writer is too fine (though perhaps too defensive) to welcome a neat tweak by another hand. But even an **ideal reader**'s improvement may be all wrong. Writing, no matter who manages to mess with it, is the responsibility of the writer, who should be its final arbiter: quality control. What gets into print under Yeats's name is Yeats.

(Compare the signs a catcher gives to the pitcher, calling for a fastball, a curve, and so on. Pitcher has the last word, because he can always shake a sign off. Catcher may well *know best*, but the pitcher has to throw it.)

See **revision**.

➤ *eerie*

RHU: "uncanny so as to inspire supernatural fear." Comes from the Middle English *eri*, a dialect variation of *argh*. So there you have it: why pirates talk that way.

➢ *egg*

I don't see how other cultures can feel right without *g*'s in their eggs.
French *oeuf* would be a good word—but not as good as *soufflé*—for a soufflé.
German *Ei* and Greek *ooion* (from which *oology*, study of eggs; rhymes with
zoology if you pronounce *zoology* right) also seem too airy.

Even the **PIE** roots for *egg* fail to evoke breakfast: *owyo-* and *oyyo-*, perhaps related to *awi-*, bird. The *g*'s, I gather, first showed up in Old Norse,
none too soon. We get *leg* and *keg*, too (but not *beg*), from Scandinavian
sources.

Omelet doesn't seem fluffy enough for my taste. It is probably so called,
says Chambers, "from the omelet's flattened shape," from Latin *lamella*,
a small, thin plate, diminutive of *lamina*, from which we get *laminated*
and *lamé*. But no omelet worth its whisk (see **symbolic/presentive**) is flat.
Oeuf would be a good word for omelet.

How is a poem like an egg? There's no such thing as a pretty **good** one.

➢ *eggcorn*

From a misspelling of *acorn*, this is a linguist's term for amusingly not
quite right, but perhaps sort of logical, versions of words and established
phrases. Apparently many eggcorns crop up in students' papers. "Whoa is
me" and "mute point" are examples that I have seen cited. For all I know,
these will take over from "Woe is me" and "moot point." I might mention,
though, that *mute* and *moot* don't really sound alike, to anyone who is paying attention, nor do *eggcorn* and *acorn*. See **figures of speech, gotten all
wrong**.

➢ egg jokes

Chicken and egg in bed together having a postcoital smoke. Disgruntled-
looking chicken to egg (or vice versa): "Well, I guess that settles that." Did
this joke originate in a cartoon? I can almost picture it, except how would
an egg be shown smoking?

➢ *either*

You say "eye-ther," maybe, and I say "ee-ther," but I'll bet both of us had always taken this useful word for granted until I started looking into it. Turns out to be a contraction of the Old English *aeghwaether*. Breaking that down: *ae* for "always" (compare *aye* as in "I'll love you for aye"), *g* just a bit of connective tissue, and *hwaether* meaning "which of two, whether." The earlier Germanic form was the phrase *aiwo gihwatharaz*, literally "ever each of two."

See **unscribable**.

➢ electricity/chewing tobacco

What do these things have in common? They both involve juice, and then there is the amber factor. We know from the writings of Thales of Miletus (or more likely, as in my case, from encyclopedias) that the Greeks knew as early as 600 BCE that amber when rubbed would take a magnetic charge. When in 1600 Sir William Gilbert found ways of generating that charge by rubbing other mineral substances (notably sulfur), he called the charge *electricam*, from the New Latin *electrum* for "amber," which is from the Greek *elektron*, which is related to *elektor*, meaning "the beaming sun." (Apparently no connection to *election*. Certainly not to any election I can think of.)

And from the *Dictionary of Smoky Mountain English*, here is a usage of the word *ambeer*: "Hit doesn't look nice to see a woman cuddin' this home-made tobacco, that's strong enough to kill a snake, and squirtin' ambeer around everywhere." Presumably from the amberish (and also beerish) color.

➢ elegant variation

When Henry Watson Fowler coined this term, in *The King's English* (1906), he was not invoking Bach. He was pinning a tongue-in-cheek name upon a cheesy syntactical maneuver: reaching beyond pronouns, such as *it*, *they*, and *he*, in order to avoid repeating either those pronouns or the nouns, such as *raspberry*, *dittoheads*, and *Fowler*, to which they (the pronouns in question) refer. "Many writers of the present day abound in types of variation that are not justified by expediency," Fowler wrote, "and have consequently the air of cheap ornament."

I would rather not plunge any deeper into this matter. By "this matter," I mean, of course, strained synonymy—*a rose is a blossom is a posy*; *grasping at equivalents*; *whatever hat he wears, it's always Charley*—in other words, elegant variation. This is not going to be pretty.

But okay. Say you feel obliged to warn future generations against inter-planetary entanglements, at some length. You don't want to keep saying "future generations" and "interplanetary entanglements." Nor do you want to use *they* in such a way as to be unclear whether *they* means "future generations" or "interplanetary entanglements" or some other plural thing altogether. You are tempted therefore to write, "If future genera-tions do not beware of interplanetary entanglements, then these eventual fruits of the present generation's loins will find themselves . . ." Your in-ner arbiter of elegance hollers "Foul!"

Old-fashioned baseball writers gave Fowler the raspberry. Those ven-erable locutioneers, fed up with repeating words like *hit*, *home run*, *pitcher*, and *ball*, came up with substitutes like *clout*, *four-bagger*, *moundsman*, and *spheroid*. With no apologies. (See **baseballese**.) They drank a lot, too.

Here's how I avoided elegant variation in the first sentence of the preceding paragraph. I went back to the last sentence of the paragraph before that paragraph and changed "inner Fowler" to "inner arbiter of elegance." That freed me up to refer to Fowler *simply* as Fowler in the aforementioned preceding paragraph (the one right up there that begins "Old-fashioned baseball writers"). It—the avoidance—didn't work too well. Robbing Peter to pay Paul. And I liked "Your inner Fowler hollers 'Foul!'" I believe I might have found peace as an old-fashioned baseball writer.

In the second sentence of that paragraph (you see the one I'm talking about?—now it's the one before the one just before this one), I didn't avoid elegant variation. I meant to avoid it, by starting that sentence with *They*. But then, to insure clarity, I thought maybe I should recast the first sen-tence into the passive: "The raspberry was given to Fowler by old-fashioned baseball writers. They . . ." But the passive is **perhaps** even more deplorable than elegant variation. Instead of forging ahead, the passive backs into linkages of convenience. So, what the heck. I indulged in some elegant, even swellegant, variation, not to mention a bit of locutioneering. Just to show what a mess a person can get into, in words.

Stringing English together is like rewiring an old house. When as readers we are treated to the true elegance of due concatenation, we may recall what Spencer Tracy says about Katharine Hepburn in *Pat and Mike*: "Not much meat on her, but what's there is cherce." Those nondescript words *what's* and *there*, well placed, conduct juice. Elegant variation would have been, "Not much meat on her, but the muscle mass she does have . . ."

Whew. Let's not discuss this again.

(*To give the raspberry*, or, in short, *to razz*, is to make a rude noise: from *raspberry tart*, rhyming slang for "fart.")

➤ *e-mail*

Call this hyphen fussy if you will, but you wouldn't write *Abomb* for *A-bomb*, or *opositive* for *O-positive*, or *Xray* (which looks like the name of a science fiction villain), or *fstop* or *Bgirl* or *Bside* of a record (not that there is any such thing anymore) or *Csection*, *Fword*, *Gman*, *Vchip* or *Xfactor*. And *ecommerce* is not good, not good at all. It looks like it should be pronounced ecko-merce. You like *echecking*, *efiling*, *evoting*? No. No. No. *Eticket* looks like it should be pronounced more or less like *etiquette*. New words should be formed in such a way that they evoke as closely as possible how they are pronounced. Other words beginning in *e* followed by a single syllable beginning in *m* are *emend*, *emote*, *emit*, *emerge*. In each case, the *e* is pronounced *ih* and the following syllable is stressed. So *email* looks like ih-*mail*. The spelling *email* is an *e*-barbarism.

Strunk and White, *The Elements of Style*: "Do not use a hyphen between words that can better be written as one word." To that, a big yesindeedy. But *e* isn't a word. Advocates of *email* argue that it conserves storage space. Much, do you think?

See **mic**.

➤ English

Long before there was an England, people started using *English* to refer collectively to the people and the dialects of three Germanic tribes that moved into what is now England from what are now Denmark and northern Germany: the Angles, the Jutes, and the Saxons. Why not Jutish or Saxonish? (If the latter, you and I would be Saxophones.) Maybe the Angles were better talkers. Why not Anglish? It sounds kind of rustic. Once I brought two college professor friends of mine along when I was working on a story about coonhunting, and they were at pains not to come off hoity-toity, so when a coonhunter established that they were teachers and asked them what they taught, they said, "Anglish." See **spin**.

Esperanto is a regularized, scholar-designed system of Greco-Latin derivations idealistically aspiring to can't-we-all-get-along universality. Blah. English is an outrageous tangle of those derivations and other multifarious linguistic influences, from Yiddish to Shoshone, which has grown up around a gnarly core of chewy, clangorous yawps derived from ancestors who painted themselves blue to frighten their enemies. English is the only western European language whose verb for "to write" doesn't come from the Latin *scribere*, and one of the few whose verb for "to read" doesn't come from the Latin *legere*. Our *write* comes directly from the PIE root *wreid-*, to cut, **scratch**, tear, sketch an outline. Our *read* comes from the Old English *raedan*, to advise, which, like a number of other words involving the concept "to fit together" (*army*, *harmony*, *art*, *order*, *riddle*, *arithmetic*, *rhyme*) goes back to the PIE root *ar-*. The core of English is gritty, sonorous Anglo-Saxon. The rest of it comes from all over.

Italian is more melodious, German more precise, and I daresay Russian plumbs more nearly ineffable sorrows, but English embraces three times as many words as any other language, and they come from an unparalleled range of sources—Tagalog, Persian, Hawaiian, Mandingo . . . The reaches of empire have not only established English but enriched it: *juggernaut* from conquest of India, *Oklahoma* (originally Muskogean for "red people") from displacement of Amerindians, *hip* from American slavery. The scribes of imperial Greece and Rome helped to seize and (by their standards) to civilize the earth but ploughed it less tenaciously. English, both formal and casual, connects with catchiness, with the vernacular, with **kinesthesia**.

➤ *equally as*

"If we are to stamp out corporate fraud, we must be *equally as* committed as the people who profit by it." Sets off redundancy bells.

But to say, "Either word can be used, alone, and be perfectly correct" (OAD) isn't quite right.

Losing *equally*, you have ". . . we must be as committed as . . . ," which is adequate. But losing the first *as* doesn't quite work: ". . . we must be equally committed as . . ." Sounds, at least at first, as if you're saying that each of us, the people involved in *we*, must be committed to an equal extent.

To hold on to *equally*, which has a certain ring to it, you'd have to recast the sentence: "The people who profit by corporate fraud are deeply committed to it. We must be equally committed against it."

Simplest solution: ". . . we must be *just as* committed as . . ."

➤ ethnocentrism

Maybe better than no centrism at all. But see **common**.

➤ *etymology*

From the Greek for "the true sense of a word." That goes back to when roots showed through a lot more than they do today. But just as you appreciate a vegetable more if you know how it grows, you have a better hold on a word if you use it in acknowledgment of its roots, its background, some of the soil still attached.

➤ *Eve*

Derives from the Hebrew *haya* (not using any of the little diacritical marks that go with the letters), meaning "to live." Whereas *Adam*, in Hebrew (again, leaving out the *jots* and *tittles*), means "human being." Presumably some profoundly invidious gender significance there, but is it safe to assume that Adam was the namer of things? Why, because he was louder? According to John R. Rickford in an introductory essay to the AHD, "women frequently lead linguistic change," perhaps because of "their closer association with the very young, who are often linguistic innovators; others hold that women are more expressive, using language more often as *symbolic* capital and as markers of personal style." This is, or traditionally has been, more likely true of spoken language, as opposed to all those un-*sonicky* words that the scribes of ancient Greece and Rome pulled out of their heads.

But let's say that whatever words Eve came up with, Adam thought they were too cutesy. He was the decider of their names. For himself, he assumed he was the template of humanity, He who is Who. The thing that struck him about Eve was, she was always moving around and making noises—buzzing about—on her own. And when some other creature was doing that, and Adam, naturally, went to kill it, sometimes Eve would say, "Let it live." (Ironically, the first thing she said that about with absolute insistence was baby Cain.)

So Adam is First Noun, but Eve gets to be a verb.

➢ *even*

One of those words whose placement in a sentence is crucial. Rasheed Wallace of the Detroit Pistons said, regarding the Cleveland Cavaliers after the latter won a fourth game, tying the playoff series in 2006 (which the Pistons eventually won): "Even the sun shines on a dog's ass sometimes." What this says is that everything—even the sun, sometimes—shines on a dog's ass at one time or another. Should be "The sun shines on even a dog's ass sometimes," or more loosely, "The sun shines even on a dog's ass sometimes." "Sometimes, the sun shines on a dog's ass, even." "Sometimes, the sun shines even on a dog's ass." "Sometimes, even a dog's ass catches the sunshine."

See *odd*.

➤ *evening*

No etymological connection between this word's meaning "time for a drink" and its meaning "establishing equilibrium," except in this song-title **zeugma**:

"Things Had a Way of Evening Out, Till I Spent One Out with You."

➤ exclamations

Exclamation points are to be avoided in writing, but in *quoting*? Hey!

Joey Heatherton, after returning from Vietnam: "There's a hill at Da Nang. Every inch had a marine on it. A mountain of men, a sea of green. And all good-looking. What an audience. You would say 'Hi,' and the whole mountain would yell, 'Wow! Wow! Wow!'"

Once at a pro basketball game I attended, the visiting coach protested a referee's call by loudly expressing incredulity: *"Whaaa??!!"*

The referee called a technical foul.

The coach responded, *"For saying 'Whaaa??!!'??!!"*

➤ *eye*

This word and *I* don't have a common root, but they share more than phonetic identity. The *I* of the beholder. "For as you were when first your eye I eyed," Shakespeare could not restrain himself from writing. In French there's a similar correspondence between *je* and *les yeux*.

f · **F** · f

All of us who have blown up a balloon or fallen back on a fluffy (see **stuff**) feather comforter (see **Goody Two-Shoes**) know the invariable sound of *f*. Or do we?

"I ask you to pronounce *s-o-w*," wrote Mark Twain, "and you ask me what kind of a one. If we had a sane, determinate alphabet . . . , you would know whether one referred to the act of a man casting the seed over the ploughed land or whether one wished to recall the lady hog and the future ham." If we had a sane, determinate literature, we wouldn't have a Mark Twain, but heaven only knows he had a point. Consider:

Oof. Fine.

Oaf. Fine.

Off. Fine.

Of. Please explain. How can the second most commonly used English word be the only one I can think of that pronounces *f* as a *v*? *Of* comes from the same root as *aft*, *after*, *off*, and *offal*, no *v* sounds in them. And *ablaut*, which suggests that maybe *of* should have been *ob*, as in "de land ob cotton." The letter *f*'s ancestor was the Phoenician *vau* or *waw*, which stood for the *v* or *w* sound, but it was shaped like a *u* on a stick, and after turning it into something that looked like a backward *f*, the Greeks decided they didn't need those sounds and dropped it altogether. The Romans restored it, turned it right way around, and eventually linked it to the *f* sound we know and love except in *of*.

How has that one *f*-as-*v* survived, 2,500 or so years later? Well, *of* is related (however tenuously) to the Old Norse *ofugr* (turned backward), whence the *awk* in *awkward*. (The land awk cotton?) And in Old Norse, *f* was pronounced either *f* or *v*. The Old Norse *hafa* was pronounced hava and meant "have."

So it's the Vikings you can thank for locutions like "a heap o' loving."

➤ familese

I suppose most families have special words they use among themselves.
One family calls windshield wipers "windle-shibers," after their toddler's stab at pronouncing *windshield wipers*. (My own son said "potato
quarter" for *tape recorder* before he got it right.) The first time I heard that
the president of Russia was named Putin I thought it sounded like a family
name for an intimate body part: "Don't forget to wash your putin, pud-
din'." But Sara Coleridge, wife of the poet Samuel T., was **perhaps** the most
prolific familese-coiner ever. In 1821 the poet Robert Southey, Mrs. C.'s
brother-in-law and childhood friend, wrote of her "Lingo Grande" in a
letter to a friend:

> I have carefully composed a vocabulary of it by the help of her
> daughter and mine, having my ivory tablets always ready when she is
> red-raggifying in full confabulumpatus. True it is that she has called
> us persecutorums, and great impropnetors . . . , and has often told
> me not to be such a stuposity; threatening us sometimes that she will
> never say anything that ends in lumpatus again; and sometimes that
> she will play the very dunder; and sometimes bidding us get away
> with our toadymidjerings. And she asks me, how I can be such a
> Tomnoddycum (though my name, as she knows, is Robert), and calls
> me detesty, a maffrum, a goffrum, a chattcrpye, a stillycum, and a
> great mawkinfort . . .
>
> On one occasion . . . I was fortunate enough to see this
> extraordinary language in the mint, if I may so express myself, and
> in the very act of its coinage. Speaking of a labourer, she said, "the
> thumper, the what-d'ye-callder—the undoer,—I can't hit upon it,—
> the cutter-up." These were the very words, received and noted as
> they came from the die; and they meant a man who was chopping
> wood . . .

Mrs. C. and her children were living with Southey and his family because Mr. C., a slave to laudanum, depression, and the muse, had de-
serted them. "She was of an ironic turn of mind: a dangerous thing to be at
the best of times," suggests Coleridge's biographer, Molly Lefebvre. "By
using a private language she was able to give vent in safety to her irony . . .

By using a method of verbal shorthand she could reach to the heart of things in a flash: for instance, to describe a man chopping wood as a 'thumper,' an 'undoer' and a 'cutter-up' is to express . . . a myriad of associated ideas and comments ranging from the sexual to the social."

I don't mean to suggest, *of course*, that *your* family's language has anything to do with anxiety.

➤ fart jokes

No, the pun is not the lowest form of *humor*. Anyway, who cares? See *partridge*; words, naughty.

Someday I hope to write a Western novel with a character in it named Silent Bud Dudley.

➤ figures of speech, clean

They are more ingenious, less on-the-nose, when not everything goes. The 1932 movie *Blonde Venus*, in which Marlene Dietrich dances her way out of a *gorilla* suit, is not demure, but back then movie dialogue stopped short of words regarded as obscene. In that movie somebody says, "That tightwad? He wouldn't give you the fleas out of his vest." That, I submit, is fresher than "the sweat off his balls," and just as *sonicky*.

Mark Twain's friend William Dean Howells bade him change, in *Huckleberry Finn*, "they comb me all to hell" to "they comb me all to thunder." The former might have been pushing the envelope at the time, but the latter has more of a ring to it.

➤ figures of speech, folksy, which so far as I know have not yet been used in literature

"I feel like a hog starin' at a wristwatch."

"So ugly he looks like a homemade child."

"A wink is as good as a nod to a blind horse."

"She ran home so fast you could play dice on the tail of her coat."

"Tea so strong you could trot a mouse on it."

"Quiet as a mosquito doing push-ups on a lemon meringue pie."

"He lives so far up in the woods, the sun sets between his house and the road."

"He looked like he'd been sortin' wildcats."

"Quick as a hiccup."

➤ figures of speech, gotten all wrong

I'm enjoying a story in *The New York Times Magazine* about a town trying to absorb, or repel, a large influx of Spanish-speaking immigrants. But then a cloud falls over my Sunday morning. A woman who is trying to get English established as the town's legal language is quoted as saying, "I don't want to get my butt in a ringer."

How can anybody expect first-generation Mexican-Americans to master English if neither a Middle American defender of that language nor the best newspaper in that language can get the expression "to get one's tit in a wringer" right? Of the activist, I would ask, "How in the world can anybody get his or her *butt* in a wringer?" Of *The Times* I would ask, "What in the world would be a *ringer* in this context?"

On the part of *The Times*, there may be an element of Freudian slip here, since it was *The Washington Post*'s publisher Katharine Graham who was warned by John Mitchell, then the nation's attorney general, not to get her tit caught in a wringer when her paper, and not *The Times*, was exposing the Watergate scandal. On the part of the activist, you can see why she wouldn't want to make the anatomically correct reference to herself, but that's no excuse for butchering an expression that is unpleasant and sexist but also—if you have any sense at all of what an old-fashioned washing machine was like—vivid and coherent.

➤ *first*

Long story short, this word is a combination of *fore*, as in front, and *-est*, used to form the superlative. So *first* is a boiled-down version of *foremost*, or *before-est*. That which is the most in front. Is that cool, or what?

➤ flack/flak

The former is often used for the latter. Sanctioned (unenthusiastically) by dictionaries. I say "unenthusiastically." RHU, for instance, defines *flack* for what it is, and then it says *flack* with a little ² next to it, which doesn't mean "to the second power," it means "yeah yeah okay this too if you insist" (as I interpret it), and then it says *flak*. It doesn't say, "These two words are six of one and a half-dozen of the other."

These words deserve to be kept distinct. A *flack* is a press agent. Engages in puffery. Here's what *flak* is:

Explosions! All around your plane in which you are way up in the air, over enemy territory! Concussions from flak are rocking your plane, and fragments of flak are blowing bits off your plane, and a hit of flak in the right place on your plane will send it down in flames. And maybe you'll be able to parachute out, but maybe not, and maybe some of the flak will tear a hole through you. You're way the hell up in the air, and people are flinging explosive missiles at your plane!

Flak comes from the anti-aircraft gun the Germans used in World War II: the Flak gun, a syncope (see **aight**) of *Fliegerabwehrkanone*, which breaks down literally into "pilot-ward-off-cannon." In English, *flak*'s lack of a *c*, which we would expect in a word that rhymes with *lack*, accents the harsh alien nature of that terrible stuff in the air.

Flak may also mean, figuratively, harsh criticism. But if you write that someone has "caught a little flack," you are writing that someone has chased down and grabbed a diminutive pufferist.

➤ Flaubert, Gustave

He rolled on the floor in agony for hours (compare Ford Madox Ford, at **ideal reader**) trying to think of *just* exactly the right word, *le mot juste*. At least that's what he is said to have done. In fact *it* sounds like something in Flaubert's satirical *Dictionary of Accepted Ideas*, for instance:

> TOAD. Male of the frog. Its venom is very dangerous. Lives inside a stone.
> LION. Generous animal. Always plays with a large ball. "Well-roared, lion!" "To think that lions and tigers are just cats!"

Flaubert wrote to George Sand: "You don't know what it is to spend an entire day with one's head in one's hands, taxing one's poor brain in search of a word." No, she didn't, she replied, perhaps stifling the impulse to say, "And you never got it on with Liszt." Maybe there were no thesauri in French then, but Peter Mark Roget's English one appeared five years before *Madame Bovary*. If Flaubert did in fact agonize more than, say, Mark Twain, who wrote while smoking cheap cigars in bed, it may in part have been because French has too few words in it: no more than a third as many as English.

By the way, *mot*, like *mutter*, comes from the Latin *muttum*, a grunt or word. *Mute*, however, comes from the Latin *mutus*, silent or dumb, from the **PIE** *mu-*, "imitation of a dull sound made with tight-pressed lips" (Chambers). See **M**; **D**.

➤ *flinch* and *wince* family, the

Eloquent tighten-up words from various roots: *flinch*, *clinch*, *clench*, *cinch*, *inch* (the verb), *pinch*, *winch*, *Grinch*, *wrench*, *cringe*, *whinge*, *mingy*, *stingy*, *mince*, *wince*, *tense*, *shrink*. And **think**? Maybe, if you do it, like **Flaubert**, with your head in your hands. What do all these words have in common? If you pronounce any of them pronouncedly, so to speak, your nasal passages constrict and you make the sort of face you make when you encounter a *stench*, or *stink*. The English word *French*, a contraction of something Germanic along the lines of *fränkisch*, may reflect a prejudice against *les Français*. The *eh* vowel is less tight than the *ih*, to be sure— *mensch* is a favorable word, perhaps mellowed by the *m*. According to OAD, the original Yiddish is *mensh*, which is softer and more expansive at the end. According to RHU and *Born to Kvetch*, the Yiddish is *mentsh*, which is less simply pinched. (WIII, inexplicably, omits *mensch*, though it includes *schlemiel*, *schmo*, and *schnorrer*.)

Compare **funky**, which also has to do with strong smells and may well connote offensiveness, but replaces the narrow *ih* or *eh* sound with the deeper, heartier *uh*, and therefore can connect to what is uptight in the original jazz sense of in-a-good-way together. No one in an outgoing mood would exclaim "Get finky!" or do the Finky Broadway.

➤ folk etymology

I'd like to tell you that this entails people in festive local costume doing the PIE-root dance while someone plays traditional airs on the *etym*, a kind of balalaika, but that would *be* folk etymology. Sometimes the folk is better than the scrupulous, if all you care about is a good story, but the etymologies that people send me by *e-mail* are usually, to quote a Roger Miller song, "pure-d B-U-double-L bull." Junk etymology. For instance, under the heading "Life in the 1500's":

> England is old and small and they started running out of places to bury people. So they would dig up coffins and would take their bones to a house and reuse the grave. In reopening these coffins, one out of twenty-five coffins [nice statistical touch] were found to have scratch marks on the inside, and they realized they had been burying people alive. So they thought they would tie a string on their wrist and lead it through the coffin and up through the ground and tie it to a bell. Someone would have to sit out in the graveyard all night to listen for the bells. Hence on the "graveyard shift" they would know that someone was "saved by the bell" or he was a "dead ringer."

Big Bill Broonzy once said that all music, as far as he knew, was folk music, in that it was all made by folks. But music is not *arbitrary*, and neither is etymology. I don't know the origin of "graveyard shift," but OED doesn't even find *graveyard* in print until 1825. "Saved by the bell" is *of course* a boxing reference, and a *ringer* is a sneak substitute, a professional player *rung in*, as the saying goes, to pose as an amateur. (There may be a connection to brass rings substituted for gold, but a ringer in effect is a gold one pretending to be brass.) *Dead* means absolute, exact, as in *dead on*. A dead ringer is such a thoroughgoing look-alike that he or she could pass for someone else.

I recommend *The Facts on File Encyclopedia of Word and Phrase Origins*, by Robert Hendrickson, which pleasingly relates stories about how figures of speech originated and also points out which ones can be supported by scholarship, which ones may be true but we don't know, and which are "strained imaginings." (He's less than all right on *okay*, though.)

I consider myself a shade-tree etymologist, like a shade-tree mechanic, who (back when you didn't need a computer to fix cars) set himself up independently by the side of the road and knew what he was doing. As opposed to a jackleg etymologist, like a jackleg lawyer or preacher, who was similarly self-appointed but incompetent and maybe crooked.

(Another form of folk etymology is the evolution of a term into something that sounds better to folks. *Welsh rabbit*—the original phrase, a jocular suggestion that the closest thing to rabbit the Welsh could afford was melted cheese on toast—thus became *Welsh rarebit*.)

See **arbitrary**; **fungo**; **kibosh**.

➤ *foot*

A triumph of **sonicky** evolution. Its ancestor is *ped-*, whence *podium, pad, pawn, pedal, podiatry, impede, expedite* (originally, to free someone's foot from a snare), and *peccadillo* (from the Latin *peccare*, to stumble, sin).

Now consider all these versions of *foot*:

Greek: *pous* or *peza*

Sanskrit: *pat* [long *a*], foot, and *padam*, footstep

Latin: *pes* [long *e*] (genitive *ped-*)

Middle Persian: *pai* [long *a*, long *i*], leg, foot—from which we get our *pajama*

German: *Fuss*

French: *pied*

Dutch: *voet*

Old Icelandic: *fotr* [long *o*]

Armenian: *otn*

Gothic: *fotus*

English (about 1125): *fot*

None of these works as well, for me, and I suspect for most native English-speakers, as *foot*: *f* for the sensitive cushioned padfall of ball and heel, *oo* for the aloofness of the arch, and *t* for the tip of the toe pushing off.

You can get a taste of three different cultural rhythms in English's brisk iambic *pedestrian*, the persnickety French *piéton* (*Voici m'sieu piéton*), and the heavy German *Fussgänger* (*Yo ho . . . Fuss . . . gäng*).

A metrical unit is called a foot **probably** because the rhythm of verse derives to some extent from walking. An *enjambed* line is one that doesn't end at the end of a sentence or clause—*enjamb* from the French for "stride over," *jambe* meaning "leg." John Hollander illustrates this admirably in his book *Rhyme's Reason: A Guide to English Verse*:

> A line can be *end-stopped*, just like this one,
> Or it can show *enjambment*, just like this
> One, where the sense straddles two lines: you feel
> As if from shore you'd stepped into a boat.

See **cush-footed**.

➤ footballese

Mind-body issue: "We didn't let down, we just mechanically didn't hold on to the ball."—Bill Fulcher, coach of Georgia Tech at the time, after a loss.

➤ Ford, Ford Madox

See **ideal reader**; **James, Henry**; *tango*.

➤ *franglais*

On an extra feature of the DVD of the Claude Chabrol movie *La Cérémonie* we learn what the French for "the making of" is:

Le Making Of.

➤ *frankly*

After it was disclosed that eight U.S. attorneys had been ousted, presumably for political reasons, even though their job ratings were high, President George W. Bush said, "Mistakes were made. And I'm frankly not happy about them." What's frank about that? Frank would be, "Mistakes were made. And frankly, I made them," or "Mistakes were made, and frankly, I am going to kick some butts."

See **interestingly**.

➤ *free*

Oddly enough, to anyone who has given much thought to trying free love, the word *free* comes from a **PIE** root (*pri-*) meaning "to love." Indeed, the Old English word *freon* meant both "to love" and "to set free." (One's loved ones were free, as opposed to the slaves in one's household.) As *pri-* words (*friend* being an exception) began to lose their love connection, words like *luba* (Old High German) and *lufu* (Old English) took over. These words—and their offspring, our *love*—derive from the Sanskrit *luby-ati*, meaning "(he) desires." We begin to see the problem.

➤ *friend*

From the same root as *free*. It used to rhyme with *fiend* (same long-*e* sound as in *field* and *piece*), according to Chambers. The vowel shortened under the influence of -*ship* in *friendship*. And a good thing, too.

➤ *fungo*

According to all references I have seen, the origin of this term, for a kind of bat used by a coach to hit practice ground balls and flies (tossing the ball up himself before hitting it) to his team's fielders, is unknown. But I have a theory. The purpose of a fungo bat is to narrow the range of the batted ball, to hit it not where the fielder ain't but where he is. The fungo bat used in the big leagues today, specially made for controllability, is a long thin handle that swells to a somewhat larger hitting surface toward the end. But I have seen old-school coaches using these bats with tape wrapped around the hitting part. What is the point of that? To lessen the deflectiveness of hard round wood. *Fungo* in Italian (compare the English *fungus*) means "mushroom." An Italian-American player in the thirties or forties might well have likened such a muffled bat to a mushroom. Or maybe it all boils down to the fact that a ball struck by a fungo bat, even without tape, doesn't go *crack*, it goes more like *fung*.

➤ *funky*

"When asked which words in the English language are the most difficult to define precisely, a lexicographer would surely mention *funky*," says an AHD Word History note.

Maybe it's one of those words, like *doo-wah-diddy*, about which if you have to ask, you'll never understand. Funk has to do with smell. Early blues and jazz music was played in rooms full of body odor, and food odor, and smoke odor, and booze odor, and the smell of deep feeling.

As far as I know, that about covers it.

➤ *funny looks*

Peculiar expression, that. To whom do we give a funny look? Someone who looks funny, that is to say peculiar. The other day I gave a fellow a funny look, without meaning to, and stopped to think that the reason I gave him a funny look was because he had a certain expression on his face—mouth held just slightly open, he seemed almost to be chewing on a toothpick, maybe, but not quite, and his eyes were fixed as if on something in the distance but you could tell he was just self-consciously trying to look like he was focusing on something other than himself—he wore, in short, the fake-casual air of someone who was afraid someone was going to give him a funny look. He must have done something at a formative age to attract a particularly searching and confounding funny look, and as a result he acquired that expression, and ever since then people have been giving him funny looks, not because he does anything to warrant them but because he has that expression. What he should have done: become a comedian.

Can writing capture any equivalent to facial expression? (Emoticons are cheating.) Certainly facial expression can be tellingly written about.

Quentin Crisp (see **arts, the**): "Without knowing it, I was acquiring that haughty bearing which is characteristic of so many eccentrics. What other expression would you expect to find on the face of anyone who knows that if he turns his head too quickly, he will see on the faces of others glares of stark terror or grimaces of hatred?"

See *logocentric*.

➤ *f*-word, the

In her review of *Network* (a terrible movie, by the way, for all its quotability), Pauline Kael took the screenwriter, Paddy Chayefsky, to task: "What happened to his once-vaunted gift for the vernacular? Nothing exposes his claims to be defending the older values so much as the way he uses four-letter words for chortles. It's so cheap you may never want to say ******** again." That was back in 1976, when *The New Yorker* didn't print "four-letter words."

In 1995 Random House published *The F Word*, edited by Jesse Sheidlower, who is now the editor of the Oxford American Dictionary. *The F Word* billed itself as "the complete story of the word still considered the most vulgar utterance in the English language." I believe it sold quite well. I contributed a foreword. The *f*-word had become so bandied about, I suggested, that perhaps the trend would be toward homespun euphemism:

> *Effing* will come back, and other eff-words.
>
> "You're looking mighty effable this evenin', Miss Effie—pardon my effrontery in bein' so effusive."
>
> "Why thank you, Eph, don't mind ef'n I do. And may I say you're lookin' mighty efficacious, y'sef."

I was not prophetic. From a discussion on the Poynter Institute website, which deals with ethical issues in the world of journalism, I gather that it's considered sexual harassment these days to say "fuck" in a journalistic workplace within earshot of anyone who objects to it, and many "journos," to use an irritating term often resorted to on that website, do. Object to it. (Whereas in my day it was not utterly unheard of—oh, never mind.) But I get the impression that double entendre such as the above would be frowned upon as well.

In less refined venues than newsrooms have apparently become, however, "fuck" is rampant. Little children shout it at each other as they walk past my house. According to a letter to Barbara Wallraff, who conducts the Word Court column in *The Atlantic*, the *f*-word "often simply means 'Omigosh' or 'Oops!'" Maybe they're trying to prove that they're not journos or anyone else confined to a corporate setting.

I guess it's a feminist thing, the stigmatizing of the *f*-word (also known as the *f*-bomb). According to Steven Pinker in *The Stuff of Thought*, a veteran male journo at *The Boston Globe* "was forced to apologize and to donate $1,250 to a women's organization when a female staffer overheard him in the newsroom using the word *pussy-whipped* with a male colleague who declined his invitation to play basketball after work." (See **ironically enough**.) "While it's tempting to ridicule the backlash against sexual swearing as a throwback to Victorian daintiness, it remains true that an atmosphere of licentiousness may be less conducive to women's interests than to men's." I have to say that I am glad to be able to look back on a period when that eternal truth was lost track of, but I know I *shouldn't* be glad. And I thank feminists for restoring some pungence to the awful old word.

As for the *p-w*-word, its offensiveness has held up from era to era. In 1981, Kael showed me the galleys of her review of *Reds*, in which she had described Warren Beatty's character as pussy-whipped. "You can't say that in *The New Yorker!*" I exclaimed. She didn't see why not. I suggested *uxorious*. She rolled her eyes. In the end, she let it be changed to *timid*.

Urbandictionary.com's number-one definition of *pussy-whipped* is judiciously couched: "The state of being influenced so greatly by your female significant other that you a) unreasonably change the way you act around your friends, family, and others so as not to upset said significant other and b) feel that you deserve a reward for not acting in a way that would upset said significant other." The second and third ones are harsher. Number four, I would hazard, is from a female:

"What a guy is called by his loser friends . . . Trying to sway the man or deter him from seeing the female . . . The friends try to be macho, or never really loved a woman or are jackasses. Also jealousy and ignorance related."

Getting back to the *f*-word, the cheap chortles Pauline deplored in *Network* are reborn in text messaging. According to Urbandictionary.com, the standard exclamation *OMG!* has expanded to *OMFG!*

See **bullshit**.

g · G · g

There is the soft one: *geranium*, *gymnasium*, *gestation*. I don't know how to generalize about that, but see **giblet**.

The hard *g* gets a guttural grip: even dictionaries acknowledge that *gag*, *gaga*, *gargle*, *gargoyle* (from the Old French *gargouille*, throat), *gurgle*, *glug*, *grunt*, *guff*, *grunt*, *gulp*, and *ugh* are at least **probably** of imitative origin. Furthermore, you don't have to be *gullible* (willing to swallow anything) to concede that **glottis**, *growl* (grrr), *grumble*, *grumpy*, *grudge*, *grouchy*, *gruff*, *groan*, *gush*, *gob*, *gobble*, *guzzle*, *glug-glug*, *chugalug*, *gaggle* (from *gagelen*, to *cackle*), *giggle*, *gourmand*, *glutton*, *glut* (from the Latin *gula*, throat—what do you point to when you say "I've had it up to here"?), *gizzard*, *gullet*, and *gorge* connect physically as well as referentially (like the regionalism *goozle*, and see **Google**, the Twainisms *goo-gooing* and *googling*) to the back of the throat. As do things that *disgust* us (a *gut* reaction), make us *regurgitate* or at least make the *gorge* rise or turn us *green* around the *gills*: *gunk*, *gurry*, *guff*, *glop* (which furthermore imitates the sound of mushy food dropped onto a plate), *garbage*, *gummy*, *goo*.

So how about *gravy*? You may well ask. A lovely thing, gravy, but the word sounds scratchy. (You need a *gravelly*, perhaps *grog*-induced voice to "Talk Like a Pirate"; see YouTube.) The etymology of *gravy* is unclear, but may go back to a misreading of a derivative of a Latin word for stew: *granatus*, consisting of many grains. The French have a better, lingering-on-the-palate word for gravy: *jus*, whence our *juice*.

Getting back to the gag reflex, how about references to things that make you swallow hard: *gory*, *gruesome* (from the obsolete *grue*, to shudder), *ugly* (from an Old Icelandic word meaning "fear"), *ugsome* (an old word for "disgusting"), *gasp*, *Gargantua* (supposed to have been derived from the Portuguese for "gullet"), *grief*, *Grinch*, **grisly**, *grizzly*, **gorilla**. Lots of insulting terms start with the hard *g*: *geek*, *goy*, *guinea*, *gringo*, *gook*, *greaser*, *goo-goo*, *goat*, *goon*, *goose*, *git*, *gink*, *goof*, *gimp*, *gawky*, *gangling*, *gauche* (from French *gaucher*, to walk clumsily).

Let us not, however, be glibly overcategorical. *Disgust* is after all the flip side of *gusto*, which is from the same root as *choose* and *chew*. As we have seen with *catch a crab* on the one hand and *catchy* on the other, *g* works one way in *snag* (or *nag* or *haggle* or *gig*) and another in **good** grip and related complimentary words: *gumption*, *get-up-and-go*, *go-getter*, *grit*, *guts*, *gung ho*. When something grabs you, it may not be good, but to grab hold may be life-saving, and when you get a grasp of something you're in business. *Grab* and *grasp* go back, says AHD, to "parallel (imitative) Germanic creations," which share a root with *Satyagraha*, Mahatma Gandhi's word, from the Sanskrit, for the policy of passive resistance that won India away from Britain and gave rise to the sit-ins and Freedom Rides of the American civil rights movement. The *-graha* has to do with seizing, and determinedly holding on.

Tradition holds, according to Richard A. Firmage in *The Alphabet Abecedarium*, that *g* was invented by a particular Roman: "Spurius Ruga, about 230 B.C. (and it appears that he derived some immediate benefit from it)." Perhaps Ruga was awarded a *g* to insert into his name anywhere he wanted. Since *spurius* in Latin meant "spurious," or "false," if I had been him I would have slipped it into my first name somewhere, Spurigus or Spurgius. But it's hard to put ourselves in the shoes of a person who lived that long ago. At any rate, the Roman *c*, *gamma*, inherited from the Semitic via Etruscan (which did not differentiate between the *g* and hard *c* sounds), was stuck with designating both the *g* and the *k* sounds. (What about *k*, or *kappa*, which the Romans had inherited from every civilization that came before them? See **C** and **K**.) Confusion resulted. Spurius came up with the notion of putting a little squiggle on the *C*. And that's how *G* was born.

How would you like to be able to tell your grandchildren that you invented one of the twenty-six letters we use today? Not that they would be as impressed, much less admit to being as impressed, as you would expect them to be, if I know grandchildren. But—what if there were things just that basic today that you could put a little squiggle on, and . . . There probably are such things, but my grandchildren won't tell me about them.

See **cog**.

➢ *gas*

To a scientist, no glass or anything else is even half-empty. The word *gas*, which came to mean, roughly speaking, a form of matter, like air, that is neither solid nor liquid, was coined by the seventeenth-century Flemish chemist Jan Baptist van Helmont, probably from the Greek *chaos* meaning "chasm" or "empty space." Van Helmont used it "in the sense of an occult principle supposedly present in all bodies" (Chambers), perhaps with a nod to the sixteenth-century alchemist Paracelsus, who used *chaos* to mean "proper element of spirits such as gnomes," gnomes being mythic dwarflike creatures who lived underground. So presumably their element—what they breathed?—was dirt.

Later in the seventeenth century, the philosopher Baruch Spinoza wrote: "Nature abhors a vacuum." That is a translation from his Dutch. He lived in Amsterdam in a community of Spanish and Portuguese Jews who had fled the Inquisition. Their synagogue put a curse on Spinoza: "The Lord blot out his name under heaven . . . There shall no man . . . come nigh to him." This for his clearheadedness, regarded as blasphemy. By trade he was a lens-grinder. He is said to have died from the effects of glass dust he inhaled.

➢ gender

See *he/she/his/her*; **sexism** and **pronouns**.

➢ *giblet*

Pronounced jib-let, which may look like "the cut of one's jib," but no connection: AHD says the root is the Middle English *gibelet*, from French for "game stew."

Why is the *g* pronounced like a *j* in *giblet*, and in *gimcrack*, *gibbet*, *gibe*, and (preferably) *gibberish*, but as a hard *g* in *gibble-gabble*, *gimmick*, and *gimlet*?

Well, *giblet*, *gimcrack*, *gibbet*, and *gibe* derive from French, in which *g* before *i* is very soft, as in *Gigi*. And *gibberish* is perhaps an extension of *jabber*, which is imitative. On the other hand, *gibble-gabble* is an extension of *gabble*, nobody knows the provenance of *gimmick* except that it first popped up in the U.S., and *gimlet* may come from Middle Dutch. So why the soft *g* in *gin*, a spirit invented in Holland? It's an English shortening of the Dutch *geneva*, from the Dutch *jenever* for the juniper berries that traditionally give gin its flavor.

You know what giblets are, I presume. RHU says "the heart, liver, gizzard, and the like, of a fowl, often cooked separately."

"And the like"? What part of a fowl that is cookable is *like* the heart, liver, and gizzard? Testicles, as in "rooster fries," but I've never heard of their being included in giblets. Do **chicken**s have kidneys? Edible ones? Let's not pursue this.

The main thing I want to contribute with regard to giblets is a personal example of what is known as "back-formation." My mother, who fried chicken giblets whole but cut turkey giblets up to make giblet gravy, used the **verb** "to gibble," always with "up," as in "Our best snack when I was a girl was to gibble up some cornbread in a glass of cold buttermilk," or "Now just look: you've gibbled up that Styrofoam all over the floor."

As we have seen, a giblet is not, etymologically, something that has been gibbled. But I think *gibble* (pronounced, **of course**, jibble) ought to be in the dictionary and that my mother should be credited.

➤ *glottis*

Another word for the vocal apparatus of the ***larynx***, but you don't learn it in school because the class—okay, the boys—would find it comical. A *glottal stop* is when you jam your vocal cords together so tightly that no air can get through, pressure builds, and then you release the air explosively. As in *uh-oh*. This you definitely do not want the boys to start doing, since it comes perilously close to a belch, and the *tt* in *glottal* is a great place for such a stop. On the original cast album of *My Fair Lady* you can hear the great Stanley Holloway glottal-stopping for the *t* sounds in "a li[ ]le bi[ ] of bloomin' luck." Recently we hear it in the catchphrase "No, you di[ ]n't."

Many of the vestigial, now-silent *t*'s in English words (*listen*, *whistle*) were previously glottal stops. As such, they got in the way. Didn't fit the appropriate sound. But we didn't want to go all the way to *lissen* and *whissle*. We could use the glottal stop in *wrestle*, given the grunting and groaning involved.

➤ Goldwynisms

As Samuel Goldwyn departed on an ocean liner, he cried out to his friends onshore, "Bon voyage." Goldwyn was a powerful figure in Hollywood before, during, and after its golden years. He produced notable movies, winning an Oscar for *The Best Years of Our Lives*. He is remembered, however, for his unintentional turns of phrase, which include "Include me out."

He was born in Warsaw somewhere around 1880 as Schmuel Gelbfisz, later Anglicized to Samuel Goldfish. It was by that name that he began—after having become one of America's leading glove salesmen—to produce movies, in 1914, but after forming the Goldwyn Company with two men named Selwyn, he took the merged name as his own. The company's symbol was Leo the Lion, who roared over the unlikely motto *Ars Gratia Artis*. By the time that company and lion had become part of Metro-Goldwyn-Mayer (MGM), Goldwyn had been ousted from it, and had set himself up as an independent studio. Anyone who is credited with saying "Don't talk to me when I'm interrupting" works best as his own only partner.

Others of his alleged utterances resemble **Berraisms**:

> "Anyone who goes to a psychiatrist should have his head examined."

> "My wife's hands are very beautiful. I'm going to have a *bust* made of them."

> "Flashbacks are a thing of the past."

Others are relatively straightforward:

> "We'd do anything for each other; we'd even cut our throats for each other."

> "A hospital is no place to be sick."

> "Go see it for yourself why you shouldn't see it."

Others have a certain tactical force:

> "For your information, I would like to ask a question."

At least one was prophetic:

"We want a story that starts out with an earthquake and works its way up to a climax."

And one, dating from the thirties, is incongruous only because the meaning of **verbal** had already been corrupted:

"A verbal agreement is not worth the paper it's printed on."

Goldwyn pretended to laugh along with those who quoted his **malapropisms**, many of which were no doubt concocted by writers who resented his sway over their work. But he chafed. According to the biography by A. Scott Berg, he spent time with a therapist to whom he blurted, teary-eyed, "I hate my mouth!" The therapist asked him "whether he wanted to be a master of these Goldwynisms, or slave to them." So he pretended to embrace—if not exactly to enbosom—his isms.

➤ *good*

PIE root *ghedh-*, to unite, join, fit. Other derivatives: *together*, from the Old English *togaedere*, from the Germanic *gaduri*, in a body; *gather*, from the Old English *gad(c)rian*, from the Germanic *gaduron*, to come or bring together. So the slang "together," meaning solid, "emotionally stable and effective in performance" (AHD), not only makes sense metaphorically but goes way back. See **well**.

God comes from a different root, *ghau*, to call or invoke, shared with *giddy*, from the Germanic *gudiga-*, possessed by a god.

➤ good letters, bad letters

From *The New York Times Magazine*, September 18, 1994: "Even the alphabet can be suspect. Surveys indicate that the letters *A*, *B*, *S* and *M* produce the most favorable feelings in people, while *Q*, *X*, *Z*, *F* and *U* evoke the worst."

AB (or *BA*) is my degree,
S and *M* is what I'm into—
Not—but either is better than *Z*:
So *terminal*, almost akin to

F U. We know what that suggests,
And as for *X*, nobody knows.
QU's for *QU*ota—that, and *QU*est's
Too arduous-sounding. *QU*id pro *QU*o's

Are *QU*estionable. The *QU*iZ *F*i*X* out-
Raged the *F*i*F*ties more than the *Bomb* (a
Specter relieved by its *B*'s, no doubt).
Anyway, now, let's have a *SAMBA*!

➤ *Goody Two-Shoes*

This time-honored term for an unbearable ray of sunshine has a more
interesting provenance than is generally known. Maybe you are the J.B. of
Dallas who wrote this to the lively syndicated source the Straight Dope
(from *The Straight Dope* by Cecil Adams, www.straightdope.com):

> We all know that grown-up liberals are sometimes called
> "do-gooders," a rather self-explanatory term. However, that same
> do-gooder at a younger age might have been called a
> "goody-two-shoes." Could you sort through the semantic thicket
> and tell us just where that term came from?

Here is the dope you got:

> "Little Goody Two-Shoes" was the heroine of a children's story of the
> same title, first published in 1765 and often attributed to that
> favorite of English graduate students everywhere, Oliver Goldsmith.
> The story, such as it is, concerns a poor waif who has somehow
> managed to make it through life with only one shoe. Finally
> rewarded with another, she scampers over hill and dale pointing at
> her feet and crying "Two shoes! Two shoes!" in so cloying a manner
> that her name has lived through the ages as a symbol of puerility.

In fact, Goody's story is (and this is a term I don't use loosely or often) a
hoot. Its anonymous author was undoubtedly Goldsmith, but he was too
fine a writer and too great a character to be favored by graduate students
alone. He might make us think of Harpo Marx if the sprites Harpo por-

trayed on-screen had been in any way benevolent. From Washington Irving's biography of Goldsmith:

> Among the anecdotes told of him while at college is one indicative of that prompt but thoughtless and often whimsical benevolence which throughout life formed one of the most eccentric yet endearing points of his character. He was engaged to breakfast one day with a college intimate, but failed to make his appearance. His friend repaired to his room, knocked at the door, and was bidden to enter. To his surprise, he found Goldsmith in his bed, immersed to his chin in feathers. A serio-comic story explained the circumstance. In the course of the preceding evening's stroll he had met with a woman with five children, who implored his charity. Her husband was in the hospital; she was just from the country, a stranger, and destitute, without food or shelter for her helpless offspring. This was too much for the kind heart of Goldsmith. He was almost as poor as herself, it is true, and had no money in his pocket; but he brought her to the college gate, gave her the blankets from his bed to cover her little brood, and part of his clothes for her to sell and purchase food; and, finding himself cold during the night, had cut open his bed and buried himself among the feathers.

People who knew Goldsmith laughed at and with him about equally. Dr. Johnson, the great lexicographer, who loved Goldsmith so much that Boswell was jealous, said, "No man is more foolish than Goldsmith when he has not a pen in his hand, or more wise when he has." Horace Walpole called him an "inspired idiot." Inspired, he was. I don't know of any other writer—much less one from the eighteenth century—who produced a play, poems, a novel (why no one has made a movie of *The Vicar of Wakefield* since 1917, I don't know), and a children's book that are still well-known and highly enjoyable—droll and affecting—today. The latest *Bartlett's* has seventy-four Goldsmith quotations, including "Silence gives consent," "the very pink of perfection," "Ask me no questions, and I'll tell you no fibs," this from "Elegy on the Death of a Mad Dog":

The man recover'd of the bite,
The dog it was that died.

and this niftily metrical sketch of his friend David Garrick, the actor:

> On the stage he was natural, simple, affecting;
> 'Twas only that when he was off he was acting.

(See **subjunctive**.)

Thanks to Project Gutenberg, *The History of Little Goody Two-Shoes* is available for free online. Goody's given name is Margery. Her parents die when she and her brother, Tommy, are but tykes. Here is how the mother passes: "Poor Woman, it would have melted your Heart to have seen how frequently she heaved up her Head, while she lay speechless, to survey with languishing Looks her little Orphans, as much as to say, Do Tommy, do Margery, come with me. They cried, poor Things, and she sighed away her Soul; and I hope is happy." How do you like that last little pivot? Goldsmith, who was addicted to gambling, wrote the book for money, which he was always short of, but he was too much of a mooncalf to be a hack. Without giving itself away as a semi-send-up, the story of Goody pushes the moralizing, heart-heaving conventions of the period's stories for children just a smidge, so as to poke some fun at preachy-soppy lit. Yet the story evokes genuine feeling. To quote Lillian Gish in *The Night of the Hunter* (as she sits rocking on her porch with a shotgun in her lap, ready for would-be child-snatcher Robert Mitchum), "It's a hard world for little things."

Goody is left with nothing in the world but an outfit of rags and just one shoe. Her brother has two, but maybe not her size, because much as the siblings dote on each other, he never offers to share. It is easy to imagine Goldsmith himself limping around with one shoe on, as a result of his sympathy for a barefoot one-legged man. Eventually, some kind person gives Goody a full pair, and she exclaims with beamish gratitude and forgivable pride, "Two shoes!"

You can tell it's a real writer's book by all the good crazy alphabet stuff. Goody rescues a raven from some cruel boys, names him Ralph, and teaches him to read and write. Ralph is her aide as she selflessly introduces other poor children to letters. "Put them right, Ralph!" she cries when her students get their alphabet blocks out of order, and he does. The raven is referred to as "that rogue, Ralph," at the point where the roguish author portrays him as not only a versifier but a plagiarist. Ralph is said to have "composed" the couplet "Early to Bed, and early to rise; / Is the way to be healthy, and wealthy, and wise"—a slightly looser version (hey, he's a bird) of the adage published in *Poor Richard's Almanac* thirty years before.

Other bits of the story must have provided satirical amusement to parents. After Goody grows up, still saintly, she invents "a Considering Cap"

almost as large as a Grenadier's, but of three equal Sides; on the first of which was written, I MAY BE WRONG; on the second, IT IS FIFTY TO ONE BUT YOU ARE; and on the third, I'LL CONSIDER OF IT. The other Parts on the out-side, were filled with odd Characters, as unintelligible as the Writings of the old Egyptians; but within Side there was a Direction for its Use, of the utmost Consequence; for it strictly enjoined the Possessor to put on the Cap, whenever he found his Passions begin to grow turbulent, and not to deliver a Word whilst it was on, but with great Coolness and Moderation. As this Cap was an universal Cure for Wrong-headedness, and prevented numberless Disputes and Quarrels, it greatly hurt the Trade of the poor Lawyers, but was of the utmost Service to the rest of the Community. They were bought by Husbands and Wives, who had themselves frequent Occasion for them, and sometimes lent them to their Children: They were also purchased in large Quantities by Masters and Servants; by young Folks, who were intent on Matrimony, by Judges, Jurymen, and even Physicians and Divines; nay, if we may believe History, the Legislators of the Land did not disdain the Use of them; and we are told, that when any important Debate arose, Cap, was the Word, and each House looked like a grand Synod of Egyptian Priests . . . I myself saw thirteen Caps worn at a Time in one Family, which could not have subsisted an Hour without them.

➤ *Google*

I wondered whether anyone had thought to write, "I've Googled so much I'm googly-eyed." So I Googled that expression. Several people had. Thought to write it. That's one thing Google is good for: checking to see whether something you think of has e'er been so well expressed. The downside is, it **probably** has been. For instance, I thought it would be a jolly fresh notion to call this book *Writing from* **Scratch**. I Googled that title and found that notion to have been around for a while, long enough to have taken on a technical computer-code application beyond my area of competence. If Shakespeare had been able to Google . . . oh, never mind.

The founders of Google, who aspire to digitize all human knowledge (but see **cancan/Cancún/cooncan**), have confessed that they spelled their company that way because they didn't realize that *googol* is spelled *that* way. *Googol*, meaning ten to the one-hundredth power (or ten duotrigin-tillion, one tick higher than the figure at which most pocket calculators max out), was coined around 1938 by the late Milton Sirotta, who was nine years old at the time. His uncle, the American mathematician Edward Kasner, had asked him to come up with a name for the biggest number he could imagine. (Some sources claim that this happened in 1920, but Kasner didn't use the word in print until 1940. It's hard to believe he would have kept *googol* under his hat for so long.) When I was a child (and I can say the same of my children in their turn), we would sit around saying, "I'm a jillion times more [something] than you."

"Well, I'm a squillion."

"Well, I'm a squillion padillion."

Young Milton (**probably** trusting his uncle not to top him) was better than that.

But numbers are made to be topped. If you think a googol is big, how about a googolplex, which either Milton or more likely his uncle or a colleague came up with after realizing that too much is never enough. A googolplex is even bigger than a googol, way way way bigger, biggledy-bigger: it's ten to the googolth power. At that, Milton and Edward rested. And so, so far, have we all.

Googleplex, on the other hand, is the headquarters of Google, in Mountain View, California. I have visited there. It looks like Berkeley in the sixties without any faculty. A form of heaven. No employee is ever more than a hundred feet from free food, either a cafeteria or a fruit stand or a candy stand. There's a sand volleyball court.

Let's hope that there will never be a need for the word *Googleth*, as in to the Googleth power, because it looks like it ought to be the archaic first-person singular of the verb: He Googleth me to lie down in the still waters.

Getting back to Milton, I assume it was his uncle who decided how to spell *googol*. Looks vaguely Arabic maybe, which befits a mathematical term (see **algorithm**), and is also more intimidating (compare *ghoul* and *Mongol*) than *Google*, which is friendlier, a better household word. Chambers suggests that Milton may have been influenced by the comic-strip character Barney Google. (See **heebie-jeebies**.) We don't know that, but let's consider it.

Barney was a man—to quote the 1923 hit-song tribute to him—with "goo-goo-googly eyes." *Googly* presumably derived from *goggly-eyed*. To goggle is to stare. Goggles are bulgy protective glasses. *Goggle* may be said to derive from a combination of the Middle English *gogelen*, to roll about, and *gogel-eyed*, squint- or one-eyed. (See **louche**.) OAD makes a nice syncretic stab: "probably from a base **symbolic** of oscillating movement." We've seen that in animated cartoons.

Shakespeare never used any form of the word *google*, but its present participle appears in *Huckleberry Finn*: "The duke he never let on he suspicioned what was up, but just went a goo-gooing around, happy and satisfied, like a jug that's googling out buttermilk."

The duke was communicating in goo-goo noises at that juncture because he was pretending to be mute. Perhaps those noises influenced Huck's choice of words. But if we picture the action of a thick liquid pouring *glug glug glug* out of a jug, we might infer that *googling*—its admirable **onomatopoeia** aside—aptly invokes the bobbing of an Adam's apple during prolonged swallowing. The *Dictionary of Smoky Mountain English* defines *google* (or *goozle*) as "the throat, Adam's apple." (In 1859 a resident of the Smokies was said to have relished a meal of turnip greens cooked with hog's google.) The Adam's apple (larger than Eve's, hence deeper in pitch) is the voice box, which in infants googles out goo-goo noises. (See **diaphragm**; **larynx**.)

Has Google rounded up a googol of data bits yet? Depends on when you read this. What if this one was to be the googolth one? Wait a minute. Has anybody gotten credit for *googolth*? Which, now that I think about it, is not felicitous. Looks like *Golgotha*. I'm no Milton Sirotta.

In cricket, a *googly* is a ball bowled in a distinctively deceptive way. My understanding is that it is delivered more or less the way a *screwball* is in baseball, but since it strikes the ground before it reaches the batsman, it breaks the opposite way. But I may be oversimplifying.

➤ *gorilla*

A word that ancient Greek translators made up for very hirsute creatures reported around 500 BCE by a Carthaginian named Hanno who voyaged along the coast of Africa. Hanno presumably wrote his account in the Phoenician alphabet, which had no **vowels**. That, or the fact that Hanno had been at sea for a long time, may account for the translators', or Hanno's, impression that the creatures he sighted were, as RHD puts it, "a race of hairy women."

➤ *gossamer*

If you have had the good fortune to catch sight of these marvelous long fine filaments aglint in the sun and floating on air, you will wonder why the word comes from "goose summer." It's because gossamer occurs on certain sunny, very faintly zephyrish days in the fall, or Indian summer— the season when, back in the day, English people traditionally ate goose.

The Old English for "goose" was *gos*. That which we call a goose, either the bird or the poke, clearly cried out for the move to *oo*. For gossamer, the softness of *oss* works, as does the unstressed *a* replacing the heavy *uh* of *summer*. Cole Porter lyrically captured a magical but fleeting romance, "just one of those things," as "a trip to the moon on gossamer wings." No fabric is that delicate, but the connection to capricious travel is apt. Morgan Bulkeley Sr. sheds light on the gossamer phenomenon:

> Only when we look in the direction of the sun do we perceive this dazzlement of day ribboning from . . . bushes, trees, or even free-floating in the air. Look in another direction, and you will not see it at all. Walk through it, and you will feel nothing.
>
> Still, it is real enough . . . The day being somehow salubrious, myriad small spiders are moved by wanderlust. With deliberate intent, they . . . spin out their long, invisible strands that will bear them off on the slightest air current . . . Like animate seeds they disperse their kind to fresh fields and pastures new.
>
> It is usually very young spiders of many different species that exhibit this aeronautic proclivity. Their weightier elders are shackled

by the webs they spin. Chains for the one prove wings for the other, as if it were the privilege of the young to soar . . . Should they fall upon water, their infinitesimal weight will not break the surface tension, so they may be wafted ashore or aloft again. These little Argonauts have been caught in ships' rigging hundreds of miles at sea.

➤ *gourmet*

An etymology here that no gourmet would be eager to dwell on. The word is from the Old French *groumet*, servant, valet in charge of wines, from the Middle English *grom*, boy, valet, whence also *groom*. Granted there's a food-related influence: the earlier form *gourmand*, which still means a hearty, not necessarily very discriminating overeater.

Gourmand, despite its relative lack of refinement, has kept a firmer grip on the Frenchy sound of its *ou* than *gourmet*, whose first syllable is now most often pronounced gor- by Americans, and sometimes (by the Gormet Deli on Route 19A below Tarpon Springs, Florida, for instance) even spelled that way.

➤ *graffito*

The singular of *graffiti*. Here's one reportedly seen on the underside of a stairway in New York City:

> The law of gravity is a friend of mine –
> He's a sensible law—I like him fine.
> What go up must come back.
> It's a bona fide justified natural fact.

Here's one I saw in Tuscaloosa, Alabama: "I think I won't put this here because I am the only one who really appreciates it and it will be defaced but I don't care because I really know. M."

See **Here I Sit, All** . . .

➤ *gray/grey*

To me, *grey* looks greyer. The Middle English form (AHD) was *grei*. And the British, who see a lot of it nearly every day, prefer *grey*. OED points out, however, that Dr. Johnson's dictionary spelled it *gray*, that *grey* is "phonetically ambiguous" (I suppose it *could* be mispronounced to **rhyme** with *key*, by someone unfamiliar with *bey*, *fey*, *hey*, *lei*, *obey*, *prey*, *they*, *trey*, *whey*, and *oy vey*), and that there are other linguistic arguments for the -*ay* spelling.

OED also notes that some nineteenth-century printers asserted that *grey* and *gray* were not quite the same color: the former being only a mixture of black and white, while the latter might be lighter or warmer— or "any broken color of a cool hue," according to *Field's Chromotography* (1885), which insisted that "the distinction between grey and gray should be carefully observed." A voice in the wilderness. (See **weatherese**; *livid*.)

➤ great one-word sentences

Fuhgeddaboudit.

C'm'ere.

Touché.

Look!

And the actual last line of *The Maltese Falcon*, which is not, as most people believe, Bogart's "This is the stuff that dreams are made on," but Ward Bond's response: "Huh?"

➤ great three-word sentences

Omit needless words.

Ain't she sweet?

The game's afoot.

Call me Ishmael.

Baby it's you.

And they're off!

I got it!

(According to Ira Berkow's biography of Red Smith, that distinguished sportswriter's "least favorite player" was a third baseman named Bill Werber, who was so proud of his college education (from, you guessed it, Duke) that he would correct other players' grammar. He even admonished his teammate Skeeter Newsome for shouting "I got it, I got it" to signal, as is traditional, that a pop fly was his to catch. "It's 'I have it, I have it,'" insisted Werber. He was wrong, *of course*, because grammar is to some extent situational: when two people are attempting communication while running toward roughly the same spot while looking straight up in the air, something as forceful as a hard *g*—or the ur-consonant, **M**, in the alternative "Mine! Mine!"—is required.

➤ great two-word sentences

Jesus wept.

Nooses give. (From Dorothy Parker's poem about the drawbacks of various suicide methods. The next, and final, line is "You might as well live.")

Go figure.

Non serviam.

I'm home.

➤ *grisly*

Means "gruesome" (which is from the obsolete English *grue*, to shudder). Understandably confused with *grizzly*, which strictly speaking means "greyish," from the French *gris*, but hey, the Latin for the grizzly bear's subspecies is *horribilis*.

It's a good chewy word, *grisly*, even tougher than *gristly*. What you don't expect to learn is that its **PIE** root, *ghrei-*, to rub, is also that of *grime* (from the Germanic for "to smear"), *Christ* (from the Greek for "to anoint"), and *cream*.

The *New York Times* TV listings once described *Bundle of Joy*, a 1956 movie with Eddie Fisher and a pregnant Debbie Reynolds, as "a grisly little sunbeam." I tell you what, though, I like Debbie Reynolds. I was on *Politically Incorrect* once with her and Allen Ginsberg, and he was interesting, but she was a lot more down-to-earth. (See **hyphen**.)

➤ *groin*

AHD says this is perhaps from the Old English *grynde*, meaning "abyss" or "hollow," influenced by *loin*. WIII agrees on *grynde* (related to *ground*) but says the *oin* influence is from the British-dialect *groin* (related to *grunt*) meaning "the nose and sometimes the upper lip of an animal (as a swine)."

(Omigod, I just discovered where *oink* comes from.)

If you ask me, *groin* is a **portmanteau** of *grind*, as in bump and grind, and *loin*.

➤ *gussy*

As in "gussy up," that is, to dress up elaborately. AHD says: "perhaps from Australian slang *gussie*, an effeminate man, from *Gussie*, diminutive of the personal name *Augustus*." OAD is more cautious: "perhaps from *Gussie*, nickname for . . . *Augustus*." RHU is not having it: "origin obscure." WIII doesn't even acknowledge the word. I don't know about you, but I'm already thinking TV movie. Father named him for a great Caesar, but little Gus had other interests, and—long story short—now the boy's empowered as a verb.

h · **H** · h

Geoffroy Tory maintained that *h* "is not a letter; nonetheless it is, by poetic license, given the place of a letter." It's silent in *honest*, *hour*, and **rhythm**, dropped by Cockneys, contracted out of *could've*. The English word for the letter has no *h* sound: *aitch* lost one of its aitches when it came into English from the French *hache* (which, by the way, is also French for *ax*). Frequently, complains David McKie in *The Guardian*, contemporary Britons overcorrect by pronouncing the *h*-word *haitch*. McKie is not happy:

> Aitch suggests something amenable, affable, amicable, where haitch
> is harder, harsher, more hostile. Aitch P Sauce, I think, may be
> expected to seep more gently and co-operatively out of the bottle
> than the possibly balky and truculent Haitch P Sauce. Haitch G Wells
> sounds to me a more aggressive man, and writer, than Aitch G Wells.
> An Aitch R Aitch might be expected to proffer a limp regal
> handshake, where Haitch R Haitch sounds more apt for trouble in
> nightclubs and service in Iraq.

To be sure, *h* heads up a heap of effortful words. Heigh-ho, heigh-ho, it's off to work we go: *hack*, *haggle*, *hammer*, *handle*, *hard*, *harness*, *harry*, *harsh*, *hatch*, *haul*, *hawser*, *heavy*, *hectic*, *heft*, *heist*, *hew*, *hie*, *hike*, *hit*, *hitch*, *hod*, *hoe*, *hog*, *hoist*, *honcho*, *hoof it*, *hop*, *horse*, *hound*, *huff*, *hump*, *hunch*, *hunt*, *hurdle*, *hurl*, *hurry*, *hurtle*, *hustle*, *hype*. Soldiers trudge to *hup-two-three-four*. Football players get off on *hut-one hut-two*. Soldiers brace to *atennn-hut*. Sled-dog drivers don't say "mush," they say "hike." Sailors hauling in sail chant "yo-ho heave ho." Ward Bond heads the wagon train west with "wag-guhhhnns *ho*!" "Hunh," said steel-driving men each time they swung their heavy hammers. "Whew," we say when something *ex-hausting* is over.

Ben Jonson was *hip* to *h*: "Be it a Letter, or Spirit; we have great use of it in our tongue." *Spirit*, like *inspire*, comes from the Latin for either spirit or breath. In the Book of Genesis, *h*umanity is born when Je*h*ovah (*JHWH*) ex*h*ales into some eart*h* (in Latin that would be *humus*, same root as *human*) and *h*up-la*h*: Adam. I'd have called him Hadam, but it wasn't up to me. (See *Eve*.)

The "power" of *h*, says OED, "is that of a simple aspiration or breathing, with just sufficient narrowing of the **glottis** to be audible before a vowel. It is often silent, or lengthens the pronunciation of a preceding vowel." Ohhhh. Ooohhh. Ahhhh.

We *hum*. We *hem* and *haw*. We *huff and puff*, *hoot and holler*. We *hiss* or (if we're a Southern dog) we *hassle*, we *howl*, we raise a *hue and cry*. We laugh: *ha ha*, *hee-haw*, *heh heh*, *ho-ho*. We shout: *hurrah*, *huzza*, *hi-ho*, *hoo-hah*, *yo-ho-ho*, *hip hip hurray* or *hurrah*, *wa-hoo*. We announce that we've caught on to something: *aha!*, *oh-ho!*, *unh-hunh*. We grunt: *hmm?*, *hunh?*, *humph*, *harumph*, *ahem*, *pooh*. We greet: *hello*, *hey*, *hi*, *ho*, *how*, *howdy*, *ahoy*. When we want someone to hear what we think we're hearing, we say "Hark!" or "Hist!" or "Hush!" We raise a *hubbub* or a *hullaballoo*. We *hiccup*. We *whistle* and we *whisper* (originally *hwistle* and *hwisper*; see **wh-**). When we are *hoarse*, our voice is *husky*. We breathe heavy: *hubba-hubba*, *hamada-hamada*, *hotcha*. We weep: *boo-hoo*. We worship with *hosannahs*, *hallelujahs*, and *holy*, *holy*, *holy*'s. We blow into or puff on a *horn* or a *hookah*. If something is overinflated, blown out of proportion, we call it *hooey*, *hype*, *hyperbole*, a *hustle*, *huckstering*, *humbug*, *ballyhoo*, *hoohah*, *hot air*. A big blow is a *hurricane*.

Chambers notes that "in common words beginning with *exh-*, the *h* is generally silent" and was therefore left out of the Middle English *exalen*, exhale, and *exort*, exhort—only to be restored in the 1500s and 1600s by scholars imitating the Latin spelling. But might not those learned men have been motivated as well by the apt breathiness, however subliminal, of *h*? The Latin *exhalare* was a combination of *ex-*, out, from the **PIE** *eghs*, and *halare*, to breathe, of unknown origin. Well, *ex-* ends in an outward hiss (as *in-* ends in an inward tuck), and the *ha* in *halare* sure sounds **son-icky** to me.

In blends, *h* lends breath: it turns labial *p* or guttural *g* into fricative *f*, for instance. And how about the *h* in *ghost, ghastly, aghast*? It doesn't induce audible catch-of-breath as in *abhorrent*, but it's there, in spirit.

Consider the *h* in *oh*. The difference between "O beautiful, for spacious skies . . ." and "Oh, beautiful."

How about *sigh*? In 1250 it appears as *sigen*, but people must have thought, Come on, there's got to be an *h* in there somewhere. By 1303 it was *syghen*.

Rheumy is pronounced the same as *roomy*, but there's a difference—for one thing, the silent *h* evokes the laryngonasal. Similarly, the *h* in *catarrh*. The silent *h* in *rhapsodist* helps make him or her poofier than a *rapper*. In *rhetoric* it adds a touch of inflation.

Hey, *h* is personal. Originally, *he, she, it,* were *he, heo, hit; they* and *them* were *hi* and *hie*. Before *I*, the first-person singular pronoun in English (as it breathily still is in German) was *ich*. *You* used to be *thee* or *thou* (originally pronounced with the soft, breathy *th* as in *thorn*). We still have *he, her, him, his, hers, who, whom,* and *whose*. Other intimate *h* words: *have, hold, whole, heaven, human, hope* (aspiration), *head, hand, health, heart, hearth, here, hug, hubby, honey,* and *home*.

H is the symbol for hydrogen, the first element of the periodic table, the lightest element, and the element most prevalent in the universe, though not on earth, where it is highly volatile and usually found combined with oxygen as water, hence its name from the Greek for, roughly, "water-producing." It is also the simplest element, a single electron orbiting a single proton.

H is a slang term for heroin, whose name comes unfelicitously from *hero*, for its supposed, temporary effect on its user's self-esteem.

See *hmmmmm*.

➤ *has-been*

A bee that is over the hill.

➤ *hater*

In 2006 Representative Alcee L. Hastings of Florida was passed over for the chairmanship of the House Intelligence Committee because he had been impeached and removed as a federal judge in 1989 in connection with a bribery case. (He was not convicted of any crime.) His public statement was: "Sorry, haters. God is not finished with me yet."

Sorry, Haters is an enigmatic movie first screened at festivals in 2005 and available now on DVD. It's a making-sense-of-9/11 psychological thriller that some respondents on IMDb.com hated, some loved, and most (including me) found highly interesting and uneven. As Pauline Kael used to say, it "has something."

The sixty-five definitions of *hater* on **Urbandictionary.com** (as of April 2008) constitute a redolent stew of ***subjective/objective***. The number-one definition (1,237 votes for; 149 against): "A person that simply cannot be happy for another person's success. So rather than be happy they make a point of exposing a flaw in that person."

Definition number three (640 for; 468 against) is "Overused word that people like to use because someone else expresses a dislike for a certain individual."

Definition number nine (94 for; 80 against), submitted by "straight up snitch":

1. A person who hates others unprovoked.

2. A person who hates out of jealousy, depression or racism.

3. Someone who hates someone superior to them.

4. NOT someone who hates a hater.

5. NOT someone who hates someone after being provoked.

6. Adrian C. from Glenmore Park High School.

Followed by ten lengthy "scenarios" involving said Adrian C. as a hater or as rightfully hated.

Hater has become a ***meme***, it seems.

➤ headlinese

If literal news*papers* die out, so will headlines like this one from the *Berkshire Eagle* of August 14, 1998:

REPRESSED-MEMORY

CANNIBALISM CASE

HAS SHRINK IN PICKLE

The story, by the Associated Press, began:

Illinois has moved to discipline a prominent psychiatrist accused of convincing a patient that she was a cannibal who ate human flesh meatloaf and the high priestess of a satanic cult.

In most any medium, careless syntax can give rise to brief, startling misimpressions—as, here, that the shrink convinced the patient that she ate, rather than was, a high priestess. But only the printed page has column widths, which give rise to a distinctive surreal poetry, as in this from the *New York Post*: SAY SLEUTHS EYE AXED AIDE. The spatial exigencies of ink-on-newsprint are comparable to regular meter in verse. Online, the *Eagle* permits itself flaccid free-verse headlines like this:

CITY PLEDGES STRICT ENFORCEMENT OF

LAW

As headlines cease to be column-determined, newspaper words like *deem* and *slain* and *vie* and *woes* (MONEY WOES THREATEN THEATER OF THE DEAF)—space-saving versions of *consider* and *murdered* and *contend* and *problems*—may fade from the language. Too bad. And *garner*, which is not a space-saver so much as just the sort of word that looks right in a headline—HYBRIDS GARNER LOCAL INTEREST—and nowhere else.

Columnar compression and framing lends intensity. Here's a headline that plunges us into a scene:

HOGS LOOSED AFTER COLLISION

CREATE HAVOC ON A HIGHWAY

It sets up the story's first sentence, a quote from a police sergeant on the scene:

"It was just hogs flying through the air and people hitting hogs."

➤ *hear that*, ambiguity thereof

African-American street-corner beggar, to well-dressed African-American passerby:
"Hey, man, I need some money."
Passerby (passing on by) to beggar:
"I hear that."

➤ *heebie-jeebies*

A more **sonicky** term for the jitters coined in the 1920s by Billy De Beck, in his comic strip *Barney* **Google**. Billy also gave us *hotsy-totsy*, meaning, in a fully affirmative sense, all right, hunky-dory, as in "everything is hotsy-totsy."

Why do so many reduplicative or near-reduplicative expressions start with *h*? To wit: *hacky-sack, hamada-hamada, handy-dandy, Handy Andy, hanky-panky, hardeharhar, hari-kari, harum-scarum, Heckle and Jeckle, heebie-jeebies, helter-skelter, herky-jerky, heehaw, heyday, hickory dickory dock, hi-fi, higgledy-piggledy, hillbilly, hinky-dinky, hippy-dippy, hip-hop, hobnob, hobgoblin, hocus-pocus, hodgepodge, hoi polloi, hoity-toity, hokey pokey, holy roller, hoochy-coochy, hoodoo, hoo-hah, honeybun, honky-tonk, hotchpotch, hotshot, hot spot, hotsy-totsy, Howdy Doody, hubba-hubba, hub-bub, huckaback, the hucklebuck, hugger-mugger, hula-hula, hullabaloo* (originally *hollo-bollo*), *hully gully, humdrum, Humpty Dumpty, hunky-dory, hurdy-gurdy, hurly-burly, hustle and bustle,* and *hysteron proteron*.

That's fifty-four, and I've left out a couple of obscure ones. *H*'s closest competitor in this department is *w*, with sixteen. Five of those start with **wh-** (and tend toward obscure English or Scots dialect: *whim-wham* (a trinket), *the whim-whams* (the jitters), *whimsey-whamsey, whilly-whaw,* and *whittie-whattie*), which, according to dictionaries and me, should generally be pronounced *hw-*.

You will note that many of those *h* expressions refer to disorder and jumblement. Most are of unknown origin. (No matter what you may have learned at your mother's knee, *hunky-dory* probably does not come from a street in Yokohama where sailors could find a bit of all right.) They're the sort of expressions that people pull out of the air to convey something otherwise indefinable, like *whatchamajig*. Could it be that those *h*'s betoken intakes of breath? See *H*.

➤ *Here I Sit, All Broken-Hearted: A Treasury of Restroom Verse,* all I have so far

The title.

➤ *he/she/his/her*

In his book *Words*, Paul Dickson lists a number of genderless pronouns that have been suggested in various quarters, including *et*, "from the *e* in *he* and *she* and *t* in *it* . . . created by Aline Hoffman of Sarnia, Ontario"; *per*, used by Marge Piercy in per book *Woman on the Edge of Time*; *hirm*, a *her/him* composite; and *hesh*, from *he/she*, courtesy of Professor Robert Longwell of the University of Northern Colorado. None of these work for me, especially *hesh*, which will forever evoke for me one of my favorite characters on *The Sopranos*.

Then there is *thon*, an all-purpose third-person about which Dickson quotes William Zinsser as saying, "Maybe I don't speak for the average American, but I very much doubt that thon wants that word in thons language or that thon would use it thonself."

Personally, I have no problem using "he or she" or "she and he" and "his or her" or "her or his," which brings everyone to the party without lumping them together in the singular *they* or *their*, which seems to have settled into general preference, but which puts me off. For instance, someone on **Urbandictionary.com** defines *mirrorface* as "the unintentional look of coolness, focus and determination" that people give themselves in a mirror. That's interesting. But the definer goes on: "a self-preservation technique in which one fantasizes about looking way better than they really do." You can't tell me that *they* goes well with *one*.

I suggest contracting *his or her* into *his'r*. And, maybe, just maybe, *she or he* into *sh'e*. I realize that the latter, especially, does not look like English, but neither do other contractions that we've grown accustomed to, like *I'd've* and *mustn't*.

See **if/whether**; **sexism and pronouns**; **statistical rhetoric**; **ze**.

➤ *hip*

AHD and other references suggest that *hip*, the adjective meaning "keenly aware" and the verb meaning "to make aware," comes from the Wolof *hipi* or *hepi*, "to open one's eyes, be aware." That makes sense to me. I visited Senegal, where Wolof is spoken (also French), in the late seventies. People in the markets seemed on top of things, all right. The standard way of haggling was to *laugh*. Not dismissive sarcasm, but spit-take, uproarious, what-fools-we-mortals-be laughter of delighted disbelief. Seller names price, prospective buyer guffaws, chortles, wheezes, comes back with a counteroffer, which seller finds equally preposterous, and so on until they settle.

It may be worth mentioning, however, that the 1811 British *Dictionary of the Vulgar Tongue* (see **dictionaries, gender-skewing**) defines *hyp* or *hip* as "a mode of calling to one passing by," with this example of its use: "'Hip, Michael, your head's on fire': a piece of vulgar wit to a red haired man."

Then there's the *hip* in the old exclamation (which a friend of mine sent to a friend who had successfully weathered an operation to replace both hips): "Hip hip, hooray."

See **name, scientific, they couldn't think of anything** . . .

➤ Hittite

In one online dictionary of Hittite, grandfather is *huha*, which sounds lively; in another, it's *huhha*, which sounds like breathing hard. I am a grandfather, but I am not as old as Hittite, which died off in the twelfth century BCE along with the Hittite empire, which had dominated most of Asia Minor. In the Old Testament, Bathsheba's husband, poor jerk, was Uriah the Hittite. David seduced Bathsheba while Uriah was off in a war somewhere, and got her pregnant, so he brought Uriah back and bade him sleep with her so the child would seem to be his, but Uriah smelled a rat, so David sent him back into battle with a note instructing Uriah's commander to abandon him to the enemy. As a result, a curse was laid upon the house of David. You might say, then, that Uriah had the last laugh. Hittite for "to laugh" is, or rather was, *hahhars-*.

The reason I looked into Hittite was that popular writers so often use it as a virtual synonym for gibberish: "He might as well have been speaking Hittite." And yet there are grounds to believe that Hittite was the first derivative of **PIE** to be set down in a form of writing (which survives on clay tablets), and that Hittites were the first to spread an Indo-European language to other cultures. In Hittite *watar* means "water," *puggant-* means "repulsive," *huelpi-* means "a young animal," and *hand-* means "sincere, honest." Hittite for **partridge** is *kakkapi-*, which I'd call **sonicky**.

Here is a passage from an online translation of a Hittite account of two gods fighting dirty (I don't know what to make of "knees"):

> Kumarbi bit Anu's "knees" and his manhood went down into his inside. When it lodged there and Kumarbi had swallowed Anu's manhood, he rejoiced and laughed. Anu turned back to him, to Kumarbi he began to speak: "Thou rejoicest over thine inside, because thou hast swallowed my manhood. Rejoice not over thine inside! In thine inside I have planted a heavy burden . . . Three dreadful gods have I planted in thy belly as seed. Thou shalt go and end by striking the rocks of thine own mountain with thy head!"

There again, the last laugh.

➤ *hmmmmm*

The thesis, which I find persuasive, of *The Singing Neanderthals*, by Steven Mithen, is that the first stirrings of language were *hmmmm*: Mithen's acronym for *holistic*, *manipulative*, *multi-modal*, *musical*, and *mimetic*. In other words, early hominids were like me in Japan: using every aspect of the body and imagination in pursuit of rough intelligibility.

Hmmmmm is also a hum, shades of Winnie the Pooh. We might imagine the first conversation:

Hmmmm. (With a wink)

Hmmm? (You mean . . . ? As if she didn't know.)

Mm-hmm. (You *know* what I mean.)

Hmmmmmm. (Thinking it over)

And eventually, if all goes well, a **mutual** (or anyway complementary) *Mmmmmmhhhhh.*

Many English words are similar to *hmmmmm*: *hum*, *ham*, *him*, *hymn*, *hem*, *ahem*, *helm*, *homonym*, *honeymoon*, *hum*, *hump*, *hymen*, *home*, *humble*, *humor*, *humus*, *human*. (The last two derive from the PIE root *dhghem*, whence *earth*.) Swift's *Houyhnhnms*. And how about **whom**? And *humuhumunukunukuapuaa* (a trigger fish with a snout like a pig's). And *humph*. On a desert island with someone, you could **probably** get by with just those, and plenty of winks and inflections.

➤ *hocus-pocus*

This bit of magician's patter may derive from part of the Latin liturgy, *hoc est corpus (meum)*, which is intoned at the moment when a bite of bread is transubstantiated into the body of Christ—deemed appropriate then, for the production of a rabbit from a hat. From *hocus-pocus* itself may derive *hoax*, *hokey-pokey*, and *hokum*, from which *hokey*, *hoke it up*, and *hanky-panky*.

➤ *honest broker*

A broker expects to reap a benefit, a commission or fee, from negotiating a deal between or among other parties; an honest one is otherwise **disinterested**. This the United States once presumed and tried to be, in attempting to foster peace in the Middle East, say. The regime of Bush II, however, has had no qualms about being (**perhaps** not quite knowingly) an **unreliable narrator**. The word *broker* stems from the Spanish *alboroque*, a ceremonial gift at the resolution of a business deal, which in turn is from the Arabic *baraka*, divine blessing. Barack Obama's first name comes (by way of his father, same name) from that word.

I am told that today's Wall Streeter no longer uses *broker* as the **verb** form, but instead endeavors *to broke* a security. One reason I'm not rich is that I am broker-phobic. I assume they are always trying to unload dreck on people like me and lining up something underhandedly predetermined for insiders: if it ain't fixed, don't broke it.

And I resent how often we hear "keeping Wall Street analysts happy" as a reason for cutting back on the quality of products and the enjoyability of work.

➤ *honey*

The Latin for it, *mel*, gives us the appropriately sweet-flowing word *mellifluous*. But I'll tell you what: At a roadside stand in Tallahassee, Florida, I once heard an, I'd say, about seventeen-year-old young woman, blond and—if I were to say "full-bodied," I would not mean that in a prurient way. Nor would I mean she was heavy. She was wholesomely well put together, fresh, sort of buttery. I heard her pronounce the plain old English word *honey* (one of her stand's wares) in a way—closest I can come is *hunnih*—that I doubt I will ever forget. There was no element of come-on implied or inferred. If she called her boyfriend "honey," I'll bet it was in a more personal tone. This was her matter-of-fact, congenial, over the counter, public *hunnih*. It did honey such unforced justice, I wish I had it on tape.

➤ *hoo-hoos*

Back in the early eighties I was to make a speech in some out-of-the-way place in Pennsylvania. A driver picked me up at the Pittsburgh airport. He was an affable sort, but he kept saying things that seemed oddly off, somehow. We were going to pass by Gettysburg, he said. That didn't seem right, especially when he said, "That was where they spent the winter, you know, without any shoes. Feet wrapped in rags, if they even had that. And we think we have it hard."

Oh, I thought, he means Valley Forge.

I asked him about a sign in front of a private home we passed: BARB'S BIG PIES!

"Oh yeah," he said. "That lady bakes *famous* lemon pies. They're *real* big. Like a chef's hat. The *meringue* part alone is this thick!"

He held his fingers about an inch apart, which didn't seem particularly thick for meringue, especially on a pie comparable to a toque.

Then he started talking about his wife. "I made her a Valentine for her birthday. Out of Styrofoam and copper wire? The heart went right through the middle of the arrow."

Well, you could, after all, look at the depiction of a pierced heart that way, but I was still trying to sort out what seemed askew about the image—in fact, I was beginning to wonder about being way out in the middle of nowhere with this man when he said, "She's smart, you know. We grew up together. I wasn't good in school, at all. She was. Oh yeah. She was a hoo-hoo."

"I'm sorry?" I said.

"A hoo-hoo. You know. *Hoo-hoos Among American High School Students.*"

We got where we were supposed to. He was good at what he did. But I hadn't realized that anybody's dyslexia extended as far as pie.

But back in the day when New York cabdrivers were much more likely to chat nonstop in English with their passengers than in some exotic native tongue over their ear-clip phones, I did have a cabbie who, after nearly running over an elderly lady, said in a reassuring tone, "Nah, you don't wanna hit a pedestrian. 'Cause you have to fill out a form. And if you don't dot all your *t*'s and cross your *i*'s . . ."

➣ *hopefully*

This word—as in "Hopefully, my prince will come"—has been a great bone of contention between people who think of themselves as realistic latitudinarians and people like me, whom the other people think of as cranks. Most people are in the former camp, and blithely use *hopefully* as a sentence-modifying adverb, as in "Hopefully, Satan's legions will surrender." To me, that suggests hopeful surrender. Similarly (now there's a sentence-modifying adverb), the sentence "Thankfully, all the evildoers have been burnt to a crisp" suggests, to me, that the evildoers are grateful for their immolation—and I don't know of any examples of saints, even, of whom that could be said.

The American Heritage Dictionary Usage Panel, on which I thankfully and even hopefully serve, was asked whether to vote *acceptable* or **unacceptable** on three sentences.

1. Hopefully, the treaty will be ratified.

I voted *unacceptable*.
Hopefully, here, is obfuscatory shorthand. I want to know who's hoping: "I hope/We hope/A great many people in both countries hope/Polls show that 84 percent of Israelis and 61 percent of Palestinians hope the treaty will be ratified."

2. The new product will be shipped by Christmas, hopefully.

I voted *unacceptable*.
Hopefully, here, is irritatingly semi-noncommittal. Doesn't give us anything to base a shopper's decision on. More helpful would be honestly unpromising: "We at L. L. Bean cannot guarantee that the new product will be shipped by Christmas, but we hope so."

3. Mercifully, the game ended before the opponents could add another touchdown to the lopsided score.

I voted *acceptable*.
Hope is most often used as a verb, a verb that tilts toward desire. That makes *hopefully* a hotter and looser wire than *mercifully*. Who's hoping? "Here's hoping we'll meet now and then," in the context of Cole Porter's "Just One of Those Things," is far from bullish, but it's vernacular and personal and leaves no doubt that it's the speaker who, however unlongingly, is doing the hoping. "Hopefully, we'll meet now and then" would be chillier, more distancing, more corporate. Maybe it's *you* who hope that new product will be shipped by Christmas.

Sentence 3 is unambiguous about who or what was being merciful. Not the dominant victors, obviously, but the game: the clock. This is a respectable **pathetic fallacy**. To ascribe mercifulness to a game's ending is fanciful, but not so fanciful that the quality of mercy is strained. Had the intention been to say that the winners were showing mercy, this option was available: "The winners mercifully ran out the clock without trying to score again."

On the other hand, if an announcer says, "Hopefully, the Steelers will run out the clock . . . ," he may be implying, without being plain enough to say so, that he represents a right-thinking consensus. My response would be, "Maybe *you* hope so, but I hope they'll squeeze in several more touchdown passes to Hines Ward."

Regrettably, an announcer is likely to toss *hopefully* into a sentence almost anywhere: "The Steelers hopefully will run out the clock," or "The Steelers will run out the clock, hopefully," or "The Steelers will hopefully run out the clock." Maybe that doesn't bug you. It does me.

How about *regrettably*, then? We can readily take it to modify the rest of its sentence because we can say "It is regrettable that." (Same goes for *fortunately*: "It is fortunate that.") We can't say "It is hopeful that." And there is no such word as *hopable* or *hopably*.

Would we say, "Fearfully, Iran will get the bomb"? Or "Expectfully, it's going to rain"? Or "Dreadfully, the market will crash"? Would we say, "Hopelessly, the day will come," to mean that we hope it won't? Martin Luther King did not say, "Dreamfully, one day this nation will rise up and live out the true meaning of its creed . . ."

On the analogy of *generally speaking* or *conservatively speaking*, you can say that *hopefully* is short for *hopefully speaking*. Grammatically speaking, that may pass muster, but semantically, isn't there something cheesy about, say, "Hopefully speaking, we will be able to move on from *hopefully* soon"? "Generally speaking, people need people" is a nod to inevitable exceptions. "Conservatively speaking, the bake sale will pay for itself" is a lowball estimate. Begin a sentence with "Hopefully speaking," and whatever follows sounds like hot air.

Construably, *hopefully* is so popular in contemporary rhetoric because it serves as something like an **elegant variation** of sound and rhythm. After droning along through a humdrum series of sludgy truthisms, you can shift gears. Without committing yourself to anything anyone could object to, you can kick off a new sentence with a small sigh of an *h* floating a bold long *o* bumped by a peppy *p* on puffy *f* on quick *uh* followed by two flowing *l*'s, a bit of long *E*, and a beat-skipping comma, and you've given your discourse a bounce. It even sounds sort of statesmanlike.

But it's not. "Our goal is to fully and finally remove a real threat to world peace and to America," said George W. Bush on signing the congressional resolution that authorized his use of force in Iraq. "Hopefully this can be done peacefully. Hopefully we can do this without any military action."

And now: "Hopefully, we'll get out of this war" instead of "I hope we'll get out of this war" (or "Let's hope . . .") is like "Thoughtfully, we'll get out of this war" instead of "I think we'll get out of this war," or "Fearfully, we'll never get out of this war" instead of "I'm afraid we'll never get out of this war." To be sure, "I hope we will get out of this war" is such an obvious sentiment as to be hardly worth saying, but so is "Hopefully, we will get out of this war," except for the sake of its spurious lilt.

➤ hopeless

"You're hopeless," often spoken with as much fondness as rue, means there is no point hoping to change you, you're incurable. Hence you may fondly/ruefully describe yourself as "hopelessly devoted" to someone, or as a "hopeless romantic." I guess it would take a foolishly strict literalist to ask why you sound so fond of being fond in the archaic sense of *foolish*, as in "Why so pale and wan, fond lover?" But when someone calls himself or herself "a hopeless optimist," *hopeless* is overextended. You might call *hopeless optimist* oxymoronic (from the Greek for "pointedly foolish"). But I don't think it's pointed. Not, for instance, in this self-description from a website where Russian women advertise themselves as marriage material:

> I am a hopeless optimist and the soul of any company. I still believe in fairies . . . I am waiting for some magic in my life and I hope I will be able to find that man who will bring this fairy in my life.

➤ horror story, all I have so far

"It was all knots and bulbs and slime and veins and it was squirming in the undergrowth making a noise like *k-k-k-k*, like telling a horse to go only harder."

➤ *humor*

To speak of "dry humor" is odd, if you know *humor*'s history.

Originally, in English (spelled *humour*, as it still is in the U.K.), the word betokened wetness (hence *humid*) or bodily fluids. Medieval medicine held that people were governed by four humors: blood, phlegm, yellow bile or choler, and black bile or melancholy. Too much phlegm, and you were phlegmatic; too much choler, choleric. Jaques, in *As You Like It*, spoke of "a melancholy of mine own . . . , in which my often rumination wraps me in a most humourous sadness."

Against this background, a person's humor came to mean his or her temper or whim—to humor someone is still to indulge that person's mood. Here and there in Shakespeare a comic character puns on *humour* in such a way that we may see it beginning to connote funniness, but the word still had to do primarily with serious fluxes. In *Much Ado About Nothing*, indeed, *humour* crops up in direct opposition to drollery. When Benedick, a wisecracking confirmed bachelor, is led to believe that Beatrice, an equally sharp-witted confirmed maiden, is sweet on him, his love starts coming down, as they say in blues songs. He thinks maybe he should stop trading bookish barbs with the lady and go with the flow of natural manly juice: "Shall quips and sentences and these paper bullets of the brain awe a man from the career of his humour?"

Not until late in the seventeenth century does OED find *humour* or *humor* meaning what it means today: that which excites amusement, "distinguished from *wit* as being less purely intellectual, and as having a sympathetic quality in virtue of which it often becomes allied to pathos." Humor is more moist (and what a juicy word is *moist*), we might say, than wit. The overlap, though, is essential. Humorless wit is arid, witless humor soppy.

In his choleric declining years, the distinguished humorist James Thurber could wax grandiose about humor—arguing in his cups that *some* humorist, ahem, should get the next Nobel Prize, and proclaiming, in print, "It is high time that we came of age and realized that, like Emily Dickinson's hope, humor is a feathered thing that perches in the soul." A bit wet, that.

➤ hyphen

This tidy horizontal connective hardly resembles a can of worms (that is to say, a can-of-worms sort of doohickey). Indeed, it is a highly efficient sense-clarifying tool, which has come down to us (in a catch-as-catch-can sort of way) from the Greek for "in one" and in part from the same **PIE** root as *simple*. Nevertheless, its use, by and large, is hit-or-miss. Online, we may find a New York University editing workshop, worked up by Sonia Jaffe Robbins, that includes a thoroughgoing breakdown of the hyphen. Hyphen-phobia arises at the get-go:

> Hyphens cause writers more trouble than any other form of
> punctuation, except perhaps commas. This may be because the
> hyphen has no analogue in speech; it is punctuation created purely
> by the needs of print.

It's always heartening to see **punctuation** related to the senses. To me, even the hyphen has some sonic, or kinesthetic, force, at least in a construction such as "that deer-in-the-headlights look." Aloud or on the page, hyphens quicken the pace, the connectedness, yet provide enough separation to avoid confusion.

Consider:

Run down to the store for me. A distinct sliver of pause between *run* and *down*, because they are closely related but separate words: a verb telling what to do and an adverb telling what direction (roughly) to do it in.

Give me the rundown on that store. No pause at all in the compressed noun *rundown*.

It's just a little run-down country store. Just enough pause in the compound adjective to evoke, perhaps, the passage of time—at any rate a process.

Why, then, does *run-on sentence* require a hyphen, whereas *chemical runoff* doesn't? The first, after all, is a jammed-up thing, the second something dismayingly loose. It's because *runoff* is unmistakable to the eye, but *runon* looks weird. Of course so does *thoroughgoing*, but in a not-un-English sort of way, and we've become used to it.

Here is the sort of hyphen error I encounter most often as a reader: "Orson Welles's fevered ego was only reined-in one time." Better all around would be "Only once was Orson Welles's fevered ego reined in," but at any rate *reined in* is like *run down*, above. "Welles's reluctantly reined-in ego soon reasserted itself" would be okay, like *run-down*, above.

Even when it isn't ungrammatical, heedless hyphenation may be a means of forced marriage. Consider *much-awaited* (from a baseball story that also had someone "shutting the door on a milestone"). You don't await *much*, you await *long*. A *much-awaited* event is like a *much-lost* relative or a *muchtime* employee or a *muchstanding* friendship. It is not English. It is not any language.

➤ *hypocoristic*

This is a good example of how un*sonicky* (not to mention creepy) words that are derived from the ancient Greek can be. A hypocorism is a pet name, from the Greek *hupokorizesthai*, to call by endearing names or (OAD) "to play the child," from *korizesthai*, to caress, from *koros*, boy, or *kore*, girl, and *hypo* beneath or secretly. If you call your granddaughter "Toots," you are being hypocoristic. I'll bet the old Greeks didn't use *hypo-coristic* around the house. See **familese**.

i · I · i

From what AHD calls the "pronomial stem" *i*-, we get *ilk*, *yonder*, *identity*, *id*, *it*, *yes*, and *item*. Quite a range there.

I is different. We don't get *I* from *i*-. We get *I* from *eg*-, which has given us only *I*, *ego*, and the German *ich*. There's an ilk for you.

The first person singular. (The last person singular, globally, at least to date, was Adam.) I believe there is an inspirational book entitled *I Come Third*, but you notice what the first word in the title is. According to Wiktionary.com, *you* is the most commonly used English word and *I* is second. But we must remember that *you* is subjective, objective, singular, and plural. *I* and *me* together—not even including *we*—are much more frequent than *you*.

That's the way people are. But other languages don't *capitalize* the first person singular. Is English especially egotistic, or insecure? Well, it's a little-known story, but *I* has emerged from a long line of indignities.

The Old English for *I* was *ic*. Not good for self-esteem. In the Middle English period it evolved into *ich*, pronounced itch.

"Will you take this woman to be your lawfully wedded wife?"

"Itch will."

Not a good start. Over the years, the *ch* fell away. For a while it attached itself to adjacent vowels, as in *cham* for *I am* and *chill* for *I will*.

"Will you take this man to be your lawfully wedded husband?"

"Chill."

Not a good start.

The *ch* lingered longer in some parts of England than others. When Edgar, in *King Lear*, adopts a dialect to conceal his identity, he uses *chill* for *I will*. According to OED, as recently as 1875 people in "remote parts of Somersetshire" were saying "utchy" for *I* and "utchil" for *I will*. *Utchil* from bride and groom would suggest that the rehearsal dinner was coming back on them.

At length, *ich* became *i*. Without the **dot**. Such a piddly little pen-scratch of a word kept getting lost. The dot (the *tittle*, that is) helped, but not enough. So: capitalization. At long last, *I* came into its own.

Now if only people would stop substituting it for **me**. "He ran into Mickey Mantle and I," *The Times* quotes Whitey Ford, the former Yankee pitcher, as saying.

Why would *Whitey Ford* talk like that? Whitey Ford is cool. Once, hanging around the Yankee dugout before a spring training game, I heard somebody tell Whitey he was looking rocky that morning, and he said, "Yeah, last night, I think I got some bad ice cubes." I've used that, since.

Surely Whitey Ford wouldn't say, "He ran into I." So why "Mickey Mantle and I"? Does *me* sound too personal, physical somehow? To *Whitey Ford*?

When Cole Porter, in "I Get a Kick Out of You," explains why he doesn't get one out of air travel, he gets an extraordinary amount of juice out of the sound of long *i*: "Flying too high with some guy in the sky / Is my idea of nothing to do." That *i* keeps ascending in the mouth, pushing against the roof, and just when you think it's as high as 'twill fly—to the *sky*—it double-clutches, up, again, to *my* and then, again, to the initial *i-*; and tumbles: *-dea of nothing to do*.

" 'S Wonderful," I would say, but that's Ira Gershwin.

➤ *id*

Odd that this and *ID* are so different: the latter makes you (and your ego) respectable, the former *au contraire*.

➤ ideal reader

In 1911 Ezra Pound, who at this point in his life tended to wear "trousers made of green billiard cloth, a pink coat, a blue shirt, a tie hand-painted by a Japanese friend, an immense sombrero, a flaming beard cut to a point, and a single, large blue earring," presented himself to the influen-tial novelist and editor **Ford Madox Ford**—a corpulent Britisher conventionally dressed and heavily mustachioed, whose highly readable memoir is our source for Pound's attire. Pound had poetry for Ford to read. As Hugh Kenner describes it in *The Pound Era*:

> The summer was the hottest since 1453. And into these quarters marched jocund Ezra Pound, tending his new book that chaunted of "sprays . . . of eglantine above clear waters," and employed such diction as "hight the microcline." Ford saw that it would not do. The Incense, the Angels, elicited an ultimate kinesthetic demonstration. By way of emphasizing their hopelessness he threw headlong his considerable frame and rolled on the floor. "That roll," Pound would one day assert, "saved me three years."

They became friends. (*Hight* is archaic for "called"; *microcline* is a kind of feldspar used in making *porcelain*.)

Ten years later, Pound served as T. S. Eliot's ideal reader. Eliot gave Pound "The Waste Land" to read, Pound cut a good deal of it out (a wasteland is no place for fat), and Eliot dedicated the finished product to "*il miglior fabbro*," the better craftsman, Pound. Pound went on to be a friend of the Mussolini regime beyond the time such a thing was appropriate (**Will Rogers** liked Mussolini in the thirties), spouted anti-Semitism in wartime, and wound up incarcerated in a mental hospital.

Ford created, in *The Good Soldier*, perhaps the best-known **unreliable narrator**. He was himself dependably, zestfully unreliable in his memoirs. Here he is (with an assist from Guy de Maupassant) recollecting **Henry James** (a triplex of unreliable narration) on Algernon Swinburne:

> He mimicked the voice and movements of Swinburne with gusto. He let his voice soar to a real falsetto and jerked his body sideways on his chair extending his hands rigidly towards the floor below his hips . . . And he particularly refused to believe that Swinburne could swim. Yet Swinburne was one of the strongest salt-water swimmers of his day. One of Maupassant's *contes* tells how Swinburne's head with its features and hair of a Greek god rose from the sea beside the French writer's boat three miles out in the Mediterranean and how it began gloriously to converse. And so conversing, Swinburne had swam beside the boat to the shore. No

doubt Maupassant had his share of a poet's imagination. But
Swinburne certainly could swim.

And see **prose rhythm; readers, fashioned out of suet and squash.**

➤ *if/whether*

If "then" is implied, use *if*:

"If the river don't rise too high, [then] we will get Mama to the family
burial ground before she gets too ripe."

If "or not" is implied, use *whether*:

"I don't know whether [or not] we will get Mama to the burial ground
before she gets too ripe." (These are literary allusions to the great American novel *As I Lay Dying*.)

We might very well *of course* say, "I don't know if we will get Mama to the
burial ground . . ." without confusing the issue. But here's something I
heard on National Public Radio:

"The agreement did not address if detainees or their lawyers would be
able to see any classified evidence."

That *if* sticks out like a sore conjunction. "Damn it," that *if* cries, "this
is not my job."

Here is what the NPR sentence would be if everything implied in it
were made explicit: "The agreement did not address the question of
whether or not detainees or their lawyers . . . ," etc.

There's nothing wrong with leaving out "the question of" and "or not."
Furthermore, this is an *if* you can get away with. It bothers me, but most
people would pooh-pooh my purism. In other statements, however, an *if*
that ought to be a *whether* can get you in trouble.

If a candidate said, "I won't debate if troop levels are high enough,"
people might well think he was saying, "If troop levels are high enough, I
won't debate."

And even though the NPR sentence may not be downright misleading,
it "catches a crab." If you're rowing crew and one of your oars enters the
water at a bad angle so that it hangs up, (then) you have caught a crab. Your
whole boat is thrown out of *rhythm*, and the other end of your oar may jab
you in the midsection. You shouldn't let that happen. To avoid **sexism and**

pronoun issues, let's call that reader or listener Pat. You don't want to bring Pat up short, unless there's a point in doing so. If Pat gets brought up short for no reason, Pat is going to find another boat.

If I'm Pat, (then) I'm expecting "did not address whether . . ." When I hear "did not address if . . . ," I'm thrown back into what came before—did I miss something? Has the announcer already said what the question to be addressed is, and is she now (it was a she) tossing in a note of contingency?

When asked in a press conference whether, if his generals thought a surge in troop levels was a bad idea, he would overrule them, President George W. Bush might have caused confusion if he'd said, "I'll report back to you if I support a surge." He did not. He went too far in the other direction, though: "I'll report back to you as to whether or not I support a surge or not."

Using *if* to mean *whether* can also lead us into the senseless **subjunctive**, as in (Michiko Kakutani, *The New York Times*): "One biographer asserted that the queen once asked if Dante were a horse—or a jockey." In his generally well-written book *The Glorious Deception*, Jim Steinmeyer writes that an audience "never questioned if he were really a Chinese magician, or a New York theatre professional, or a Lancashire lad. They didn't ask whether he was a loyal husband, a good father, or an honest man." The *whether he was* is right. Maybe the *if* isn't wrong, but it brings out the *were*, which is.

To be sure, plenty of fine utterances have used *if* for *whether*. In the movie *Roxie Hart*, reporters and photogs ask the murderess Roxie (Ginger Rogers) to do the black bottom for them. She's having a press conference in jail. She replies, blushingly, in a Noo Yawk accent, "I don't know if I ought." (*Ought* sounds more like ooo-utt.) And then she commences. Zestfully. The press and her jailers join in. I question whether *whether* would have worked there. Usage ain't always a matter of ought.

If is a great little word, used well. It's probably the shortest title of any famous poem. And here, legendarily, is a message from ancient Athens: "If we take Sparta, we won't leave one stone on stone." Reply from Sparta: "If." Except that in ancient Greek that would have been *an* or *eiper*. *If*, which was *gif* in Old English and comes from the tiny **PIE** root *i-*, whence also sprouted *yonder*, *yes*, and *identity*, is better.

See *he/she/his/her*.

➤ *if you will*

Dick Cheney, in his heyday, used this expression often:

"We also have to work, though, sort of the darkside, if you will." (In other words, we have to make captives feel the sensations of drowning until they tell us what we want to hear.)

"I think in fact there has been over a time a restoration, if you will, of the power and authority of the president." (In other words, the president is above the law.)

"And then we'll fall back into the pre-9/11 mindset, if you will." (In other words, electing Democrats would increase the risk of terror attack.)

There were many more instances, in each of which Cheney was saying in effect "whether you will or not," and to each of which the all-American response would have been, "No, we won't."

➤ *incredible*

Is there any way to rehabilitate the literal meaning of this word? Currently people use it, or *unbelievable*, to mean "wonderful, amazing." "You look absolutely incredible." "She's an unbelievable role model," literally an indictment, is meant as a resounding endorsement. People who speak of an "incredible story" **probably** intend to mean that it is astonishing, not dubious.

So how can we mean *incredible* anymore? We can call a story *implausible*, but that might mean no worse than unlikely (untruthy, even; see **truthiness**). Neither *questionable* nor *unreliable* is quite the adjective for something that downright defies belief. *Uncreditable*, maybe, but I doubt that will catch on. It doesn't exactly **trip off the tongue**. Maybe *uncreditworthy*. An account that nobody can take to the bank.

➤ *inkling*

Isn't this a great word for (Chambers) "slight suggestion, vague notion, hint"? We might imagine a spermatozoa-resembling little fella swimming around the edges of our cognition. An informal group of writers, including J. R. R. Tolkien and C. S. Lewis, at Oxford University in the 1930s called themselves the Inklings (they met at a pub called the Eagle and

Child, which they referred to as the Bird and Baby), but *inkling* has nothing to do etymologically with the far more definite *ink*, which is from the Greek *enkaiein*, to burn in. (See **Times, The New York**.)

AHD says *inkling* may be related to *ningkiling*, a Middle English variation on *nikking*, meaning possibly "a whisper, mention." If I may, I would like to quote a couplet I wrote once from the viewpoint of a puppy dog standing, with a look of bemusement (from the French *muser*, to stare stupidly), on a sheet of newspaper:

> Who is born with the faintest inkling
> There's anything wrong with spontaneous tinkling?

See **groin**.

➤ *intelligible*

We say something is unintelligible or barely intelligible, but we never say, "That argument of yours sure is intelligible." Why doesn't *intelligible* come up in positive contexts? Maybe because *-ligible*, the clump of three unstressed syllables at the end of the word (see **artisanal** and **lamentable**), cries out to be stumbled over or mumbled indistinctly. We do use *distinctly* as a positive—*tinct* is nice and pointed and unencumbered by a train of unemphasis.

We don't often use *comprehensible* approvingly either. It's not burdened by a draggy terminal threesome, but it is shlumpy five syllables with only one real stress and that one beginning softly with an *h*. If you add the prefix *in-*, however, you get something livelier: a double **dactyl**, *in*-com-pre-*hen*-si-ble, in which the foreshadowing *in-* and the ditta rhythm of *-compre-* bring out the *-hen-* sharply and huffily:

> Biggity-wiggity,
> Henry A. Kissinger
> Turned on a liberal
> Critic and grumped:
> "I find your reasoning
> Incomprehensible!
> Umpity umpity
> Umpity umpt."

➤ *interested*

From the Latin for "to be between." Say we're walking along and see a foot-
print with seven toes. "Here, this is interesting," I'll say, and there it will be
between us, appealing to the curiosity of both of us, if I'm correct in my assumption. If in this sense you are interested, then you are not *uninterested*.

Or say I'm putting together a deal. I lay it out on the table to see if you
want to get in on it. If you do, you are interested in that you have a stake,
you stand to gain or lose from it. In this case you are not *disinterested*.

So if you are to comment trustworthily on a deal—business, political,
romantic—you need to be *disinterested* in the deal, not working your own
gain-seeking angle.

Why insist that a scrupulous writer heed this distinction? Because if
the use of *disinterested* to mean *uninterested* becomes common enough—as
seems to be happening—then the word has lost its distinctive meaning
and we will have taken one more step down the slippery . . .

This just in: *disinterested* has lost its distinctive meaning.

See **truth**.

➤ *interestingly*

It is often tempting to begin a sentence—one containing information that
the writer considers interesting (so what were the previous sentences,
chopped liver?)—with this word. But might not the reader prefer to be the
judge of that? *Incidentally* might leave the writer less vulnerable. But let's
face *it*, that's false modesty.

➤ internal letters

A friend **e-mail**ed me this:

> Tihs is smoe crzay stfuf . . . psleae raed.
>
> *The paomnnehel pweor of the hmuan mnid.*
>
> Aoccdrnig to rscheearch at Cmabrigde Uinervtisy, it deosn't
> mttaer in waht oredr the ltteers in a wrod are, the olny iprmoetnt
> tihng is taht the frist and lsat ltteer be at the rghit pclae.

The rset can be a total mses and you can sitll raed it wouthit a porbelm.

Tihs is bcuseac the huamn mnid deos not raed ervey lteter by istlef, but the wrod as a wlohe.

Amzanig huh?

My reply was this:

That's bushlilt.

However, later that same day, in *The New York Times Magazine*, I read a description of the writer Susan Minot's hands as follows: "Three hundred silver rings on as many fingers . . ."

Wait just a minute here, I thought to myself.

I did the math. Crunched the numbers, *if you will*. (Interestingly, I was good at math in school. Less so, *now*. Age is just a number, but I'm getting number every day.)

I read again:

"Three hammered silver rings . . ."

➤ interviewese

People so often fall back on the question, "What (or who) is your favorite . . . ?" I hate this question. I almost never have a genuine answer for it. (See *chicken*.)

Here is an exchange between a radio interviewer and *me*.

"Do you feel comfortable *verbal*izing what you've written?"

"Ah, er. Let's say, 'Sometimes.'"

"Well, do many people tell you they see a little bit of them*self* in what you've written?"

"Well . . . Not in so many words."

Beck, on being interviewed: "It's almost like reporters are guys that see a pretty girl and want to talk to her, but they don't know what to say. So they say all the things they think they're supposed to say." Easy for a rock star to say, of course, but one knows what he means. When my friend Danny Klein, in his sixties, had a book suddenly pop up on the *New York Times* bestseller list, a young reporter from a local weekly paper asked him, blithely, "What are you going to do if you make a lot of money? Find a younger wife?"

➤ *ipsilateral*

This is not a word that you'll ever need, but I thought it might cheer you up. *Ipsilateral*. Means "located on or affecting the same side of the body" (AHD). For the life of me I can't think of a way to use *ipsilateral* in a sentence, except *of course* the way I did just then. If it applied to the street instead of the body, you and the girl next door would be ipsilateral. Not to mention abutting and bounding.

A nonforward pass thrown by an intoxicated football player would be a tipsy lateral.

➤ *ironically enough*

Can anything be? So perhaps best not to try. Perhaps best to go after things straight-on. But you'll miss a lot that way. See *inkling*.

➤ irony, lost on someone

I wonder how much irony is lost on how many people annually. Perhaps a Bureau of Irony could generate statistics, with an eye toward conservation.

➤ irony, presidential sense of

A microphone, which wasn't supposed to be open, picked up George Bush sharing with Tony Blair his impatience with regard to conflict in Lebanon: "See, the irony is what they need to do is get Syria to get Hezbollah to stop doing this shit and it's over."

American news media focused on the four-letter word. They should have on the five-letter one, *irony*. There is cognizant irony, and inadvertent irony, and free-floating irony, and . . . oh, never mind.

And we wonder why Brits insist that Americans have no irony. Once when the name Darryl came up in an Anglo-American discussion, one of the Anglos actually took me aside to inform me that "Darryl seems to us a comical name." His name was Nigel.

➤ *it*

In the usual list of third-person pronouns *it* comes third, and it isn't even a person at all. I daresay *it* is the skinniest of all two-letter words. But *it* casts a much wider net than either *he* or *she*. *It* could be anything, from a booger to everything.

And that'll be *it* for you? That's *it*. *It* would seem. She thinks she is *it*. The *it* girl. Get with *it*. Ain't *it* the truth. *It*'s cold out here.

Brevity is the soul of *it*. Promiscuity is its weakness: *it* (and when I say *it*, there, I mean *it*, not *weakness*) is likely to hook up, at least temporarily, with whatever noun most closely antecedes it. So keep a close watch over *it*'s, from clause to clause, sentence to sentence. Be sure you are sure what each *it* refers to and that it—that is to say, each *it*'s antecedent—is clear to the reader. Otherwise, it—that is to say, your usage of *it*—can at the very least cause your reader to catch a crab (see **if/whether**). Consider: "It's **incredible**—you better believe it." The main problem there is, **of course**, the loose, heedless use of *incredible*; but the two differently referential *it*'s compound it. The problem.

➤ *its, it's*

The last *it*'s in the previous entry is **of course** the plural of *it*. The word *it*'s is a contraction of *it is*. The possessive of *it* is *its*. Many people do not care. I know, you *want* to make a citizen's arrest of anyone whose menu lists "Idaho potato baked in it's skin," but you can't.

j · J · j

J is for *jump, joy, jet, jig, jingle, jiffy, jolly, jelly, J-Lo, jest, jitterbug, June, jazz, Judeo-Christian ethic*. Are there any downer words that start with *j*? Oh, I guess so, *jaundice, jerk, jeer, jail* (see **truly**), *jinx, jihad, jingoism*. Up or down, it's an energetic letter: *jolt, jog, jitters, judo*. As for *jejune* (from the Latin for "empty, dry, barren"), it doesn't sound right:

> Exclaimed her swain: "Petunia,
> Let me importune ya
> Not to be jejune, ya
> Sweetie-pie. Petunia?"

No! *Jejune* should be a positive word, a staple of love songs along with *m'moon* or *la lune*.

Perhaps this is the place for me to pop a key question:

When you linger mentally and orally over the word *juice*, do you flash, as I do, on "Ode on Melancholy," by John Keats? I mean this part: "Though seen of none save him whose strenuous tongue / Can burst Joy's grape against his palate fine."

Consider, in this light, the word *taste*. It derives from the Latin for "to touch" under the influence of the Greek for "to assess." In forming *taste*, the tongue executes a bit of a burst upon the palate. Call that **arbitrary** if you will.

➤ James, Henry

If you have dipped into James's late novels, you may have wondered whether in the name of all that is holy anyone ever talked like that. Here, from our friend **Ford Madox Ford**, is a firsthand account of James himself in conversation:

> "A writer who unites—if I may use the phrase—in his own person an enviable popularity to—as I am told—considerable literary gifts and whom I may say I like because he treats me"—and here Mr. James laid his hand over his ear, made the slightest of bows and, rather cruelly rolling his dark and liquid eyes and moving his lower jaw as if he were revolving in his mouth a piquant titbit—Mr. James continued, "because he treats me—if again I may say any such thing—with proper respect." And there would be an immense humorous gasp before the word "respect," ". . . I refer of course to Mr. Kipling . . . has just been to see me. And—such are the rewards of an enviable popularity!—a popularity such as I—or indeed you, my young friend, if you have any ambitions which I sometimes doubt—could ever dream of, far less imagine to ourselves—such are the rewards of an enviable popularity that Mr. Kipling is in the possession of a magnificent one thousand two hundred guinea motor-car. And, in the course of conversation as to characteristics of motor-cars in general and those of the particular one thousand two hundred guinea motor-car in the possession of our friend . . . But what do I say? . . . Of our cynosure! Mr. Kipling uttered words which have for himself no doubt a particular significance but which to me at least convey almost literally nothing beyond their immediate sound . . . Mr. Kipling said that the motor-car was calculated to make the Englishman . . ." and again came the humorous gasp and the roll of the eyes . . . "was calculated to make the Englishman . . . think."

The story, to be found in Ford's *Return to Yesterday*, goes on much longer. I recommend the whole of it. A *cynosure*, **of course**, is the center, the focal point, of attention—someone of whom the culture is making much. And yet the word comes from the Greek for "dog's tail." That's because Greek mariners steered by the constellation Ursa Minor, in which the Greeks apparently saw neither a little bear nor a little dipper. I for one have never been able to see, and therefore do not believe in, any of the constellations except the Big Dipper. See **Wilt: A Tall Tale.**

➤ *jingoism*

From the "refrain of a bellicose 19th-century music hall song, from alteration of *Jesus*" (AHD). For me this connection takes some of the pleasure out of the rousing old hymn "Onward, Christian Soldiers" and the even more rousing gospel song "I'm a Soldier in the Army of the Lord."

➤ *jot* and *tittle*

A jot is the tiniest bit, from *iota*, the smallest Greek letter. A tittle is more or less the same thing (the dot over an *i*, for instance), except that it can be traced back to Medieval Latin for a little mark over or under a letter, such as an *accent ague* or a cedilla. I don't know whether an umlaut is one or two tittles. Maybe it's a jot and a tittle side by side. Another word for tiny bit is *whit*, from the Old English *wiht*, a living being or creature. In the expression "suits me to a T," the *T* probably derives from "Suits me to a *tittle*."

➤ journal

I've never been good at keeping a journal as such, partly because I can never figure out who it is that I'm writing to. But I've written lots of things down in notebooks over the years. I'm glad of nearly everything I have written down (legibly) and tucked away. I kick myself for all the things I haven't. Here's something I wrote down that my friend Lee Smith said, when somebody, maybe me, I don't remember, asked her if she ever got lax about writing down something good that occurred to her: "I may be a fool, but I'm not that kind of fool."

➤ *Jr.*

Why don't I use a comma before the *Jr.* in my name? It's one stroke of fuss that I can spare the world—as when Disney stopped drawing a tail on Mickey to save ink during the Depression, or the war effort, or whenever it was.

But people *will* put the comma in. And when you use a comma before it, in a sentence, you've got to use another one after it (unless you end the sentence with *Jr.*, in which case it's hard to tell whether the period marks the end of the sentence or just of the *Jr.*). To take an **arbitrary** example, here's Adam Gopnik in *The New Yorker*:

> . . . the best of all books about pro football, Roy Blount, Jr.,'s "About Three Bricks Shy of a Load" . . .

That's five punctuation marks—a comma, a period, another comma, an apostrophe, and a double quotation mark—in the space of three letters. Too much. As to why *The New Yorker* puts quote marks around book titles, I don't know. I do know more than anyone else on earth about *Jr.*'s.

Walt Whitman (Jr.): "Song of Myself"

Muhammad Ali (born Cassius Clay Jr.): "I am the greatest"

Robert DeNiro (Jr.)'s most famous line: "You talking to *me*?"

Marshall Herff Applewhite (Jr.) grew up being called Herff, founded a cult called Heaven's Gate, had himself castrated, took the name Bo, then the name Do, and induced all thirty-eight members of the cult to commit suicide along with him so they could be taken into outer space. *Don't you see? It's about the lengths a person will go to, when forced to make a name for himself.*

➤ *just*

Except in rare cases, such as in this sentence, *just* is generally not *le mot juste*, or just the right word, but rather *le mot intense et vague*. Nor is *just* infused with much of what we might call *mot jus*. Though come to think of it, maybe the *j* and the soft *s* have a gratifyingly juicy mouth-feel, as in *joyous* or *juice* itself or *Jesus*. And the *uh* sound feels earnest, effortful.

But just what is *just* meant to mean? It is supposed to mean "right and fair" or "exactly" or "really" or "appropriate" or "simply," but so often people say, "It's just . . . It's just . . . I don't know, it's just . . . you know."

I overuse *just* myself. I don't know why. I just do.

See **Flaubert**.

k · K · k

"I find the letter K offensive, almost nauseating," **Kafka** wrote in his diary. "And yet I write it down. It must be characteristic of me." That was Kafka being Kafkaesque.

Without the *k* sound, the world's languages would be mush. From *coochy-coo* to the one-side-of-the-tongue *k-k* noise that makes a horse get moving or that goes along with a sly wink, the *k* or *q* or hard *c* sound is provocative, stimulating. Even a silent *k* (*knot*, *knack*, *knob*, *knuckle*, *knickers*) has a certain presence. Indeed, this vestige of our Teutonic-tribal heritage cries out to be sounded, as when Andy Stein on *A Prairie Home Companion* does knock-knock jokes:

> "K'nock, K'nock."
> "Who's there?"
> "Canoe."
> "Canoe Who?"
> "Canoe let me in so we can canoodle and coo?"

In *The Sunshine Boys*, Walter Matthau's old-school comedian character can't bring himself to do a commercial for a cereal called Frumpies, because it's not an intrinsically comical word. "If it was funny, I'd say it. Like *Alka-Seltzer*, *cupcake*, *pickles*, **chicken**—words with the *k* sound. You don't get laughs with tomatoes or lettuce. Or Frumpies."

It is an awkward-looking letter, *k*, like someone with hands in the air putting one *foot* tentatively forward, and we may think of *kitsch*, *kooky*, *kaka*, *klunky*, *klutz*, and *kleagle*. But then there's *king* and *kiddo*.

Why do we use the prefixes *ker-* and *ka-* in words like *kerplunk* and *kaboom*? RHD says this derives from the Scottish Gaelic *cearr*, meaning "wrong, awkward, left-handed." That may apply to *kerfuffle* or *kerflooey*, but is *kerchoo*, as opposed to *ahchoo*, an awkward sneeze? How about *ka-ching*? I think *k* deserves credit here for providing **sonicky** kick.

➣ Kafka, Franz

"I notice that I am afraid of the almost physical strain of the effort to remember, afraid of the pain beneath which the floor of the thoughtless vacuum of the mind slowly opens up, or even merely heaves up a little in preparation. All things resist being written down."—Franz Kafka, *Diaries*.

If it were easy, everybody would do it. It can't always be like Harpo Marx, in *Duck Soup*, writing with a long quill pen for the sake of tickling his face with the plume.

See **switcheroo, the old**.

➣ Keillor, Garrison

Before we became pals, I reviewed his first book, *Happy to Be Here*, a collection of pieces, in *The New York Times Book Review*. I noted "some nifty punctuation in the story 'Don: The True Story of a Young Person,' in which the narrator quotes a newspaper quoting a youth worker quoting someone else: '"She spoke for the conscience of a community when she said, 'Have we become so tolerant of deviant behavior, so sympathetic toward the sick in our society, that, in the words of Bertram Follette, "we have lost the capacity to say, 'This is not "far out." You have simply gone too far. Now we say "No!"'"?'"'"

I added one of those layers, *of course*, when I quoted that passage in my review, at which time I felt I had **probably** set the record for number of quotation marks in a row. I have added another layer just now, quoting the review. But most of the layers are Garrison's, and my hat is off to him.

Now. Imagine this:

In the 1983 Penguin paperback edition of *Happy to Be Here*, some proofreader apparently threw up his or her hands, because all the layers before the question mark are *omitted*. No quotes around the words of Bertram Follette, nor around what Bertram Follette believes we have lost the capacity to say, nor around the expression "far out," nor around what the narrator says we say now. You think you have set a standard for the ages, and poof.

Now the construction is back on course. Feel free to quote it.

➤ *kibosh, the*

To put the kibosh on something is to squelch it, debunk it. Origin is uncertain, though *bosh*—a word for nonsense, borrowed from the Turkish—may have had an influence.

So I'd say a kibosh is **perhaps** a ceremonial squash or truncheon, deriving from Istanbul (not Constantinople—I know, Constantinople goes back further, but Istanbul sounds more Turkish, as indeed the Turks themselves concluded, officially, in 1930).

Worth organizing a whole secret society around. Sons and Daughters of the Mystic Kibosh. Haul a bit of bosh or a boshical person before the Great Turk (in pro football, the man who goes around during summer camp telling players they have been cut from the squad is called the Turk) and bring the kibosh down, *kabonk!*

➤ *kid*

Newspaperman in a Raymond Chandler short story answers the phone: "Werner speaking. Go ahead. Kid me." A bit of slang (from the Old Norse for "young goat") that doesn't go out of style ("You gotta be kidding me"). Short, snappy, good mouth-feel. The *k* helps. AHD's example of *kiddo* is also hard-boiled: "I have a trade, kiddo, I'm a detective" (Ross Macdonald).

➤ *kind*

The two kinds of *kind*—the one meaning "sort" and the one meaning "humane"—come from the same Old English parent, *gecynd*, race or offspring. (With an *e* added, *gecynde*, it meant "natural.") Whence *kindergarten*. *King* and *kin* belong to this family. Further back we find the PIE *gene-*, whence *gene, gender, genital, gentle, generate*, and so on. Kiss my *foot* if all this ain't organic. As opposed to **arbitrary**.

➤ kinesthesia

From the Greek for "to move" and "to feel." A dancer's kinesthesia is a heightened and cultivated sense of his or her limbs and joints, motivated by a need for expression. A writer's kinesthesia is an appreciation that words, spoken or written, catch and carry meaning most effectively when they capture the feeling of physical movement. *Sphincter* is tight; *goulash* is lusciously hodgepodgy. *Swoon* emerged from the Old English *swogan*, to suffocate, because the mind and the mouth conspired to replace *og* with *oo* in order to register a different motion feeling.

You could, I suppose, construe *kinesthetic* as a dash of sensitive *esth* injected into "your thighbone kinetic to your hipbone, your hipbone kinetic to your backbone . . . ," but that is a stretch. *Kinesthesia* itself is only vaguely kinesthetic English. There is no Anglo-Saxon-based synonym, but *sprachgefühl*, borrowed from the German and meaning a feeling for language, an ear for idiom, smacks of oral kinesthesia, and then there is *mouth-feel*, for the chewiness or slipperiness or crunchiness of food.

Cinema comes from the same Greek word as the first half of *kinesthesia*. *Movie* works better.

See **synesthesia**; *arbitrary*; *sonicky*.

➤ *kiss*

A pleasant word by association, and it bounces right along in love ballads, but except in the sense of "to strike lightly, barely brush against," it's hardly **sonicky**. Instead of perhaps proceeding to the back of the mouth, it begins there, and travels by way of *ih* into a final hissing sound. *Smooch* is much better.

Snogging, though—I can't warm up to *snogging*. *Sn*- is not a friendly sound. Well, there's *snuggle*, but it's got that *-le* going for it. *Snog* sounds too much like *slog*.

Canoodling sounds like fun, but apparently applies only to entertainment-world celebrities in public places. Why would you go to a restaurant to make out? No wonder they stay so trim.

Make out is not a great term either, come to think of it. *Petting* has never struck me as strong enough. *Stroking*—well, now. You know that Clarence

Carter song? "I be *strokin'*!" That's the one, I think, where he gets to the point of crying out, as if in his strokin' partner's voice, "*Cla'ncecotta-Cla'ncecotta!*" If you're going to be self-referential, why be coy?

➤ *know best*

You have one opinion, I have another. I give in, saying, "You know best." Since there are just two of us, shouldn't it be "You know better"? But that has a different connotation—you know better than (to argue with me, maybe). Maybe "You know best" is short for "You know what's best," but still, if there are only two choices . . .

➤ *knowledgeable*

On the face of it, this is one ugly word. My fingertips resist the typing of it. Bad enough that it takes *dgea* to spell the sound *ja*. Worse is the semantic mismatch of *knowledge* and *able*. *Changeable* means liable to change. *Marriageable*, suitable for marriage. *Knowledgeable* doesn't mean liable to knowledge or suitable for knowledge, either of which would be nonsense; it means having and showing knowledge. Would you say "understandingable"? "Expertiseable"? "Eruditionable"? "Knackable"? However, you can't substitute *knowing*, because that connotes a sly sort of awareness. And when you get right down to it, there's something stodgily show-off about *knowledgeable* (often preceded by **quite**) that fits.

➤ *kvetch*

Here is a great example of language's bodily nature. In *Born to Kvetch*, Michael Wex tells us:

> Not only do Judaism in general and Yiddish in particular place an
> unusual emphasis on complaint, but Yiddish also allows considerable
> scope for complaining about the complaining of others, more often
> than not to the others who are doing the complaining . . . The best
> response to a complaint is another complaint, an antiseptic counter-
> kvetch that makes further whining impossible for anybody but you.

Kvetching, then, is not just chronic but also intense, projective complaining. Standard dictionaries trace *kvetch* back to the Yiddish *kvetshn*, to squeeze or strain (which derives from the Middle High German *quetzen*, to squeeze). Wex connects it to the Yiddish *kvetshn zikh*, to squeeze oneself. Not just to strain, but to "strain at stool"; to make an effort to move the bowels. (Which is what Elvis died doing, but we don't associate him with kvetching—"Don't Be Cruel" is schmaltzier than that.) As Wex puts it, *kvetch* connects with its alimentary roots

> in the tone of voice: someone who's kvetching sounds like someone
> who's paying the price for not having taken his castor oil—and he has
> just as eager an audience. A really good kvetch has a visceral quality,
> a sense that the kvetcher won't be completely comfortable,
> completely satisfied, until it's all come out.

The *v* after the *k* adds tensile force, but *kvetch* also goes back to the root *kakka*- or *kaka*-, to defecate, which according to AHD is "imitative of glottal closure during defecation." Hence *poppycock*, from Latin *cacare*, to defecate, and *cacophony*, from Greek *kakos*, bad.

I wouldn't be surprised if *squeeze* (not to mention *squash*, *squat*, *squeak*, *squeal*, *squelch*, *squib*, *squinch*, *squint*, *squirm*, *squirt*, *squish*, and *squoosh*) gets some of its juice from that primordial tightening, the constriction of the **glottis** that enables us to focus on the other end of the digestive tract.

1 · L · 1

I don't know the song of the *willow warbler*, but its name is like water rippling over pebbles, a flame fluting, compatible willowy limbs mingling. Flow.

The role of *l*: *love, ooh la la,* the *roll* in *rock and roll, liberty, luscious, lascivious, lips, belly, lovely, beautiful, lubricate, jelly roll, fully packed, lick, lilt, lyrical, lollipop.* Lovely to look at, delightful to hold.

Tralala. Allemande left with your left hand. *Ballet. Waltz.* Usually graceful, maybe slow, maybe contemplative. *Lull, loll, lullaby. Deliberate.* Dwelled-upon movement. *Lallygag, shilly-shally, loll.* (But *chill, still.*) *Flouncing. Fly, flutter, lift, land, aloft, lofted, vault, mill around, mull, wallow, spill, dollop, pull, haul, flop, fall, lurch, allez-oop, gallop, gallivant, slouch, slip, slide, slither, slow, mellow, limber, loose, lax, slack, lissome, luscious.*

Let us pause to enjoy the movement of *l* between *sliding* and *sidling.*

In *gallop,* the *g* and the *p* are the get-up elements, the *l* is the flow. The *g* is the gathering, the *p* is the clop.

Swallow, glug-glug, gulp.

Mellifluous, malleable. Elegant. Ululate. Oil. Owl.

Longing. The *ng*'s do most of the consonantal work there, but *l* is a prolonging letter. *Fall. All. Will. Full. Hill. Well,* well, well. *Tall. Slow. Linger. Stall. Hold. Fold.*

Smolder. The *l* and *d* together there—the *d* holds the slow progress of *l,* as *t* abruptly halts it in *halt. Mold. Old.*

Lulu. Lily. Lilith. Lillian. L'il.

Lalapalooza. La-la land.

Ball. The *b* is the bounce, the boost, the bop; the *l* is the roll. You can't tell me that it's wholly **arbitrary** that *ball* rhymes with *all,* or *fall.* The Old English of *ball* is believed to have been *beall.*

Lip. The tongue sound, *l*, introducing the lips proper, *p*.

Loblolly has come to mean a kind of pine, oddly enough, but before that it was a lolly that went *lob . . . lob*, according to AHD: "a combination of *lob*, probably an onomatopoeia for the thick, heavy bubbling of cooking porridge, and *lolly*, an old British dialect word for 'broth, soup, or any other food boiled in a pot.'"

People like saying *l*. Did I mention **language**?

➤ *lamentable*

RHU wants this to be pronounced with the emphasis on the first syllable. (Doesn't even give us the second-syllable-stress version as a backup option, as it does with *despicable*.) I'm sorry, that dog won't hunt. Its tail is too long for the tongue.

➤ *language*

I trust that you get your back up, as I do (that is to say, I get *mine* up), when this word is used pejoratively or dismissively. As in, "At the moment the two sides are primarily talking language." Until you've agreed on the language, you haven't agreed on anything, unless you're in love or something, and even then . . . you're going to be surprised.

➤ language, attempting to converse in a foreign

One American on a cruise ship, to another:

"Have you met that French fellow, named Bong Appety or something? Very friendly, for a Frenchman."

Other American:

"Bong Appety? That can't be his name."

"Yes it is. As I was about to sip my drink, he said, 'Bong Appety,' or whatever. So I introduced myself."

"Idiot! He was saying '*Bon appétit*.' Means 'Hope you enjoy it.'"

"Oh."

So the next time the first American encounters the Frenchman at the bar, they raise their glasses to each other and the American says (putting a bit more stress on the last syllable, now that he knows it's French), "Bong ap-pa-*tee*."

And the Frenchman, pleased to have learned, in his previous encounter, the proper American response, says, "Carl McCormack."

Note: I stole this from the **uneven** but frequently sublime British humorist Beachcomber (J. B. Morton). But I thoroughly rewrote it, except for the Frenchman, to Americanize Morton's Brits. In his version, the Frenchman says, "Harris." Maybe better. But no **K**.

See **readers, fashioned out of suet and squash**.

➤ *larynx*

The voice box, located between the mouth and the windpipe. Here we find the mucous-membranal vocal cords, the lower pair of which resonate in the sounding of **vowels** and voiced **consonants** such as *r* and *n*. Note that the *n* comes after the *y*, so don't pronounce it lar-nyx. See *glottis*.

➤ *laugh*

Doesn't sound much like laughter, does it, even if you consider that the *gh* sound was originally like the *ch* in German *ach* (see **Z**). I've known people whose laughs were like that *ch* repeated, and those weren't bad laughs, but don't we want more of a *haha* element as well? Our *laugh* may be related to the Greek *klossein*, to cluck (see **chicken** and **weevil**), from the PIE *klok-/klek-*. I wish we had adhered more closely to the more **sonicky** *laugh* of Old English: *hlaehhan*. From the proto-Germanic *HlaHjanan*.

It is hard to write humorously about people laughing. Max Beerbohm managed this trick in an essay of 1920, entitled "Laughter," which comes out in favor, and regrets the scarcity, of all-out, helplessly surrendering laughter. Beerbohm recounts a scene of such hilarity back in 1813, which he had read of in Thomas Moore's *Life of Lord Byron*.

Moore and Byron, "already in high spirits," pay a call on the poet Samuel Rogers. Though Beerbohm can hardly believe it, the young and lively Moore and Byron sincerely "venerated Rogers (strange as it may seem to us) as the greatest of living poets." And Rogers "was ever the kind of man, the coldly and quietly suave kind of man, with whom you don't take liberties, if you can help it—with whom, if you can't help it, to take liberties is in itself a most exhilarating act."

Rogers showed Moore and Byron a copy he had just received of a new book by a friend of his, one Lord Thurloe. When the young men opened this book, they found in it "much that was so execrable as to be delightful." They paged through it together "in throes of laughter, laughter that was but intensified by the endeavours of their correct and nettled host to point out the genuine merits of his friend's work."

Moore and Byron come upon a Thurloe poem that may in part explain Rogers's defensiveness: it is a panegyric on Rogers. "We were, however," recalls Moore, "too far gone in nonsense for even this eulogy, in which we both so heartily agreed, to stop us." The first line of this poem was "When Rogers o'er this labour bent." Byron tried three times to read it aloud, but each time could get no further than "When Rogers" before he and Moore would go off in another laughing fit.

Finally, according to Moore, "Mr. Rogers himself, with all his feeling of our injustice, found it impossible not to join us; and we were, at last, all three in such a state of inextinguishable laughter" that Moore felt Thurloe himself, had he been present, would have joined in.

"The final fall and dissolution of Rogers, Rogers behaving as badly as either of them, is all that was needed to give perfection to this heartwarming scene," writes Beerbohm, who joins the three of them—regrettably from a distance, less boisterously—in their hoo-haws. I have joined the four.

And I can add a note. *A Literary History of England*, published in 1948, has room, since it is 1,673 pages long, for a passing consideration of Rogers:

"He returned in *Human Life* (1819) to the sedately reflective manner best suited to his slender talent. *Italy* (1822), his best-known poem, is a collection of fifty-two sections" in which "only once, in the touching tribute to Byron's memory, does the writing approximate to poetry."

Another example of comic laughter: In the inimitable P. G. Wodehouse's *The Inimitable Jeeves*, Bertie Wooster says of the overhearty and too-strapping Honoria Glossop: "She chucked back her head and laughed with considerable vim. She had a penetrating sort of laugh. Rather like a train going into a tunnel." It's better in context: To Bertie's great alarm, his aunt Agatha is trying to get him betrothed to the willing Honoria, who persists ("You funny man") in interpreting Bertie's evasive tactics as diffident courting. Bertie is scheming to offload her affections onto his frequently smitten friend Bingo Little, whose head is conveniently over his heels (odd expression, come to think of it) as regards Honoria at the moment. Bertie plans to push Honoria's younger brother into a handy lake, so that Bingo can save him. Here is how confident Bertie and Bingo are, against all odds (Jeeves not being involved), that this stratagem will work: Bingo has "chuckled," in the previous chapter, "like the last drop of water going down the waste-pipe in a bath." In the confluence of this simile and the one for Honoria's laugh, we may detect a swirl of cross-purposes.

➤ laughter in text messaging

ROFL (pronounced and sometimes written *roffel* or *roffle*) stands for "rolling on the floor laughing."

ROFF, according to an **Urbandictionary.com** definition, means "less funny than rofl, as heh is for stuff less funny than haha."

ROFLMAO, sometimes spelled *roffelmayo*, is "rolling on the floor laughing my ass off."

ROFLMAOWTIME is "rolling on the floor laughing my ass off with tears in my eyes."

And so on.

A medium that requires such terms is not a happy medium.

➤ *lava*

A Neapolitan dialect word, originally meaning a stream of water created by a downpour of rain. Then molten rock came coursing down the sides of Vesuvius, near Naples, and the word took on another meaning. *Lava*—and *lavish*, from the Old French *lavasse*, deluge of rain—comes from the Latin *lavare*, to wash. So does *laundry* (a contraction or syncope of the Middle English *lavendry*). It has been speculated that *lavender*, whose oil was often added to laundry, was influenced by *lavare*, though *lavender* probably comes more directly from the Latin *livere*, to be bluish. See *livid*.

➤ *-le*

What do all these words have in common, besides the ending *-le* preceded by two different consonants: *jingle, jangle, tingle, tickle, tangle, wrangle, wangle, dangle, mangle, angle, gargle, handle, fondle, dandle, rustle, bustle, gristle?*

They all entail, in their meaning, a certain prolonged ragged friction or sustained uneven engagement, rendered, in their spelling, by the sustained uneven engagement of those three different consecutive consonants (*ngl*, for example): dense in the first two, finally liquid in the *l*. This is nitty-gritty Anglo-Saxon **sonicky**-ness, ingeniously derived, through eons of trial and error.

In this connection, the suffix *-le* has a force that is called *frequentative*, which is defined in AHD as "expressing or designating repeated action." (To me, *frequentative* is not as good a term for this as something with an *l* in it would be—*lingerative*, maybe, or *prolongative*.) The derivation of *tickle*, according to AHD: "Middle English *tikelen*, perhaps frequentative of *ticken*, 'to touch lightly.'"

The suffix *-le* indicates "repeated action or movement especially of a trifling or small-scale character," says WIII, citing *prattle, wiggle, hobble*.

RHU points out that the *-le* suffix may also have the sense of "apt to," as in *brittle*, apt to break; and it may indicate "agent or instrument," as in *thimble* (thumb gizmo). According to WIII, *juggle* comes from the Latin for "little joke" (*joculus*), but surely there is something physically imitative in the word—compare *joggle, jiggle, toggle.*

No one seems to detect or even suspect any etymological connection between *-le* and *-ly*, but is it too great a leap to suspect something similar in the effect—the sought-after effect—of the fluid *l* in both cases?

➤ *let's hope*

More straightforward and gracious, if you ask me, than **hopefully**.

➤ *lightning*

In 1879, in a speech to a men's club on "the science of onanism," Mark Twain put forth this critique of masturbation, ascribing it fancifully to Brigham Young: "As compared with the other thing, it is the difference between the lightning bug and the lightning." Nine years later, in a letter to a man who was editing a book called *The Art of Authorship*, Twain wrote: "The difference between the almost-right word and the right word is the difference between the lightning bug and the lightning." By extension, then, a writer who settles for less than the *mot juste* (see **adverb** and **Flaubert**) is what the British would call a tosser. Circumstances, of course, may be mitigating. "I cannot describe what I owe to this gentle art," the speech on onanism quoted Robinson Crusoe as saying. But for all his freehandedness, Twain attended to words in minute detail. Writing *Huckleberry Finn*, he first had Huck speak of an undertaker's "softly soothing ways." Then he scratched out *soothing* and replaced it with *soothering*. (Compare the spiritual "The Old Ark's a-Moverin', a-Moverin'.") As a result, observes Victor A. Doyno in *Writing Huck Finn: Mark Twain's Creative Process*, "the undertaker remains continuously busy in our memories."

A small syllable more or less can make a big difference. For centuries, the job of representing aerial bolts of electricity was up in the air, flickering back and forth between *lightning* and *lightening*. (More elaborate shots in the dark included *lyghtenynge*, which looks like more than one flash.) Like *brightening*, *whitening*, *thickening*, *sickening*, *stiffening*—and even *shortening* and *hastening*—*lightening* held on to that extra beat in the middle. Accordingly, it settled into the more leisurely work of making things lighter. Nothing's quicker than *lightning*, which is why it's so hard (unlike bleach, say) to catch in a bottle.

And *lightning* **bug** is no slouch. It's a nicely **rhythm**ic slick-and-chunky eighteenth-century American improvement over the British *firefly*, which evokes *froufrou* and fairies at the bottom of the garden. Anyone who has accidentally squashed a lightning bug can imagine how greased lightning might smell.

➤ limerick

This term has come to be used far too loosely. A limerick (named, I don't know why, for the Irish town) is a specific, time-honored verse form: two rhyming lines of trimeter (three feet) followed by two lines of dimeter (two feet) with a different **rhyme**, and one more of trimeter returning to the first rhyme. Generally the intended effect is spicy. For example:

> There once was a lady named Dot,
> Who said as we found a nice spot,
> > "I never undress
> > At a picnic, unless
> It's warm, and it is, so why not?"

The U.S. Army has published a manual regulating every detail of certain formal dinners in mess halls that involve guest speakers, exchanges of toasts, and what the manual calls "limericks and ditties" but thereafter refers to only as limericks. According to USAREC Pamphlet 600-15, section 24, any member of the mess may rise to deliver a limerick. Said limerick may rag on any other member, of any rank, who is then "bound by honor" to respond in kind before the dinner is over. Or a member of one group dining in the mess may address a limerick to any other group, a representative of which must work up a corresponding comeback. Regulations require these limericks to be "in good fun and taste." Specifically, "personal vendettas, attacks upon notable or sacred institutions, politics, and matters of the heart are never in good taste." But you know how rhyme schemes strike sparks:

> Oh we have a lieutenant colonel
> Who reads the *Ladies' Home Journal*.
> > And happens to be
> > Not a he but a she—
> But boy, is she not maternal.

And the response, perhaps:

> If I *were* your mom, Private Ryan,
> I'd make you stop whinin' and cryan,

And stop being sexist—
 'Cause I am from Texas,
And I will kick your behyan.

However, the Army manual's "example of a limerick to a recruiting station that lost a sporting challenge to another station might be, 'Your ability to shoot baskets is worse than someone in a casket.'" Taste aside, this raggedy-ass couplet is no limerick. It is not even a ditty, defined by AHD as "a simple song." Limericks may be sung to the tune of "Waltz Me Around Again Willie." It is hard to imagine any tune that would accommodate the Army's example. See **meter**.

➤ lists

Writers love a good list. Here's one from Margalit Fox's obituary of Jimmy Lee Sudduth, the Alabama outsider artist, in *The New York Times*:

> To expand his palette further, Mr. Sudduth colored his work with an
> astonishing array of available ingredients, either by mixing them
> into the mud or rubbing them directly onto his wooden canvas. They
> included flour, coffee grounds, instant coffee, dye wrung from
> sodden red crepe paper, ground brick, ground charcoal, colored
> chalk, crushed coal, turnip greens, flower petals, pokeweed berries,
> ivy, soot, axle grease, elderberries, crushed green tree buds, boiled
> jimson weed, sap, walnut shells, burnt matchsticks, tobacco, egg
> yolk, grass and leftover house paint donated by neighbors.

Two keys to a good list: extraordinary miscellaneity—not random, though—and rhythm. The rhythm is in the items' arrangement. Many a list have I rearranged ten, twelve, twenty-five, or fifty times without ever quite making it flow like, say, "The Atchison, Topeka and the Santa Fe." Here, in verse, is the latest version (still not quite right) of a list of the kinds of peas I have seen on Southern grocery or farmstand shelves:

A PAEAN TO PEAS OF THE SOUTH

Though English peas or snow peas
 Do have their appeal,

Those who grow and know peas
Will always tell you: *"We'll*
Have black-eyed peas or pinkeye peas, or
Zipper peas, or crowder peas, or
Purple hull, or mush peas, or
Lady cream, or butter peas, or
Medium early or very young small sweet peas,
Please.

Or perhaps
Fancy tiny field peas with snaps.

The list doesn't have to be long. Here is my favorite Beatles lyric: "Vera, Chuck and Dave."

➤ literacy

Is too important to be left to the literati.

➤ *literally*

Listen up, folks. This word, which derives from *letter*, as in "the letter of the law," means just what it says, which is to say: "meaning just what it says." It should not be used to mean its opposite: *virtually*, or *figuratively*— or "as if rilly and truly I swear ta God!" If you say, "I literally went through the floor," it means that somehow or another the floor opened up and you physically passed through it. Or else it doesn't mean anything.

My friend Dan Mayfield, who invests people's money for them in Memphis, recently told me that the Federal Reserve Board head Ben Bernanke had come out in favor of "throwing money out of helicopters, literally," if necessary. Literalist that I am, and innocent as I am as to economics, I was startled. I wondered how in the world this would help the economy, and whether it would be assumed that people would *catch* . . . He said he meant that Bernanke had literally *said* he was willing to resort to "throwing money out of helicopters," which, he informed me, is a common economic metaphor for government's printing money and pushing it into the economy some way, as Japan did—hiring people to count train cars for $100,000 a year, for instance—in order to burst the bubble that had lowered Japanese interest rates to 0 percent and therefore stagnated cash flow. I had connected Dan's *literally* to be the wrong verb.

Another figure of speech, from Dan: Keeping an economy afloat by going deeper and deeper into debt "is like your baby is peeing on a mattress, and you keep checking underneath, and it's still dry, so far—but as soon as one drop comes through, there'll be a flood." The system swamped with debt.

Figures of speech are my bread and butter (so to speak). Trying to intensify them by attaching *literally* to them spoils them. Even when a figurative expression *does* apply literally, as when a man at a field trial of bird dogs informed me that "every dog has its day," it is best to allow the pleasure of its literalness to speak for itself.

➤ *livid*

Like many color words, this one is muddy. Because *livid* has come to be used as a synonym for furious, I thought it meant "red-faced," as in fact RHD says it can: "reddish or flushed." But it comes from the Latin *livere*, to be bluish. (*Liveo*, then, would be "I am bluish," an odd thing to say.) A livid bruise is a "bluish leaden color," says OAD. AHD has "discolored, as from a bruise; black and blue," or "ashen or pallid: *a face livid with shock*." WIII chips in "ghastly," and also cites the color of lead. Well, *leaden* sounds leaden, but *livid* doesn't. Maybe there's a subliminal association with "in living color." I once sat on a plane next to a woman who had never flown before, and was frightened. "I am sitting here just vivid," she said.

According to Chambers, *blue* itself is etymologically related to *yellow*, *white*, and *pale*. According to AHD, the **PIE** root *bhel-* has given rise to various words meaning "to shine, flash, burn: shining white and various bright colors," including *blue*, *bleach*, *blond*, *blend*, *bland*, *blush*, *flagrant*, and *black*. And *blind*.

➤ *logo*

Short for *logotype*, this term is from the Greek for *word*, but a logo is generally not a word. It aspires to be a ***meme***.

➤ *logocentric*

This is a fascinating area to get into. The only way in, perhaps unfortunately, is by word. Look at it this way: What other kind of too-narrow focus provides, for one and all, a diagnostic name for itself? If you're ethnocentric, does your culture include a folk dance acknowledging the limitations of your outlook? Is there a beeper that goes off when you get too technocentric? If you're iconocentric, where's the visual image that's going to tell you that you are? Maybe if somebody videoed you staring at a video screen for hours on end, it would be a picture of videocentrism—but if you were willing to watch that, the video of yourself watching video, you would be more egocentric than anything else.

I am logocentric. I know it. More than once I've been told so, in effect, by someone, for instance let's say a woman, who said, "Stop picking on every word I say!" to which I responded, "I'm not 'picking on' your 'every word,' I'm just trying to figure out what you are saying, exactly . . ."

But better logocentric than not centric at all. And call me logocentricentric, but I think logocentrism is about the best darned old centrism there is. How else than in words could the limitations of words be expressed as well as by Faulkner's Addie Bundren in *As I Lay Dying*:

> . . . how words go straight up in a thin line, quick and harmless, and
> how terribly doing [as opposed to words] goes along the earth,
> clinging to it, so that after a while the two lines are too far apart for
> the same person to straddle from one to the other; and that sin and
> love and fear are just sounds that people who never sinned nor loved
> nor feared have for what they never had and cannot have until they
> forget the words.

➤ *Lolita*

This fine twisted novel has lovely fluid opening lines: "Lolita, light of my life, fire of my loins. My sin, my soul. Lo-lee-ta: the tip of the tongue taking a trip of three steps down the palate to tap, at three, on the teeth. Lo. Lee. Ta." Peter Sagal, the host of National Public Radio's *Wait, Wait . . . Don't Tell Me!*, uses this to warm up his speaking apparatus before the show. I sometimes use what Wynn Handman, director of the American

Place Theatre, advised me to use when I did a one-man show there: "Over the lips the teeth the tongue," and "beed'n beed'n beed'n." I don't know where *beed'n* comes from, but it does seem to help. Then there's the phrase Warren Beatty, as Bugsy Siegel in *Bugsy*, keeps repeating: "Twenty dwarves took turns doing handstands on the carpet." In that movie Bugsy does a good crisp job of straightening out another mobster when the latter uses dis*interested* to mean *uninterested*: "*Disinterested* means impartial! *Uninterested* means you're just not interested!"

➢ *louche*

AOD's definition is nice: "disreputable or sordid in a rakish or appealing way." Agreement seems to be general that the word is from the French for "squinting." The connection is not clear to me. Nor can I quite see why *goggle*, meaning "to stare with wide-open or bulging eyes" (picture Esky, the personification of *Esquire* magazine back when it was sort of *louche*, and maybe now again), seems to have been influenced by the Middle English *gogel-eyed*, meaning "squint- or one-eyed." See **Google**.

➢ *love*

The Old Frisian version was *luve*, which may make us think of Woody Allen's character in *Annie Hall*, trying to convey to the Diane Keaton character how much he loves her by saying, "I looove you. I lerve you . . ."

See *free*; *U*.

m · **M** · m

Mammalia, the word for the class of animals that includes humans, derives from *mammary* (milk-producing glands being a key characteristic), and *mammary* derives from *mama*, baby talk for mother. This is undisputed.

It is also generally acknowledged that *mum*, as in "Keep it mum" or "Mum's the word," is imitative of tightly closed lips.

As in suckling lips.

Languages (sixty-one) in which the (or at least a) word for "female parent" begins with *m* (or, in a few cases, a vowel sound followed by *m*) include Afrikaans, Akkadian (*ummu*), Apache, Arabic, Aragonese, Armenian, Avestan, Belorussian, Bengali, Bosnian, Breton, Bulgarian, Catalan, Chinese, Czech, Danish, Dutch, Estonian, French, Frisian, Gaelic, German, Gothic, Greek, Hebrew, Hungarian, Icelandic, Ido, Indonesian, Interlingua, Irish, Italian, Korean (*eomeoni*), Latin, Lithuanian, Lojban, Malay (*emak*), Malayalam, Navajo, Norwegian, Novial, Old Prussian, Old Norse, Persian, Polish, Portuguese, Russian, Serbian, Sinhala, Slovak, Slovene, Spanish, Sumerian, Swahili, Swedish, Tamil, Telugu, Thai, Tok Pisin, Ukrainian, and Vietnamese.

Languages (nine) in which that is not the case include Esperanto (which was made up and has never caught on), Finnish, Georgian (whose word for *mother* would appear to be spelled with a square root, an *f*, another square root, and an upside-down question mark), Guarani, **Hittite**, Japanese, Kurdish, Tupinamba, and Turkish.

From the same **PIE** root as *mother* we get *matter* (as in the substance of the universe and what's botherin' you), *material*, and *matrix*. The international Muslim community calls itself the Umma.

I'll run a few more *m* words by you: *me* (the receiving self), *my*, *mine*,
moo, *mouth*, *milk*, *maw*, *munch*, *mug*, *yum*, *num-num* (baby wants food),
smile, *meal*, *meat*, *morsel*, *much*, *more*, *magnificent*, *mountain*, *minute*,
moment, *magma*, *common*, *moral*, *mortal*, *medicine*, *meaning*, *moan*, *hum*,
murmur, *mumble*, *mutter*, *mute*, *mellifluous*, *mutual*, *memory*, *meme*, *medi-*
tate, *Ommmmmmm*, *moi*, *mot*, *Mr.*, *Mrs.*, *Mary*, *Moses*, *man*, *madam*,
human, *humus*, *mulch*, *middle*, *mild*, *mollify*, *meta-*, *moon*, *mimesis*, *imi-*
tate, *muster*, *muse*, *music*, *may*, *might*, *must*, *muster*, *magic*, *malice*, *mature*,
manus (Latin for *hand*), *manage*, *manifest*, *must*, *mind*, *mingle*, *mix*, *match*,
meet, and *motel*.

Amen.

(See *Y*.)

➤ malapropism

In his play *The Rivals* (1775), Richard Brinsley Sheridan created Mrs. Mal-
aprop, from the French for "inappropriate." She says things like, "She's
as headstrong as an allegory on the banks of the Nile."

Her predecessors were Dogberry, in *Much Ado About Nothing*, who says
things like "comparisons are odorous," and Mrs. Slipslop, in Henry
Fielding's *Joseph Andrews*, who says things like, "How have I deserved that
my passion should be resulted and treated with ironing?" and "Want of
shame was not the currycuristic of a clergyman."

Her successors have included William Archibald Spooner, Sam Goldwyn, Yogi Berra, and George W. Bush. See the last name of each of these
plus -*isms*.

➤ man

I know there is much to be said against men. But there must be some
deep-structural reason why it is so expressive, when we of either gender
feel afflicted, to say, "Aw, *mannn*." Or impressed: "Oh, *man*!"

➤ *mange*

Derives from the French *manger*, to eat. Hence the expression "all et up with the mange."

➤ *mansuetude*

My logophilic, life-form-loving friend Jon Swan—poet, gardener, woods-man--brought me this specimen, with the smile on his face of a lad who has captured and is eager to share an unforeseen but richly explicable small animal. *Mansuetude* (man-swi-tood) means "gentleness of man-ner, mildness." It came into Middle English, by way of Old French, from a Latin verb meaning "to tame." The *man* part comes from the Latin for "hand"; the *-suetude*, from a Latin verb meaning "to accustom."

So we can see how the word arose: a gentle animal, from a human per-spective, is one that has become accustomed to . . . how shall we put it: to being *handled*? Yes, that's **probably** the root barnyard truth of the matter—a gentle horse is one that has been broken, turned to human purpose—but we could also say with justice that a gentle animal—a gentle cat, say—is one that is used to being petted, touched gently. Before Jon had his coat off, he had fondled *mansuetude* a couple of times, vocally, aurally, and with his deep sense of history. Now, next morning, I'm turning it over in my mind's sonarium and with fingertips on the pliant keyboard, and eyes on the generous screen, of my Apple.

It's a word that takes well to being probed, dissected. To get back to the *man-* part: *manufacture* today is generally accomplished by machinery (and in countries where labor is cheap), but it dates back to when people did metalworking (Latin *factura*, from *facere*, to make) by hand. A *manu-script* is still handwritten, though seldom with a pen (from the Latin for "feather"), technology having rendered most people, if they are like me, virtually incapable of writing legibly at any length on anything but a com-puter. Handtyped, anyway. Manual dexterity is still to do with a person's being *handy*, though not exclusively with the right, or *dexter*, hand. A *manual* is a handbook, or an organ's handplayed keyboard, or, as in *man-ual of arms*, certain manual manipulations of a rifle. *Manual manipula-tions* (the latter word from the Latin *manipule*, a handful, as of grain) would have been redundant a century and a half ago (except in the figurative sense of psychological *management*), but it isn't now that handling is so seldom done by hand: during a prolonged air-travel delay "due to equipment" recently, I heard the following semi-apologetic announcement: "We are trying to manually get the bags on the plane." (See **split infinitive**.)

Here are some more words from that same *man-* root: *manacle*, *manner*, *amanuensis*, *maintain*, *maneuver*, *manicotti*, *manicure*, *manifest*, *mastiff*, *manqué*, *emancipate*, *mandate*, *Maundy Thursday*, *command*, *demand*, *recommend*, and even, unexpectedly, *manure* (from the Middle English *manuren*, to cultivate land). AHD does not connect the hand-related *man-* root to a second *man-*root, whence *man*, *human*, *mensch*, and Walt Whit*man*. But I wonder.

Let's look at -*suetude*. Its root, *s(w)e-*, according to AHD, is a "pronoun of the third person and reflexive (referring back to the subject of the sentence): further appearing in various forms referring to the social group as an entity." The reflexive aspect gives us our *self*. The "various forms" include, from the Latin *consuescere*, our *accustom*. We can intuit how *accustom*, with regard to taming an animal, relates in meaning to *self*.

Now I leap to the assumption that -*suetude* (with an eye to *desuetude*, which, alas, we will come to) is also related to *used*, meaning "accustomed," as in "My wife's horse is gentle because he is used to being treated gently. He is used to her." AHD, however, eschews any such connection, telling us only that *use* comes from the Latin *usus* by way of the Old French *us*.

Might we be so bold, then, as to propose that the English *us*, as in "We believe that our cat genuinely loves us," comes from the self-reflexivity of *s(w)e-*? Not according to AHD, which connects our *us* to the root *nes-*, whose influence is more evident in the Latin *nos*, French *nous*, and German *uns*.

We can get back to *mansuetude* by way of *mastiff*, a big useful dog whose name may have picked up its -*stiff* from the Old French *mestif*, mongrel, but derives primarily from the Latin *mansuescere*, to tame (by handling). Having rejoined this word of which we have grown so fond, however, we must bid it farewell, for it has fallen into *desuetude*, "a state of disuse or inactivity." Neither RHU nor AHD calls *mansuetude* archaic, but OED did back in 1905 (when Volume VI, containing the *m*-words, went to press)— citing Robert Browning's use of it in 1869 as its most recent appearance.

OED's first citation is from Geoffrey Chaucer's "Parson's Tale," 1386: *mansuetude* is called a remedy against anger. Does this benign concept stand a chance of revival? No, because look at the word: neither its meaning nor its pronunciation is apparent. (And, for some reason, when I type it out I keep putting the *e* before the *u*.) Even if a reader or listener somehow made a connection to *manhandle*, that would be regrettable, for to manhandle is to handle roughly. Given the recent proliferation of such metrosexually suggestive terms as *man-purse*, *man-boobs*, *man-date*, and *mankini* (a very brief men's bathing suit), and the rhyme with *dude*, this distinguished old word might mockingly suggest, to the ear, male sweetness. And to the eye, with that *suet* in there, male fatness. We honor *mansuetude* best by putting it back out to pasture.

(*Pasture*, by the way, comes from the same root as *food*, *fodder*, *forage*, *fur*, *foster*, *pasta*, *pantry*, and *company*.)

➤ marriage, impact of word choice upon

A woman once told me that she made a point of mispronouncing words in fine restaurants because she knew it drove her husband crazy. "What's this gunnotchy?" she would ask the waiter, pointing to *gnocchi* on the menu. Once she even pronounced *steak* to rhyme with *leak*. Why? Because years earlier, in a snooty French eatery, her husband had expressed embarrassment over her pronunciation of *huîtres*, and she was still getting back at him.

I thought about that couple as I read of marital problems between Jason Kidd, the basketball star, and his wife, Joumana. The former had filed for divorce, contending, as the New York *Daily News* put it, that "his wife resorted to punching, kicking and throwing 'nearby household objects' to resolve marital disputes." Her lawyer pooh-poohed this claim, and mentioned that Jason, to quote the *Daily News* again, "was once busted for punching his wife in the mouth in a fight over his eating their son's French fries."

Over his eating his son's . . . ? It's hard to write that scene.

"Who says they're *his* French fries? You always take his side."

"Aw, look, he's trying to pry them out of your hand."

"Okay, okay, jump ball!"

Possibly the French fries masked some deeper issue. Asked whether Jason was unfaithful, Joumana's lawyer said, "Do they sell pantyhose at Macy's?" That's a new one to me. I like it better than "Does a bear go poop in the woods?" It's edgier, more urban.

Speaking of figures of speech, the *New York Post* quoted Joumana as saying, "Home is where we lay our hat." Maybe it wasn't nearby-object-throwing or even infidelity that undermined that marriage, so much as her tendency to get expressions slightly wrong. And he can't refrain from snapping at her: "The expression, damn it, is 'Home is where I *hang* my hat'!" And she comes back with "Lay our hat! Lay our hat! Lay our hat!" Not the sort of thing you'd put into court papers, so we may never know.

➤ marriage, to a writer

Anton Chekhov, whose stories are justly renowned for their compassion, in a letter to a friend:

> Very well, then, I shall marry . . . But under the following conditions: everything must continue as it was before, in other words, she must live in Moscow and I in the country, and I'll go visit her. I will never be able to stand the sort of happiness that lasts from one day to the next, from one morning to the next. Whenever someone talks to me day after day about the same thing in the same tone of voice, it brings out the ferocity in me . . . I promise to be a splendid husband, but give me a wife who, like the moon, does not appear in my sky every day. I won't write any better for having gotten married.

➤ *marvelous*

Try not to use it unless you mean it in full from its roots.
   See **muskrat**.

➤ *me*

"He disrespected Goofy and myself."
   "He took the mickey out of Mickey and I."

Why? Why? Why? Has the word *me* become obscene? It wasn't long ago that referring to oneself unreflexively (that is, when it was not a matter of doing something to or for oneself) as "myself" was widely recognized as uncouth. Now a great many people seem to assume that it's classy. Nor was it long ago that well-spoken people shuddered to hear *I* used as the object of a verb or a preposition. In his highly recommendable and **sonicky**-conscious book on English, *A Mouthful of Air*, Anthony Burgess offers "a good, or infuriating, example" of the sort of "linguistic solecism" actors will utter when they don't stick to a script. It occurred in the shooting of the 1974 film *Moses the Lawgiver*, whose screenplay Burgess helped to write:

> Aaron, played by Sir Anthony Quayle, was permitted by the Italian director to say, "God has chosen people like you and I." A former director of the Royal Shakespeare Company should have known better. The offending *I* was uttered in close-up and could not easily be plucked out. The expense of reshooting the scene to accommodate the correction *me* would have been prohibitive. Looping to put right a single grammatical error would have been dear enough. A piece of film was taken from a different scene, in which Aaron has presented his back to the camera, and this was cut in to cover the *me*. The pronoun itself was uttered and recorded by a mere cutting-room technician, and nobody seemed any the wiser.

Hard to imagine moviemakers going out of their way to make such a correction today. They might go the other way: sparing no expense to change "between you and me" to "between you and I," regarded as tonier.

In fact *me* is more flexible grammatically than *I*. Using *me* instead of the strictly speaking correct *I* in time-honored idiomatic expressions such as "It's me," "Woe is me," and "me and my big mouth" is unimpeachable. "It's I, it's I, it's I, oh Lord, standing in the need of prayer" would put off the Almighty.

Maybe the expression "the Me Decade" helped make *me* seem selfish somehow. Or maybe *me* seems too homey for public speech. But there's something icky about "This is an injury that myself and the Lakers' medical staff will just have to monitor" (Kobe Bryant).

➤ *meadow muffin*

A plop of cow manure in a field, according to the *Dictionary of Smoky Mountain English*.

➤ *meatspace*

The sphere of actual flesh-and-blood interpersonal presence and contact, as opposed to cyberspace.

Yes, it's creepy. We here in Paper Kingdom would never think to deprecate the, uh, real world in such a way. I didn't make the word up. I ran into it—the word, not the space—on **Urbandictionary.com**.

Creepy, but good. Here's a bad word: *meatus*. The meatus of the ear, for instance. A dictionary will tell you it's pronounced mee-*ay*-tus and means "a body opening or passage." Our inner ear tells us something else. It's what Mike Tyson bit off of Evander Holyfield.

➤ *media*

This is a plural of *medium*. Other Latin plurals have come to be regarded as singular in English—*agenda* for instance—but a statement like "The media distorts the truth" is indiscriminate. There are various news media, various mass media, even various corporate media. To treat all these media collectively as a monolithic institution is to create a bugaboo or punching bag. "The press" made more sense as a singular, because a press is a single thing, standing for many print media.

➤ *meme*

A bit of information or fashion that goes viral, spreading through a given culture: *bling*, chronic fatigue syndrome, *baby mama*, "Let go and let God," low-riding trousers, "the war on terror," a Scooby-Doo ending, *agenbite of inwit*, that thing where you put your forefinger and middle finger to your eyes and then point them toward the other person, betokening the making of eye contact . . .

A meme is not necessarily valuable or cogent, just catching. In that sense it reproduces itself. Theoretically, it can also adapt and evolve, though how that applies to, say, the YouTube video of OK Go dancing on treadmills, I don't know. Once something's frozen on YouTube . . .

The word *meme*, from the Greek for "to imitate," was coined by Richard Dawkins in analogy to the gene, in his book *The Selfish Gene*. We human beings, Dawkins argues, are in fact primarily carriers of our genes, which care no more about us than we do about, say, the ozone layer.

If we are but means for our genes, are we **merely** meme **media**? In that case, according to Marshall McLuhan, we are the message. Maybe memes (behind our backs) take a meme-first attitude—everything with them is *me me me*—but do they get to eat fresh strawberries? I do.

The word *meme* is a meme. And surely part of its survival value is that it is **sonicky**. It doesn't get much catchier than the *m* for "mama" and long *e*, first sound out of an infant's mouth, and then another *m* sound, rhymes with *dream*, *gleam*, *deem*, and *scheme*. *Meme* might even be the quintessential selfish phoneme cluster. (Some Americans, apparently believing or hoping that *meme* derives from French [*la même la-même?*], pronounce it mehm. They are posers, or, if they prefer, *poseurs*. For all I know, the French pronounce it like their colloquial word for "grandmother," as in the expression *Faut pas pousser Mémé dans les orties*—literally, "Don't push Grandma into the stinging nettles," figuratively [I found this on the Internet], "Don't exaggerate, don't push a notion too far." You can only push a notion as far as the alphabet will bear it.)

Many of the best words—*queasy*, *groggy*, *frank*, *haunch*, *spritz*, *rubble*, *catch*, *clog*, *articulation*, *swamp*, *pivot*, *dapper*, *gristle*, *finicky*, *nudge*, *lob*, *blob*, *bubble*, *hoist*, *crisp*, *swelter*, *quibble*, *fudge*—are mimetic, not in the sense that they reproduce themselves, but in the sense that they imitate, however indirectly, how the human body, brain included, senses and tries to transmit what obtains in the world.

Words do adapt and evolve. Let's see how *meme* holds up to natural selection.

See **Snakes on a Plane**.

➤ *memorabilia*

Mementos, souvenirs. So what's the singular? *Memorabilium?*

> Up in the attic we have got
> Many a memorabilium—
> For instance, that's the spot
> Where you'll find Uncle William.

No, according to RHU, it's *memorabilie*, rhyming with *slobbily*. No wonder nobody ever uses it. Then too, who ever has just one? (I have three co-
conuts from the 2007 Mardi Gras Zulu parade alone.) It's not as though
you don your Cub Scout cap for the first time thinking, I'll bet this is going to be my first memorabilie.

There might be a way to drag the Latin *mirabile dictu*, **"marvelous** to
say," in here, especially since it might lead us into "too marvelous for
words" and other philological lyrics by Johnny Mercer—but we've got to
move along, if this book is to have any narrative drive.

➤ menu-ese

The **verb** *to au poive* (an *r* lost and none the worse for it): "Blacken or Au
Poive your steak, $1 extra."

Different ways I have seen *hors d'oeuvres* spelled on the menus of
America: *orderves*, *Hor'devours*, *h'orvedurs*. It's a wonder that the French
version is still operative at all. Means "outside the (main) work, or
course"—awfully close to "out of work." Americans generally feel no need
to master the sound of *vr* (except in *vroom*), hence the last name of Brett
Favre, the distinguished quarterback, is pronounced Farve and the Army
(at least when I was in it) remembered the battle of Le Havre as luh Harve.
It's a wonder *canapés* hasn't replaced *hors d'oeuvres* on menus. Literally,
though, a canapé is limited to a dab of something on a cracker or a bit of
toast—the bready part serving as a settee for the dab. *Canapé* comes from
the French for "couch," which in turn derives, waywardly, from the Greek
for "mosquito netting," hence *canopy*.

While we are on this, whoever came up with the expression *appetizer?*
What appetizers tend to do, in practice, is eat up the appetite. An *apéritif*

works, though. From the Latin *aperire*, to open. Thus *aperture* and, speak of appetizing: *pert* (in Middle English, unconcealed, bold). German for "pert," by the way, is *schnippisch*.

"Turkey sausage one dollar extra than regular." *Extra than?*

➤ *merely*

"Not merely content to sue you, they've been making noises in Washington about the need to get tough on the insurance companies." "Not merely content," which means "They're not just content to sue you, they're downright smug about it," is presumably a pointless and confusing avoidance of the **split infinitive** in what is intended: "not content to merely sue you." But why the *merely*? Who needs it? There's something snarky or whiny (as in "a mere mortal like me") or nudgy about *merely*. "Not content to sue you" is fine.

➤ *meta*

Meaning, how shall I say, "at a level of, like, likety-like," as in *metafiction*, which is fiction rolling its eyes in our (or its own) direction with respect (or disrespect) to fiction. It may be time to bring that meme down a peg.

The Greek word *meta* meant "beside" or "after." *Metaphysics*, the mother of all *meta-* words, comes from references to Aristotle's treatise on first principles and primary substances, which, according to the *Stanford Encyclopedia of Philosophy*, was "to be studied only by one who has already studied nature (subject matter of the *Physics*), so 'after the *Physics*.'" Before you could take up the matter of matter and the subject of what is a subject, you needed to study the physical world.

The *Stanford Encyclopedia* notes that "it is important to remember that for Aristotle, one defines things, not words. The definition of a tiger does not tell us the meaning of the word *tiger*; it tells us what it is to be a tiger."

The essence of tigerness, then. Well, then again, the *Encyclopedia*: "'Essence' is the standard English translation of Aristotle's curious phrase *to ti en einai*, literally 'the what it was to be' for a thing. This phrase so boggled his Roman translators that they coined the word *essentia* to render the entire phrase, and it is from this Latin word that ours derives.

Aristotle also sometimes uses the shorter phrase *to ti esti*, literally, 'the what it is,' for approximately the same idea."

And people got all outraged when Bill Clinton said, "It depends on what the meaning of the word 'is' is."

From the Wikipedia entry on *meta* (as of December 1, 2006):

> The sentence "This sentence contains thirty six letters." along with the sentence it is embedded in are examples of sentences that reference themselves in this way.

Well now. If I were more of a wiki-person, I would do something about that sentence. Consider:

- The number *thirty six* should be hyphenated.

- The verb and subject don't agree: "along with . . . are examples" should be either "along with . . . is an example" or "and the sentence it is embedded in are examples."

- And what's that period doing in there after *letters*? If the writer feels required to put a period at the end of the embedded sentence in order to make it a sentence, then a sentence with a period in the middle of it is not a sentence. What we have here is either a grammatical anomaly embedded in something other than a sentence or something other than a sentence embedded in a grammatical anomaly. And whichever one is the sentence and which the grammatical anomaly, each of them, independently, is ungrammatical.

- Which goes to show, not that what the writer means to be saying is wrong, but that if you are going to get so meta as to wax authoritative about *meta*, you ought to pay more attention to what you're saying. However meta *meta* gets, there's always room beyond the meta, and some mess out there for someone to clean up.

> ➤ metaphor

Here's a good one: "You're just the wave, not the water" —Jimmie Dale Gilmore. See **simile**.

➤ metaphor, mixed

Micheal Ray Richardson, when he was playing for the New York Knicks, said his team was "a sinking ship." How far did he think the ship might sink? "The sky's the limit."

➤ meter

When, in the writing act, you feel as though you're slogging, trudging, dragging along, getting nowhere except deeper and deeper into abject tediousness, stop. Take a breath. And ask yourself this: WWJMD? What would John Milton do?

He would do what he was doing when, in *Paradise Lost*, he rendered Satan flung from heaven,

> *With hideous ruin and combustion down*
> *To bottomless perdition, there to dwell*
> *In adamantine chains and penal fire.*

He was doing what you've been doing: putting one foot in front of another. Only he was getting jiggy with it. He was stepping *metrically*.

So can you. Fewer *of*'s and *the*'s, more irregular verbs (*lit* not *illuminated*), absolutely no sluggish globs of unstressable syllables as in *tediousness*. Get a beat going, not just in your head but on the page, and even despair—even derivative despair ("I'll roll myself into a ball of dung, and wait for Kafka's bug to come along")—gets livelier, and you get surprises, like that *dung/along* off-**rhyme**, which you probably want to avoid in prose, but you're just getting yourself grooved here.

Even if you're reduced to singsong nonsense for a while (not that singsong nonsense is easy), pretty soon natural robust American English will be elbowing its way into your rhythm. And with it, your sense of purpose and command. Maybe. I ought to do something about that *it*, which should clearly connect to "natural robust American English," but "your rhythm" is in the way.

Here's a difference between writing and dancing: in writing it's okay to look at your feet. Anapest (da da *dum*), trochee (*dum* da), spondee (*dum dum*), dactyl (*dum* da da), mix 'em as required. But who's your daddy? Iamb. (Da *dum*.)

➤ *mic*

We need to preserve as much phonetic fiber in English as we can. That is why we have *trafficking*, not *trafficing*. I hate to see *mike*, short for *microphone*, rendered as *mic*, which is how it tends to be spelled these days, especially by people who use microphones. *Mic*, dammit, should be pronounced mick. As in *sic, tic, picnic, public, music, politic, Vic, hic* (the sound of a hiccup in comic strips), and *Bic* (the pen—short for *bicycle* is *bike*). The colloquial abbreviation of a word is not limited to letters taken from that word. If it were, we wouldn't be able to shorten *refrigerator* to *fridge*. We would have to spell it *frig*.

Here's all AHD has to say about *mic*: "*n. Informal* Variant of *mike.*"

A noun. But *to mike* is also a verb. And when you spell it *mic*, the past tense becomes what? In the subtitles to the DVD of a French movie I was watching the other day, it popped up as *mic'd*. Uggggly. The alternative is *miced*. Do you like the way that looks? Now, how about the present participle: *micing*. Does that look like it should be pronounced to rhyme with *liking*? No. That looks like it should be pronounced to rhyme with *icing*. (It also, **of course**, looks like something the cat can claim to have been out doing all night, why he looks so tired.)

Mike for *microphone* dates back to the 1920s. Like *bike*, *trike*, and the comparable *picnicking* and *politicking*, it has served us well, representing the hardness of the *c* sound with a *k*. But people seem to want something different now. Something that serves as a prime example of pissing away alphabet juice.

Maybe people favor *mic* because it looks like **chic**. In that case, it should be pronounced meek.

Rolling Stone, the venerable rock 'n' roll magazine, spells it *mike*.

See **e-mail**.

➤ *mignon*

Isn't it swell the way the *g* and *n* go together there to make that *ny* sound? (Same in *chignon*.) The way we spell that sound in English, *ni* as in *senior*, makes more sense, but it's not the same; it grabs hold of the palate with the tip of the tongue, for steadiness, before bringing up the edges of the tongue for the glide. The French goes right into the glide. Well, maybe a teeny tap of the tip first. Let's see, in *junior* it's *n-y'*; in *mignon* it's more . . . Now I'm confused—it's hard to keep track of exactly what your tongue is up to.

At any rate, compare the chuggy sensible English *gn*, as in *dragnet*, or the *ugh*-nasty *gn* in *repugnant*. And the heartier, less exquisite Italian *gn* in *lasagna*. That word, incidentally, may come from the Latin for "chamber pot" or "cooking pot." (That's a big *or* there.) Spanish approximates the French *gn* with a squiggle—a *tilde*—over an *n*. See *jot* **and** *little*.) Words should have as few squiggles as possible.

See **muscle/mussel**; **diaphragm**.

➤ *mingling*

Mingle is one of those -**le** frequentative words, prolonging an Old English word meaning "to mix." The present participle richly evokes mingling, to my ear—maybe because of the subsonic -*e* that becomes a phantom when the word is formed not by adding -*ing* to make *mingle-ing* (which would sound a bit clanky, like *ding-a-ling*) but by blending the middle syllable with the suffix.

➤ minimalism

A little of it goes a long way.

➤ *mishit*

Should be hyphenated, for decency's sake.

➤ misnomers

The War Between the States, which staunch Southerners used to insist upon as the only proper term for the 1861–65 conflict between the Union and the Confederacy—not the American Civil War, because a civil war is between parts of the same country and the South had seceded. But *between* is one-on-one. The Confederate States of America never got—or wanted to be—cohesive enough to be a state.

➤ *mistletoe*

The good news: the *-toe* part comes from an Old English word meaning "twig." So nothing to do with kissing feet.

The bad news: the *mist-* part derives from Germanic words for "dung." Mistletoe seeds, apparently indigestible, are deposited, and in the process fertilized, by birds that eat the berries.

➤ *mnemonic*

I would much rather appreciate words than criticize them, but this word, which means a ditty or formula designed to help you remember something—a word like that should be easier to keep in mind. You hear people pronouncing it noo-monic, when it should be neh- according to OAD, nih- according to RHU and AHD.

Forget the first *m*. I know, you'd think a word that has to do with memory and that begins with the letter *m* would begin with the *sound* of *m*. But if you start trying to pronounce that first *m*, the next thing you know you'll find yourself saying "m'n'm'nonimc." And then, "Thanks for the m'n'm'nies." And, "In my day, we had to m'n'm'n'ize whole long poems—of course back then you had poems that were a lot more m'n'm'nizable."

The only way I have found to cleanse my palate, so to speak, after falling into this pattern of speech is to think of something I *didn't* think of to say, once, until too late.

A friend of mine was looking at a lush stand of ferns in my yard. I liked those ferns, but my friend didn't think much of them for some reason. "You ought to plant some anemones," he said.

"With fronds like these, who needs anemones," I *should* have said, but I didn't think of it until later that day, when I was alone. It just popped into my head. *Then.*

Not saying that when it would have been so quick is one of the great regrets of my life. Occasionally I tell the story of not having said it, but that way it doesn't come off so witty. I have gone so far as to edge visitors over toward the ferns and say, "How do you like these ferns, here?"

"Nice."

"Think I ought to, maybe, replace them with something else? Some other . . . plant?"

"No, I think they're fine."

Some things, you can't set up. If it's not in the moment—well, a moment is something that you can't set up.

I find that saying "With fronds like these, who needs anemones?" a few times untwists my tongue enough that I can pronounce *mnemonics* and *memorandum* and *remnemb . . . remember* and so on again. But why should I have to go through that? What if we dumped the *n*? If Mneme and her mom Mnemosyne, the Greek muse and goddess, respectively, of memory, become Meme and Memosyne, then *mnemonic* becomes *memonic*, and we can connect it to **meme**: a bit of collective memory.

I am not, however, advocating such a change, because I have been reading *The Sound of Greek*, by W. B. Stanford. That book has done much to correct my bias against words beginning in *mn* or *pn* or *pt* or *tm* or *phth* and ending in *gm*. My prejudice—which in some cases, *see* **ptarmigan**, was well-founded—had been that such words must have been forced upon English by tin-eared Grecophile scholars who just wanted to show off their learning at whatever expense to **kinesthesia** and **sonicky**-ness. The word *phthisis*, meaning a wasting disease and pronounced *tie*-sis (*why? why?*) according to etymonline.com, used to irritate me no end. (A fine romance, my dear, phthisis.) My feeling was, let's rid English of all its counter-phonetic Greek-derived words. (Okay, *tisicky*, from *phthisic*, meaning asthmatic, was good, but not as good as *wheezy*, from the Scandinavian.)

But then (thanks to Sedge Thompson) I found Stanford's book. The Greeks of old, he points out, always read out loud, even to themselves. So did the Romans after them, except for Julius Caesar, whose ability to absorb written material silently was regarded as a sign of his uniqueness. Not even Quintillian, the Roman rhetorician who came along a century or so after Caesar, foresaw "that the quicker-moving eye would someday completely abandon the slower voice."

Don't worry, I won't advocate a return to reading aloud on trains and in airports, although the resultant cacophony would at least drown out cell phone chatter. But Stanford convinces me that the glory that was Greece included a much richer appreciation of the physicality of language, because "among well-practised readers their eyes, voices, ears and minds received the message almost simultaneously." An attentive reader of the Greek classics today can detect their appeal to "a kinesthetic sense . . . by which the brain receives from the ear not only an awareness of sounds but also a feeling of the vocal actions causing those sounds."

That's what I've been talking about! Holistic reading. You can move your lips. You can move your *hips*. Okay, your inner lips and hips. If you read only visually and cerebrally, it's like eating just for the vitamins.

Stanford leads us to the *Cratylos* of Plato, in which "Socrates is asked to join in a discussion on whether words have a natural affinity with what they denote or are merely conventional and arbitrary signs as Demokritos believed." Socrates weighs in on the affinity side: the short *i* sound "is apt for thin and narrow things"; the *o* sound "expresses round things . . . ; *t* and *d* express binding and stopping, on account of the throat and pressure of the tongue . . ." Words that begin with a *gl* sound evoke glueyness, as the hard *g* "holds back the movement of the tongue" and the *l* sound "with its gliding movement gives an impression of liquidity." In *glukus*, (or *glykys*, if like WIII you prefer the Romans' version of upsilon), meaning sweet (whence our *glucose*), "the tongue moves as if tasting a pleasant, sticky liquid," the *gl-* being followed by the *ew* (more or less) sound of upsilon, "which flattens the tongue," and the *k* sound of *kappa*, which "raises it to the palate"—as in, similarly, our *succulent*.

There. If you won't listen to me about kinesthesia, maybe you'll listen to Socrates. Who, to be sure, in his next breath turns around and weighs in on the other side, pointing out as do linguists today that there are too many counter-examples and so on, and condemning people "who care nothing for the truth but only for the way they shape their mouths."

Are we going to let this old bird divide people into truth-speakers and mouth-shapers? "With all due deference," says Stanford, "I would add a third type which hardly existed in Plato's time: those who care nothing for the physical substance of words and thereby miss a good deal of what authors are trying to convey to the reader." Mouth-deniers! Ear-ignorers!

Stanford doesn't say anything about *mn-* words. (He does observe that words beginning in *pn-*, like English words beginning in *sn-*, significantly move our nostrils.) But he has given me a feel for classical Greek sounds that I never got in college, although I was a Sigma Chi. For instance, he presents evidence that *chi* was pronounced not like a *k* but breathily, *c-h*, which greatly enhances a word that is an old Greek throat-clearing equivalent of *h'rumph*.

He even makes me feel the limitations of **honey**, which "is rich and euphonious, but hardly mimetic in any obvious way. Contrast the sound of Greek μελι [*meli*], Latin *mel*, French *miel*, Irish *mil*: the lips close on the *m*: the tongue rises with the *l*: we are going through the actions of tasting something deliciously sweet."

We can always try to work *mellifluous* into a conversation. And it might do us some good. "Modern psychologists," Stanford points out, "have suggested that the process of adopting a particular physical gesture," for instance turning up the corners of the mouth in a smile, can produce "the habitually corresponding emotion and mood. The Greeks probably knew this by intuition and experience."

So let's concede that Mneme and Mnemosyne knew a thing or two about memory. Browsing in *Finnegans Wake* recently (see **scratch**), I came upon "What a mnice old mness it all mmakes!" and "Everyday, precious, while m'm'ry's leaves are falling deeply," and "mememormee!" Memory is a tricky thing, more elusive than, by definition, memes are.

I can't even remember any mnemonics, except for one: "*i* before *e*, except after *c*, or when sounded as *a*, as in *neighbor* and *weigh*." I can even remember the exceptions to it—"the weird foreigner seizes neither leisure nor sport at this height"—because, for one fleeting moment, I become that foreigner.

➤ Moebius statement

You can make a Moebius strip by taking a narrow slip of paper, twisting it once, and gluing the ends together. Now run your finger along its surface and you'll find that it has only one surface, which goes on forever. A Moebius statement is one that seems to make sense—you know what it means to say—but the more you run your mind over it, the less it seems to track. An example is Robert E. Lee's famous remark at Fredericksburg: "It is well that war is so terrible; we would grow too fond of it!" Are we just fond enough of it *now*, at its going level of terribleness? If it got *considerably less* terrible, say down to the level of Ivy League football, wouldn't it be okay to become too fond of it? Couldn't it get *somewhat* less terrible without really getting to be all that fond-making? Could you plot on a graph an ideal nexus of fondness and terribility at which war is just terrible enough to take all the pleasure out of it, so that people hardly ever resort to it anymore, without being *so* terrible that when they *do* resort to it . . .

➤ monkeys

A monkey on one's back may seem a friendly companion, but whoever came up with that term for addiction had *probably* had a monkey. "Nobody ever has more than one," Billy Carter, brother of Jimmy, told me. The monkey Billy had was cute, the children loved him, he used to ride the family's pet rabbit around, but the rabbit didn't like it, and the monkey jumped onto the Christmas tree and started throwing the ornaments, and when Billy grabbed him the monkey bit him down to the bone and held on, had to be prized off.

I can't find the newspaper clipping now: one academic quoted as accusing another of being "a philosopher monkey." It's a striking image—I wouldn't want a philosopher on my back either—but it's likely that the reporter misheard "philosopher *manqué*," meaning someone who puts himself forward as a philosopher but falls short.

➤ movie dialogue

Nobody writes dialogue like this anymore:

> "My liver works like a buttered eagle." —Joel McCrea in Preston Sturges's *The Great Moment.*

Nor like these exchanges between Robert Ryan and Barbara Stanwyck, circling each other and closing in, in *Clash by Night*:

> *RR*: I need a drink. What do you need, Miss Doyle?

> *BS (after a beat)*: Well, let's say a drink.

RR: You're like me: a dash of Tabasco or the meat tastes flat.

BS: If I ever loved again I'd bear anything. He could have my teeth for watch fobs.

Nor like this Rudy Vallee line in *The Palm Beach Story* (Sturges again): "That's one of the tragedies in this life, that the men who most need beating up are almost always enormous."

Nor like this, from Judy Holliday in *Born Yesterday*: "If there's a fire and I call the engines—so who am I double-crossing—the *fiyah*?"

Movie dialogue isn't written anymore. It's improvised by the stars. And it shows. You know one big reason why *The Sopranos* was so good? David Chase was the godfather of all the words in it, and the actors had to speak the script as written.

➤ movies, French

The first adventurous use I made of my Georgia driver's license, at sixteen, was to hurtle in the family station wagon to an obscure drive-in theater way the hell off, forty-some-odd pre-Interstate miles out of town in Fayette County somewhere, with *guys* (it wasn't the kind of thing you'd take a nice girl to, and anyway making out would distract you from the movie, and anyway at the time none of us had girlfriends) to see Brigitte Bardot in . . . *And God Created Woman*.

To this day, if I had the power to change one evening of my past, it would be to turn the movie that evening into a different one—I don't care, *An Affair to Remember*, whatever *she* wanted to see—and to turn the people in the car with me into Brigitte Bardot, as she was then.

Except that, no—that's just bluster. I, as I was then, would have gone insane. B.B. (pronounced bay-bay) would've had to leave me out on the highway, gibbering and moaning—"a blithering idiot," as my mother would say.

It is impossible to re-create how inflammatory Brigitte Bardot was to a sixteen-year-old Methodist Georgia boy in 1957—those lips, that long dark-honey hair, and the rest of her always on the verge of getting naked *comme une jaybird*—because you'd have to re-create Georgia in 1957, and me at sixteen, and nobody in his or her right mind would want to do either of those things.

But Brigitte Bardot in Fayette County in 1957 was just a dream. Whereas when I went off to graduate school in Cambridge, Massachusetts, 1963–64, there was this series—every Wednesday night a different *serious* French movie. *Shoot the Piano Player. Zero for Conduct. The Rules of the Game. Hiroshima, Mon Amour.*

Way off beyond spicy, now. Maybe life could actually *be* French. Truth be told, the way these movies moved was more like the way my own mind moved than anything my mind had been exposed to back home.

Resnais, though, was pushing it. Trying himself, as my mother would say. Not jumping like the jumping in the Lead Belly song:

> *Jumpin' little Judy,*
> *Was a mighty fine girl.*
> > *She brought jumpin'*
> *To the whole wide world.*

But jumping by design. Jumping trying to pound some kind of abstract point home. That's the French for you. They can't be content with all that *oo, la la* they got working (take it for granted, maybe), they got to push it so far off into theory that you begin to wonder, *Où est la là là?* Where is the there there?

➤ *muscle/mussel*

Ancient Romans called both the former and the latter a *musculus*: little mouse. The former for its darting in and out of sight as it flexes and unflexes, and the latter for its shape, more or less like the torso of a mouse. Ancient Romans must have had unpretentiously developed bodies and unsuggestible stomachs. They ate dormice, but to be fair, the fat or edible dormouse (*Glis glis*) looks more like a squirrel than a mouse and was served with a glaze of honey and poppy seeds.

➤ museumese

"That hacked-off lumps of human and animal flesh were offered to the niche-held fetish idols we know." (Notice in witchcraft museum in Boscastle, England.)

George III "went to bed willingly but sillily at nine" (display in the British Museum).

➤ *muskrat*

This is a product of **folk etymology** that makes sense. A muskrat looks like a big rat and smells musky. However, though ordinarily I feel life is too short for dwelling on obsolete words, the original English word for this animal—derived from the Western Abenaki *moskwas*, perhaps equivalent to the proto-Algonquin roots for "head bobbing above the surface of the water" (RHU), does have a *sonicky* appeal. Here that original word is, in an indoorsy quote from James Russell Lowell: "I do not believe that the way to a true cosmopolitanism carries one into the woods or the society of musquashes."

Perhaps Lowell was being *snarky* about Henry David Thoreau, who wrote in *The Maine Woods* of shunning a moose hunt, for which he lacked the stomach, and instead taking a *marvelous* trip through wild northern Maine country with an Indian named Polis (punctuation Thoreau's):

> Just before night we saw a musquash (he did not say muskrat), the only one we saw in this voyage, swimming downward on the opposite side of the stream. The Indian, wishing to get one to eat, hushed us, saying, "Stop, me call 'em;" and sitting flat on the bank, he began to make a curious squeaking, wiry sound with his lips, exerting himself considerably. I was greatly surprised,—thought that I had at last got into the wilderness, and that he was a wild man indeed, to be talking to a musquash! . . . He seemed suddenly to have quite forsaken humanity, and gone over to the musquash side. The musquash, however, as near as I could see, did not turn aside, though he may have hesitated a little, and the Indian said that he saw our fire; but it was evident that he was in the habit of calling the musquash to him.

An *electrically prompt* (see **adverb**) word, that *wiry*. Makes me think of telegraph lines (see **wrought**), and the "high mercury sound" that Bob Dylan spoke of reaching for in music.

The Indians Thoreau met spoke an English much like that of Western-movie Indians. Except that they said *l* for *r* (*loots* for *roots*, for instance), like Chinese people in movies. Thoreau learned Indian words, for instance *Madunkehunk-gamooc*, Height of Land Park, and *Paytaywecon-gomec*, Burnt Ground Lake, which seem unwieldy, but less pretentious than the white man's word for the latter: *Telos* Lake, which would be the Greek for "Ultimate Object Lake." The Indian word for "echo" was *pockadunkquay-wayle*. More **sonicky** than *echo*, which comes from the Greek for "sound."

Polis asked Thoreau in turn to explain what the words *reality* and *intelligent* meant. Thoreau doesn't tell us how satisfactorily he managed to do that. He does tell of "the attitude that the Indian, who could not tell what we were talking about, assumed" when he and another white man had a "discussion on some point of ancient history":

> He constituted himself umpire, and, judging by our air and gesture, he very seriously remarked from time to time, "you beat," or "he beat."

➤ *mutual*

Alan Delynn, a theater and film producer I used to run into when I took part in New York nightlife, once said of two people, "They hold each other in mutual contempt, which speaks well of both of them." I've never read or heard that anywhere else, and assume it was original. It deserves recording.

"The feeling is mutual." Is that ever quite true?

Heard in a bar in Cheyenne, Wyoming: "I believe in the Golden Rule, and I assume he does. Means when he shot at me, he must want me to shoot at him."

➤ *myself*

If you say to me, "I hurt myself," I want to know how I can help. If, however, you refer to yourself as *myself* instead of *I* (as in "Can Trudy and myself go dig in the sandbox now?"), I have to tell you that you're making a spectacle of yourself. Not an entertaining spectacle, but rather the kind of spectacle that makes people think to themselves, "Oh, jeez." Which is fine with me. Go right ahead. But I'll bet Trudy will go play with somebody else in the sandbox next time, you watch.

If you think you're being **meta** or something, you're not. You're just being tedious. And just wait till your mother gets home.

n · N · n

In *Wordplay*, the excellent documentary film on the world of crossword-puzzle competition, one champion puzzler says he has a thing for *q*, but doesn't care for *n*.

Not care for *n*? It's true that *no* in every language I can think of begins with *n*. But just think how low you feel when you have a cold in your nose and can't say *n*: "A trib to the mood ode gossamer wigs."

N gives things a tang, a nip. Quintillian, the Roman rhetorician, praised the *quasi tinniens*, or ting-a-ling, effect of *n*. Without *n*, Snoopy would be soupy. Granted, without *n* an infant's *waaaanh* would not be such a disturbing sound. But *unh-unh* and *unh-hunh* don't convey dissent or assent without that back-of-the-palate *n* that's like French nasality—*uh-uh* and *uh-huh* do not get it.

The *n* sound (and I am not talking about the *n*-word, which has been noised about enough) has great negative resonance in Southern culture: "You ain't nothin' but a hound dog, cryin' all the time."

➤ name, in the news (you don't know what love is)

From the Cleveland *Plain Dealer* one day in 1974:

> Dr. David S. Love, under indictment for voluntary manslaughter in the death of his wife, was released yesterday on $1000 personal bond after pleading innocent . . .
>
> Love, 42, an assistant professor of anatomy at Case Western Reserve University, is accused of suspending his wife, Virginia Lee, on a rope from the third-floor window of their home . . . to perform a sex act June 22.

Mrs. Love, also 42, was hanging by a rope tied around her ankle,
according to George J. Sadd, assistant Cuyahoga County prosecutor.
She fell when the rope slipped from Love's hand, he said.

➤ name, scientific, they couldn't think of anything better than the common term so they got all sniffy

A medical term for the *hip*bone is the innominate bone. Which means
"unnamed."

➤ name, shrub's, self-assumptive

The shrub or small tree called *euonymus*, which is from the Greek for
"good name."

➤ name, stadium's, self-contradictory

For a while after the domed baseball stadium was built in Minneapolis, it
was called the Homerdome, because so many home runs were hit there.
Then, the rate of home-run-hitting there declined. So a baseball writer
(see **baseballese**) in *The Sporting News* suggested that the stadium be called
the Misnomerdome.

➤ name, wine's, with entitlement issues

There's a cabernet (rated quite highly by *Wine Enthusiast* and priced at
$62.49) called Eponymous 2002. Well, an eponymous character is one from
whose name the title of the work he or she appears in is taken. Hedda Gabler,
or Old Yeller. So this wine is apparently named for itself's being named for—
no, wait. This wine appears in a book, or movie, or play, entitled *Eponymous*?
That seems unlikely. Perhaps the wine's *label*, which did have quite a bit of
reading matter on it, as I recall (if you think I brought home a wine that ex-
pensive, you must think shade-tree lexicography is more lucrative than it is),
and might therefore be regarded (or might regard itself) as a literary work—
perhaps the *label* is named for the wine. But when is that not the case? When
it's old wine in a new bottle? Or vice versa? What this name is saying is, this
wine is what it's called. And I've lost track of what that second *it* refers to.

➤ names, famous, whose correct pronunciation is essential
   if you are going to be regarded as well-read, even though
   how would you know from reading?

Evelyn Waugh is *Eev*-lyn. P. G. Wodehouse is Wood-house. Roger Angell is
Angel. Isaiah Berlin is I-zi-ah. (Unlike Isiah Thomas, who is I-zay-ah.)
J. K. Rowling rhymes with *bowling*, not *growling*. Martin Scorsese rhymes
with *Desi*, not *daisy*, as it's more often pronounced.

Anthony Powell's last name rhymes more or less with *bestowal*.

If I had known thirty years ago that Edward Albee is All-be, not Al-be, I
would not have found myself in the embarrassing situation, on an air-
plane, of having tried for several minutes to carry on a conversation about
Albee's work with an increasingly mystified professor who had told me he
specialized not in Albee, as I thought I'd heard him say, but in algae.

➤ names, famous, whose correct pronunciation is so
   narrowly known that if you use it, you'll seem wrong

It was her daughter Amy who told me that Diane Arbus, the photographer,
pronounced her first name Dee-ann; but try telling that to all those arty
people impeccably dressed in black who pronounce it Dy-ann. And there
I am wearing God knows what.

It was his biographer, David Levering Lewis, who informed me that
W.E.B. Du Bois, author of *The Souls of Black Folk*, pronounced his last
name Duboyce. OAD gets it right. But educated people generally say
Duboyze. Indeed Richard Nixon, during his 1968 campaign for president,
charged that Communist-front youth organizations named for Du Bois
were trying to hide behind a name, the Du Bois Clubs, that sounded sus-
piciously like the Boys Clubs of America. I have laid this out for more than
one Duboyze-saying person who responded by kindly informing me that
Du Bois was not French. *Listen to me*, I say to these people, *I am not saying
Dubwah, I am saying Duboyce. Sss! Sss!* Those are hissing noises. For the
terminal soft-*s* sound. You see. Never mind.

Similarly, Édouard Manet. Having grown up around people whose minds
art never crossed, when I went to college and read this artist's name I steered
by my high school French and called him Mah-*nay*. When my wife, who *is*

an artist, heard me say this the first time she flinched visibly. Apparently you're supposed to say *Man*-ay. Well, no doubt the British do. Perhaps even the French do (my wife lived in Paris for a time, before meeting me, and may have been influenced by that city's rough-and-ready usage). But OAD agrees with me. I mean, it agrees with the way I said it before being set straight by her, who is no doubt right anyway. AHD says either Muh-*nay* or Man-*ay*.

Let us now consider Tootsie Bess, the late proprietor of the famous Nashville bar where country singer-songwriters of the sixties and seventies hung out: Tootsies Orchid Lounge (no apostrophe, as on the sign out front). In a video tribute to that institution, Kris Kristofferson, Justin Tubb, Tom T. Hall, and Buddy Emmons pronounce the first syllable of Tootsie's name to rhyme with *foot*, which is how I've always heard it and said it, and which makes sense given that *tootsie* is an affectionately diminutive term for **foot** as well as for a fetching female person. However, Willie Nelson, who knew Tootsie well, rhymes it with *boot*, and so do Roger Miller, Mel Tillis, Marty Stuart, Bobby Bare, and Tootsie's stepson Steve Bess. Got to go with the latter, then, even if it makes people other than Willie and them look at you like you must have never been in Tootsie's in your life.

A friend of mine in scholarly circles says that her colleagues make a point of pronouncing Walter Benjamin's last name Ben-ha-*meen*, but if someone were so bold as to ask them, "Who's Ben Hameen?" they would say, "Walter," not Val-ter.

Chico Marx's first name: Chick-o. They called him that because of his chick-chasing.

Back in Wyoming where he comes from, people pronounce Dick Cheney's name the way his family always did, "to rhyme with genie, not zany," as the *Chicago Tribune* puts it.

The *Couch* in Sir Arthur Quiller-Couch (see **darlings**) is pronounced cooch. Puts a little different spin on the man, doesn't it? Especially if you knew his sister Hootchy.

➤ names, fictional, good and bad

If the connection between words and their meaning is **arbitrary**, why is it so important to give fictional characters names that fit them?

I don't mean names that fit them heavy-handedly, as in Thomas

Pynchon's novels: Yashmeen Halfcourt, Alonzo Meatman, Ruperta Chirpingdon-Groin, Professor Heino Vanderjuice, the Reverend Lube Carnal, Pig Bodine. Pynchon builds interesting structures, but when it comes to grace notes he has the touch of an engineer.

Dickens's hand wasn't heavy, it was lavish: Ebenezer Scrooge, Wackford Squeers, Uriah Heep, Abel Magwitch, Mr. Pickwick, Wemmick, Pip. They aren't labels, those names, they're fitting, organic. You can muse endlessly about what makes Miss Havisham's name right for her—traces of *have*, *ravish*, *shhh*, like the notes discriminating tasters find, or say they find, in wine.

James Fenimore Cooper had a screw loose: Who else would call his romantic pioneer hero Natty Bumppo?

Among living novelists Charles Portis is an excellent namer: Rooster Cogburn, Lamar Jimmerson, Sir Sydney Hen, John Selmer Dix, Dr. Buddy Casey, and a little boy who never says a word, in *Norwood*:

> He was very well behaved and Norwood remarked on this.
>
> Mrs. Remley patted Hershel on his tummy and said, "Say I'm not always this nice." Hershel grinned but said nothing.
>
> "I believe the cat has got that boy's tongue," said Norwood.
>
> "Say no he ain't," said Mrs. Remley. "Say I can talk aplenty when I want to, Mr. Man."
>
> "Tell me what your name is," said Norwood. "What is your name?"
>
> "Say Hershel. Say Hershel Remley is my name."
>
> "How old are you, Hershel? Tell me how old you are."
>
> "Say I'm two years old."
>
> "Hold up this many fingers," said Norwood.
>
> "He don't know about that," said Mrs. Remley. "But he can blow out a match."

If I get around to writing my epic Western novel, the bad guy's henchmen will be either Plug, Twist, and Fancy (three different kinds of tobacco in an old advertisement) or Slim and Nunn.

➤ names, great, of people I have known in real life

Snake Grace, Ariel Stout, Candy Love, Love Beavers, LaMerle Tingle.

➤ names, pleasing to the eye and tongue

If you're like me, you like to savor certain names. For instance, the eponymous hero of a song that Jerry Leiber and Mike Stoller wrote for the Coasters: D. W. Washburn.

Why is *D. W. Washburn* so pleasing to pronounce? Because once you start saying it, it almost says itself. It carries your tongue through an agreeably rangy workout, and when it is over, it's over. Also I think there's something gratifying about the *D* followed by a letter whose name (double-u) starts with a *d*, followed by a word that starts with *that* letter. (I can now breathe the sigh of relief I have been nursing since 1994, when it hit me that I had spelled *Leiber* wrong several times in my anthology of Southern humor. I spelled it with the *i* before the *e*—which of course is the way it should be spelled, but who am I to tell people how to spell their names?)

Among many reasons New Orleans should not die is that the spokesman for the New Orleans Housing Authority, as of June 2006, was Adonis Exposé. Other New Orleans names from the *New York Times* story in which Adonis appears are Contresse Wilson, Terry Pierre, Pamela Mahogany, and Cliffie Pettigrew.

Bob Wills, the great Western Swing bandleader, had a manager named O. W. Mayo.

➤ names, power of

From the *Berkshire Eagle*: "If W.E.B. Du Bois had been named George Washington, everything in town would be named after him." An example of how you can seem to be—and in fact, I guess, be—making a commendable political point (that Du Bois is underappreciated in his hometown of Great Barrington, Massachusetts), without literally making any sense whatsoever. Or maybe this is a **Moebius statement**.

➤ names, some good ones I've picked up here and there

Marthalove Huge. A lady who died.

D'Brickashaw Ferguson. Offensive tackle, New York Jets.

Rosetta Shinboom. Driver of a Chicago cab that Walter Iooss Jr., the great sports photographer, and I took once.

➤ naming a song

Thelonious Monk played a new song. Somebody said, "What we going to call this one?" Monk said, "Let's call this . . . ," and he stopped talking. So it's called "Let's Call This."

➤ neologisms, created by typos

Destoryed (for *destroyed*): to be deprived of one's narrative.

➤ neologisms, needed

A word for the practice of quoting oneself (with or without attribution) because one can't quite resist it even though one looks down on others' quoting themselves.

A word for effects in writing that . . . that . . . well, that are like this one, achieved by William J. Broad in *The New York Times*: "Four million of a newly discovered microbe could fit into the period at the end of this sentence." I love that sort of thing. It isn't hard to picture the little fellas crowded into—more precisely, onto—the dot in question, jostling in their natural eagerness to spread infection but, for the moment, cooperating with the writer. But the image works only on paper. On a computer screen, the writer can't determine the size of the period. For all Broad can know, the online reader may have zoomed in on his passage so closely that four million cats, or at least one, could be dozing at the end of the same sentence. Not that a cat would do so at anyone's behest.

➤ neologisms, suggested

From time to time I have been informed by steely-eyed copy editors that I was coining or attempting to coin a word. Generally, I was using one that

I assumed already existed—*ructious*, for instance, which *The New York Times Book Review* was dubious of but eventually let stand.

Because to me *accomplice* connotes subordination—an accessory or henchman—I have occasionally felt I needed the word *complicitor*. But I have been persuaded by dictionaries, every time, that my sense of *accomplice* rests upon misinference. (Is there such a word as that? If not, why not?) And whereas a solicitor solicits, there is no such **verb** as "to complicit." You would not of course want to write, "According to his testimony, he did not know of the plot until he found himself complicited in it." Or even "He was unaware of the plot until he became one of the complicitors." "Until he became complicit in it" will do fine. Though it's awkward (*licitinit*) to pronounce. Maybe there should be a word like *licitinity* for linguinfelicity caused by too many short *i*'s; except that when you turn it into *licitinity*, it bounces right along. *Bounces* is not quite the right word. *Binces*, maybe? Combining *bounces* and *minces*?

Aside from nonce puns like *sub-blurb* for a blurb that seems half-hearted (a dear friend of mine once . . . oh never mind), the only word I can think of that I've coined on purpose is *antepenultimatum*. I've never had occasion to use it till now. It's when, for instance, you're absorbed in something outdoors, and you hear your mother calling, "For the last time, *come in for supper*," and you know from the tone of her voice that you really will absolutely have to come in, not this time, and not the next time she calls you, but the time after that.

Perhaps *postmature*, as regards a stage in life or something put off too long, has (so to speak) possibilities. Is there a word for that "so to speak," whereby a writer attempts to point out—to make sure the reader notices that the writer is aware of—certain or rather uncertain sort-of-notable, we might say "infrapunny," verbal reverberations that have cropped up . . . Never mind. See **of course**.

Scraction: tires getting going on a loose surface.

Schnicker: a drunken snicker.

Scrimptious: opposite of *scrumptious*.

Scrotch: crotch-scratch.

Exuality: your feelings and behavior toward people you have broken up with.

Bemusiast: one who makes it a practice, for personal or professional reasons, to go about being bemused.

If sportswriters covered fashion shows, they might come up with *clingage*, regarding a gown: "Some nice clingage along the haunch." They might also write: "As to Halston's version of a little summer dress, it is too little for words. From the high longstemline right on up to the plunging ahemline, there's too little material to work with. It will have to shift for itself."

Peekaboobs.

Swagamuffin.

Ah, but you can't force (foist? it's from the same root as *fist*) these words on the language—counterfeit coinage. They have to be inspired, like *chortle*. See **portmanteau word** and **giblet**.

➤ nerd

If you are a fan, as I am, of the Word History notes in AHD, see the one for this word.

➤ nicknames

The Hall of Fame infielder Jud Wilson, who starred in the Negro Leagues and in Cuba back when you had to be white to play in the U.S. big leagues, was given his nickname, Boojum, by Satchel Paige. For the sound his line drives made when they hit the outfield walls. That is a **sonicky** nickname.

➤ *niggardly*

This, of perhaps Scandinavian origin and meaning stingy or measly, is not, **of course**, a racist word. But it sure does sound like one, and there are plenty of handy and more current synonyms. Only a damn fool would use *niggardly* in a political setting in the presence of African-Americans and expect no one to be offended. That's what an aide to the mayor of Washington, D.C., did in 1999. He lost his job. Anti-p.c. columnists waxed indignant. He was rehired, as he should have been, assuming his judgment in other regards is better. Not even genuinely racist words can or should be erased from the language, but doesn't an alarm go off in your head well before you come out with *niggardly* in any company today? If it doesn't, it should. By the same token, Philip Roth's academic protagonist in *The Human Stain* should have had better sense than to ask a black student, "Are you a spook?" Hey! It just means ghost! Or CIA agent! Right. No educated person has grounds for *innocence* about traditionally insulting words.

> *nitpicking*

Let us consider that **monkeys** *enjoy* having their nits picked, and enjoy picking other monkeys'. (*Grooming* is a less pointed term.) It's how they bond. We should feel the same way toward copy editors, and yet we are wary. Monkeys, in this regard (though not, heaven knows, in every regard), have a certain tact. Which comes from the past participle of the Latin *tangere*, to touch, hence *tangible*. (**Tango**, however, is from quite another root.) When a quarterback, in football, can throw a pass that is forceful yet congenial to the intended receiver's hands, we say that he "has touch." A godlike quarterback could throw a ninety-yard pass that a three-year-old girl could catch. Clumsy, hasty copy editors don't have touch. A scrupulous, sensitive copy editor, such as the one who will go over (has gone over) this book, does have it, bless him or (in my experience, more likely) her.

A nit, *of course*, is the egg of a louse. From the Old English *hnitu*. Nature favors those animals who have fingers, are social, and find louse eggs tasty. That pretty much boils down to monkeys. Copy editors find grammatical nits nasty, and throw them away. A good one, however (I mean a good copy editor), must have a taste for this process.

According to John Tierney in *The New York Times*, there is an anthropological theory that gossip (the word, oddly enough, is from the Middle English for "godparent") is the human equivalent of monkeys' nitpicking, and that it is the mother of all language. But I'll bet it was first called schmoozing.

It is said that Demosthenes, the greatest Greek orator, once used a nitpicking audience to his advantage. He and his archenemy, Aeschines, the second-greatest Greek orator, had denounced each other back and forth in the most scurrilous terms for years, but neither had managed to put the other away. In their last face-off, Demosthenes made his greatest speech. After mocking Aeschines' assertion that he had visited Alexander the Great as a guest friend, Demosthenes presented to the assembled citizens this question:

"Men of Athens, which do you think? Is Aeschines the hireling or the guest-friend of Alexander?"

"Hireling! Hireling!" the assembly presumably shouted, because the next thing in the surviving text is Demosthenes saying to Aeschines, "You hear what they say."

According to the Roman commentator Ulpian, however, Demosthenes had drawn this response by deliberately mispronouncing the Greek word for hireling, putting the accent on the first syllable instead of the last. The fastidious Athenian crowd shouted out the correct pronunciation, which was the answer Demosthenes wanted. Aeschines went into exile.

➤ noir novel, all I've got so far

When she walked in the joint she looked like the poem framed on the wall—perfectly typed, but key words mispelled:

> In everone there is a bit
> Of the devine. Just fined it.

Or is it *misspelled*. Nobody's perfect. That's what makes it so hard to know for sure how wrong. You start thinking, "Maybe those words aren't so key." Because she did look very good. Pretty soon you aren't thinking at all.

➤ *no question*

When we say, for instance, "No question Saddam Hussein had nuclear weapons," do we mean "no doubt," or "out of the question"? I see it used both ways, or in such a way as to fudge which way.

After George W. Bush began to be challenged on his assertion that Hussein had nuclear or at least mass-destruction weapons, he fell back upon insisting—in a tone that admitted of no ambiguity or doubt—that Hussein definitely, unquestionably *did so* have . . . "weapons."

➤ *no-see-um*

Also called *biting midge* or *punkie*, this is one of those flies or gnats that are almost too small to be seen, but that pack a wallop by coming in clouds and biting harder than mosquitoes. For all their damnability, the more I learn about these mini-imps of Satan the more I think there should be a no-see-um museum. According to the *Columbia Encyclopedia* (third edition, 1963), "some species ride the wings of dragonflies and lacewings, sucking the blood of their hosts." Their family is Ceratoponidae, which is Latin for "horned and bearded." Good thing they're not as big as goats.

Sinclair Lewis, according to the excellent, lamentably unfinished *Random House Historical Dictionary of American Slang*, once wrote that "Seattle . . . is so big I feel like a no-see-um in a Norway pine reserve."

Gnat **probably** comes from the same Old English verb as *gnaw*.

➤ *nosism*

This means arrogance on the part of a group of people, but it's not to do with noses in the air or looking down noses or noses getting out of joint. It's from the Latin *nos*, and its more specific meaning is the delivering of one's opinions in the royal or editorial or corporate *we*. There is also *illeism* (from the Latin *ille* for "he"), meaning referring to oneself in the third person. And *tuism*, as in "You wake up in the morning and you get dressed and you go to work and you sit there in your cubicle and you say to yourself, 'You know what? You deserve more than this.'"

After radio shocktalkmonger Don Imus (known to friends as the I-man) caught *flak* for idiotically referring to the Rutgers women's basketball team as "nappy-headed ho's," he first offered a nosist apology: "We want to take a moment to apologize for an insensitive and ill-conceived remark we made the other morning . . . It was completely inappropriate, and we can understand why people were offended. Our characterization was thoughtless and stupid, and we are sorry."

When that statement did not suffice and it seemed he might actually get fired, the I-man at last began to single himself out, so to speak: "I understand there's no excuse for it. I'm not pretending that there is. I wish I hadn't said it." And, "I'm not a bad person. I'm a good person, but I said a bad thing. But these young women deserve to know it was not said with malice."

That was certainly less lordly: just good old-fashioned egotism. Such consideration of others: "these young women deserve . . ." What if these young women don't give a big jump shot whether malice was intended. What if they find it *more* objectionable, not to mention less hip, if Imus thought it would pass for lighthearted.

If you're going to call people names, you should have the decency to mean it. See **demean**.

➤ *not about me*

When I think of how many things fall into this category, it's humbling, I'm here to tell you. It is even a **bit much**.

➤ *now*

In print, this term is meaningless, now . . . these days . . . lately. Come to think of it (I just now thought of it, this very minute), that (the preceding sentence) has always been true. Even in a daily paper, the closest the printed word *now* can come to "this moment" is the day before. Now (loosely speaking), in electronic media, we have the new *n* . . .

Has anyone else come up with that phrase? "The new now"? Have I maybe struck upon a potential original **meme**? Got to Google that . . .

Oh, "about 38,400."

Including an album, *Then Is the New Now*, by someone named Denison Marrs. I learn of this from a "blogcritic," Craig Lyndall, who appears in his accompanying photo to be about fourteen. He says (or, wait—he *said* on April 22, 2004, or at least that's when he posted on Blogcritics.org) in effect that *Then Is the New Now* is not happening. Not that it is so five seconds ago (as is so much supposedly "live" TV and radio, owing to the tape-delay buffer designed to protect the world from dirty words and any recurrence of Janet Jackson's breast) . . .

Here's a review: "If you want to skip this album altogether, you should try releases by Jimmy Eat World, or even the latest from Hey Mercedes."

There is so *much* now out there these days, and the bulk of it . . .

But wait! Lyndall has I guess gotten the title wrong. According to a Web reviewer named Peter Bate, the Denison Marrs album is called *This Is the New Now*, it is "Christian powerpop/metal," and it includes a song "begging Christ to unlock the secret of enemy loving." I suppose what is meant is *enemy-loving*, with a hyphen: Love thy enemy. As opposed to inimical loving. Anyway, Bate says, "Denison Marrs squeeze every ounce of energy into this CD as if their life depends on it. Now could be their time."

But wait! According to Answers.com, the album's title *is*, after all, *Then Is the New Now*. And it came out in 2002. And . . . since Web surfing and note-taking are such incompatible operations, I've lost track of who said what, but somebody accused the album of falling "between two stools of power pop and metal, and the other two stools of hooky pop and bland anthem." Somebody else: "bland anthem rawk." (See **rock criticism**.)

And someone else says *Then Is the New Now* was rumored to be "the death of the group, but the rumors were obviously just that, *of course*."

I don't know what "Then is the new now" means, but I know this: there is no *now* on the Web, even. Fast as it is, the Web is layers on layers, in no chronological order.

In a paper-and-ink medium such as this book, the only version of *now* that makes any sense is "as I write." Which is to say, "as of the last time I put any finishing touches on this and stopped to think whether what it says is still . . . still."

And if there is no *now* here, there is no *is* either, nor any *here*.

Roy Wilder Jr. says "She has everything up to now" is a Southernism for "She has everything in good order." Nobody does anymore.

➤ *now-bashing*

Deploring what goes on in the present time compared to some idealized time in the past.

➤ *nuclear*

New-klee-er. Not noo-kyul-ler. How can people blithely mispronounce a word that refers to the center of everything? Do people say "noo-kyu-lus"?

o · **O** · o

O *O*, how empty yet how full
You are; how like the moon you pull.

You're just inside the door of *home*,
You calm us down when we say *Om*,

You couldn't be more in the middle of *now*.
If it weren't for you, we couldn't go "Wow!"

You're shaped like a mouth making your sound,
You're a ring, orgasm, the essence of round,

The egg in *mom*, the bubble in *pop*.
Hip is static without your *hop*.

Origin-omega, *okay* to *no*,
Yo ho ho, good old *O*.

According to Lynn Berry, former editor of *The Moscow Times*, here's a joke that went around Moscow in 1980, when Leonid Brezhnev, leader of the Soviet Union, was getting rapidly less young. Brezhnev begins his speech opening the Moscow Olympics as follows:

"O! O! O!"

An aide breaks in with a whisper: "Leonid Ilyich! The speech starts below! That is the Olympic symbol."

➤ obituaries, quotes from

"A careful man with a dollar, he would be furious to know how much this notice costs."

"A master of the inappropriate witticism."

➤ *odd*

Derives, according to AHD, from the Old Norse *oddi*, meaning "point of land, triangle, odd number." Something that is odd, then, sticks out. Two's company, three's a crowd; a fifth wheel. How about, on the other hand, **even**. RHU traces that back to the Old English verb *efnan*, to lower. Consider all the uses of *even*: don't they seem to come out of the leveling aspect of the root word . . . everything else being even.

➤ *of a*

"Is there a danger about racing to this big of a lead?" asks the *New York Times* sports page. In writing, that will not do. The *of* has no function there. "This much of a lead," okay, but "too big a lead." A simple inversion of "a lead that's this big." You can say, "I don't like much of that," or "I would like more of that," or "I like a lot of that," but you can't say, "I'd like a big of that."

Tossing words into a sentence for no reason is like adding ingredients to a recipe just because they come to hand.

➤ *of course*

Called "the lazy writer's crutch" by Robert Gottlieb, the former editor of *The New Yorker*, in a book review. One sees his point, *of course*, but how else (*obviously* being too heavy) can one indicate that one knows that what one has just said is undoubtedly already known, or heaven knows ought to be known, to the reader? Otherwise the reader is likely to be saying "Duh," and one doesn't want that, of . . . it goes without saying. Maybe I'm living in the past, though. Editors and English professors keep telling me that you can't assume anyone knows anything anymore. When I was growing up I took it as a given that any reference I didn't get was a gap in my knowledge. If I was ever going to become a reader worthy of, for instance, *The New Yorker*, I would have to be assiduous in filling in those gaps. These days, I keep being told, a writer has to explain everything or readers will fling him or her aside. And then you write a book that explains things you'd rather assume people know already, and a knowing reviewer says you sometimes seem to be addressing an audience of Martians, people who have never heard of anything on earth. *The New Yorker*, by the way, is a distinguished weekly magazine.

Addressing a niche audience, *bien sûr*, is a different matter. This from a fishing column: "Flavored soft baits are not new, of course . . ."

Then there is what we might call the cute *of course*, as in this from George Will: ". . . the greatest piece of music since Mozart ('Take Me Out to the Ballgame,' of course)."

➤ *oink*

Pronounced *oingk*; the *g*, as in *boing* or *boin(g)k*, gives it reverb. "What is that pig doing?" "Just going *oink*." An oinkling might be a piglet.

Oink originated, says OAD, in the 1940s. RHD narrows it down to 1940–45. The war? And how were pigs going before that?

See *groin*.

➤ *okay*

I'm not comfortable with *O.K.* H. L. Mencken praised *O.K.* and *C.O.D.* and *P.D.Q.* as "American masterpieces" of abbreviation, but back up now and look at that mess: "*O.K.* H. L." Capital letter, period, no space, capital letter, period, space, capital letter, period, space, capital letter, period.

Feh. *OK* is better in some ways, aside from looking like the cry of a giant throttled bird; but my vote is for *okay*, if only because it enables us to render the past tense of the verb as *okayed*, which looks like English, instead of *OK'd* or, worse, *O.K.'d*.

However you spell it, the sound of *okay* is eminently catchy—brisk, basically upbeat but modulatable. All the more reason to spell it right. I find it regrettable that Okeh Records, the label that was pronounced Okay, and

which put out so much great vernacular American music, took upon itself
that alternative, now obsolete spelling. I can't help thinking -*keh* should
rhyme with *feh*. Or *meh*. Or *bleh*. Or at least *Tecumseh*. Woodrow Wilson is
said to have favored and popularized *okeh*, having decided to go with the
unsubstantiated theory that the expression came from a Choctaw/Chicka-
saw word, *okah* or *okeh*, meaning "it is indeed" or "amen."

   Woodrow Wilson?, you are probably wondering. *How about Old Kinderhook?*

   Okay. Many people will tell you that *O.K.* meaning "all right" was inspired by one of the least inspiring American presidents, Martin Van
Buren. They may even tell you that Van Buren initialed state documents
"O. K.," for "Old Kinderhook." That story, like the expression, is good
and snappy, easily remembered. But it's not quite right.

   Van Buren as president was what George W. Bush has more recently
been called: a post turtle. Like a turtle that wakes up on top of a fence post,
Van Buren knew he hadn't gotten where he was by himself, and he didn't
know what to do there. He was his predecessor Andrew Jackson's boy. I
won't go into why Jackson liked him so much, but it had to do with Van Buren's courtesy toward a highly appealing scandalous character, whose
maiden name was Peggy O'Neale. (She married John Eaton, Jackson's
secretary of war. You should look her up some time.) Thanks largely to
Jackson's residual popularity, Van Buren was elected over the Whigs'
William Henry Harrison in 1836. But then came the Panic of 1837, which
brought on a national depression, which Van Buren failed to lift. The
Whigs were calling him Martin Van Ruin.

   When Van Buren ran for re-election in 1840, again against Harrison,
his party, the Democrats, needed a better nickname for him. He was from
Kinderhook, New York, so someone came up with Old Kinderhook, which
was sort of like Old Hickory, Jackson's nickname, or Old Tip, which is
what the Whigs were calling Harrison: short for Tippecanoe, the battle in
which Harrison had razed an Indian village and made himself a military
hero. There was apparently a Democratic organization called the O.K.
Club, and "O.K." was a rallying cry for the Van Buren campaign.

   However, *O.K.* meaning "all right" was already current in Boston and
New York City newspapers before it was applied to Van Buren. And it was
tongue in cheek. As RHD puts it, O.K. were the "initials of a facetious folk

phonetic spelling, e.g. *oll* or *orl korrect* representing *all correct*." "The joke being," as AHD explains, "that neither the *O* nor the *K* was correct."

Here's how the catchphrase went, to take an 1839 example—"The suspension of the U.S. Bank . . . is O.K. (*all correct*) in this quarter." Not much of a joke. And as a political slogan, "O.K." was no "I Like Ike." Quotations in *The Random House Dictionary of American Slang* suggest that "O.K." was used to mock Van Buren as much as to energize his supporters. By the account of Sean Wilentz in *The Rise of American Democracy* (which doesn't even mention the role of "O.K."), the Harrison campaign was almost modern in its anything-goes irrelevance. "The electorate learned from Whig partisans," for instance, "that the degenerate widower Van Buren had instructed groundskeepers to build for him, in back of the Executive Mansion, a large mound in the shape of a female breast, topped by a carefully landscaped nipple." The incumbent lost badly to "Tippecanoe and Tyler too" and the refrain "Van, Van is a used-up man."

The Van Buren campaign does deserve credit for spreading *O.K.* around the U.S. But within decades Old Kinderhook was forgotten and *O.K.* had replaced *right-o* in England. Now of course it is part of the global lingua franca. But the juice wasn't in the candidate, or in the obscurely waggish provenance. It was in the word. Okay?

> onomatopoeia

Refers *of course* to words (*buzz, murmur, gong*) that sound like what they mean. It's a fun word to pronounce and an easy one to remember—perhaps the only literary term that many of us retain, if we retain any at all, from our schooling. But fond of this word as we may well be, we need a better one in English, because *onomatopoeia* (besides being hard to spell) is itself un-onomatopoeic (or non-onomatopoeic, if you prefer). If you had never seen the word before, you wouldn't suspect, from the sound of it, that it means what it means. Nor would you from its etymology: it comes from the Greek for "coining names," not from the Greek for "sounding like what it means." And if I were commissioner of spelling I would drop the *o* after the *p*: this word looks plenty Greek enough without clinging to a *poe* pronounced pee. Furthermore, *onomatopoeia* tends to be rather narrowly applied, to words like *bang* and *jingle* that specifically try to capture sounds in letters. We need a word to get at the quality of a great many words, especially those deriving from the Anglo-Saxon, that are kinesthetically evocative of, or appropriate to, their meaning, without necessarily involving imitative noise: *chunky*, *blink*, *squeeze*, *foist*, and so on. I propose **sonicky**.

The Greek for "sound" is *phthongos*. Hence *diphthong*, for two sounds— a glide from one to the other—within the same syllable (*oi* in *foist*). Do you think *phthongic* could catch on? See **piss**.

➤ *orange*

Ever wonder which came first, the fruit or the color?

In English, at least, the fruit. From the Arabic *naranj*.

➤ *ornery*

This word, meaning "mean, contrary, stubborn" (though lately it is taken as having a kind of cutesy, because folksy, ring), evolved from *ordinary*. A syllable got slurred out and the word began to sound begrudging and contrary. As the sound changed, the meaning changed, and vice versa. See **cantankerous**.

➤ *out of*

William Whitworth, former editor of *The Atlantic*, complains of this "slightly dopey usage":

> "He's out of San Antonio, Texas." Said when "he" is still *in* San Antonio and seldom leaves. The dictionary has an "out of" listing, but only for the sensible use—"He works out of the home office," meaning that he comes and goes from there. My guess is that it arose from such office designations and from references in the thirties and forties to what were called "territory bands." Like, "The McIntyre band works out of Dallas." Same as the office. Their headquarters is Dallas, but they play all over the Southwest.
>
> But now when a radio sports guy is talking about an offensive line

recruit in Cabot, Arkansas, he'll say that the kid is "out of Cabot," though he may never get out of Cabot unless someone gives him a football scholarship.

My only suggestion is that this *out of* might have been influenced by horsebreeding terminology: "Bless-my-stride, by Legman out of Beatitude." The offensive line recruit seen as a son, then, of Cabot.

I once asked Steve Blass, when he was pitching for the Pittsburgh Pirates, whether he was the only major-league ballplayer to come out of Falls Village, Connecticut. He said, "I'm the only *person* to come out of Falls Village, Connecticut."

p · P · p

Why don't we say, "On your mark . . . Get set . . . *Gop!*"?

Because all those straining runners, instead of exploding out of their blocks, would freeze and tip over onto their proboscises. *P* at the end of a word is a sound that stops: no vibrations, and just a piffly escape of airflow. The *k* at the end of *mark* and the *t* at the end of *set* are also unvoiced (no vocal-cord vibrations) plosives (blocking air), but they don't clamp the lips down as firmly as *p*.

Which is why *p* is so much fun at the *beginning* of a word—all that pouty prim pompous bottled-up air finding explosive (hence *plosive*) release: *pooh*, *poof*, *poot*, *pop*, *pfft*. Or, with a little hiss of air let out up front to build suspense: *sproing*.

So why do we go *giddup* (or *k-k*) to make a horse go and *whoa* to make him stop? Well, if you have a magnificent horse that you trust implicitly, it's "Hi-yo Silver! Away!" Otherwise, it's about control, isn't it? You're not saying, "Haul ass, take off." You're saying, "Let's get into a gait." And as to *whoa*, that derives from *ho*, a way of getting attention—and *whoa* shudders gutturally at the end, h-h-h . . . can that be the **uvula** I hear? Maybe *whoa* should be spelled *woah*, or, no, *wo-h-ho*, something like that, to capture that little sympathetic whinny at the end.

The *ll*'s in *gallop* and *wallop* and *dollop* and *trollop* help make them good bouncy words. Pronouncing a series of *p*-words can be like popping Bubble Wrap, fun but far from fluid: "Peter Piper picked a peck of pickled peppers and put them in a pot." Poky. But if you get the right rhythm going, you've got *pitter-patter* and "Pick her up and pat her on the po-po."

Papa: often the first word out of baby's mouth. *Mama* comes from getting milk, *Papa* is just an accident, just playing around with the lips, but it makes the old man light up (and he does seem to have a certain standing), so what the heck. Lip service.

Pumped. Potentate. Pompadour (see **spelling bee**). Paparazzi. The pope.

My daughter, whose family has just got a puppy, says that according to current thinking you're not supposed to say "no" to a puppy. You say, "Ep, ep," which simulates a mother dog's admonitory yap.

➤ *palate*

The roof of the mouth, without which the nasal and oral cavities would be one and I shudder to think how conversation would sound. Up front is the hard, or alveolar, palate. Further back is the soft, or velar, palate. The tongue interacts with the hard palate in making *d*, *t*, and *s* sounds and with the soft palate in making *k*, *r*, *y*, and hard *g* sounds, which may be called guttural, from the Latin for "throat." See **consonants**.

Palate is also used for a person's sense of taste, in food and drink or more generally. *Palette*, pronounced the same, is the range of colors that a painter has on that flat board with the thumb hole, or by extension the range of elements employed by any artist. A chef's palette appeals, or doesn't, to a gourmet's palate, a writer's to a reader's. The two words don't share any roots. *Palette* is from the French for "little shovel." If there is any metaphorical texture to *palate*, from the Latin *palatum*, meaning "palate," it is lost in the mists of time. No known connection to *palatium*, meaning "palace." But there was something palatial about Enrico Caruso's palate: it was arched so high that he could hold an entire un-cracked egg in his mouth and from looking at him, no one would know. You try it.

➤ palindrome, spontaneous and ingenuous

I was in a village along the river Huallaga in Peru. I shared a mango with a local boy.

"Yum," I said to him.

"*Muy* yum," he replied.

➤ *pareidolia*

A term of recent coinage. The prefix is from *para-*, which in a medical or psychological (but not parapsychological) context denotes functional disorder. In common words from the French, however, it refers to protection, as in *parasol* and *parachute*, *chute* being French for "fall"; and in *paradiddle* it imitates the first two of four even strokes on a drum with alternating hands, left-right-left-left or right-left-right-right. The rest is from *eidolon*, an idealized or phantom image.

Pareidolia is "seeing things." Seeing, that is, what you want to see in ambiguous patterns or images. The Virgin Mary on a piece of toast (never, you notice, on a bagel), weapons of mass destruction in Iraq.

And, more reliably, the Man in the Moon. Apparently different cultures see different faces on the moon, but the one I see is the best and least deniable one. Any of them, I suppose, may serve as an absolute standard of comparison: "You are no more going to do what I say," my mother would tell me, "than the Man in the Moon." He was sent up there, I was taught, for working on Sunday, but there are juicier theories.

See **cherry-picking**; **subjective/objective**; **arbitrary**.

➤ *partridge*

The name of this "plump-bodied Old World game bird" (as AHD puts it, mostly spondaically) **probably** comes from the Greek *perdesthai*, to fart, in tribute to the sharp whirring noise a partridge makes when flushed. (Yes, I know, your uncle Sidney did the same thing.)

To show you how discriminating Proto-Indo-Europeans were, there are two **PIE** roots for *fart* words: *perd-*, whence *partridge* and *fart* itself (via the Old English *feortan*, to fart); and *fezd-*, whence *feist*, a little disagreeable dog, and *petard*, which in French is a loud fart and in English an explosive device (he who is "hoist by his own petar," as Hamlet puts it with Rosencrantz and Guildenstern in mind, is blown up by his own stratagem). None of this should dampen anyone's enthusiasm for partridges in pear trees, but you might want to think twice if you mean to compliment a small plucky person by calling him or her feisty.

In *Origins*, his book of etymology, the late noted lexicographer Eric Partridge, who as a rule did not shrink from four-letter words, tells us that the Latin *perdix*, meaning "partridge," "was adopted from Gr: ? echoic of the whirring wings of the rising bird." Doesn't bring farting into it. Can't blame him.

➤ pathetic fallacy

Ascribing feeling, not necessarily pathos, to an inanimate object.

Lincoln, after Grant took Vicksburg: "The Father of Waters again goes unvexed to the sea." (As if the river gave a silt who "controlled" it.)

Aristotle maintained that a falling body accelerated because it became more jubilant as it found itself nearer home.

➤ *perhaps*

What a weasel word this is. "This, then, perhaps, is the one thing we must do if the human race is not to be extinguished, perhaps, or did I say that already." Means *maybe*, **of course**, but at bottom it's even vaguer: by chance. *Maybe* is a more assertive word: Maybe, baby, something going on there. *P'raps* is faux-diffident.

The prefix *per-* is one of an amazing range of derivations from the **PIE** root *per-*: *far, paradise, furniture, afford, first, protein, privy, probable, pristine,* and *priest.* As for *hap*, it's Middle English for "luck." Hence *happy.* And *hap'nin'*, perhaps.

See **probably**.

➤ *pfft*

See *P, F,* and *T.*

➤ *pharynx*

Larynx and *pharynx* sound like sidekicks in a Greek comedy, perhaps *The Frogs.* In anatomy, the former lies behind the latter. In a Greek comedy,

Larynx might be lying there so that someone can push Pharynx over, but in the human vocal apparatus, larynx and pharynx work together. See ***glottis***.

➤ *phenomenon*

This word seems to be dying out, at least in speech—I hear even professors using *phenomena* as the singular. All the dictionaries, however strong their inclination toward description rather than prescription, flatly condemn the practice, but what are you going to do? I can't come over there and grab you by the scruff of the neck and march you over to the library and—oh, never mind.

➤ *phlegm*

The *g* is silent, but doesn't it add something? Sure it does. Captures **teh** nature of the thing. (Here is an expression I have long longed to find an occasion for: "strumming his catarrh.") From the Greek *phlegma*. The *g* leaves in the Middle English *fleume*, but comes back in the sixteenth century thanks to scribes influenced by the classics. Good for them. We wouldn't want it to be *phlem*. Though Faulkner's Flem Snopes is a funny name, short for Fleming **perhaps**, but only trash would call a son Flem. The *g* comes up audibly in *phlegmatic*. See ***humor***.

Latin for "phlegm": *pituita*, literally "the spit thing." The Latin for "phlegmatic" is *pituitosus*, "hence French *pituiteux*," says my old Latin dictionary. My old French dictionary has *pituite* for "phlegm" (but also *flegme*, with the *g* pronounced, and *flegmatique*). The pituitary gland was so named because it was originally believed to produce mucus. Today we may have many beliefs that are just as dumb.

The vocal cords are mucous membranes. We must have a lining of mucus to lubricate any body passage exposed to the air. It does its job, and let's be grateful. And move on.

➤ *phooey*

This is here mostly to separate the entry above from the one below, for tastefulness' sake, but I must say that in ejaculations or inter-

jections such as "Oh, phooey," it's a breath-of-fresh-air alternative to the
f-word.

Pfui, Yiddish, from the German, works too—is even a bit juicier, if only
because more compressed.

Etymonline.com says *phooey* was popularized by Walter Winchell in the
thirties and that *phoo*, as a "vocalized gesture expressing contemptuous
rejection," goes back at least to 1642. I'd say further.

➤ *pie*

Sweet, fruity pie didn't show up in print until the sixteenth century. Before that, pies were assumed to be meat pies—game pie, eel pie, pigeon
pie. So the king may have been quite pleased to be served four-and-
twenty blackbirds in pastry, until they popped out alive, in what, come to
think of it, might make, if inventively staged, a great Broadway musical
number:

> Whether you're a commoner,
> Whether you're a king,
> Remember sweet Philomena,
> And don't eat birds that sing.

Philomena being that unfortunate young woman who, in recompense for
being horribly misused, is turned into a nightingale by the gods. Preferred, *of course*, is *Philomela*, but we can work around that. Otherwise we
have to fall back on *phenomena*, and we lose the classical touch.

Come to think of it further, isn't there a Betty Boop cartoon in which
Louis Armstrong and band are depicted as performing in a pie? Oh my.

All that aside, etymologists' best bet is that pie owes its name to a black
and white bird, which we now know as the magpie. Originally the bird
was called simply pie. In recognition of its tendency to chatter, it was
personified, sexistically, by various nicknames for Margaret: *maw pie*,
maggoty pie, and the one that caught on, understandably: *magpie*. Similarly, the daw, known for boldness, cunning, and a willingness to eat
parasites off sheep, became the jackdaw. There may have been magpie
pies, but *probably* the pastry struck people as being like the bird because
its miscellaneous ingredients reminded people of the magpie's pro-

pensity for collecting odd (not to say **arbitrary**) mixed troves of glittery objects.

To me (see Y, however), *pie* sounds much juicier not as a Yankee diphthong, *pi'ee*, but as a simpler sound, unspellable but more open-mouthed—as Bessie Smith pronounces it, for instance, in "St. Louis Blues":

> I love that man like a schoolboy love his pie.

The mathematical *pi* is the first Greek letter in the Greek word for "periphery." It's useful in calculating a pie's circumference.

➤ PIE

Proto-Indo-European. One day in the 1780s it struck Sir William Jones, an English judge (see **arbitrary**) in India, that Sanskrit, Latin, and Greek had so many similar words and forms of grammar that they must have "sprung from some common source, which, perhaps, no longer exists." Indeed that language was not only dead, it had died before history could record it. No one even knows what the people who spoke it were called, or exactly where they lived. They apparently left no artifacts.

But by assiduously comparing all Romance, Germanic, and Slavic languages, philologists have been able to reconstruct PIE in the form of roots like *pleu-* (to flow) and *tong-* (to think, feel), from which have blossomed the languages native to one-third of the world's people. Most good English dictionaries connect the words they define to these roots, where possible. AHD goes so far as to include in a wonderful appendix a thoroughgoing (ooh, that's an ugly word to look at, isn't it?) PIE-ological breakdown. I urge you to venture back there, if you haven't already: *ghend-*; *medhyo-*; *sleubh-*. You can hear English groaning to be born.

Which is the juiciest root, the one that has produced the most unlikely range of flowers? Maybe *wegh-*: *vogue, weight, wiggle, way, earwig.* Maybe *pag-*: *fang, newfangled, peace, pact, palisade, travel, peel, pole, pagan, peasant, paisano, propagate, pectin, compact, impinge, pace, pageant.*

Or *gere-*: *crack, grackle, pedigree, cranberry,* and *geranium.*

I don't know. I love them all.

(AHD has another appendix dealing with Proto-Semitic roots, from which Hebrew, Arabic, Aramaic, and other languages have sprung, and which have had an influence on English through those languages.)

See **Hittite**; **Pokorny**; *vulva*; *blend*.

➤ *pip*

Put two *p*'s around a short *i* and you get a handy little item whose applications range in and out, up and down:

A *pip* is one of the dots on dice and dominoes; also a short, high-pitched radio signal; also a blip on a radar screen.

A *pip*, short for *pippin*, is a seed, as of an orange or an apple, and it's also something admirably realized: a pip of a girl.

The pip is a slang term for a vague draggy ailment that people come down with, and a proper term for a specific disease of birds.

The verb *to pip* is to break through a shell—a chick hatching—and also to peep, like a chick that's hatched. See *double entendre*.

➤ *piss*

Robert Hendrickson calls this "a fine old echoic word, echoing the sound of a bladder being voided," which "derives from the Latin *pissiare*, 'to piss,' just as does the Italian *pisciare* and the French *pisser*. 'Urinate' derives from the Latin *urinare*, which is what the cultured Romans called the same thing that the common man called *pissiare*." I'm reading this and thinking, Yes! As so often, the vernacular . . .

And then it occurs to me that a bladder being voided doesn't make a sound like *piss*, unless it's onto a hot rock—anymore than *tinkle* does (at my house, when I was a child, we tinkled), unless onto a tiny bell. Still, Hendrickson is right: *piss*, unlike the abstract *urinate*, does somehow evoke pissing. You could say the same thing about *spurt*, *squirt*, and *trickle*.

How does this evoking work? Take another hydraulic word, which OAD calls "*probably* imitative": *gush*. Hard *g* way back in the **glottis**, *uh* surging forward from there, *sh* releasing the breath outward. *Piss* is less obvious, but it starts with pursed lips—holding something in—and then *ih*, which is similar to but appropriately narrower than the *uh* in *gush*, and finally *sss*,

which is less sploshy than *sh* but also a release. In both words, airflow imitates waterflow. A *spurt* is quick and comes to a stop; *squirt*, too, but that
kw sound constricts it more. A *trickle* is tight and extended; see *-le*.

➤ *pixelated/pixilated*

No etymological connection, but if you're pixilated (tipsy, or mentally
influenced by pixie dust), things may get fuzzy, ill-focused, in something
like the way a digital image is blurred when its resolution is off to the
point that you see a pattern of pixels instead of what the pixels are supposed to seamlessly represent. Pixelation may be used on purpose to
muddle naughty bits of the body so as to render something on video fit for
viewing by easily offended families (the Public Broadcasting System **now**
requires that the lips of someone cursing be pixelated so that they can't be
read). For *pixilated*, see *Mr. Deeds Goes to Town*.

➤ *pizzazz*

OAD: "Said to have been invented by Diana Vreeland . . . in the 1930s."
How'd you like that on your résumé? Oh, I suppose Diana Vreeland never
needed a résumé. But let's say she did—and let's say, further, that she's
the heroine of a big Broadway musical, and we're cutting to the midst of
the showstopper right now:

> I'm the girl who invented pizzazz.
> Lexicographers agree
> 'Twas me who put the *p*—
> Not to mention, if you please
> The one who put the *z*'s—
> In pizzazz.

> For in the womb, *peut-être*,
> At least **avant la lettre**,
> I possessed enough pizzazz to burn.
> Who better, then, I ask you, to discern
> Who . . .

Else . . .
Has . . .
Pizzazz?

➤ *planet, the*

Nobody says "the biggest nincompoop in the world" anymore, or even
". . . on earth." It's always "on the planet." As if there were only one—so
this is more parochial than "on earth." But maybe it's ecological. E. B.
White:

> Before you can be an internationalist you have first to be a naturalist
> and feel the ground under you making a whole circle. It is easier for a
> man to be loyal to his club than to his planet; the by-laws are shorter,
> and he is personally acquainted with the other members. A club,
> moreover, or a nation . . . offers the right to be exclusive . . . The
> planet holds out no such inducement. The planet is everybody's. All
> it offers is the grass, the sky, the water, and the ineluctable dream of
> peace and fruition.

➤ Pokorny, Julius

When it comes to **PIE**, he wrote the book: *Indogermanisches Etymologisches
Wörterbuch*, published in 1959. He was born in Prague (about the same time
as Kafka), studied in Vienna, learned Irish in County Mayo. He was a professor of Celtic philology in Berlin, a practicing Catholic, and both a German and an Irish nationalist until 1935, when the Nazis found out that all
four of his grandparents were Jewish. He managed to get out of Germany, to
Switzerland, in 1943 because the Irish issued him a visa. Went on to teach
Celtic in Zurich, Berne, and Munich. He's mentioned in poetry by Flann
O'Brien and in *Ulysses* by James Joyce. A latitudinously European person,
then, and one disowned evilly by Germany: So why did he call Indo-
European roots Indo-Germanic? Does German nationalism go that deep?

Germany is of course *Deutschland*'s name in English—from the Latin
Germania, which *may*, or may not, come from the Celtic (aha) for "neigh-

boring people," which comes from words related to the Old Irish *gair*, neighbor, and *maon*, people.

The word *germane* would seem to be germane here somehow, but . . .

➤ *polyurethane foam*

Why do I derive so much pleasure from saying, to myself or out loud, "polyurethane foam"? No one seems to get anything out of hearing me say it. From my perspective, feeling it running around in my mind's ear and mouth is like watching otters play in the water.

I don't think it has anything to do with the nagging question of whether the substance in question, based on the *poly* and *ure* parts of its name, is made out of many kinds of pee, but I can't rule that out as a subconscious factor. Unquestionably, it has to do with how many different **vowel** sounds are involved, the fluidity of the sort of off-anapestic meter (so unlike that of, say, "in the sweet by and by"), and the conjunction of that *y* pronounced like a long *e* and that *ur* like *yoor*. It's *just* so *sayable*.

> I built my home
> Of polyurethane foam.

➤ *ponder*

"Edna Earle could sit and ponder all day on how the little tail of the 'C' got through the 'L' in a Coca-Cola sign." —Eudora Welty, "The Wide Net."

➤ *porcelain*

What conceivable pig-in-a-china-shop connection can this word have to *pork*? Well, the shiny finish of porcelain is like that of a cowrie shell. And the French for cowrie shell is *porcelaine*, from the Old Italian *porcellana*, of a young sow. At this point, dictionaries scatter. AHD cites "the shell's resemblance to a pig's back." RHU says the shell was apparently "likened to the vulva of a sow." OAD stays away from sow anatomy altogether. Chambers says, "The curved shape of the cowrie shell was thought to be suggestive of the curve in a pig's back," and then there's "the added similarity of color between the two." I take *the two* there to mean the shell and a pig's back. As opposed to porcelain and a pig's back. WIII's entry seems to suggest (I hate to say this, but I swear I think it's inadvertent) that *porcus* in Latin meant either "pig" or "vulva."

I should never have gone into this. Actually I thought I might be reaching out to a segment of the audience that I don't usually feel I'm connecting with, the segment that cares about porcelain. And here we are—

Oh, what the heck. How do you feel about the word **vulva**? It's a mite heavy-sounding, not a name you'd give to your little lapdog, your bichon frise, but it does have an agreeably enfolding quality for a cold winter's night. It's from the same root, *wel-²*, as a number of words involving turning, rolling, enclosing: *waltz, whelk, walk* (that's interesting—from the Old English *wealcan*, to roll, must have been a sailor involved), *valley* (sure), *helix* (there's half of your DNA for you), *willow* because of the flexibility of willow twigs, and, well, *wallow*.

Cowrie has no connection, you'll be relieved to learn, to any aspect of a cow.

➤ portmanteau word

Portmanteau (from the French for, literally, "carries the cloak") is a British term for a suitcase that opens out into two halves. Portmanteau words are inspired combinations such as *guestimate* from *guess* and *estimate* and, less obviously, *chortle* from *chuckle* and *snort*. I thought I might have made up *mizzle*, coarser than mist, finer than drizzle, until I found it in dictionaries.

My mother used a vivid one: *squirmle*, combination of *squirm* and *wiggle*, I assume. She would say to a small child she was trying to wash the ears of, "Don't squirmle so much."

Is *fribble*, as in "fribble away an opportunity," a portmanteau of *frivol* and *dribble*?

Might there be, for the page only, the word *flurt*, blend of *flirt* and *blurt* (or even *hurt*), to flirt heavy-handedly? If so, I want nothing to do with it. From my deep past I can recall—can't help recalling though I would profoundly **rather** not—three literally heavy-handed flirts, that is to say I reached out and my hand landed, somehow, heavily—not I hasten to say as a blow, but as lurching contact, like connecting with a tennis ball wrong, only it was a woman not a ball. A woman who didn't want to be connected with by me. Oooooh, that felt bad.

And should have been avoided. In the words of Kinky Friedman, "Never try to climb a fence leaning toward you or kiss a woman leaning away from you."

➤ possessives

It seems to me simple to decide whether to add *'s* to a word ending in *s*: Do you pronounce the *'s*? In *Charles's*, you do. In *Hank and Audrey Williams'* house, you **probably** don't. *For righteousness' sake*, you don't.

➤ *possum*

Latin for "I can," American for "opossum." Basil Clark, who used to hold possum shows and sell "Eat More Possum" bumper stickers in Clanton, Alabama, would say, "The *o* in *opossum* is silent, like the *p* in swimming." That is an **unscribable** joke.

➤ *potable*

There is no reason to pronounce this as if it were spelled *pottable*. Yet many people do just that.

➤ *preposterous*

From the Latin for, roughly, "foreafterward." *Pre-* means "before" and *-posterous*, "after," so the elements would seem to be in order; but absurdity lurks, somehow. Think in terms of a junk-mail announcement that you have been "pre-selected" for a new credit card, which means that if you apply for it, you may, or may not, be selected to get it.

➤ *probably*

A less weaselly word than **perhaps**. Lurking in its roots is the sense of "(conceivably) provable." Whereas *perhaps* at its roots is "by chance." (The Greek *hapax* means "once.") You might even say that *probably* is a sign of scrupulousness. But sometimes it's a **bit much**, as when AHD says *roughy*, meaning "a small fish . . . with rough scales," comes "probably from *rough*."

Probably is a big leap for political pundits, who would basically like to say, "The apocalypse [or whatever] probably won't happen, but if it does, I won't be surprised." How's this for hedged probabilism, from George Will: "At the moment, however, it remains possible, perhaps even probable, that . . ."

See **scientese**; *arbitrary*.

➤ *problem*

From the Greek *proballein*, to throw before, *ballein* meaning "to throw." Surely related to *ballizein*, to dance, whence cometh *baller*, French for the same, and *ballet*, and *ball* as in a dress-up dancing party. I'd like to start pulling a lot of things together by saying that *ballein* is also behind *ball* meaning a throwable sphere, but that, according to AHD, is from the unrelated **PIE** root *bhel-*^{2}, which has yielded many words "referring to various round objects and to the notion of tumescent masculinity," such as *boulder*, *phallus*, *balloon*, *bowl*, *bull*, *ballot*, and *fool*. Perhaps we should leave *it* at that.

➤ *prolific*

Mandy Patinkin, playing some kind of sleuth on TV: "We are pursuing the most prolific serial killer in history." No. You've got to have more respect for words than that. *Prolific* means giving lots of life, producing lots of creations. Not making lots of corpses.

➤ prose rhythm

You never know where you're going to find a fresh sense of it. Back in the early seventies this sentence jumped out at me from the Frankly Frances column in the *People's Press* of Yazoo City, Mississippi:

> I feel Charlotte Pinson is being selfish in not hanging her recently framed examples of her mother Hazel Gholson's superlative crewel work embroidery, for a short time at the club.

It keeps on rising, gathering or at least sustaining momentum, for so *long*, and yet in such a ladylike way, and then, with no haste, hitch, or waste motion, it smoothes its skirt behind and sits down.

Now here is a bit of Max Beerbohm on the speaking voice of Swinburne (see **ideal reader**) from his essay about visiting Swinburne at "No. 2, The Pines":

> The frail, sweet voice rose and fell, lingered, quickened, in all manner
> of trills and roulades . . . The whole manner and method had certainly
> a strong element of oddness; but no one capable of condemning as
> unmanly the song of a lark would have called it affected.

No one ever thought of Beerbohm as athletic, but the way that last clause bends in on itself and then springs free may remind you of the great Earl "The Pearl" Monroe gathering himself on the way to the basket and then inimitably elevating. See *laugh*; *rhythm*.

➤ *prothonotary*

The prothonotary warbler (so named *probably* because its bright plumage suggested that of—I mean, the robes of—certain ecclesiastic functionaries) figured prominently in the testimony of Whittaker Chambers against Alger Hiss, *of course*, but a prothonotary is also the chief clerk in certain civil courts of law.

Thereby hangs a tale, famous in Pittsburgh but not widely known elsewhere, and even in Pittsburgh I have never seen it printed except in slightly but crucially bowdlerized form. Here it is as I heard it in 1973 from an authoritative source:

In Allegheny County (whose heart is Pittsburgh) in the late forties, the prothonotary of the civil division of the court of common pleas was a man named Davey Roberts. He weighed some three hundred pounds, he never got past grade school, he once disparaged an opponent as "high-kalutin'," and in some respects he exercised considerable political clout. His duties were limited (indeed I believe his office and three others have since been merged under one person), so he had plenty of time to be officious about them. And he was.

Word came that President Harry Truman was coming to Pittsburgh. As prothonotary, Roberts claimed the prerogative of welcoming the president to town.

For weeks Roberts began every conversation with, "As you know, I'll be the one greeting the president." He prepared and rehearsed exhaustively, going over and over the slightest details to make sure every point of protocol was covered and no flourish of ceremony would be spared.

The day came. Roberts was at the airport hours ahead of time, fussing around and telling people what to do. The president's plane was late. An imposing assemblage of politicos waited on the tarmac, Roberts at the fore. When the mayor said he had to pee, Roberts adjured him to remember the occasion, and the mayor stayed in place.

At last, the plane appeared in the sky. One of the dignitaries waved. Roberts told him to cut it out, it wasn't proper. The plane landed. Secret Service men emerged, looked around, nodded as if to say everything was in order. Roberts nodded back, as if to say, "You bet it is."

President Truman, himself, emerged. The finest marching band in Pittsburgh struck up "Hail to the Chief." The president approached. Roberts stepped forward, shook the president's hand, and said, "Welcome to Pittsburgh, Mr. President. I am David B. Roberts. The prothonotary."

"What the fuck's a prothonotary?" said the president.

➤ *ptarmigan*

The English language is strange enough without scribes making it stranger, which is what happened in the case of this word. The Scots Gaelic *tarmachan* looked, to scholars with some Greek, as though it could use a silent *p* (see **surds**) at the beginning of it. These scholars were guilty of what the first edition of the AHD judgmentally (which I love) calls "pseudo-learned association." They fancied a connection with the Greek word for "wing": *pteron*. That *pt* is okay when buried in *helicopter* or leading off a beast as exotic as the *pterodactyl*, but a ptarmigan is just a kind of *grouse* (origin unknown) with feathered feet. It lives in cold climes and mostly shuffles or flutters around. It isn't putting on neoclassical airs.

Ptomaine, the poisoning, is from the Greek for "fallen body, corpse." The downside of wings. And by the way, the Greek for "down," "soft feathers," or "plume" is *ptilom*. In the abstract, okay, the wing association (*feather* and *petal* and by the way *pen* come from the same **PIE** root); but where's the softness there? Maybe if you get a soft feather in your mouth, you go *pt*—but no: you go *tp*.

The *p* in *pneumonia* does seem to work. AHD says its root, *pneu-*, to breathe, is imitative. In pronouncing *pn* words, argues W. B. Stanford in *The Sound of Greek*, "the nostrils are moved as in the process of smelling."

In linguistics, *breath* means (AHD) "exhalation of air without vibration of the vocal cords, as in the articulation of *p*." So. Why silence that Greek *p*-before-a-consonant? It works in *prompt* (see **adverb**) and *ptui* (see **saliva**). Maybe the Greeks pronounced *pneuma* (breath, also "soul or vital spirit") as *puh*neuma, anyway p'neuma. If that is the case, we should pronounce *pneumonia* that way. What's the use of a silent, unpopped, *p*?

And come to think of it, *puh*terodactyl might get that flying reptile aloft.

➤ *pun*

The lowest form of wit, it used to be said, but that was before Ann Coulter. A great punster was the late singer-songwriter Roger Miller, who came up with the term *shellout falter* for what so many people do, around the restaurant table, when it's time to put in money for the check.

The origin of the word *pun* is unknown, but **perhaps**, acccording to the *Oxford Dictionary of Word History*, "an abbreviation of the obsolete *pundigrion*, as a fanciful alteration of *punctilio* 'petty point' (from Italian *puntiglio* 'little point')." An unnecessary synonym, from, yes, the Greek, is *paronomasia*.

> *Chico*: What is it has a trunk, no key, weighs two thousand pounds, and lives in the circus?
>
> *Prosecutor*: That's irrelevant.
>
> *Chico*: Hey, that's the answer!
>
> *Judge*: That sort of testimony we can eliminate.
>
> *Chico*: Atsa fine, I'll take some.
>
> *Judge*: You'll take *what*?
>
> *Chico*: Eliminate. A nice cool glass eliminate.

➤ punctuation

Here is something that popped into my head: The point of punctuation **rhythm** timing clarity.

How might we punctuate that? "The point of punctuation is rhythm and timing: clarity." "The point of punctuation is rhythm, timing, clarity." "The point of punctuation is rhythm, timing—clarity." "The point of punctuation is the clarity and memorability derived from rhythm and timing."

One thing to consider is the pun or semipun in "point." A multipun, since *punct* means "point."

Punctuation comes from the Latin *punctum*, point, from *pungere*, to prick, hence *puncture*.

Punctuation makes writing more pointed, and more punctual, in the sense of apt timing.

Once I tried to work up a noirish novel with a bad guy who, for emphasis, would enunciate his punctuation: "You may not wish to accompany me, semicolon. You nonetheless must, period." Never got very far with it, but here's some punctuational verse:

> In the Senate, an ill-tempered solon
> Expostulated (:)
> *"My distinguished colleague's momma—"*
> After a while (,)
> He awoke, with injuries myriad.
> You just don't go there (.)

"One man can't punctuate another man's manuscript any more than one person can make the gestures of another person's speech" —Mark Twain.

q · Q · q

This is the only letter (except for *J* in script) whose capital has a bit that breaks the base line. **Geoffroy Tory**'s personificational explanation: "*Q* extends below the line because he does not allow himself to be written in a complete word without his trusty comrade and brother *V* [Latin form of *U*], and to show that he wishes always to have him by his side, he embraces him with his tail from below."

Ben Jonson, on the other hand, perceived *q* to be female. He pointed out with some asperity that Anglo-Saxons used *k* instead of *q*: they "knew not this halting *Q* with her waiting-woman *U* after her."

To me, capital *Q* is an upside-down apple, but much depends on typeface. In a font called *Apple Chancery*, it looks more like a cherry, or a simplistic cat whose head hasn't been drawn yet: Q.

In **Braggadocio**, it looks like a *South Park* character: Q.

In Goudy Old Style, it's . . . I don't know, looks like it's got a high heel on: Q.

In **American Typewriter**, its tail is piggy-curly: Q.

In DESDEMONA, its tail is almost internalized: Q.

In Onyx, it's a chili pepper: Q.

A character in fiction whose name starts with *Q* tends to be strikingly peculiar—queer, in the old sense—on the surface but to have, deep down, a redeeming quality. Queequeg, Quasimodo, and Quixote, *of course*, are good guys at heart and even in effect, but there's also something appealing (down too deep to register in a Q rating) about Captain Queeg in *The Caine Mutiny*, Quint in *Jaws*, ghostly Peter Quint in *The Turn of the Screw*, the excitable but slow-witted Mistress Quickly in Shakespeare's Henry plays, the Questing Beast (which makes in its belly a noise like thirty pairs of hounds) in *Le Morte d'Arthur*, and Faulkner's Quentin Compson, who has incestuous longings for his sister and even tells his father that he has acted on them and therefore may have sired his own niece, also named Quentin—but he was probably lying to his father, trying to shift the blame away from the sister (he drowns himself eventually). Even the shady Quilty did free Lolita from the horrible Humbert. In an appearance-versus reality class by himself is Quetzalcoatl, the plumed serpent ruler-god of the Aztecs, who introduced maize to his people and encouraged the arts, and didn't realize how awful he looked till someone held a mirror up to him, and he burst into holy flame and his heart became the planet Venus and the ashes of the rest of him were birds.

In history, many Q's have been questionable, at best: Vidkun Quisling, who became a synonym for traitor by ruling Norway as a Nazi puppet; William Quantrill, the larcenous and murderous guerrilla leader during the Civil War; the eighth Marquess of Queensberry, who warrants an entry of his own. And Sayyid Qtub (pronounced *Sye*-yid *Kuh*-tahb), the philo-sophical father of al-Qaeda. Qtub was radicalized by his exposure to, of all things, a church dance in Greeley, Colorado: "Every young man took the hand of a young woman. And these were the young men and women who had just been singing the hymns! Red and blue lights, with only a few white lamps, illuminated the dance floor. The room became a confusion of feet and legs: arms twisted around hips; lips met lips; chests pressed together." He didn't hate just America; he hated puberty.

On the other hand, I give you the fair-minded American patriot Josiah Quincy of Boston. In the 1760s he boldly opposed the British occupation, but when a mob of Bostonians tormented British troops into shooting some of them—the Boston Massacre, it was called—and the troops were charged with murder, he and John Adams defended the redcoats and saved their lives. Remember when American leaders did things like that? The country wasn't just threatened by jackleg terrorists, it was *occupied* by an army, and yet people like Quincy and Adams felt strong enough to fo-cus on due process—to resist the occupation but still identify with the oc-cupiers as people. Those were the days.

Let's give *q* credit. In WIII, the words that start with *s* take up 329 and a half pages, *q*-words only twelve. Any letter that manages, within so little space, to range from *quiet* to *quarrelsome*, *quotidian* to *quixotic*, *quasi* to *quintessence*, *quest* to *quit*, *quark* to *quasar*, *quill* to *QWERTY*, is okay in my book. And say you've been arrested for spreading gloom about the government. Would you want your lawyer to write on your behalf, in his or her briefs, things like "Kwoting Thomas Jefferson on this kwestion, the U.S. Court of Appeals held . . ."? No. Not after all these years with *q*.

The word *queue* is another matter. We Anglophones have preserved, from the Latin *qu*, the sound of *kw*. So when I see *queue*, I have to bite my tongue not to say something like kwuh-ew.

To be fair, I suppose English already had a *cue*, and a *coo*, and an old man from Kew who found a mouse in his stew. Said the waiter, "Don't shout and wave it about, or the rest will be wanting one too."

Still.

Before *queue* meant a line of Brits, you know, it meant a pigtail, from the Old French *cue*, tail. Hence *curlicue*, which brings us full circle.

➤ *qualm*

Here's a word, like **terrific**, from which much of the force has been leached, by usage influenced by sound. According to Chambers, *qualm* comes from the Old High German for "death and destruction," then the Middle English for "pestilence, plague." It has come to mean no more than a sudden uneasiness, perhaps a bit of nausea, or just, by extension into the abstract, a misgiving. That's what it sounds like it ought to mean. Similar-sounding words have had closely related meanings. OED defines the verb *to walm* as "to swell, bubble, as in boiling," and *walming* as a "turning (of the stomach), nausea." According to Jesse Sheidlower, "a specific application" of the obsolete noun *walm* "is 'one individual motion of boiling water.'" When I see the first sign of boiling-water turbulence, *walm*, or *qualm*, seems about right. It might be the water going, "Uh-oh, this is trouble."

See **seethe**.

➤ Queensberry, the eighth or ninth Marquess or Marquis of

In American reference books (AHD, WIII, and RHU, for instance), this man, whose name was John Sholto Douglas, is identified as a marquis. In OAD, *The Oxford Companion to English Literature*, and the *Oxford Dictionary of Phrase and Fable*, he is a marquess. OAD draws this distinction between the titles: a marquess ranks "above an earl and below a duke"; a marquis ranks "above a count and below a duke." So which is higher, an earl or a count? Oh, I guess the British don't have counts. Do we care?

I'll bet I know where you think I'm going with this: "Put up your dukes." No. It is true that one of the two reasons this marquess is remembered to this day is that, in 1865, he and a boxer named Chambers drew up rules that still apply to the sport of boxing. These are still referred to as the Marquess (or, in the U.S., Marquis) of Queensberry Rules. In marriage, or dogfights, or investment banking, you will frequently hear, there are no Marquess (Marquis) of Queensberry Rules.

Many reference books will tell you that the rules banned gouging and hitting below the belt. Not true. Those things were already prohibited under the London Prize Ring Rules of 1838. The Queensberry Rules outlawed "wrestling and hugging" and "shoes or boots with springs." They also established a ten-second knockout count and a three-minute round, and required boxers to wear padded gloves. (Gloves actually made boxing more damaging to the brain, because a padded puncher can swing harder and connect to the head more solidly without breaking his or her knuckles, but that consequence was presumably unintended.)

Be all that as it may, *dukes* as a synonym for fists has nothing to do with the possible aspirations of a marquess. It's Cockney slang: *Duke of Yorks* rhymes with *forks* (fingers).

The second thing for which this M of Q is remembered is what I would draw your primary attention to. He set in motion the downfall of Oscar Wilde. The M's son, Alfred "Bosie" Douglas, got up to some hanky-panky. (See **hocus-pocus**.) There was talk, which infuriated the M. He left a card at Wilde's hotel that was addressed, in plain view, to "Oscar Wilde, posing as a Somdomite." Or maybe just "posing Somdomite"—the M's handwriting was hard to read. But the *Somdomite* is clear enough.

Why would a nobleman take such an ignoble shot? If a legislator of boxing is going to insult another man, you'd think he would do it to his face, or at least spell it right. One consideration may have been that Wilde was not only witty but large. The M had previously barged into Wilde's apartment, with a bodyguard, and Wilde had run them off. What if the M had tried to thrash Wilde, and Wilde had not only come up with an epigram, on the spot, that established the M as, between the two of them, the distinctly more vulgar, but also had knocked the M down? Never mind how that would have reflected on his lineage. Think of the embarrassment to boxing.

Speaking of lineage, the M of Q in question is usually called the eighth, but sometimes the ninth. The question being, whether to count as the third marquess a James Douglas who was violently insane from early childhood. After many years locked up in an institution, he escaped, killed a kitchen servant, roasted him on a spit, and was eating him when recaptured.

That was bound to make future M's of Q touchy. People must have been forever saying, "Eighth, are you? I heard ninth. Something about—oh, sorry. But tell me: a marqu*ess*? Thought that would be a marquis's lady fair." And when the M would explain that he was something that ranked above an earl: "How about an earless?" And here's something I would have wanted to ask the M, were it not for my natural democratic manners: "What exactly is a queensberry?"

As counterproductive as the M's note-leaving was, in establishing him in history as a poofter's dad, Wilde's reaction was even more so. He sued the M for libel, and lost, and testimony in the case eventually put the theretofore nonchalant Oscar in prison at hard labor. Well, here is one of his remarks in *Bartlett's Quotations*: "A poet can survive anything but a misprint." Maybe he kept grumbling to himself, "Somdomite? *Som*domite? From a mar-*quess*? Of Queens*berry*?" until at last he struck back.

The word *berry*, by the way, shares a root with *beacon*, *banner*, *fantasy*, and *epiphany*. And *pugilism* shares one with *pointillism* and **punctuation**.

➤ *quick*

"Be quick," the great UCLA basketball coach John Wooden told his players, "but never hurry." Writing, however reflective or cumulative, needs to be quick, so it's readable at first glance and also worth lingering over. Making it so is tedious, but that's a *writer's* **problem** (as they say in moviemaking when they need something **preposterous** worked into the script). We keyboard our fingertips to the bone, or at least to the point of calluses, from doggedly cutting toward what's meaty and sensitive: the quick. From the Old English *cwicu*, alive.

➤ *quirky*

The origin of this synonym for *idiosyncratic* is unknown. But I'm going to speculate that *quirk* is the union of *quick* and something more pejorative, perhaps *jerk*. OED says the original sense of *quirk* was **probably** "a sudden twist, turn or curve," as in Ben Jonson's "young Frenchman . . . that . . . knew every quirk within lust's labyrinth."

Lust aside, I find that the closer attention I pay to something, the more quirks it reveals. Writing may be called quirky when its humble intention is to pull an honest focus. When its arch/cuddly intention is to be quirky, on the other hand: feh.

➤ *quite*

It strikes me as sloppy that this is sometimes used to mean "completely" or "exactly," as in "Are you quite finished?" or "That's not quite accurate," and other times to mean "rather" or "more or less," as in "Our visit was quite pleasant." My strict policy is to use *quite* in the absolute rather than the relative sense, so that "Quite so" is not noncommittal. Can't we reach, however gradually, a consensus that *quite* is the opposite of *not quite*?

Quite shares a root with *quiet*, *quit*, and *quietus*, all of which suggest settlement or finality. The crisp sound of the word suggests a cutoff, unlike the mumbly *somewhat*.

See *rather*.

r · **R** · r

Is there something about *r*? I think there is, but then I would, my name starts with one. I can't say what that something is.

There's the *R* rating, which indicates a movie that is worth a teenager's time trying to sneak into.

There are the three R's, ***of course***. And the *er*, *ar*, *or* sounds in *are*, *earth*, *earnest*, *origin*, *hormone*, *urge*, *urtext*, and "murder your **darlings**."

There's dog-growl: *rrrrrr*; and pirates' favorite letter: *arrrrr*. And *roar*, which I heard the poet David Wagoner describe as "obviously a word from before language."

There is the old signage joke (which is **unscribable**, I see **now** that I am writing it down):

"'RAILROAD CROSSING, LOOK OUT FOR CARS'—can you spell that without any *R*'s?"

"Gee, no, I don't see how such a thing would be humanly possible."

"Easy. T-H-A-T."

And in related news:

In July 2006, a total of 103 plastic *R*'s disappeared from the signs of business establishments in Greencastle, Indiana. Then a surveillance camera outside the local police station caught a woman leaving a shoebox on the station's doorstep. The box was found to contain the missing *R*'s.

The woman turned out to be the mother of a teenager who, with his girl-friend, had driven around swiping *R*'s from the signs of some two dozen gas stations, doctors' offices, repair shops, and restaurants. The girl-friend, according to the Associated Press, "collects letters and nicknacks."

"It started out as a couple of *R*'s for her collection," said Police Chief Tom Sutherland, "and before it was said and done, they were stealing *R*'s all over town."

The teens "are going to have to do some community-work service and do some apologizing to some of the people they took the *R*'s from," said the county prosecutor.

R is used by a lazy person, or one who is extremely pressed for time (in either case, *let's hope*, a teenager), for the word *are* in *e-mail* and text messaging.

Socrates, in the *Cratylos* of Plato, says that *rho* (a rolled *r* sound) expresses motion because of the tongue's vibration. (Think boys making noises for their cars.)

> *rather*

May be used to express a preference: "I'd rather be turned on a spit, myself, than eat the flesh of a fellow human being so overdone."

But also to express either vagueness or exactitude.

On the one hand, to fuzzify adjectives or adverbs that if genuinely intended might be a *bit much*. "It's rather stupendous, this . . . rat terrier of yours, isn't it?"

On the other hand, to mean "more precisely." "This so-called enchilada is all I need to know about New England, or rather northwestern Connecticut."

Because we can readily gather which of these senses is attached to a given *rather*, we are not faced here with anything like the regrettable ambiguity of *quite*, which someone should do something about. But it's interesting to speculate, just for the *sheer* giddy hell of it, how *rather* got so various.

Undoubtedly, preference-expression came first, because *rather*'s ancestor is the Old English *hrathor*, meaning "sooner" or "more quickly." "I'd sooner be turned on a spit . . ." and so on.

I'd say the next meaning to develop was the "more precisely." More quickly. Not as in closer to hand or easier to get ahold of, because a language in its early formative stages is no casual matter; but rather more quickly as in closer to the mark, closer to the actual life and nature of the thing.

And then sophistication, adulteration, set in. Use of a word to mean its opposite. All rather *marvelous*, I'm sure.

➤ read, how to

I heard Quincy Jones being interviewed on NPR. He had a new recording
out, a departure from his recent work. The interviewer, *rather* tensely:
"What would you tell people to listen for in this music?"

Jones: "Don't listen *for* anything. Listen *to* it."

➤ reader, underzealous

Here's a website that came up when I was Googling something: *The 1024*,
"a U.C. and Cal State University targeted publication" published by Pinet
Multimedia Group, devoted to "Fashion, Life, Art and Sexxes" (the last *s*
is backward). A policy statement: "The 1024 is not intended for the
overzealous, intelligent readers."

➤ readers, fashioned out of suet and squash

From *Cram Me with Eels*, a collection of humor by the **uneven** but frequently sublime Beachcomber (J. B. Morton):

> *PRODNOSE*: Why do you often give a paragraph an utterly
> meaningless headline?

> *MYSELF*: To excite interest. Most people who read "Clergyman's
> Niece Bites Dog" or "Duke Hidden in Chimney" will read on avidly.

> *PRODNOSE*: You must have a pretty low opinion of your readers.

> *MYSELF*: Who has a better right to such an opinion?

➤ reading one's own stuff

Frequently disagreeble, at least until the stuff in question has cooled off
for at least a full calendar month. Before that, one peers at it out of the
corner of one's eye. One suspects—let's call one Pat.

Pat suspects . . . and it's *true*! This stuff is *beneath contempt*. Pat flings it
against the wall (unless it is on a costly laptop) and stomps on it (once it
reaches the floor), again and again and again.

Then Pat regains a semblance of composure. Grits teeth. Reads . . .

And reading, Pat recalls how good it seemed until it began to congeal into literal words, and what a nightmare of intricate fiddling went into it thereafter, and yet—it must be fiddled with further.

And if by chance it is sweet? Whom can Pat in all modesty—in *any* modesty—share that with? As someone says in *Romeo and Juliet*, "'Tis an ill cook that cannot lick his own fingers." But to urge someone else to lick them—no, not even the **ideal reader**. For you see, it's not about the fingers, it's about the stew.

I am making too much of this.

See **Flaubert; clarity;** *he/she/his/her*.

➤ *really*

In conversation I really overuse this word. I'm trying really hard to stop. I shouldn't use it at all in writing, really. The word comes from *res*, Latin for "thing." Let the thing speak for itself.

➤ Realtor

Real-tur. Not Ree-luh-tur. Pronouncing it the latter way is like singing off-key on purpose.

➤ *recursion*

In computer programming, this means, to quote the to-me-incomprehensible Merriam-Webster's Online definition, a "technique involving the use of a procedure, subroutine, function, or algorithm that calls itself one or more times until a specified condition is met at which time the rest of each repetition is processed from the last one called to the first."

In linguistics, according to Noam Chomsky, *recursion* means the ability to embed phrases and clauses within sentences, ad infinitum, and it is a uniquely human faculty and the cornerstone of every language. Maybe so, I don't know. I do know it can be run into the ground:

> In *Goodbye, Little Rock and Roller*, Marshall Chapman tells us that her
> song "Betty's Bein' Bad" was inspired personally by our mutual

friend Betty Herbert (who never shot anybody so far as I know but
back in the day might well be seen as, to quote Marshall's book, "a
lady in a pink linen dress and pearls . . . standing on a table
screaming, 'Raise Hell in Dixie!' at the top of her lungs," and her
husband, Bobby, would say, in a philosophical voice, "Betty's bein'
bad") but musically by "Short'nin' Bread" ("A .45's quicker than
409 / Betty cleaned the house for the very last time").

I wrote that. It's in one of my books. I have got to stop writing like that.

➤ redundancy

My sister, Susan, is in the business of editing corporate prose into English. She was sent this:

> The specific services to be performed will vary, based on each
> individual customer's individual requirements. The service is
> therefore tailored to a Customer's specific requirements to deliver
> the particular range of services required.

She boiled it down to this:

> The scope of this service is tailored to meet the customer's particular
> requirements.

In the July 30, 2007, *Berkshire Eagle*, I am drawn to a small local news
item by the photos that go with it: two faces, bright and beautiful, strikingly similar yet different, one pensive, one sparkly. The same person
in different moods? Or do the pictures capture two different personali-
ties?

Something called the Stephen Phillips Memorial Scholarship Fund has
awarded educational grants to these young women. They are twins—
daughters of the same couple, at any rate, and in the same college class. They
both "look forward to a career with the Federal Bureau of Investigation."

Cool. You know that great movie *Out of Sight*, from the Elmore Leonard
novel, J-Lo as a U.S. marshal? I project these twins as two Feds of that cal-
iber (but Irish, by their last name). Maybe two beautiful Feds pretending
to be one.

But look at this: "Both women were two of 170 recipients who received an award this year."

Aw, man. "Both . . . were two . . . recipients . . . received"? Why did no one at the paper instinctively cringe and start slashing away at that sentence?

And trim it down to, say, "The women were among 170 recipients of an award this year." That's what I did, but then I looked at the next sentence in the story, "The Phillips Scholarship annually awards approximately 600 new and renewed grants . . . ," and I wondered: How come just 170 this year, in July? Don't know. But I can do this: go back and make it ". . . recipients of an award from the Phillips Scholarship Fund so far this year. The Fund . . ." Or, better, ". . . recipients of Phillips scholarships so far this year. The fund . . ."

I shouldn't have to do that. Somebody connected to the fund should take pains to write a nice clean news release, and somebody else should take pains to rewrite it for the paper. If it still needs tightening up, there should be a copy editor. Think of the person-hours wasted when a paper leaves all those pains up to each individual reader. No wonder newspaper circulation is in decline.

On the other hand, things are looking up for the FBI.

➤ reference

As a verb? Instead of *refer to*? "In his diatribe against imaginary cats he referenced Felix, Garfield, and the one in the hat"? You're okay with that?

Why?

Are we to inference that your use of the verb *to reference* conferences you a right to be deferenced? I beg to difference you.

➤ relationship, the, between reader and writer

Have you ever had a conversation in which the other person hears whatever you say as "fault fault fault," and therefore that other person is responding, "No it isn't, it's yours, no it isn't, it's yours"? The only way to deal with that—well, there are other, temporary but perhaps more sensible, ways, involving a lot of hugging and giving in—but one way, which I think of as the high road, is using words meticulously, but with feeling, and counting on the other person to perk up to such usage. Maybe this only works between writer and reader, if then—never between combatants or lovers. All the more reason to improve the prospects between writer and reader.

I got off into the writer-reader relationship as a child, because nobody I could talk to was as attentive to words as I was, or as scrupulous with words as the writers I responded to were. You could have recited the Declaration of Independence to my mother and her reaction would have been, "You don't love me." That level of discourse was pulling me into the trap she was caught in. I couldn't save her but she saved me, by teaching me, intimately and early, to love reading and to play close, sensuous, even obsessive attention to words. She must have realized at some level how impossible she was, and even though she was enabling me to move away, leave the church, and break her heart, she cared enough to convey the keys to my escape. Or maybe my DNA made me obsessive about words, and that made *me* impossible. Anyway, everywhere I've gone, I've written my way there. You got to go with what you got. See **arts, the**.

➤ *reservationist*

I heard a word that was new to me the other day when I called to reserve a car to take me to LaGuardia the following morning because I know from experience how few available cabs there are around 8:30 to 9:00 in the morning. I got a recording. "Please hold on," it said. "Our reservationist will be on in a moment."

And it hit me: Can this, at last, be my religion? I'm not an *indifferentist* or a *nothingarian* (see **wrought**), I'm a *reservationist*. One who refuses to believe in anything—even the reservations—without reservations. I'm not boasting. I'm not trying to proselytize. I'm not even saying I'm a good one. I'm just saying, that's what I am, **perhaps**.

➤ revision

John Berryman, *Paris Review* interview, on his meeting with Yeats:

"He said, 'I never revise now'—you know how much he revised his stuff—'but in the interests of a more passionate syntax.' Now that struck me as a very good remark. I have no idea what it meant, and still don't know, but the longer I think about it, the better I like it."

See **editing**.

➤ rhyme

Many a poet these days will call *pucker* and *pocket* a rhyme. Will in fact prefer that kind of rhyme to *skillet* and *chill it*. Me, I'm just a versifier, but *pucker* and *pocket* put me off. *Skillet* and *chill it* get me to thinking. I bring them together just because of the sound, but then it hits me that they both relate to heat:

> If you're going to tell me to "Chill," it
> Would help if you'd put down that skillet.

I grant you, I'm an old crank. That's my muse down there at the end of the bar explaining how everything went wrong after the Truman administration. (See **prothonotary**.) But to me, a rhyme like *pucker* and *pocket* is an off-rhyme, or a slant rhyme, and I don't trust it. If I'm going to traffic in semi-rhyming, I'd rather go with words that look like they almost rhyme, or ought to rhyme, but don't. *Dyslexic* rhymes, you might say. Put them side by side and watch them melt and swim:

> *miseries/miniseries*
>
> *wrapper/reappear*
>
> *baseline/Vaseline*
>
> *Iowan/loan*
>
> *topmost/compost*
>
> *veracity/intra-city*
>
> *shoulda/shoulder*
>
> *subtitles/subtleties*
>
> *pewter/twerp*

toolshed/sloshed

scaly ears/fiscal years

Oslo/also

heroes/theories

aides/ideas

warring/earring

knowledge/window ledge

mildewed/wild-eyed

jauntily/Aunt Lily

amulet/omelet

unseated/nauseated

sniper/worshiper

sing-along/signaling

elbow/wobble

wrought/*sloughed*

Whac-A-Mole/guacamole

➤ *rhythm*

"Just as we should take the trouble to preserve our historic buildings and cultural diversity, we also should take the trouble to keep the 'y' in rhythm"—Rebecca Sealfon, 1997 National Spelling Bee champ.

> Words: Rebecca gets down with 'em—
> She's the girl who keeps the *y* in rhythm.

I stand with Rebecca, on grounds of tradition. But why is that *y* there? It's a *u* or a *y* (upsilon, or ypsilon) in the Greek *rhuthmos* or *rhythmos*, meaning "measured flow," metrical movement in verse. The Romans didn't have a *u*. They used *v* for both *v* and *u*, which is why Enoch Emery in Flannery O'Connor's *Wise Blood* takes what is carved on the front of the local museum to be a sacred, unutterable word, like YHWH:

> He pointed down through the trees. "Muvseevum," he said. The
> strange word made him shiver. That was the first time he had ever
> said it aloud. A piece of gray building was showing where he
> pointed . . . It was round and soot-colored. There were columns at
> the front of it and in between each column there was an eyeless stone
> woman holding a pot in her hand. A concrete band was over the
> columns and the letters, MVSEVM, were cut into it. Enoch was afraid
> to pronounce the word again.

The Romans didn't start out with a *y* either, but found it handy when they started taking in a lot of Greek words. So in Latin: *rhythmus*, or as they would have written it, ʀʜʏᴛᴍᴠs. Now you ask me, Why not *rhythmys*, or *rhvthmvs*, for that matter, and I say to you, Maybe you had to be there.

In English, *rhythm* was originally pronounced the same way (and sometimes had the same meaning) as *rhyme*, which was originally spelled *rime*. Sometimes, as late as the eighteenth century, people spelled *rhythm* with an *i* (OED cites a medical text, in 1722: "Rithm . . . is used to express a certain number of pulses in a given time"). But the *y*, we may assume, struck literati as classy (and in English there's another *rime* of long standing, meaning white frost), so *rime* became *rhyme*.

And *rhythm* went off on its own. pronouncing its *th* and becoming that rare thing, a two-syllable word with just one vowel. (Other examples are *spasm*, from the Greek *spasmos*, and *ism*, which is from the Greek suffix *-ismos* and which I'd be willing to bet is the shortest one-vowel, two-syllable word in English.) In the mid-nineteenth century *rhythm* began to be applied in print to regular patterns of movement beyond the page and the pulse. OED cites the following: "Rhythm is the rule with Nature;—she abhors uniformity more than she does a vacuum." One thing we can say about English, it doesn't get bogged down in uniformity.

As to why the first *h*? You may almost always assume, when you see an *rh*, that the word it appears in derives from Greek. Early English spellers wanted the reader to know that they knew that. The Greek *r*-sound letter is spelled, in English, *rho*. The *h* in *rho* betokens a touch of rough breathiness, which I would say survives in English words, subliminally—as in (harrumph) *rheumy*, (ah) *rhapsody*, and (ahem) *rhetoric*. The American word *rhumba*, for the Cuban dance, is not from the Greek but from the Spanish *rumbo*. What is that *h* in there for, if not to contribute a trace element of *huh*!

An *h* before *r* is another matter. Hrothgar, the Danish king in *Beowulf*, may have been more imposing than if he'd been Rothgar, but only marginally. In Old English *ring* was *hring*, *roof* was *hrof*, and *ridge*, if you can believe it, was *hrycg*. Who needs that? No words beginning *hr* survive in modern English except for a surname here and there. In these, the *H* may suggest overinflation. I doubt that Vera Hruba Ralston would be so notorious as a bad actress without the *Hr*. True, her stardom in twenty-six movies between 1941 and 1958 was in large part responsible for bankrupting Republic Studios, whose head, forty years her elder, had left his wife and children for her. But she was not unappealing as a native girl named Kim Kim with a heavy Czech accent in *Fair Wind to Java*, and was even less awkward as a French debutante in *The Fighting Kentuckian*. The latter movie is worth checking out if only because her costars were, reluctantly, John Wayne (the studio had to grant him profit participation in his *next* film) and, unexpectedly, Oliver Hardy as sidekick. Another prominent *Hr* was Roman Hruska, a U.S. senator from Nebraska who is remembered only for one statement: when a Supreme Court nominee was criticized as mediocre, Hruska pointed out that lots of Americans are mediocre and deserve to be represented.

All that aside, what is rhythm? Check out the dictionary definitions. Touchingly earnest, every one, but I have yet to find one that sets my toe to tapping. Dame Edith Sitwell's pronouncement is at least interestingly impressionistic: "Rhythm is one of the principal translators between dream and reality. Rhythm might be described as, to the world of sound, what light is to the world of sight."

➤ rock criticism

Bo Diddley. The rest is commentary.

➤ Rogers, Will

Since I mentioned his approval of Mussolini (see **ideal reader**), it is only fair to point out that back in the thirties he pretty much summed up U.S. presidential politics then and today, in three remarks:

"I belong to no organized party. I'm a Democrat."

"The Republican motto is 'Boys, my back is turned.'"

"It does seem that our country could be run better by someone, if we could only think who."

s · S · s

S would seem to be **monkeys**' favorite letter. In 2003 researchers at Plymouth University in England gave six monkeys full access to a computer for a month, and—far from making any progress toward typing out the works of Shakespeare—the monkeys failed to produce a single word. "They pressed a lot of *S*'s," said Mike Phillips, one of the researchers.

"Five pages of text," reported the Associated Press, "primarily filled with the letter *S*. At the end, a few *A*'s, *J*'s, *L*'s and *M*'s." One is left with the impression that these other letters were statistically insignificant.

One is also left with the impression that no one cares *why* monkeys like *s* so much.

Let us consider what kind of monkey they were.

Sulawesi macaques.

Maybe the *m*'s were purely accidental; maybe the *j*'s, *a*'s, and *l*'s were not an attempt to spell *jail*. But maybe, just maybe, to a macaque who comes from—longs for—Sulawesi (an Indonesian island), *s* means something that a man named Phillips, in Plymouth, doesn't get.

"Another thing they were interested in was in defecating and urinating all over the keyboard," added Phillips. Anyone who hasn't felt like that has never tried writing anything.

➢ *saliva*

Like so many intimate things, saliva when we turn our attention to it is strange. We retch at the idea of drinking a glass of saliva, and may even have to repress a slight **qualm** to use the toothbrush of someone we have just been deeply kissing, and yet of course we are constantly swallowing saliva. The origin of the word (beyond its being the same in Latin) is, appropriately, unknown. Here is the AHD definition: "The watery mixture of secretions from the salivary and oral mucous glands that lubricates chewed food, moistens the oral walls, and contains ptyalin." Yuck, right? More than we want to know. Except . . . What in the hell is ptyalin?

It's an enzyme that helps break down starch. It comes from the Greek *ptualon*, saliva, from *ptuein*, to spit. Aha! Ptui! Now let's move on. (The Old English for "mucus," by the way, is *snofl*.)

➤ sayings from sports

"It's never over till it's over" is surely the one most quoted and most widely applied. It's attributed to Yogi Berra, but like many of his pearls, it may have been cultured. I dug deeply into this saying's provenance when I did a long, admiring story about Yogi for *Sports Illustrated*. I concluded that Yogi provided a seed by asserting, with regard to his team and the pennant race, "We're not out till we're out." The eventual adage, like many another by many a sage, was the product of gradual misquotation. Yogi did once say, of a pair of gloves, "I'm wearing these for my hands." And he may well have said, "You can't think and hit at the same time."

It is axiomatic that a ballplayer has to "have an idea" up there, or out there, which is to say he needs to be working to some extent from theory. But any athlete when red-hot is said to be "unconscious."

When David Cone was a young pitcher for the New York Mets and about to pitch an important game, a teammate was asked what the veterans were telling Cone. "There's no magical saying," the teammate said. "There's nothing we can say except he can't look at it like, 'Oh, my God, the earth will crash if I don't do it.' If he realizes the situation too much, that's not good."

Successful athletes do not realize the situation too much, nor does anyone else who would be pithy for the ages. If Descartes had realized the situation too much, he would have said, "I think, therefore I am—I think . . . I mean, assuming that I am who or what I think I am, or in other words, well, of course I realize you'd have to look a little further into the whole concepts of *I* and *think*, let alone *therefore*, and also consider how various noncerebral aspects of a person, like the feet, say, figure in, . . . which—I don't know what made me bring up *feet* particularly, but, you know . . ."

Successful athletes also realize that proverbs arise from action, not vice versa. As Reggie Jackson once put it, "When the ball is in the air and it starts hopping, all you can do is follow it with your eyes and sing along." He also said, "When you're hitting .175, whatever you say doesn't make much sense." He was hitting close to .175 at the time; there's the paradox.

Once on ESPN I heard Arnold Palmer say: "As my father said, ninety percent of this game is played above the shoulders. And the ten percent you don't use up there goes into trying to figure out how to get the rest of it up there." Palmer *looked* cogent, which is what counts on television.

Sports figures often have a loose grip on figures of speech. When Daniel M. Galbreath owned the Pittsburgh Pirates and let out that he might sell the team, he reported an overwhelming response: "Nibbles from prospective buyers have been running off the hook." Once Kareem Abdul-Jabbar's agent assured the media that any delay in contract negotiations would not be on his or his client's part: "We will not dangle our feet on this end." And when Buck Showalter was manager of the Yankees and was asked why he didn't bolster his own job security by pressing the front office to acquire better players, he said, "When you do that you become a prostitute toward covering your butt."

A sports person's way with a proverb of long standing may go so far as to threaten it with erosion. Willie McGee once said of Vince Coleman, when they were both Cardinals and Coleman had a lot to learn, "I can't lead him to water, but I can tell him where it is." The next step would be, "I can't tell him where water is, but I can tell him what it looks like." Then, "I can't tell him what water looks like, but I can tell him there is such a thing." Then, "I can't tell him there's such a thing as water, but I can say to him, 'H_2O.'"

Like everyone else, sports people are on firmer ground when they speak directly and unfiguratively from their own experience. Digger Phelps, the basketball coach, once said, "Being an undertaker's son, there are a lot of things that you learn about right and wrong."

And those sports sayings that are least disputable are those most limited to specific cases. An Oakland restaurateur once said of Al Davis, owner of the Oakland Raiders, "Al Davis is a fine guy—for Al."

➢ scientese

According to a molecular biologist I used to know, researchers have to be clever about the *n* factor: if you don't indicate in your report that an experiment has proved out a sufficient number of times, a peer reviewer may say, "I don't like the *n* on this one."

So you resort to language: "We have shown time and again" means "We have shown twice." "We have shown time after time after time" means three times.

➢ *scratch*

Here's a word with the feel of a well-designed tool, simple but with many uses, no extraneous moving parts. It can mean Satan, money, a slight wound or mark, chickenfeed, fluky (as in *scratch hit*), the starting line, zero handicap, to scribble, to delete, to withdraw a horse, to respond duly to an itch, and so on. Its derivation goes too far back to pin down (though Chambers would like to link it to the Albanian *gërrüej* and therefore to a PIE root that AHD doesn't even list). Sources agree, however, that *scratch* represents the marriage of two earlier words which—even more so than *splish* and *splash* or Click and Clack the Tappet Brothers—were meant for each other: *scratten* and *crachen*, both of them meaning "to scratch."

I was going to call this book *Writing from Scratch* (combining soupçons of cooking, pencils, itches, and maybe even demons), until I Googled those words. There is already a book out by that title, on how to do business writing. And among computer programmers, the expression has to do with code-writing. It means making everything up instead of piggy-backing on existing code.

According to Chambers, the expression *from scratch* first appeared in print in James Joyce's *Ulysses*, but that's not quite right. In *Ulysses* we read, "My client is an infant, a poor foreign immigrant who started scratch as a stowaway . . ." and "Or all start scratch then get out of step," but never "from scratch." It is in Joyce's *Finnegans Wake* that we find "We are once amore as babes awondering in a wold made fresh where with the hen in the storyboot we start from scratch." (See **double entendre**.)

In *Finnegans Wake* we are also treated to a brawl that begins, "They're all odds against him, the beasties. Scratch. Start." (A reference to "scratch" meaning the line drawn as the starting point in a race or a rough-and-tumble bout, from which derive various sporting terms such as "up to scratch.") And here we go: "He dove his head into Wat Murrey, gave Stewart Ryall a puck on the plexus, wrestled a hurry-come-union with the Gillie Beg . . ."

If anyone ever carried *English* back to scratch, it was Joyce in the 628 pages of multifariously rootsy punning that is *Finnegans Wake*. Don't ask me what it's all about, but it's rousingly **sonicky** fun to dip into: "Yawn in a semiswoon lay awailing and (hooh!) what helpings of honeyful swoothead (phew!) . . . Hwoah!" (See **wh-**.)

➤ *seethe*

From the Old English *seothan*, to boil. "Cognates outside Germanic are found in Lithuanian *siausti* to rage, and Avestan *havayeti* (he) stews," says Chambers.

The seething point in the boiling of water, to me, is just before the bubbles start to form. Listen: not *quite* audible, maybe, but if you could combine into one sound the sounds *s*, *ee*, and *the*, isn't that what just-about-to-boil water would at least subliminally sound like?

Huh? Huh? How about it?

Or should I go soak my head?

➤ *see through*

Can mean "sustain to conclusion" or "discern by the means of" or "perceive the hypocrisy of," as in "The No Illusions Blues":

Saw through my own eyes before I was four,
Six years later, sawed through my floor.

Disillusionment should be a good thing, right? Depends, I guess.

What's more expressive, "see-through bikini" or "transparent bikini"? I'd say the former. It's from Old English as opposed to Latin, it's more interactive, and *see* picks up all the little rhymes you want to draw out of the *i*'s in *bikini*.

➤ -self

From Reuters news service:

"The makers of popular computer game Tomb Raider issued a public apology on Wednesday to a French archaeologist who was miffed that a character appearing alongside cyber heroine Lara Croft seemed to resemble himself."

This, **of course**, should be "resemble him." If one doesn't resemble oneself, one must be out of sorts or in disguise.

Why is there such an aversion in the media, and even in polite conversation, to the simple objective personal pronouns *him* and *me*?

See *he/she/his/her*.

➤ self-contradictory or countereffective words

Frankly, **literally** when misused, *monosyllabic*, *diminutive*, *long*, *effortlessly* (cannot be pronounced effortlessly). *Microsoft Help*.

If you have a fascinating story to tell, you won't need to use the word *fascinating*, much less *utterly fascinating*. It is prejudicial to a story to begin it by saying, "Here's a hilarious story."

There is never (except to put them in the mouth of a character to show that he or she is gushy or cutesy) sufficient reason to use the following words in writing: *fabulous*, *fantastic*, **marvelous**, or **terrific**, unless they are meant full-force from their roots.

See **truly**.

➤ semicolon

It's what was born when a colon and a comma got together. Which you can almost see happening, physically, though *greater than* and *colon* (> and :) look more like they're meant for each other.

Many fine writers have inveighed against the semicolon. Donald Barthelme, for instance: "Let me be plain: the semicolon is ugly, ugly as a tick on a dog's belly." But then he mentions a German writer he admires who "averages eleven to a page." Here, from an essay by the poet Donald Justice, *Oblivion*, to do with an estimable but forgotten poet named Robert Boardman Vaughn, is a passage which, I submit to you, uses semicolons duly and well:

Whole poems have been lost, doubtless forever; and probably, in truth, it does not much matter. One from the Caribbean, a favorite subject of Vaughn's, was called "Pilgrim's Terrace"; the rhythms of this poem seemed a revelation to me at one time; now gone forever. Only my memory of the title remains. After this, who will ever mention it again?

➤ sentence fragment

Not necessarily an error. Best way to put something sometimes. Something worth putting. Unless something else was wrong with your sentence fragment (which, let's face it, is highly likely), you're right, your teacher shouldn't have taken off for it. *"Highly likely"*? Rudeness on my part? No. **Simply** the candor of a person whose first, second, third, fourth attempts to write anything . . .

. . . sentence, sentence fragment, clause, phrase, word, *ellipsis* . . .

. . . have something wrong with them most of the time. Usually several things.

And I am a professional wordsmith.

We (this is not **nosism**) must keep on attempting. **It** will get better. Eventually. Perhaps when you least expect it. It's like brushing your teeth: if you keep on brushing, and rinsing, and brushing, eventually the fresh taste will come. See **advice**.

➤ sentences, notable

From *The Texas Observer*, October 4, 1974 (unsigned, but **probably** by the late great Molly Ivins):

> We have a new nomination for The Greatest Single Sentence Ever Written by Robert Baskin. *The Dallas Morning News'* Senior Political Analyst got to worrying about amnesty for draft-dodgers earlier this month. So he sat down to warn us that the matter of amnesty is not as simple as our President might have us think. Baskin urges a cautious, case-by-case approach: "There can be no general, sweeping pronouncement about these miserable individuals."

➤ *sesquipedalian*

Describes a long uncommunicative word used for the sake of showing off. For instance, *pogonotomy* for shaving. Okay, *pogon* is the Greek for "beard," but *pogo* evokes a **possum** and "a toy for jumping around on" (OAD)—hence a reader would be excused for assuming that *pogonotomy* means removal of a possum or a pogo stick from the body. There is scant need for such a word.

For that reason, *sesquipedalian* itself (from the Greek for "foot and a half long") is useful. By the way, it comprises two metrical feet—a double **dactyl**.

> Jiggery-pokery,
> President Forty-three's
> Foot-in-the-mouth disease
> Limits his words.

> Anything longer than
> Monopedalian's
> Too much by half, maybe
> Even two-thirds.

➤ sexism and pronouns

Back in 1984, in a book called *What Men Don't Tell Women*, I addressed this issue as follows:

> The careful reader will note that sometimes my personal pronouns imply that every person in the world is male, and sometimes that he isn't. When I go out of my way to avoid saying something like, "The trouble with nuclear conflagration is that it will leave man with no sense of his sociometric place" (by saying, "The trouble with nuclear conflagration is that it will leave a person with no sense of his sociometric place, or hers either"), it is because I am suffering from Pronoun Guilt.

Just joshing, women! In point of fact, I acknowledge unreservedly that a statement such as "Everyone has a right to *his* opinion" is not only sexist but also absurd. Any sentence involving mixed company can be constructed so that both genders are duly acknowledged. However, I don't feel right about replacing the overinclusive male pronoun with the nonsensical genderless plural.

"Everyone please put down their pencils" suggests—no, states—that each person is holding several. "Everyone please put down their pencil" has the whole class holding one large common pencil. But things can get sillier than that. Speaking of pronouns and guilt, here's what Gary Herwitz, an accountant convicted of insider trading, told the Brooklyn federal court judge Nicholas Garaufis on June 8, 2006, according to the *New York Post*:

"No one's been harder on themselves than me."

Let's not be too hard on Herwitz. Let's give him credit for his willingness to refer to himself as, simply, *me*. In this case *I*—"than I have"—would have been preferable, if only because his choice of words could be interpreted as "No one's been harder on themselves than they have been on me." But at least he didn't say, "No one's been harder on themselves than *myself*."

What he more or least *meant*, I would say, is "No one has been harder on me than I have been on myself."

Or maybe not. After all, it's not true: he didn't go so far as to arrest himself, haul himself before a grand jury, and indict himself. Other parties did that, and in so doing they were harder on him than he was.

Maybe what he more or less meant was "No one has been harder on himself than I have been on myself."

Not true either. Other people have shot themelves for less. But let's say that was something like what he was driving at. Was he unable to say it because he didn't want to be sexist in a court of law? In that case he might have said, "No one has been harder on himself or herself than I have been on myself." But surely no one would have begrudged him "No one's been harder on himself." Strictly speaking that wouldn't have been sexist, inasmuch as it leaves open the possibility that some female people *have* been harder on themselves.

Alternatively, Herwitz may have been throwing up a glob of penitent-sounding but backhandedly boastful guff. And the nonsensical genderless plural helped him not to be clear.

The judge, according to the *Post*, "likened Herwitz's involvement in the stock scam as being 'like a Greek *tragedy*,' before giving him a slap on the wrist." He sentenced him just to probation.

See **adverbial or adjectival drift** and *he/she/his/her*.

➤ Shakespeare

Did somebody else write his stuff? Maybe in eternity there will be an experiment (see *S*; **monkeys**):

> The Earl of Oxford meets Francis Bacon
> And Christopher Marlowe. Hands are shaken.
> (Each, that is, doth shake his peers'.)
> Then in a room in a million years
> They type up something that is . . . a *bit*
> Like *Hamlet* at least. Resembles it.
> Not nearly as good. Bacon shrugs,
> Says, "Worth a try." Marlowe hugs
> An angel against the angel's wishes
> And storms out shouting and smashing dishes.
> Oxford (a.k.a. Edward de Vere,
> Aristocrat), huffs: "I say, look here,
> I never said anything about any *plays*. I wrote the *Sonnets*.
> Honest."

➤ *sheer*

Like most overused intensifiers, it's a fun word to say (see *E*), but how much more joyous than the joy of life is "the sheer joy of life" that we so often hear attributed to traditional peoples (in costume), otters, and the recently departed? See *simply*.

➤ silent letters

See *phlegm*, *wring*, and, on the other hand, *wh-*.

➤ simile

A comparative figure of speech, generally using *like* or *as*. For instance, "Sitting there all glassy-eyed, like a head with its *chicken* cut off."

Or, to quote something that Dorothy Parker tried but failed to get into *The New Yorker* back in its prudish infancy, "like shot through a goose."

This does not include unimaginative expressions like (I mean, such as), "Your simile is so, like, lame." In fact, we may lose the simile if we toss *like* around too loosely: "My love is, like, a red, red rose" is not so bad, but "She's, like, 'My ass!'" is confusing.

I would, however, be inclined to classify as similes figures of speech that involve *so . . . that*:

"Times was so hard . . ."

"How hard was they?"

". . . that even people who didn't intend to pay weren't buying." And *as*:

"Ugly as a stump full of spiders." (From Roy Wilder Jr.'s *You All Spoken Here*.)

"As strong as horse piss with the foam farted off: Like coffee so strong it'd swim a wedge p'int fo'most." (Ibid.)

According to AHD, *simile* comes from the same root (*sem-*, meaning "as one," "together with") as *similar*, *simple*, *single*, *seem*, *semblance*, *assemble*, *simultaneous*, *hyphen*, the suffix -*some*, and the prefixes *homo*- ("same") and *hetero*- ("one of two, other"). Also *Sanskrit*.

Here's another good one: "One sip of the poisoned drink and he dropped like six feet of chain."

➤ *simply*

Any statement including the word *simply* can be put more simply without it. It's a froufrou word: "Fabulous! Simply fabulous!" These statements by great writers are exceptions that prove the rule:

> We are absurdly accustomed to the miracle of a few written signs being able to contain immortal imagery, involutions of thought, new worlds with live people, speaking, weeping, laughing. We take it for granted so simply that in a sense, by the very act of brutish routine acceptance, we undo the work of ages, the history of the gradual elaboration of poetical description and construction, from the treeman to Browning, from the caveman to Keats. What if we awake one day, all of us, and find ourselves utterly unable to read? I wish you to gasp not only at what you read but at the miracle of its being readable.
>
> —Charles Kinbote, in Vladimir Nabokov's *Pale Fire*

We say that we perfect diction. We simply grow tired.

—Wallace Stevens

See *merely*.

➤ *sit, set*

Sitting on an egg breaks it. Setting on one hatches it. When the sun sets, it won't break until tomorrow.

There seem to be a lot of **egg jokes** in this book.

➤ *sizzle sozzle*

"Nothing so drastic as a trash-mover or a gully-washer, but not just mizzly either: a good long steady soaking rain, sufficient to pearten up the crops" (Roy Wilder Jr., *You All Spoken Here*).

➤ *skew*

From the Middle English *skewen*, to escape, run sideways, says AHD.

To "skew younger" is to "go in a different direction," which is another expression marketers use to tell you you're too old (or something) for the target audience. I would like to take this occasion to thank you for having been, over the years, the only audience I have had to skew to.

By the way—just curious—did you actually buy this book, new?

That's what I thought.

➤ *ski*

Seems a sticky sort of word (as in *skip, skimpy, skeptic*) for sliding down a glistening slope. English inherits this spelling from the Norwegian, in which it is pronounced shee, a schussier sound. Norwegian *sko* is our *shoe*, *skinne* our *shine*; but "she resort" or "a she holiday" wouldn't sound right. Other *sk-* words inherited from Scandinavian sources are *skid* and *sky*. *Shid* would be more evocative of no traction than *skid*, but we would not want to speak of *shyscrapers* or, say, the Chicago *shyline*.

➢ *sn -*

Starts off a lot of good **sonicky** words: *snag, snap, snatch, snide, snicker, sneer, snarl, snip, snoop, snarky, snip, snub, snooze, snuggle,* and what we might call the *snasal* family: *sniff, snort, snivel, sniffle, snuffle, snoot, snout, snot.*

➢ *Snakes on a Plane*

Months before the movie by that title appeared, the expression became an Internet *meme* abbreviated to "SoaP" and a popular expression that quickly generated, on the invaluable if sometimes only barely literate **Urbandictionary.com**, forty-seven different definitions, including "whattaya gonna do"; "describing overkill so over the top it's illogical"; "an idea so amazingly, naturally perfect that no amount of deep thought by experienced professionals can possibly improve on it"; and "a full house in poker consisting of 888AA, Eights over Aces" (because 8's look like snakes and AA stands for American Airlines). And check out this definition, with which, in April 2008, 744 people had agreed and 627 disagreed: "In a heated arguement, if one cannot sufficiently defend themself, stating 'snakes on a plane' automatically wins the arguement no matter what the circumstances."

ONE . . . DEFEND THEMSELF!?? There are snakes all over that sentence, and I'm not going to shrug and say, "Whattaya gonna do?" I'm going to point out crisply that it would not be gender-discriminatory to say, "if one cannot sufficiently defend oneself." See *he/she/his/her*; **sexism and pronouns**.

Snakes on a Plane might be a prime example of the selfish meme. Except that it tried too hard. It will never have legs like "a can of worms."

➢ *snarky*

Is easy, comedy's hard.

➢ *sneck*

Nice (in the sense of "precise") little word that sounds just right. RHU: "A small stone . . . inserted into the spaces between larger pieces of rubble in a wall." Origin uncertain. But can't you just hear a mason saying, "Hand me that little, uh . . . sneck there"?

➤ *sneeze*

In Old English it went from *fnesen* (which makes me think of *fnf*, the cartoonese noise Dagwood Bumstead would make when Blondie woke him up in the night) to *snesen*. The German is *niesen*, also good, and there are cases to be made for the Italian *starnutire* and Spanish *estornudar*. But the French *éternuer*? That's a sneeze to the French? The Danish *fniesen*, though, that's pretty good.

➤ *so-called*

Supreme Court Justice Antonin Scalia, in a dissenting opinion to the Court's ruling in *Lawrence and Garner v. Texas*, wrote that the Court "has largely signed on to the so-called homosexual agenda." This is dishonest: it suggests that homosexuals or people promoting their cause have put forth that expression, as in "so-called patriots." He might have said "what has been called the homosexual agenda," or, more precisely, "what homophobes have called the homosexual agenda," but more honest would have been an attempt to come up with a less pejorative term of his own. See *agenda*.

➤ *socket*

It's a good expressive word. So is *plug*. Connectors female and male, soundly evolved and universal, no **Bossom** element there. I wouldn't change a letter of either one.

And yet . . .

In "Socket Blues," Memphis Minnie sang:

> Well, the reason I love my baby
> And love him so,
> He carry me a socket everywhere he go.
> I need a socket, oohhh, I need a socket.
> Babe I've got to have a socket,
> If you want me to iron your clothes.

Minnie may have been harking back to earlier English, for *socket* derives from Anglo-Norman words for "spearhead" and "plowshare." Over the centuries, it has changed sex. The PIE root, according to AHD, is *su-*, which really leads us astray, having to do mostly with (that's right, *sooey*) pigs. *Sow*, but also *hog*. I can see how a plowshare is like a rooting pig. But that doesn't explain how a spearhead became a receptacle. AHD says *su-* is "**probably** a derivative of *seuə-*," to give birth—but the only word cited as a derivative of that root is *son*. Maybe, when you go way back in tradition, gender isn't as binary as traditional thinking would have it. "Sock it to me" is evenhanded enough.

Incidentally, the last words that Abraham Lincoln ever heard were "I know enough to turn you inside out, old gal—you sockdologizing old mantrap!" John Wilkes Booth timed his shot to this, the big laugh line in the play *Our American Cousin*, knowing that the burst of hilarity in Ford's Theatre would mask the report of his pistol and divert the house. Then he leapt to the stage, shouting "*Sic semper tyrannis*" (thus always to tyrants) and ran offstage and into the night. Talk about a moment, a coup de théâtre. Assassination thrust into the live equivalent of a Jim Carrey movie.

Terrible historical associations aside, the line is hardly boffo today. The participial *sockdologizing*, which turns up nowhere else, was the English playwright's fanciful extension of the slang noun for a knockout blow: *sockdologer*, itself an extension of *sock*, another slang term, of pre-1700 vintage but still somewhat current, meaning "to hit hard." At least one source credits the coinage of *sockdologer* (also *ripsnorter*) to Davy Crockett, but since everything we read about the barely literate Crockett was written by someone else and mostly after his death, that is questionable. Roy Wilder Jr., whom I trust, says *dologer* was "a corruption of *doxology*."

➤ solecisms, contradictions, factual errors, etc.

There are 167 in this book. See if you can find them all.

➤ *some*

The literary, quasi-intensifying *some*: "Like some avenging angel," say, instead of "like an avenging angel."

In 2005 *The New York Times Book Review* praised a novel by Thomas

Rogers by quoting this line—"Her dress came slithering off like a tarpaulin from some public monument"—and adding, "Any book containing that line is worth reading." I am willing to accept that judgment, and not just because this book, now, contains that line. But wouldn't "from a public monument" be better? Why *some*? "My love is like a red, red rose," not "like *some* red, red rose."

Then there's the political-mendacity *some*:

"Some will say that when faced with the forces of evil we should just cut and run and slit our own throats to save them the trouble, and then, with our dying breath, apologize. Isn't that just typical of Them?" Who? Who? Who are these *some*?

The following is a much less significant *some*, but . . . Am I the only person who is bothered by TV newspersons who say, "The hurricane drowned some two thousand people," giving the same lack of emphasis to *some* as one might in saying, "Pick up some beer while you're out"? When *some* is used to mean "approximately," followed by an impressive figure, it needs to be emphasized somewhat, as it is when one says, "This has been going on for *some time* now." Can it be that authors' inflationary use of *some* and politicians' forked-tongue dwelling on *some* have taken the juice out of a good straightforwardly emphasized *some*?

➤ *sonicky*

I offer this neologism as an alternative to *onomatopoeic* or *echoic* or *imitative*. Would *phonicky* be better? I don't think so; makes me think of *finicky* (which is a good sonicky word) and *phony* (which according to AHD is an "alteration of *fawney*, gilt brass ring used by swindlers").

I mean the quality of a word whose sound doesn't imitate a sound, like *boom* or *poof*, but does somehow sensuously evoke the essence of the word: *queasy* or *rickety* or *zest* or *sluggish* or *vim*. The word *nausea* comes from the Latin for "seasickness," which came from the Greek for "ship"—but even if it didn't have that pedigree, it would *sound* right. If you were a caveperson earnestly trying to communicate how you felt digestively, you might without benefit of any verbal tradition come up with something close to *nausea*.

In his essay "Not-Knowing," Donald Barthelme relates that he was once in the artist Elaine de Kooning's studio when he heard from the metal sculptor Herbert Ferber's studio, on the floor above, "a most horrible crashing and banging. 'What in the world was that?' I asked, and Elaine said, 'Oh, that's Herbert thinking.'" Working with words is also noisy.

See *arbitrary*; onomatopoeia; *qualm*; *wh-*; *symbolic/presentive*.

➤ sonnet

I picked up a book a while back that called itself an anthology of sonnets, and the things it called sonnets were eleven lines long, fifteen lines long, maybe rhymed, maybe not—those might have been poems, but sonnets? I do not hold with calling anything a sonnet (from the Provençal for "little song") that does not have fourteen pentameter lines that rhyme. I'm open to different rhyme *schemes*. Here's a Mill River sonnet:

> Baubles, bangles, beads, and ermine may
> Be quite all right on any other day,
> But when time comes for celebrating Saint
> Valentine's—and here it is—they ain't.
>
> It's Fourteen February, is it not?
> So here (assuming we can end them on the dot)
> Are fourteen lines that should be ruby red
> But may at least, I hope (perhaps in bed),
>
> By you be read. My word, that's nice—"be ru-
> By red . . . by you be read"—but you know who
> Is nicer? You. So, Pisces is your sign?
> Well here's my angle: Be my Valentine!
>
> Your present's this: another blessed sonnet.
> I sure do hope it's sort of what you wonnet.

If it's sonnet dismantlement you want, okay, here:

I. SHAKESPEAREAN SONNET SIMPLIFIED

> Wanna write a sonnet,
> Haven't got the time?
> Don your thinking bonnet,
> Grab the nearest rhyme,

Bear in mind that (*a*)
Trimeter and (*b*)
Stretcher tropes like "Hey
Nonny" and "You see"

Bring you ere you know it
To the finish—e'en
Though you're not a poet—
Under par (fourteen).

Show me where it says you're
Bound to give full measure.

II. SO, TOO, THE ITALIAN

Two-line sonnet, if you please:
Abba, abba, c-d, c-d,
Wrap the matter up with *e*'s.
See? || Yes indeedy.

III. POETRY IN ROCK?

Any two ABBA numbers, on CDs,
Make a sonnet, rounded out with ease.

IV. LINES OCCASIONED BY THE LINES ABOVE

To say there's strength in what is terse,
    And what's redundant smothers,
        Is not to say it has to sap
The vigor of a given verse
    If some of its and others'
        Felicities should overlap.

V. LINES IN DEFENSE OF THOSE JUST PREVIOUS

Although in prose I'd ne'er permit
The pesky pronouns *its* and *it*
To gad about like mice, since
That was verse I took a bit
Of referential license.

VI. A TIP ON PENTAMETER

Nearly any line that's short is fillable
With some handy (*this*, for instance) syllable.

VII. TIGHT LIKE THIS

Meter rough?
Here's what you do:
Just trim off
A syl' or two.

➤ *spatuleh?*

In *Portnoy's Complaint*, Philip Roth's eponymous narrator says that when
he was a child he thought "'tumult' and 'bedlam,' two favorite words of my
mother," were "Jewish words."

"Also 'spatula.' I was already the darling of the first grade, and in every
schoolroom competition expected to win hands down, when I was asked
by the teacher one day to identify a picture of what I knew perfectly well
my mother referred to as a 'spatula.' But for the life of me I could not think
of the word in English."

➤ *special*

"It's good that they don't make many players like Albert Pujols, because if
there were more, he wouldn't be so special, and Albert Pujols is very special." —Murray Chass, *The New York Times*. See **special**.

➤ spelling bee

Is there one for witches? Hypnotists? Have there ever been bees that
swarmed into words to save the life of a pig, as Charlotte the spelling spi-
der does with her valiant **spin**ning in *Charlotte's Web*? If so, I suspect the
orthography was **arbitrary**: sometimes things just be's that way.

I have been in only one spelling bee. I was twelve, and a hell of a speller
if I do say so myself. I went down on *silhouette*. An *h* in it? How was I supposed to know it came from Étienne de Silhouette, appointed finance

minister by his friend Madame de Pompadour? Silhouette cut down on so many expenses and levied so many taxes (on bachelors, for instance) that *à la silhouette* came to mean "on the cheap." As in portraits that were just cut out of black paper. It's a sillhy (sihc) damn word.

Pompadour, though, that's a good one: the title of Jeanne-Antoinette Poisson, which means *fish*. Madame de Pompadour adored pomp. And she fixed her hair real fancy:

> You got big old hair and a little bitty heart.
> I should've known about you from the start.
> Your pompadour is a work of aaaaart
> You got big old hair and a little bitty heart.

In fact La Pompadour was a remarkable woman. So comely was she in bourgeois girlhood that an aristocratic patron took her under his wing, declared her "un morceau du roi" (a king's morsel), and had her educated especially to be a royal mistress. In her twenties Louis XV met her at a ball and took her—though she had married some schnook (see **Hittite**)—for his own. Confidante as well as squeeze, she became not only a social arbiter but an aesthetic and political force. She named Voltaire poet laureate and fostered an alliance with Austria, which led, as it happened, to the Seven Years' War, which cost France all its foreign possessions. Louis may well have felt that she was worth it. On her deathbed she made up her face for the king.

➤ *spin*

From the Old English *spinnan*, meaning "to draw out and twist fibers into thread" (Chambers). In political-commentary jabber, to spin is to falsify. In fact, spin is essential to making sense: otherwise, fibers of significance float away. No missile in the earth's atmosphere goes in a *straight* line; to throw a baseball or a football as straightforwardly as possible, you have to put spin on it: otherwise it hops, dips, and swerves on the air currents. That's how a knuckleball behaves—unpredictably, almost unhittably, and sometimes uncatchably—because it is projected from the fingertips (not the knuckles, but "knuckle" is aptly *sonicky*) with virtually no spin. To hold your own in discourse is not to deny spin but to pick up on it (in baseball a successful batter "picks up on the spin" of a pitch quickly to diagnose it as a curve, a slider, or a fastball) and develop your own sense of spin. The TV talker Bill O'Reilly's "no spin zone" is itself, *of course*, heavy-handed spin.

After all, *english*, in the U.S., means spin. Imparted to a ball. As in these lines by Allen Tate:

> The going years, caught in an accurate glow,
> Reverse like balls englished on green baize.

That's what I call spin: capturing the action of a pool ball going out, shifting gears, and coming back—capturing that with nothing but letters on a page.

The **English**, I believe, call english *side*. Why wouldn't they call it *english*? Because they prefer to regard English as straightforward, perhaps—or because, according to etymonline.com, *english* in this sense comes from the French for "angled": *anglé*, a homophone of *anglais*.

See **U.K./U.S.**; *arbitrary*; *problem*.

➢ split infinitive

There was a time, in the nineteenth century, when persnickety grammarians categorically deplored putting anything between the *to* and the verb. These days, no one condemns "to boldly go where none have gone before," whose rhythm is catchy, or "The bishop has resolved to painstakingly separate the men from the boys." But it is wise to rigorously keep an eye on the infinitive as a unit. Consider this IMDb.com plot outline, the hitch in its getalong: "Robert Ford joins Jesse James's gang, only to become resentful of the legendary outlaw and hatch a plan to kill the fastest gun in the West." I see the *to's and of's* issue here, but to shove "become resentful of the legendary outlaw and" between *to* and *hatch* is a *bit much*.

➢ spoonerisms

For example, *kinkering kongs*, for *conquering kings*; and *This pie is occupewed, may I sew you to your sheet*, for *This pew is occupied, may I show you to your seat*. From the Reverend William Archibald Spooner, who was prone, at least by reputation, to such transpositions. See *tallywacker*.

➤ *spot*

Given that it started out meaning a small blot or stain, and that its first
form in English may have been *splot*, this is a highly appealing, short, to-
the-point word, isn't it? Good name for a dog, for a choice location, and
for a place to dine or to hear music. Heaven, wrote Emily Dickinson, was a
"spot" she'd never visited, but she knew right where it was. Milton alluded to "this dim spot / Which men call earth." Leigh Hunt extolled:

> The two divinest things that man has got,
> A lovely woman in a rural spot.

And A. J. Liebling reported this about the New York fight trainer Whitey
Bimstein:

> I once asked him how he liked the country. He said, "It is a nice spot."

Calvin Trillin claims to have produced one actual issue of a periodical
he founded called *Beautiful Spot: A Magazine of Parking*.

Speckled, in some contexts, may be almost too appealing. In Ap-
palachia, according to the *Dictionary of Smoky Mountain English* (a copy of
which should be in every home), "as cute (or pretty) as a speckled pup," as
in "Their new baby is purty as a speckled pup," or "She's as pretty as a
speckled pup under a red wagon," is "sometimes used for veiled dispar-
agement." Dolly Parton is quoted as saying of herself as a girl, "You could
not have said that I was 'as cute as a speckled pup' without expecting the
speckled pup to piss on your leg out of resentment."

➤ *spot-on*

This word for "perfect," as in "His imitation of Huckleberry Hound if he
were a pirate is spot-on," is widely used as I compose this book, but it
does not appear in any of my print dictionaries. **Books** can't keep up with
the language. But where would the language be without them?

➤ *spritzing*

Is easy, comedy's hard.

➤ statistical rhetoric

Atul Gawande, a good writer, in _The New York Times_: "One statistic seems to me to give the lie to all the rhetoric about abortion, and it is this: one in three women under the age of 45 have an abortion during their lifetime." What in the world does that mean? One in three women under 45 have had an abortion? Will have one before they die? When would people have anything except "during their lifetime"? "One in three women under the age of 45 today either have had an abortion or will have one before they die"? Maybe. Who knows? And why "one . . . have . . . their lifetime"? Too personal to say "her"?

"Among women under 45 today, one in three has had an abortion," if that is the case, would focus attention on the matter.

See _he/she/his/her_ and _if/whether_.

➤ _stock_

Our serendipitous India-paper research into **tallywacker** (I urge you to go there, and then come back here) strongly suggests that _stock_ as in the stock market derives from the tally stick. But there is also the sense of a tree's trunk and what is stored in there, hence stock in trade, taking stock, livestock, and . . . beef stock. Ooh. _Alphabet Stock_ would be a good title for this book.

The **PIE** root, says AHD, is _steig-_, to stick; pointed (whence _stitch_, _ticket_, _instinct_, _stigma_, _tiger_, _steak_), "partially **blend**ed" with _stegh-_, to stick, prick; pointed (whence _sting_, _stag_, _stochastic_). Which leads us off in the direction of a stick's pointed end, rather than the body, the trunk, the shaft, the substance—whence, surely, _stock_ as in a rifle's or an oil company's stock.

➤ _straight_

Derives from _stretch_. Things don't come straight, you have to get them straight.

➤ _stuff_

How can this be such a handy word for essence or spirit—the Right Stuff, "such stuff as dreams are made on," "show us your stuff"—and also for miscellaneous clutter, even trash? It's the liveliness a pitcher can impart to a baseball, and yet *stuffy* means unfresh and narrow-minded. People say, "She knows her stuff," and "Strut your stuff!" approvingly, but they also say, "Stuff and nonsense!" Oyster or crabmeat or even cornbread (with sage) stuffing can be a wonderful thing, and an overstuffed chair is comfy; but a stuffed shirt is full of his overinflated self.

Well, it's a word that's easy and pleasant to say. It's a breathy word. *Spirit* and *inspiration* come from the Latin *spirare*, to breathe. The Latin *anima*, from which we get *animation* and *animal*, and which meant "soul, spirit, life," also meant "breath," and derives from the root *anǝ-*, to breathe.

But that conclusive *ff*—a breathing out, an expiration (*exhale* comes from *halare*, another Latin word meaning "to breathe")—also evokes dismissal, as in *stuff it, get stuffed, fuck off,* or in the essentially unspellable sound the French make by way of pronouncing something or someone unworthy of consideration: something in the range of *buff / boeuf / bouffe / boff / beuff.* Then there's *pfft.* And *huffing and puffing,* a sign of overdoing or being out of shape. *Off, scoff, offal, toff, stuff it, poof, puffed up, puffery, powderpuff, piffle, buffoon, bluff,* even sometimes *lofty,* are all dismissive.

Let's suggest that *stuff* regarded as something retained within is good; entitles you to puff out your chest, not that you'd need to make such a show, because you know who you are. On the other hand, *stuff* as an exhalation is a response to someone or something that is full of hot air or something worse, and is to be blown off.

As to stuffy air, we might note the OED word *stufe* or *stuffe,* meaning a "hot-air bath," a steam room, apparently, used as late as 1898; these would have been unventilated, presumably, but would open the breathing passages rather than stifling them.

➤ subjective/objective

Subject is from the Latin for "to throw under." A *subject* was originally someone who was subjected to some other power, and that meaning persists in various contexts—"subject to the laws of the state," "subject to temptation." But *subject* has also come to mean a theme, the essential order of something, what a sentence is about. Power, accordingly, has accrued to *subjective*, as when feminists have resolved not to be objectified by men but to characterize themselves by their own perceptions.

Object comes from the Latin for "to throw against." Its primary meaning has always been, to quote WIII, "something that is put or may be regarded as put in the way of some of the senses: a discrete visible or tangible thing." Around the middle of the nineteenth century *objective* began to mean (WIII again) "expressing or involving the use of facts without distortion by personal feelings or prejudices."

Back in the sixties, as I recall, there was a running debate over whether a problem was subjective, solvable only by psychiatry, religion, art; or objective, solvable only by change of social conditions, the political system. This dichotomy rested on false assumptions: that social conditions or the political system can be conceived of objectively, and that subjective and objective can be separated. Which is not to say that we should stop trying.

See *hater*.

➤ subjunctive

"If I were you, I'd listen to me."

"If I were a more fabulous personality, I wouldn't have to worry about the subjunctive—the only moods that counted would be mine."

"If French toast were American, I still wouldn't eat it."

These statements unquestionably call for the conditional (*would*) and the subjunctive (*if . . . were*), betokening speculation based upon assumption contrary to fact.

A couple more, because they're so nice:

"If I had not agreed to review this book I would have stopped after five pages. After 600, I felt as if I were inside a bass drum banged on by a clown" —Richard Brookhiser.

"Even the dog, an animal used to bizarre surroundings, developed a strange, off-register look, as if he were badly printed in overlapping colors" —S. J. Perelman.

However, you will frequently see such sentences today with a *was* where a *were* should be, as in this first sentence in a *New York Times* story:

"If the longstanding fight between two professors, Alan Dershowitz and

Norman Finkelstein, was under the jurisdiction of a family court, a judge could issue restraining orders and forbid inflammatory statements."

And what with the rising tides of uncertainty and unthought-out assertiveness in Western civilization today (see **absolutely**), the subjunctive often blends with the indicative to create a syntactical can of worms, as it were. Shaquille O'Neal on Dennis Rodman as a movie actor: "If he was on fire, he couldn't act as if he were burning." That should be, If he *were* on fire, he couldn't act as if he were burning. I think. Actually to be burning and at the same time to be acting *as if* one *were* burning would be a trick. (See *-self*.) Gets you right into the question of what acting is.

There's a slangy but I'd say unimpeachable present-tense form of the subjunctive: "If I'm Vlad the Impaler, I'm thinking, So sue me." Strictly correct, I guess, would be "If I be Vlad the Impaler, I be saying . . . ," but I don't think we want to go with that.

Then there is the title of O. J. Simpson's book about the homicide of which he was criminally acquitted but for which he was civilly adjudged to be responsible: *If I Did It*. That would be grammatical only *if* he were unsure whether he did it or not.

If he hadn't done it, he would surely have titled his book subjunctively: *If I Had Done It*. But if he did it (and here I give him, for a moment, the benefit of the doubt), then he would certainly not be above going with *If I Did It*, which is catchier, in a loathsome sort of way.

➤ *surds*

Letter-sounds that are voiceless, that is to say, produced without vibration of the vocal cords, for instance *t, p, f*. From the Latin *surdus*, unheard, silent, or deaf. English *absurd*, from the Latin *absurdus*, out of tune or senseless, comes from the same root system, a Latin translation of an Arabic translation of a Greek word meaning "speechless" or "without reason." Similarly, *dumb* first meant "mute," then came to mean "stupid." *Dumb* derives from *duh* and *mute* from *umm*: inarticulate (but not necessarily voiceless) attempts to speak.

➤ surrealism

Is easy, comedy's Herb.

➢ *swell*

Staple in old movies. "Say, you're swell." Did people in real life use it so much? Presumably, though whether life imitating art or vice versa is hard to say.

➢ switcheroo, the old

A staple of humor since the cave painting that *must* have existed of a woman dragging a man around by something. Here's a relatively fresh example, which I worked up myself for the radio:

> The Family Channel has announced it will soon be airing a new comedy series inspired by Franz Kafka's "The Metamorphosis"— with a difference. *The Crawleys*, as the show is called, is not about a man who wakes up to find he's been transformed into a cockroach, it's about a family of cockroaches who turn into people. "At first they have a hard time adjusting," says Andra McCallum, who plays the mom, Ophelia Crawley. "They try to climb walls and hide under the refrigerator." But eventually their natural cucarachan cleverness comes to the fore as the Crawleys make their way into every nook and cranny of school, garden club, and workplace. They also make the life of Mr. Ketcham, the local exterminator, a living hell.

By the way, *cockroach* comes from the Spanish word for the insect (and the fittingly foot-stomping musical number), *cucaracha*. (Fittingly from a human standpoint, that is. Uh-oh, I'm starting to think of a gag for *The Crawleys*.) To approximate that sound, the British cobbled together two animals they were familiar with, the male chicken and a small freshwater fish called the roach. Genetically, that combination would make for one ugly and unhappy chimera. Acoustically, it works. Choreographically, it's not up to *cucaracha*. New Yorkers often put the first *a* sound back in: cockaroach. The first reference to this insect in printed English, so far as we know (AHD), was by Captain John Smith, the Virginia colonizer, in 1624. He spelled it *cacarootch*.

To be sure, the **bug** that Gregor Samsa morphs into was not a cockroach, except in most English translations of the story. "A monstrous vermin" is a strict translation of Kafka's words. The cleaning lady who sweeps poor Gregor into a dustbin addresses him, in death, as "old dung beetle," but Vladimir Nabokov, who knew insects, classified this one, from the details of Kafka's description, as some other kind of beetle, brown, convex, and with wing cases. "Curiously enough," Nabokov writes in the lecture on "The Metamorphosis" he gave to college classes, "Gregor the beetle never found out that he had wings under the hard covering of his back. (This is a very nice observation on my part to be treasured all of your lives. Some Gregors, some Joes and Janes, do not know that they have wings.)" Gregor also has human eyes and feelings. For Nabokov the switcheroo in the story is that the beetle acts, or tries to act, like a person, while the insensitive people around him act like cockroaches.

There is a novel, *Kockroach*, by Tyler Knox, in which a cockroach turns into an ill-mannered man named Jerry Blatta, and another novel, *Insect Dreams*, by Marc Estrin, in which Gregor does not die in his room but goes on through life as a compassionate, highly intelligent insect. He meets Wittgenstein and goes to work (behind the scenes) for Franklin Delano Roosevelt.

➤ *swive*

As early as 1300 (no, not one a.m., the beginning of the fourteenth century), this was the most common slang term for "to do it with someone." It's a good one, too, smoother—might even say more suave—than the *f*-word. It's from the Old English *swifan*, to move in a course, sweep. (I guess no connection, though, to "dust my broom.") The soupçon of *wife* in there is surely not amiss.

➤ *symbolic / presentive*

With regard to *whisk*, OED says, "The spelling with **wh**- was adopted as being symbolic." In other words, presumably, *wh*- was felt to be more **son-icky**, more representative of the sound of a whisk than *wisk* was. I certainly concur. But when you look up *symbolic* in OED, it quotes an 1877 philological work as follows: "The symbolic words are those which by themselves present no meaning to the mind, and which depend for their intelligibility on a relation to some presentive word or words." Under *presentive*, OED quotes the same work at more length:

> We will call these two classes of words by the names of Presentive and Symbolic. The Presentive are those . . . which present any conception to the mind . . . The numerals I and II and III and IIII are presentive of the ideas of one and two and three and four . . . The figures 1 and 2 and 3 and 4 are and always were pure symbols . . . The pronoun *I* . . . has also a sort of reflected or borrowed presentiveness, which we will call a subpresentive power.

Interesting reflection on *I*, that big old unitary column of a pronoun, at once the shortest (just the one letter, as opposed to *ego* or *je* or *ich*) and the tallest (by dint of its capitalization) of Indo-European first persons. But surely OED meant to say that *wh-* was adopted as being presentive, not symbolic.

WIII, which doesn't define *presentive*, has a better definition than OED's of *symbolic*: "of, or relating to, or being a sequence of phonemes occurring in a group of words connected with a common usu. vague feature of meaning but not necessarily implying imitation of a sound in nature < in *flash*, *flame*, *flare*, *flicker*, and *flimmer*, the *fl-* conveys the sense of light in motion > in *bounce*, *pounce*, and *trounce*, *-ounce* conveys the sense of rapid movement >—distinguished from onomatopoeic."

Yes. And that must be the sense in which OED was using, as opposed to defining, *symbolic*.

See **arbitrary**; **kinesthesia**; ***flinch*** and ***wince*** family; ***Google***; **wh-**.

> ➤ *synchronicity*

Jungian. Same thing as "happy accident," I would say—nothing mystical about it, but a coincidence or free-floating scrap of apparent pattern (compare **pareidolia, cherry-picking**) that you manage to jump onto like a **chicken** on a June bug and metabolize into meaning. Which is why you need to spend time at the keyboard. Catching lightning in a bottle requires having a bottle (see **conventions**) on the ready.

➤ synesthesia

"A condition in which one type of stimulation evokes the sensation of another, as when the hearing of a sound produces the visualization of a color" (AHD).

Vladimir Nabokov noticed that he associated certain letters with certain colors in childhood, when he told his mother that some of his alphabet blocks were the wrong colors. She saw nothing odd in this (possibly we are all creative in, and only in, those areas in which our mothers saw, at least to begin with, nothing odd), and when they compared notes they found that they agreed on some letters' colors.

For Nabokov, "the long *a* of the English alphabet . . . has the tint of weathered wood, but a French *a* evokes polished ebony."

Arthur Rimbaud, in his poem "Vowels," expressed the same feeling about the color, at least, of the French *a*: "a corset; black and hairy, buzzing with flies" (*noir corset velu des mouches éclatantes*).

Nabokov saw the letter *u* as "brassy with an olive sheen." To Rimbaud, *u* was viridian, a bluish green. So, considering Nabokov had in mind the English *u* and Rimbaud the French one, they would seem to have been on similar wavelengths there.

But Nabokov saw "various *e*'s and *i*'s" as different shades of yellow, and *o* as "ivory-colored."

To Rimbaud, *e* was white, *i* was red ("bloody spittle, lips' lovely laughter"—*sang craché, rire des lèvres belles*), and *o* was blue.

To Nabokov, other letters seemed black: hard *g* ("vulcanized rubber") and *r* ("a sooty rag being ripped"). Then too:

> . . . oatmeal *n*, noodle-limp *l*, and the ivory-backed hand mirror of *o*
> take care of the whites . . . Passing on to the blue group, there is steely *x*,
> thunderous *z*, and huckleberry *k*. Since a subtle interaction exists
> between sound and shape, I see *q* as browner than *k*, while *s* is not the
> light blue of *c*, but a curious mixture of azure and mother-of-pearl.
>
> In the green group, there are the alder-leaf *f*, the unripe apple
> of *p*, and pistachio *t*. Dull green, combined somehow with violet, is
> the best I can do for *w*.

And so on. As a boy I linked red with even numbers and the American League, green with odd numbers and the National League, but unless obsessing over the alphabet qualifies, I regret to say that synesthesia largely escapes me. I can connect hard *g* to vulcanized rubber, but black has too many other associations. Ripping a rag does have a more than obvious *r*-ness about it, but I don't see the soot.

Synesthesia doesn't seem to be a faculty, because it has no clear function, and it's not a short-circuit, because it doesn't kill power. It may be an overlapping of sensitivities. "The first author to discuss *audition colorée*," Nabokov notes, "was, as far as I know, an albino physician in 1812, in Erlangen." Nabokov, from old Russia, created in *Pale Fire* one of the most intricate constructions in English, and he was a serious student of butterflies. But he said, "Music, I regret to say, affects me merely as an arbitrary succession of more or less irritating sounds."

My sister, Susan, is a math major whose work in the computer business has included cutting the flab out of corporate prose (see **redundancy**), and whose volunteer work has included teaching English as a second language to literacy-impaired adults. She says she has always seen the letter *a* as "sort of beigy yellow, but it's not a clear-cut thing like the colors of numbers." A 5 (red) and an 8 (brown) together make her think of blood on dirt. Some twenty years ago, her phone number was 369-7751. The last four digits—black black red white—went together well, and the pink 3 and the blue 6 harmonized nicely, but the dark olive-green 9 made for an overall combination whose ugliness she still deplores.

Synesthetic people seldom agree as to which colors go with which numbers or letters. Steven Mithen, in *The Singing Neanderthals*, addresses something more nearly universal when he speaks of "sound synaesthesia . . . , the mapping from one type of variable—size—onto another—sound." He cites an experiment by Edward Sapir, who "made up two nonsense words, *mil* and *mal*, and told his subjects that these were the names of tables. He then asked them which name indicated the larger table and found . . . that almost all of them chose *mal*." This confirmed a suggestion by the linguist Otto Jespersen that the sound of *ih*, "which is formed by pushing the tongue forward and upward to make the smallest cavity between the tongue and lips," is readily associated with small things, while big things tend to be linked to other vowel sounds, for instance *ah* (the sound you make when you open up for the dentist or loosen your belt after a hearty dinner), which are formed by "a lowered tongue, which creates a large mouth cavity. In other words, such sounds are the product of physical gestures made by the tongue and the lips, which mimic the size of the object being named." So I guess the words *big* and *small* themselves are exceptions. But *little* and *large* work, as do *itty-bitty* and *tall*; *shrimp* and *llama*; *tick* and *whopper*. Mithen says other researchers have found that tribesfolk in far-flung parts of the world tend to use *ih* in words for small animals and *ah* or other expansive vowel sounds for large ones. (According to *The Sound of Greek*, the ancient grammarian Dionysius Thrax held that *ih* is constrained because "the breath strikes the teeth, not the lips.")

See **kinesthesia**; *arbitrary*; *sonicky*; *mnemonic*.

➤ syntax collie

Just a thought, inspired by a *New Yorker* cartoon—child coloring with dog watching him, over the caption: "He always stays in the lines since we got the border collie." So how about a dog that keeps children from saying "between you and I"?

➤ *syrup*

I am glad to see in AHD that surrup is the preferred pronunciation of *syrup*. As it's spelled, it looks like the first syllable ought to be pronounced sihr or even seer, and many cultured people do pronounce it in one of those ways. So I have long harbored a fear that surrup, which is how I have always pronounced it—

> Chewin' cane and sweatin' syrup,
> Got my foot stuck in the stirrup.
> Lord how can I straighten her up?

—might be relegated by respectable dictionaries to regional oddity. I never considered giving up on surrup, though, because—in its similarity to *slurp*—it sounds like how *syrup* ought to be pronounced. In his song "Dang Me," Roger Miller rhymes *purple* with *maple surple*.

➢ *syzygy*

There's the astronomical *syzygy*, in which, most simply, the sun and the moon and the earth (or any other three celestial bodies, but who cares?) are in a straight line. There's the *syzygy* of classical Greek prosody (two metrical feet combined into one, as in a sack race), which you need never worry about. There's Jungian *syzygy*, which is an integration of the self through the alignment of male and female elements. And then there's the *syzygy* that people toss around so loosely as to make you wonder whether people just like to find any excuse to say "syzygy": the *syzygy* meaning "any two related things, either alike or opposite" (RHU). As in, "Aunt Bootsie and Uncle Rip are out of syzygy again," or "Check the syzygy in that lady's bustier."

   See **stuff**; **bust**.

t · T · t

Frequently, *t* evokes disapproval: *tut-tut*, *tsk-tsk*, *too-too*, *tittle-tattle*, *tit for tat*, *tacky tacky tacky*, *fat*, *rat*, *catty*, *tatty*, *twit*, *twat*, *all hat and no cattle*, and, yes, *bullshit*. But how about *heart*, you may counter, and *sweet*, *delight*, and *breast*?

Right. Forget disapproval. If you would know the essence of *t*, here is what's what:

As *tav* or *taw*, it's the last letter in the Hebrew alphabet. It used to be last, as *tau*, in the Greek one, before *upsilon*, *phi*, *chi*, *psi*, and *omega* slipped in behind it. It ought to be last in ours.

You get *t* right on the tip of your tongue (at the point of contact when tongue and palate meet), and it'll fit just right, it'll hit the spot, it'll suit that tip to a T (see **jot and tittle**).

But . . .

What?

What about *but*?

Your point, I take it, is that my attempt to articulate the argument—at least, the thought—that *t* has an intrinsic terminality to it has been upset by contact against *but*, which doesn't end anything, any more than *joint* does: *but*'s a conjunction, like *if*, and *and*, or *or*.

But . . .

I've got it! *But* is trumped (pronounced trumpt) by *butt*. And by what the director says at the end of the take—"Cut!"—and by any number of words that have to do with settlement, getting it just right, confinement, or taking it to the limit: *quit*, *fit*, *splat*, *rapt*, *pit*, *rut*, *exhaust*, *sit tight*, *stand pat*, *past*, *blast*, *just*, *bust*, *rest*, *aft*, *knot*, *not*, *forgot*, *on the dot*, *exact*, *where it's at*, *direct hit*, *spit the bit*, *flat out*, *put out*, *cast out*, *die is cast*, *caught short*, *acid test*, *defunct*, *pfft*. Halt! Cut that out! Can't! *Night*, *putt*, *shut*, *shot*, *gone to pot*, *extinct*.

And *lit*, as in landed, *let*, as in blockage, and *lot*, as in fate. Is it just an accident that so many words, in particular words suggesting closure (*extent*, *pent*, *spent*, *sent*, *content*) terminate in *-ent*? Not to mention *-ment*? Furthermore, *-est* is most, best, can't get past that.

The most frequent past-tense ending in English, *-ed*, is often sounded correctly as *t*, as in *dressed*, *washed*, *finished*. In fact many such *-ed* words used (yoost) to end in *t*; and many past-tense verbs still do: *crept*, *slept*, *swept*, *wept*, *gilt*, *bought*, *bent*, *sat*. The **PIE** root of *end* is *ant-*.

So there *is* something terminal about *t*, at least temporarily, which is why *titillate*, *titter*, *teeter-totter*, *tickle*, *tempt*, *subtlety*, *kittenish*, and *tick* . . . *tick* tease us a bit, make us tense. If the *-sie* and "don't cry" did not afford release, think how hung up we'd be on *toot-toot-Tootsie*. And what about *sweet*? If sweetness didn't end, it would be twee.

Z is no ender, it's a zinger, *bzzzt*. There, look at that: if you didn't put a *t* at the end of *bzzzt* it would buzz on into infinity. *T* is the best last letter, absolutely, that is that.

➤ talking, vis-à-vis writing

I believe writing is strongest when it shares a vein with speech. But writing can do things speaking can't (and vice versa, to be sure). And chatting is something else again.

"Talking is a hydrant in the yard and writing is a faucet upstairs in the house. Opening the first takes all the pressure off the second," said—or, rather, wrote—Robert Frost.

See **marriage, to a writer**.

➤ *tallywacker*

This, when I was a boy, was the term our family doctor used for the penis. I don't know that I have ever seen it in print. It's not in AHD, OAD, RHU, Roget's Thesaurus, or even the *Dictionary of Smoky Mountain English*. Harry Peckham, when he worked in the *Sports Illustrated* reference library back in the seventies, sang a ditty that went, as I recall, like this:

Possum up a forty-foot cottonwood tree—
Why won't the girls let my tallywacker be?

Eric Partridge's dictionary of slang has *tallywag*, meaning either the penis or the testicles, and suggests a derivation from *tally* meaning "corresponding half" and the **verb** *wag*, as in what a dog does with its tail when it's happy. I don't know how that *tally* would be used in a sentence or how it might relate to the penis. RHU gives one definition of *tally* as "a stick of wood with notches cut to indicate the amount of a debt or payment, often split lengthwise across the notches, the debtor retaining one piece and the creditor the other." Hence, I suppose, the verb as it is used in "Your story doesn't tally with his." If *tallywag* is in fact the original of *tallywacker*, I would suggest that the *tally* alludes to the stick (*maybe* with notches, in a sense). See **Wilt: A Tall Tale**.

Somehow I didn't want to **Google** *tallywacker*. Our family doctor, Dr. Homer Allen, was a genial, gravelly voiced man who made house calls. He used *tallywacker* in an offhand but upfront sort of way that made me feel that having one was nothing to apologize for. Or to crow about, not that any such option would have presented itself in our household. When we had to call the penis anything, we called it the tinkle. My father may have called it something else outside the house, I wouldn't know—is it still the case, by and large, that the first term a boy learns for the distinguishing mark of his sex comes from his female parent?

I didn't want to learn of a folk-rock band called Tallywacker, or a theatrical event called *The Tallywacker Monologues*. It would be like finding my baby pictures bandied about on the Web.

But *of course* it had to be done, the Google thing. Results: 17,400 items. In Wilshire, U.K., a Tallywacker Organic Farm. On **Urbandictionary.com**, several definitions, most of them penile, one of them accompanied by an entirely fanciful derivation: "French *tallier* = pull + Western Irish mispronunciation of *wanker*."

A band called Sonic Tallywacker, with a song called "Swallow the Leader," okay, great. Some kind of music site called Slappy the Tallywacker, ha. And so on. From a site called Jim Conrad's Naturalist Newsletter I learned that when the eponymous Conrad was a boy of seven in Kentucky, his uncle informed him that *tallywacker* (not *cooter*, as he had been told by his parents) was the right word for the body part in question. And yet, muses Conrad, "the etymology sites I find claim it's a slang word from the 1970s used in southeastern England."

The Web spreads wide, but its roots (if a web had roots) are not so deep. There's nothing worse than shallow etymology.

So, back to reference *books*. Back, in fact, to my oldest dictionary. If you want to read a thoroughgoing treatment of *tally*, check the 1918 India Paper Edition of *Webster's New International Dictionary of the English Language*, "Based on the International Dictionary of 1890 and 1900, Now Completely Revised in All Departments . . . Being the Latest Quarto Edition of the Merriam Series."

Maybe you don't have a copy. So here:

> Formerly, a piece of wood on which notches were cut as marks of number; later, one of two books, sheets of paper, etc., on which accounts were kept correspondingly or in duplicate. It was formerly customary for traders to have two sticks, or one stick cleft into two parts, and to mark with a score or notch, on each, the number or quantity of goods delivered, the seller keeping one stick, and the purchaser the other. In the English Exchequer were *tallies* of loans, one part, called the counterstock, or countertally, being kept in the E, the other, the *stock*, or *tally* being given to the creditor . . .

Wait a minute! Not only does *tally* come from a stick, but so must **stock**! The stock market evolved from a piece of wood! Yes, it's true. We've gone from *tallywacker* to . . .

Look at *this*: my old India paper Webster's includes *tallywag*: ". . . pale olive, and has three rows of quadrate black blotches along each side . . ." Oh. It's a fish. A sea bass of the Gulf of Mexico. Ought to be a gulf bass then, oughtn't it?

A *tallyman*, my more recent dictionaries agree, is someone who sells merchandise on credit. Keeps a tally. "Come, Mr. Tallyman," sang Harry Belafonte, "tally me banana."

Tallyho, the **exclamation** of fox hunting, is the British adaptation of the French hunter's cry, *tayau*. What does *tayau* come from? My French-English dictionary doesn't say. *Enfin, cela me passe.* Maybe it's French for *yippee* or for *yo-ho-to-ho* or however you spell what the Valkyries sing. The only thing that counts, I guess, is that the dogs must like it. Easier to run to, I should think, than *yoicks*, which, however, may help pull you out of a stumble; and it gets a bit more traction than *hallooo*.

My French-English dictionary has no such word as *tallier* in it. ("To pull" is, *of course*, *tirer*.) Then too it doesn't have *penis* in it. It was last updated in October 1940, a year before I was born. You know what the French word for the noun *tinkle* is? Or was in 1940? *Tintin*. As in *tintinnabulation*, no doubt, but also, hey: the Belgian cartoon character, intrepid boy reporter—great stories, those. Snowy is an excellent dog (a bit like Gromit, now that I think of it), with a taste for whisky. Then there are the hapless lookalike (but unrelated) detectives Thomson and Thompson, both afflicted with **spoonerism**. Wonder how much is lost in translating spoonerisms from French to English. Something to look into.

➤ *tango*

Not from the Latin *tangere*, to touch, but from American Spanish, possibly of Niger-Congo origin; akin to the Ibibio *tamgu*, to dance (AHD, WIII).

No etymological connection with *tangle*, either. That is of Scandinavian origin. Think of a Swede trying to dance. I know, that's invidious, I take it back. Certainly neither my ethnic heritage nor I as an individual can claim any great intimacy with **Terpsichore**. Nor, I suspect, could **Ford Madox Ford**, but he tells a good tango story:

> Just after the tango . . . reached London it excited enormous controversy over whether it was or was not shocking. I was at a dance given by . . . one of the three beautiful sisters of Sargent's *Misses Wortheimer*. Mrs. Wortheimer, who was then a very old lady, asked me to take her to see the tango danced. We stood in the doorway of the ball-room and she looked long and earnestly. She sighed and said: "Yes, I suppose it is *very* shocking . . . But does it matter, if they really love one another?"

➤ *taxicab*

When we hail a cab, why do we holler "Taxi!" instead of "Cab!"? The former is much more likely to catch a cabbie's ear. "Taxi!" is two syllables ending in an extendable *eee* sound. "Cab!" is one syllable ending in a lips-together sound impossible to prolong. But there are also significant sonic differences between *cab* and the first syllable of *taxi*. In both cases, the vowel is flat *a* as in *flat*, but the oral transition from *a* to *b* is a short, uncomplicated forward thrust, as in *jab, tab, grab,* and *dab*. (Toss in a liquid *l* and you've got the floppier presence of *Lab*, as in the retriever, or *flab*, or *blab*.) In *cab* the *a* doesn't do much, just resonates mellowly in the back of the throat. But going from that same *a* to the *ks* sound of *x* requires a quick, tightening, breath-holding jerk backward (as in *acrid*) to make room for what the tongue has to do to form *k*. The resultant *a* sound itself is harsher, more energetic and ear-catching. Then you've got the hiss of tension released in the *s* part of *x*.

By the way, *taxicab* is short for *taximeter cabriolet*. The taximeter measures the tax, or fare, and a cabriolet is a light carriage that capers, or jumps about (French *caprioler*), like a wild goat (Latin *capreolus*).

➤ *teh*

From **Urbandictionary.com**:

> Originally started off as a typo for "the," but recently has changed a bit in meaning. "Teh" still means "the," however, it is mostly used in the same manner that spanish speaking people use the word "El." "I got two cookies with teh whipped cream!" makes sense, but "I got two cookies with the whipped cream!" doesn't. Get what I mean?

Originally started off as is redundant (from the Latin *redundare*, to overflow), and that **comma** before *however* needs to be a **semicolon**, or, better, *however* should be *but* with no comma after it, and of course *Spanish* should be capitalized; but otherwise that's not a badly turned definition (and the last sentence is gracious), assuming that we do know how Spanish-speaking people use the word *El*, with a capital *E*. I don't. But I gather that *teh* connotes *big-time*. Or something along the lines of the emphatic *the*, as when you tell people you are Arturo Toscanini and they say, "*the* Arturo Toscanini?"

I often type *teh* for *the*. Is this because left forefinger and middle finger coordinate from *t* to *e* faster than right forefinger can squeeze in *h*? See *H*.

Might *teh* tend toward standard for this reason? No, you can't let the keyboard's crazy QWERTYUIOP arrangement shape the language. That is a job for voices.

➤ Terpsichore

I used to think that this name for the muse of dance—the feminine form of the Greek for "dance-liking"—was pronounced *Terp*-si-core, as indeed is the street by that name in New Orleans. The *chore* part does come from the same root (Greek for a dance, a group of dancers and singers) as *chorus*. But the muse's pronunciation is more lightsome than I used to think. This is how I keep it in mind:

> The muse of dancing, Terpsichore,
> Whenever some mortal gets snickery,
> > Says, "You just keep hoofing
> > And cut out the woofing,
> Unless you got balls made of hickory."

➤ *terrific*

Originally, terrifying. Now, except in the case of a terrific headache, *terrific* usually means "splendid." How did this happen? We have a tendency to drain scary words of their juice (**awesome**, for instance). And maybe *terrific* doesn't sound terrifying (which does). Rather, it sounds kind of peppy, with that upturning *riff*. For a word to keep its force, it needs the sound of its force.

➤ theme

"This pudding has no theme," Winston Churchill is said to have said about an over-elaborate dessert.

Noted. But even worse is a theme with no pudding. Or a theme giving rise to or imposed upon a pudding that doesn't fit. For instance an "Operation Shock and Awe" that provokes prolonged defiance.

"No ideas but in things," said William Carlos Williams. No theme but
in pudding.

➤ *think*

You'd think this word would have arisen rationally, but according to
Chambers it derives from two different Old English words, *thencan*,
meaning "conceive in the mind . . . , probably originally meaning 'cause
to appear to oneself,'" and *thyncan*, meaning "it seems or it appears"
(which survived for a while in the expression *methinks*, "it seems to
me")—which two words "became thoroughly confused in early modern
English, which has led to the complete submersion of the form *think*, to
seem, to appear." Conceivably, then, when we think of ourselves as thinking, we are suppressing an old *inkling* that it only seems to us that we are.

➤ *though*

"Barry Bonds tweaked his left side during last weekend's series in New
York, though the San Francisco slugger initially tried to play through it."
Aside from the awkward insertion of who Bonds is, and the implication
that he grabbed his own side the way someone might grab a naughty boy's
ear, and the too-vague *it*, this sentence suffers from a slapdash use of
though. There's something wrong with the time: "Though he initially tried
to play through it, he tweaked his left side." That's different from an example in OAD: "Her first name was Rose, though no one called her that,"
which switches around well enough: "Though no one called her that, her
first name was Rose."
    See **conjunction dysfunction**.

➤ *through*

If it makes you feel weird to pay close attention to what goes on in your
mouth, or if you feel that paying such attention is as ill-advised as watching your feet when you dance, then skip this. To me, it's a prime illustra-
tion of oral-verbal **kinesthesia**.
    What I want you to do is this: Observe your oral activity as you pro-

nounce *through*. Your tongue starts at the front of your mouth and, with a hint of aspiration (see *H*) to glide on, it travels smoothly straight back . . . through. And then that little *h*-hint of breath, released, floats back forward and out in a sound of gratification, *ooh*, as your lips purse slightly in a wisp of *w*. (The *w* that is literally there in *throw*.) Compare *thwart*, in which a more forceful push-to-the-front *w* breaks the flow.

Compare the fitting flow-through (fittingly less open-ended than in *through*) in *thrill*, *thread*, *throat*, *thrum*, *thrust*.

Now, *throttle*: you've got your *through* thing going until *-ot-* (see *T*), as in *glottal*, stops it and the frequentative *-le* indicates prolongation.

See **sonicky**.

➤ *thusly*

No, please. There should be no such word. *Thus* suffices in any case. *Thusly* "appears to have first been used by humorists, who may have been echoing the speech of poorly educated people striving to sound stylish," says AHD. So why don't we all go around with fake arrows through our heads? Why don't we all carry rubber chickens? I believe we may say categorically that words first used by humorists are to be avoided, especially by other humorists, but also by everyone else. Rare exceptions: **blurb**; ***truthiness***.

➤ *Times, The New York*

When you consider how much there is in it every day that had to be dug up and written and edited, *The Times* is a paragon of legibility. Here is a juicy bit from a review by Manohla Dargis of Iraq-war documentaries: "There are soldier stories, lyrical meditations and wonky exegeses, propagandistic screeds, gonzo entertainments and stirring testimonials."

Wonky exegeses! Granted, there's a touch of ambiguity there, inasmuch as *wonky* primarily means "unsteady, wobbly, not sitting flat," but in context it clearly means "of a wonk," and the pure **sonicky**-ness of *wonky* draws out the vaguer sonicky undertones in the abstract Greek *exegeses*—in the plural, do I not detect a soupçon of "cheesy"?

Oh, man, I'm beginning to sound like a wine taster. Let me just say this:

Many years ago I overheard a man from out of town asking a New York news vendor how much the Sunday *Times* was. Told that it was fifty cents (this was, as I say, many years ago), the man said, "That better be some paper." It is.

And I mean *paper*. With ink on it. (See **brick-and-mortar**.) I love newspapers, even some bad ones, and this one is the best. The first time I heard someone say, "I read it on *The Times*," *on* instead of *in*, I felt a chill. Yes, I have seen the wind catch a copy of this paper and scatter its pages ever farther and wider along a relatively unspoiled beach, with first a party of three and then more and more strangers in inadequate pursuit, and seagulls wheeling overhead in consternation. I have heard people of a younger generation snort, with unfeigned disbelief, at the preposterousness of fumbling through all those big floppy sheets in search of information. Those snorts astonished me at first. Now I take their point. I take the seagulls'.

But it's not all there online. No, it isn't. I'm telling you, sometimes the last couple of paragraphs with odd details that I remember but want to remind myself of—when I go back online, they're gone. There must be less room online, somehow. And the serendipity potential is a lot lower: unless you're looking for something, good luck on finding it. And how does a household pass around the different sections?

➤ titles

They can be misleading, offering more than the work in question delivers. For instance, the 1941 movie *I Wake Up Screaming*. Anything with Laird Cregar in it, you might think, would be bound to live up to that title, but the director's name, H. Bruce Humberstone, seems hardly suitable for this sort of thing. We see a lot of Betty Grable's legs, but then there is her love interest, Victor Mature. And in the entire film *nobody wakes up screaming*. My disappointment in this film moved me to write a perfect poem—that is, I would not change one word of it—which Pauline Kael quoted in *The New Yorker*, apropos another flat thriller, *Sleeping with the Enemy*:

ON RENTING *I Wake Up Screaming*, FOR THE TITLE, AND
BEING LET DOWN, BY THE MOVIE

Blondes who don't go far enough,
Film that isn't noir enough.

➤ tmesis

Inserting a word (or a nonsense syllable) into another word for intensify-
ing effect, as in *fanfuckintastic, absobloominglutely, guaran-damn-tee*, Ben
Jonson's "how short soever," or Derrick Coleman's *whoopdee-damn-doo*.
From the Greek *tmésis*, cutting. It won't do. It's the only word in English
that begins *tm*, which is basically unpronounceable (tuh-me is as close as
we can come). **Ironically enough**, tmesis cries out to have something inserted in it. If only an apostrophe: *t'mesis*. Better, a vowel or two: *tamesis,
toomesis*. Or how about *tweenamesis*? It's a formal term of rhetoric for a
sportive conversational ploy: Would you give a clunky Greek name to the
electric glide, syncopation, sprung **rhythm**, or the pick and roll? We need
another name for it. Wraparound word?

On the other hand, sticking *f*-word-*in'* into the middle of things to intensify them gets old. Like putting *totally* or *truly* in front of *awesome* or
beautiful. Thank goodness *awefuckinsome, awetrulysome*, or *aweto-
tallysome* doesn't click. Nor do *fantrulytastic, fantotallytastic, beautitruli-
ful, awebeautifulsome*.

Maybe *jumpin* would be better. Fanjumpintastic. From Lead Belly's
"jumping Judy," who "brought jumping to the whole wide world."

Arthur Quinn's *Figures of Speech* comes from a different era than
Wikipedia: 1982. (See *different from/than*.) "In English," Quinn writes,
"only the compounds of 'ever' readily lend themselves to tmesis." He
quotes Milton: "Which way soever man refer to it." More elaborately and
beyond *ever* he quotes James Joyce's *Ulysses*:

> Want to be sure of his spelling. Proof fever. Martin Cunningham
> forgot to give us his spellingbee conundrum this morning. It is
> amusing to view the unpar one are alleled embarra two ars is it?
> double ess ment of a harassed pedlar . . .

OAD's examples of tmesis are colloquial: "a whole nother" and "any-
old-where."

AHD's ("where I go ever") and RHU's ("be thou ware") are literary and
archaic.

Wikipedia says coinages like *fanfuckintastic* are sometimes called "ex-
pletive infixations," but notes that a true *infix* is like the *izn* in raptalk's

shiznit. **Urbandictionary.com**'s most popular definition of *shiznit*, however, says it's not an insertion of *izn* into a four-letter word but a contraction of "That is the shit, isn't it?"

Wikipedia also says tmesis is sometimes called *tumbarumba*, because of frequent use of tmesis (*bloody* and *bleeding*) in Australia, where there is a town called Tumbarumba, about which there is a poem, "Tumbabloodyrumba."

Macmillan English Dictionary Online: "im-bloody-possible," "how heinous e'er it be," *Richard II.*

Dictionary.com: "the most rigged-up-marole he'd ever seen."

Chris Farley character on *Saturday Night Live*: "la de freakin' da."

Ned Flanders of *The Simpsons*: "wel-diddly-elcome."

Julia Roberts's fellow-hooker friend, in *Pretty Woman*: "Cinde-fuckin-rella."

Then there is the carnival-worker double-talk, also spoken by old-school professional wrestlers, called variously kizzarny, ciazarn, and carnese, in which *eez* or *iz* or *e'iz* is inserted into syllables, turning *carny*, for instance, into *kizzarny*, *rube* into *re'izube*. Or, theoretically, *tmesis* into *tizmeezesis*. Comparable coding traditionally excluded squares from Harlem-hipster circles. The *izzle*-y hip-hop patter readily adopted by suburban-teen gangstas **perhaps** reflects an unsystematic slackening of that line of outsider in-lingo. According to the top Urbandictionary.com definition, *fo shizzle ma nizzle* is "a bastardization of 'fo sheezy mah neezy' which is a bastardization of 'for sure mah nigga' which is a bastardization of 'I concur with you wholeheartedly, my African-American brother.'" More amusing than philological, that analysis, and none of the examples are tmetic. Leave it to the recording industry to turn *tmesis* into *tmizzle*.

➤ *to my knowledge*

"To my knowledge, my nephew has never even tried to decapitate anybody before." Does this mean "as far as I know," or "I know"? Sounds like it's the first but trying to overlap into the second. "To the best of my knowledge" means the first. "To my certain knowledge" sounds more like the second. See **chicken**.

➤ Tory, Geoffroy

A sixteenth-century French book designer and scholar. In his book *Champfleury*, whose subtitle was *The Art and Science of the Proportion of the Attic or Ancient Roman Letters, According to the Human Body and Face*, he undertook to physicalize the alphabet in harmony with ideal human proportions. His was a noble Renaissance urge, but I don't know . . . The letter *I* corresponds to prudence and the right foot? (Egotism then could be considered as getting off on the right foot.) He gets a little creepy, as we have seen, about *Q*. And is it just coincidence that he assigns *T*, his initial, to "the virile member"?

➤ *to*'s and *of*'s

I have asked other writers whether they tangle themselves up in *to*'s and *of*'s. I have received blank looks in reply. So maybe it's just me. Maybe it may be attributed to my tendency to go to too-great lengths to take into account every aspect of every part of . . . Oh, I don't know. I can't do it when I'm trying.

➤ *traditional*

Hard to say what this means anymore. A glassy-tower monstrosity of a condo building going up in Manhattan bills itself as offering "Traditional Living Like Never Before."

➤ *tragedy*

When Vice President Dick Cheney accidentally (as was widely concluded, though some commentators pointed out that the resultant media flap both reflected badly upon the media's priorities and obscured several more important embarrassments to the Bush administration) "peppered" his friend, lawyer Harry Whittington, with birdshot, it was frequently referred to unironically (by Tim Russert and Paul Gigot on NBC's *Meet the Press*, February 19, 2006, for instance) as a "tragedy" (Russert) and "a human tragedy" (Gigot).

This even though Whittington was out of the hospital within a few days, and seemed to be apologetic about getting shot. More violence was done to the word *tragedy* than to Whittington, or even to the shooter's reputation for diligence and accuracy. Also resorting to the *t*-word were *The Salt Lake Tribune*, *Editor and Publisher*, *Waco Tribune Herald*, *Time*, *The Washington Post*, Ilana Mercer on *Free-Market News Network* ("private tragedy"), *The Conservative Voice*, *Newsday* ("simple tragedy"), *Milwaukee Journal Sentinel*, Senator Richard Lugar ("personal tragedy"), *The East Carolinian* ("terrible tragedy"), the Fort Wayne *Journal Gazette*, *Chicago Tribune*, and *Slate*.

"Brush with tragedy," "potential tragedy," as other publications called the accident: maybe. But even those references reflected how watered down the word has become. A story, to qualify as a tragedy, should be full of sad developments that lead to the downfall of the central character, a downfall to which his own strengths contribute. An event, to qualify as a tragedy, should involve a lot of death and destruction.

Trouble is, it's hard to think of a good word—sufficiently but not overly sympathetic and serious—for an accident causing substantial but not irrevocable dismay.

Contretemps, which AHD defines as "an unforeseen event that disrupts the normal course of things; an inopportune occurrence," is perhaps strong enough to cover the hunting accident in question, especially in light of the term's origin, acccording to OAD: "late 17th cent. (originally as a fencing term, denoting a thrust made at an inopportune moment)." But *contretemps* today usually crops up in a comic context—sitcom characters find themselves in contretemps. Furthermore, the word derives shamelessly from French. "The shooting was a personal contretemps for the vice president" would have struck many people as flip.

Disaster, from the Italian for "ill-starred event," suggests a collapse of grand proportions. In the media, people are more likely to be "flirting with" disaster or "on the brink" of it, than in the "full-scale" experience of it, as in the case of Hurricane Katrina.

Mishap and *misadventure* sound sort of jaunty.

Catastrophe and *cataclysm*, from the Greek, for "downturn" and "deluge," respectively, are too heavy.

Calamity, from the Latin for "calamity," is too strong on the one hand and perhaps tinged with folkloric amusement because of Calamity Jane.

How about "hunting accident, in which Mr. Cheney's friend narrowly escaped serious injury and which undoubtedly caused Mr. Cheney himself considerable distress." It's great to be able to pin an event down with one word, but often you can't—in which case, trying to dragoon a word into service, in order to convey an amorphous blob of sentiment and gravity, does the word a disservice.

➤ *transparent*

If we say we see through an institution or a process, we may mean it has enabled us to see things, or we may mean that we have perceived it to be a scam. We may also see someone through a transition of some kind, meaning that we have been attentive to that person throughout the passage. If we could somehow bear all those definitions in mind more or less at once, or overlaid, we would perhaps have an organic (multigrain) approach to reading and writing.

In politics, we lately believe (however credulously) that all democratic institutions and processes should be *transparent*. Does this apply to reading and writing? Let us look at two presumably pertinent definitions, from RHU:

6. open; frank; candid: *the man's transparent earnestness*.

7. *Computers*. (of a process or software) operating in such a way as to not be perceived by users.

I am not sure those two senses of the word are compatible. See **honest broker**; **interested**; **see through**; **truth**; **unreliable narrator**.

Someday, **of course**, a trans-parent may be a father who becomes a mother or vice versa.

➤ transposition game

Rearranging the letters in one word of an existing title or well-known phrase. Aldous Huxley's *The Doors of Perception* becomes *The Odors of Perception*. The Continental Army becomes the continental Mary. I'm told that Burt Bernstein, then a writer at *The New Yorker*, learned of this game and found himself to be good at it. He hastened to his brother Leonard, who had always been better at everything than Burt, but now, finally, maybe . . . Burt explained the game. Leonard looked up from whatever major thing he was doing and said: "Icy fingers up and down my penis."

➢ *trip off the tongue*

In this expression and in "trip the light fantastic," *trip* (from the Old French *tripper*, to stamp the foot) means "to step nimbly." Hamlet's instruction to the players to speak his lines "trippingly on the tongue" assumes a spring in *trip*'s step.

But that time-honored sense of *trip* is endangered, I'll bet, because *trip* also means "to stumble," and the *p* at the end suggests a foot catching on something. As illustrations of *trip* in its graceful or fluid sense, OAD offers "they tripped up the terrace steps" and "the guest list tripped from her lips," each of which might just as well suggest missteps and stammering.

It's the *-ingly* in Hamlet's phrase that makes it jiggy. "Trip on the tongue" is halting. "Trip from the tongue" flows better, because our lips move from *p* to *f* expeditiously.

Syllables that start with *p* are frequently groovy to the vocal apparatus. My mother loved to say "Popocatépetl," the name of a Mexican volcano, and "Pick him up and pat him on the popo." And something we frequently heard in a radio commercial for an athlete's foot remedy. "Pitty-ros-poromo Valley" is what it sounded like. Many years later I happened upon the actual name of the fungus in question: *Pityrosporum ovale*. It took me back to my boyhood around the house. Trippy terms such as that one helped my mother get through the day.

➢ *truly*

The only place for this word is where it appears, twice ("and it's then / and only then / we find out who we truly are / and what we are truly made of"), in what Paris Hilton, unclean socialite, read aloud on the Larry King show as an example of the poetry she wrote in jail, only it turns out to have been sent to her in jail by a sympathetic fan who, if truth be known, wrote it.

➤ *truth*

RHU takes this back to the Old Norse *tryggth*, faith. Faith in what, is the question. Different people hold different truths to be self-evident. Which is not to say that either the truths or the holders thereof are straightforward, as to presentation.

A man who has achieved great wealth and power is not satisfied. He vows to discover the answer to the ultimate question: What is truth? He will not be satisfied, he tells everyone he knows, until he finds out what is truth and returns to spread the word. Year after year he travels, all over the world, never finding an answer, until at last he clambers up a crag in a distant Himalayan fastness where, in a dark, smoky cave, he finds an old hag stirring a pot from which arises a terrible stench. She is filthy, scrawny, twisted, toothless, dressed only in rags. Her face is covered with warts and sores. And yet, somehow, he knows that she knows the answer.

He asks her, "What is truth?"

She cackles. She looks him in the eye. He shudders. She cackles again, and spits in the pot, and looks up at him again, and says, "Hee-hee-heeee. It's meeeee."

"Oh, no," says the man. "After all these years of searching! How can I go back and tell people this?"

Again with the cackle, and her eyes flash. "Tell 'em I'm pretty," she says.

On the other hand, AHD cites the **PIE** root *deru-*, to be firm, solid, steadfast, whence not only *truth* but also *tree*, *trust*, and *betroth*.

➤ *truthiness*

A week after Stephen Colbert began his own TV show, he had already coined a **meme**. Undoubtedly it will be in the next *Bartlett's Quotations*. Well, good for Stephen (see **drawl**). Did you see the episode of Larry David's show in which Richard Lewis was trying to get credit in Bartlett's for coining the phrase "the mother of all . . . ," and he found out Larry was acquainted with the editor, and of course Larry screwed everything up? I forget the details, but something to do with the extraordinary size of the editor's young son's penis. The mother of all son-johnsons.

➤ tump

When the third edition of AHD came out, back in the nineties, I wrote a
heartfelt column for *Men's Journal*:

> Dave Barry was turned into a sitcom, so as long as there is a *Nick at
> Nite* . . . Garrison Keillor is in *Bartlett's Quotations*, the son of a bitch.
> All I ask is to be in a dictionary.
>
> There are other settings in which you have the glamor, the latent
> radiance, of various exemplars mixing casually out of their elements:
> a summit conference, an all-star game, or one of those comic books
> in which all the heroes join forces to stamp out some new evil. Only
> in a dictionary does the company range across centuries, scales and
> genera. A *tank* and a *tankard* hang with *Tanzania*, a *tapeworm* and a
> *tapir*. *Oil well*, *okapi* and *Georgia O'Keeffe* rub shoulders with *okra*. And
> all of them definitive. You could look them up.
>
> I don't ask to be defined (between *blotto* and *blouse*). I do feel that
> I am due to be cited. After years and years of using thousands of
> words, I feel entitled to go down as having provided a good example
> of at least one of them. Some years ago, while browsing in the third
> edition of Webster's Unabridged, I saw Roger Angell, who was then
> my editor at the *New Yorker*, cited for his usage of *spang*. "Spang in the
> middle of the theatre district."
>
> Hot damn, I thought. *Spang*. What a good one. At the time I was
> considering writing a baseball novel, in which the centerfielder
> would be named Cesar Spang. If I keep typing away, I told myself,
> some day I'll be in a dictionary, and I can set up a roadside stand with
> a big sign: "SEE THE CITED-IN-WEBSTER'S MAN! ONE DOLLAR!
> ALSO LIVE SNAKES MONKEYS ALLIGATORS VIDEO RENTALS
> SANDWICHES BAIT."
>
> Then Pauline Kael told me she had once used *dum-dum* to mean
> not an exploding bullet but a dumb person, and when her editor at
> the *New Yorker* questioned this usage she said let's check it out, so
> they went to a dictionary and sure enough, that meaning of *dum-dum*
> was given. The writer cited as using it in that way was Pauline.
>
> That is cool, I thought.

When the third edition of the *American Heritage Dictionary of the English Language* came out, I figured my time had come. I am in fact a member of that dictionary's usage panel. From time to time I receive a questionnaire on which I indicate whether it is acceptable to use *snuck* to mean *sneaked* (yes, sure), to refer to a woman as *suave* or a *lout* (I don't see why not, but it would seem odd), or to say "To *myself*, mountains are the beginning and end of nature" (no!). I love this stuff.

The *New York Times* called my dictionary "surely the most pleasurable dictionary ever published in this country, and one of the most useful." And I was part of it. True, my sense of myself as a maven was diminished by a story in the *Boston Globe* that said the dictionary "claims to be many things, but it does not claim to be authoritative. (Even the panel includes decidedly unauthoritative oddballs: actor Tony Randall and humorist Roy Blount Jr., to name two.)" Well, the *Globe* probably meant *unauthoritarian*. [See **Tupou IV, King Taufa'ahau**.]

On receiving—eat your heart out—a free copy of my dictionary in the mail, I plunged into it. Did you know that "the verb *carry*, which to Southerners means 'to transport (someone) in a motor vehicle . . . ,' is etymologically more precise in the Southern usage than anywhere else"? Hmm, I thought, I wonder . . . In one of my books I used the word *tump*, the copy editor asked whether I meant *dump*, and I told her no, I meant *tump*. And that was that. Could it be . . .

And there it was:

> The verb *tump*, used almost invariably with *over* in the intransitive sense "to fall over" and the transitive sense "to overturn," is in common use in the South . . . But another citation, taken from Gregory Jaynes . . . in . . . *Time*, indicates that *tump* may not be exclusively Southern: *"At the end he tumps over into his rice pudding, poisoned."*

I left a message on Jaynes's machine: "Go to a bookstore and look on page 1924 of the new *American Heritage Dictionary*. That's all I'm telling you."

Greg had got *tump*. Had in fact got credit for de-Southernizing the word. No doubt when the researchers noticed my *tump* they said yes, well, but of course he's Southern. Where do they think Greg is from? Memphis. But I was happy for Greg, the son of a bitch.

I looked up *scrooch*. I have used *scrooch* several times in writing, and you don't see it that often in, you know, writing.

Scrooch. "To hunch down, crouch," said the *American Heritage*. Well, not exactly. To scrooch is to compress oneself *in a direction*. You can scrooch down or you can scrooch over, as in "Nanette, scrooch over on the couch, Sugar, so Aunt Lotty can get situated." Once I paid a call on Flannery O'Connor, and she told of a conversation she had with a man who referred to a "scrooch owl."

"You mean a screech owl?" she asked him.

"No, a scrooch owl," he said. "That's one of those little owls that land on the same limb as another bird and then scrooch over, and scrooch over, and scrooch him all the way off the end and grab him."

Pauline Kael was in the hospital for a heart operation. By way of bucking her up, I informed her that she had been cited for *anomic*, *choirboy*, *funky*, *interiorize* and *unstoppable*. *Funky* brought some color to her cheeks, but otherwise, she said, she would prefer to be remembered for livelier words. "So-and-so got *trashy*," I said, mentioning another critic who once wrote an ill-informed (okay, semi-ill-informed) mixed review of my work so why should I give the son of a bitch any ink?

"I think I had *trashy* before him," she said.

By this time, I would have been happy with *interiorize*.

I was not turning up. What was I supposed to do, go through the entire goddamned dictionary page by page? That wouldn't be cool. Soon enough, no doubt, the phone would ring, and some friend would be telling me I had been cited for, I don't know, maybe for some high-dollar term that I couldn't even remember using. And I'd be able to chuckle and respond casually, "Oh, well, that's nice. It isn't *funky*, but it's . . ."

The phone didn't ring.

So here's what I have done, over the last few weeks. Not full-time, just a couple of hours a day, or so. I have *gone through the entire goddamned dictionary page by page*.

I was glad to see that Flannery O'Connor got *scoot*, as with a hose. Tallulah Bankhead got *slick* (*as a sonnet*, interesting). Louis Armstrong's *dig*, Margaret Mitchell's *tomorrow* and Richard Nixon's *stonewall* could hardly be faulted, and I was pleased, as a Georgian, that Jimmy Carter got *strength*. I envied Hunter Thompson for *booger*, Jimmy Breslin for *boozehound* and William Safire for *hoohah*, but I was willing to concede *snob* to Tom Wolfe, *something* to Virginia Woolf, *netherworld* to Malcolm X and *affect* to John Paul II. You know who is cited for use of the very word *define*? Gloria Vanderbilt. Okay. But I don't know about John Glenn, who, in spite of being the dullest person ever to campaign for a presidential nomination, is pictured and defined on page 770 as the first man to orbit the earth, and then *on the very next page* is cited as the first person to use, in writing, the word *glitch*. The son of a bitch.

And how about these people, all of whom I have worked or hung out with at some time or another:

Linda Ellerbee, in fact, got *hang out*. Garrison got *snuck*; also *combine*, *couple*, *octet*, *reek*, *soul* (*soul!*), *unalienable* and *unnameable*. Calvin Trillin got *collegial* and *factionalize*. Russell Baker got *clean* (*someone's*) *clock* and *not half*. Bobbie Ann Mason got *hoot* and *frag*. Stephen King got *feel*. Lloyd Rose, *Philistine*. Gary Fisketjon, *rip off*. Pat Conroy, *rootedness*. Tom Boswell, *backstab*. Curtis Wilkie, *spring* and *distinctive*. Jerry Footlick, *fountainhead*. Pete Axthelm, *troll*. Jane Gross, *dervish*. I was somewhat consoled to see that Nicholas Lemann's name was misspelled in his citation for *ticket*, but for *fluid* he was spelled correctly. Frank Deford got *shaft* (the verb).

I got nothing. Not the word *nothing*, Bosley Crowther got that. I got nothing as in not anything (Anne Tyler got *anything*, as well as *chomp*). Unless I scanned right over my name, which is unlikely, I am not cited in my dictionary for anything at all.

There are other bones I might pick with my dictionary. It doesn't seem to realize that *dickens*, as in *what in the dickens*, is a euphemism for *devil*, and it doesn't mention that a child can be called a little dickens. I disagree (as Louis Armstrong would have) that *all right* "is usually pronounced as if it were a single word" and therefore probably should have evolved into one, like *already* and *altogether*. (*Already* and *altogether* are different from *alright* in that they are adverbs— sometimes they are pronounced as two words, and when they are they are spelled that way: "Are you all ready? Okay, now, all together." All right? All *right*.) I have never seen the University of Mississippi referred to as *Old Miss* (see the definition of *Oxford*): it's *Ole Miss*.

Furthermore, whoever wrote the "word history" note for *limerick* says "Let us sum up by saying . . ." and then says one of the worst limericks I have ever read. It is a *rotten* limerick. I do not deign to quote it, for it is a *miserable* limerick. It is such a sloppy, misshapen limerick as to be no limerick at all. It doesn't scan worth shucks, it resorts to lame old-fashioned inversion ("Or from poets it came," indeed!), it only *rhymes* once. I hereby challenge whoever wrote that sorry-ass immetrical bit of scarcely even limerick-resembling twaddle to step forward and dispute the plain fact that I—just to take a random example—could write a better limerick than that in nine seconds, drunk.

Don't try to pretend that you're not reading this, either, Mr. or Ms. "Let us sum up." You are bound to have read some words I've used right. You just don't want to admit it, you drivelly, unfunny, rhyme-poor, rhythm-impaired, anonymous, slack-lined, unauthoritative . . .

Hey. No one is cited for *son of a bitch*.

In the most recent edition of AHD, it's *Ole Miss*; *dickens* is acknowledged to be "alteration of DEVIL"; there is no reference to the as-if-a-single-word pronunciation of *all right*; that execrable limerick is gone. Also Greg is no longer cited for *tump*. No one is. "Probably akin to TUMBLE," says AHD. A **portmanteau** of *tip* and *dump*, if you ask me. But what do I know.

➤ Tupou IV, King Taufa'ahau

In 1967, Taufa'ahau Monumatango became King Taufa'ahau Tupou (pro- nounced taw-fah-ah-*how*-too-po), the Fourth, of Tonga. From his *New York Times* obituary in 2006: "As king he commissioned the first diction- ary and grammar of Tongan, a Polynesian language, while promoting changes in written Tongan, notably to have the letter *b* replaced with *p* and the symbol *g* with *ng*."

Questions:

- Before his changes took effect, was he *Kig* Taufa'ahau Tu*bou*? If so, that explains the *ng* for *n* switch, but how about the *p* for *b*? Maybe he just didn't want to have the same name as I, II, and III. But I note that the king once told visiting reporters, according to *The Times*, "I'm a bit of a poo-bah, you know."

- If *p* became *b*, did *b* then become *p*? "I'm a pit of a boo-pah"? Bropaply. But I am just being silly, because *poo-bah* and **probably** are not Tongan words. (Poo-Bah is a Gilbert and Sullivan character, and *probably* is from the Latin meaning "likely to hold up if probed.")

Let's get to the real question: If you had the power to change any letters in the English language, which ones would you? Get rid of *W*? That's just an easy political joke, and a moot point. How about replacing *d* with *t*? (Which is produced by the same tongue maneuver but without the laryngeal contribution.) Consider how many *downer* words start with *d*:

Dread, dire, dank, drunk, debt, dithery, disgusting, disease, drag, duty, dumps, desperate, drizzle, dreary, dingy, drain, drastic, deaf, damp, dastardly, damned, dense, dim, depressed, down, done, dead, dud . . .

Dip would ascend to *tip*, *doubt* would become (losing the silent *b*) *tout*, *drippy* would be *trippy*.

Ah, but we need those downer words. And how about *dad*? Yes, it's close to *dead* (and in fact I often hear young people these days pronouncing the *eh* sound so that it's closer to the short *a* in *dad*), but it also probably derives from a child's first syllables, *dada*.

➤ TV, on being on

Not only viewers, but also people who appear (what should we call them—apparents?) on TV should beware of confusing it with reality. Remember William Ginsburg, Monica Lewinsky's harrumphing lawyer and old family friend, who vowed to protect her interests but wound up going down in history for (*a*) popping up on all three major network morning talk shows—"a full Ginsburg," it was called—in one day, (*b*) reminiscing about smooching Monica's plump thighs when she was a baby, and (*c*) informing the world that as a result of his video-ubiquity, Barbara Walters "has become an instant companion and friend" and that Sam Donaldson and Cokie Roberts—Sam, "a natural force of nature," and Cokie, "attractive in every way"—"could be my friends if I wasn't in this whirl." Ginsburg also let on that he'd had "a shouting match" with Peter Jennings. "A number of people have said that based on my appearances on TV, I should become a TV commentator. And I have laughed. That is not my goal. But I would be happy to take over for Peter Jennings, if that opening ever occurs."

Then, abruptly, the box closed to Ginsburg. Maybe he hangs out with Barbara and the other guys, but . . . probably not. Someday, surely, he will produce a memoir entitled *That Sixteenth Minute Is a Bitch: Getting Over Being "Over."* Asked if he will be doing media appearances to promote the book, he will say, "I *could care less.*"

I *hear that*. For in the late eighties and early nineties, I, myself, was sort of TV-famous, which is the only kind of famous that counts. TV talk shows would have me on sometimes even when I didn't have a new book out. I think it was 1989 when the CBS Morning News—which was visiting some distinguished or at least distinguishable person every Friday in his or her home—sent eleven people, several trucks, and an enormous satellite-dish vehicle to my modest country house in the tiny village of Mill River, Massachusetts, for a day and a half, to do twelve minutes of visit.

They ran a cable down to the brook behind the house, to mike the burble. They were all amiable enough, but they walked through the house saying:

"I'm stable now on battery."

"What color are you, black?"

"It's breaking up."

Evening of the setup day, I took the whole crew over to a small restaurant then operating in Mill River. As the twelve of us—*media* standing out all over the rest of them—came bursting into the place, a smallish, somewhat bug-eyed elderly man, at a table with a considerably younger woman, took one look, hunched down, waited for us to get past his table, and bolted from the place.

The TV people didn't recognize him, and I didn't tell them who he was. I only tell this now because he has passed away. It was the indubitably distinguished author Saul Bellow, dining with a temporarily local lady of my acquaintance whom I knew to be an old girlfriend of his. A character like her appears in one of his novels. He must have thought the TV people had tracked him down—what else would bring them to this somnolent backwater? It was my only encounter, if it could be called that, with Bellow, a great writer undoubtedly, and I would not have disturbed his privacy on purpose for the world, even though I have found his work, great as it is, dislikable.

Henderson the Rain King put me off. By way of introducing himself, Henderson as first-person narrator cites "my behavior in the hospital when I broke my leg. I spent all my time in the children's wards, entertaining and cheering the kids. On my crutches I hopped around the entire place in a hospital gown; I couldn't be bothered to tie the tapes and was open behind, and the old nurses ran after me to cover me, but I wouldn't hold still." Any grown man who runs around showing his ass in a children's ward, and realizes it, and tells it on himself as if it's appealing, is an exhibitionist. If the author is aware of that, then fine, let's roll with it. But I couldn't help feeling that the author was taken with this guy. None of which means that Bellow deserved to be blindsided in Mill River by some kind of proto reality show, *Get the Author* or something. As if a mass audience would care enough about authors anymore—but come to think of it, it's people like Henderson that TV reality shows thrive on today.

"Let's face it," a cameraman I worked with on another project observed complacently after we had disrupted a household and then bustled out toward the next location without so much as a fare-thee-well, "a TV crew is a train wreck."

That night I had a hard time making my way to the bedroom through thickets of cameras affixed to the floors of my kitchen, living room, and upstairs hall. Good thing Christabel isn't here, I thought. She had given up her TV news job in London to come live with me in that house, and in return I had turned down a chance to play a Southern writer in the TV series *Designing Women* because it would have meant being in Los Angeles the week of Christabel's American advent. So the role went to Gerald McRaney, who as a result married Delta Burke, one of the stars. Christabel couldn't find television work in the U.S. We had only recently broken up when the CBS crew came to visit.

The next morning I had to show them how to work my coffee grinder. But one of them taught me a useful term: when you bang on a piece of equipment to make it start working, that's called "percussive maintenance." The local phone people wouldn't install the extra lines CBS felt entitled to for these visits, and cell phones wouldn't—still won't—work in Mill River, so the entire broadcast came through my home phone number, and my ear.

I was relaying messages I did not understand ("We have lost gemlock") back and forth between New York and the truck. During breaks from these technical proceedings, I was answering Kathleen Sullivan's interview questions. She was in a studio in New York. The interview was taped. Kathleen and I got on well, I thought. It came off as a relaxed strolling chat of an interview, except when I hit my head on the ceiling, where the eave comes down by the upstairs window on the brook side, on camera. Indeed I had the feeling that Kathleen and I were vaguely attracted to each other, but of course I couldn't see her as we chatted, and we were never to meet in the flesh.

After the segment aired, a woman who runs an inn in Vermont called. I don't know how she got my number, because the words Mill River were not televised, at my request. She left a message on the answering machine, asking exactly what shade of blue my kitchen was, because it looked like exactly what she needed. That was the only response I got from the general public, or even from my neighbors.

I had said on the air that the kitchen was the same color as Monet's kitchen, because that's what the man who sold me the house told me. After the interview, Kathleen informed me in my ear that she had been to Monet's house and she didn't recall his having a kitchen. I was taken aback by this. Why wouldn't Monet have a kitchen? Artists eat. I had gone so far during the interview as to claim that Monet, himself, had painted my kitchen. I should have known that someone would get picky. The woman who called may actually have been Monet's lawyer, trying to trap me into an actionable statement.

Now, nearly twenty years later, I'm married, **of course**, to an artist. Thank goodness. She says the blue in the kitchen isn't the same color of anything in Monet's house. We're having it, the kitchen, redone.

➤ TV, being on, p.s.

I don't want to leave the impression that TV people are necessarily insensitive. Once I did an essay-to-camera about U.S. politics for BBC-TV. For
part of it, I strolled past the Washington Monument, explaining America
to the mother country. A tiny microphone was concealed on my person.
The camera crew was way over on the other side of the street, a good fifty
yards away. On the screen eventually back in Britain it would be clear that
I was speaking to the viewer, but to passersby there in Washington I appeared to be talking to myself—or else to them, the passersby. "Excuse
me?" someone would say, and we would have to start over. Before one take
I cleared my throat so loudly that a kind old lady asked me if I was all right.

"I'm on television," I explained. She looked at me sadly.

I didn't want her to think I was insane, or that I was putting her on.
"See," I confided, "I'm a writer, I don't usually do this kind of—this is the
dumbest thing!" I cut my eyes over toward the TV people, decent hard-
working folks. Clearly they had heard what I said, through our micro-
phonic connection, and their feelings were hurt.

u · U · u

The sound that comes from deepest down—the grunt vowel, the dull thud
vowel, the vowel we may utter when punched in the stomach—is the
flat *u*-sound: *uh*. It's not quite there when we think, saying to ourselves,
Hmmmmm. Nor is it in the wordless laryngeal music we make while keeping our lips together, but it is in the word *hum*. When we can't come up with
a word, we temporize by grunting *uh* or *um*. And when we say something
obvious, people say: *Duh*. Yes is *unh-hunh*, no, *unh-unh*. (Or, if you eschew
nasal seasoning, *uh-huh* and *uh-uh*.) Come again is *hunh?* (Or *huh?*)

And it's right in the middle of *love*.

➤ U.K./U.S.

To Yanks, *pissed* means "angry." To Brits, it means "drunk." (Neither is an
excuse for anything anymore.) It suits the U.S. usage mostly because of
the hiss in the sound. The U.K. usage may hint of incontinence.

"Pussy has gone to the loo in the baaath" (U.K.) means "The cat has
pooped in the tub" (U.S.).

To go over a bomb to Brits means "to have a great success"; *to bomb* to
Americans means "to flop."

Too many *to*'s in that last sentence. See **to's and of's**.

I'll tell you a British term I like: *bum*. Meaning "bottom." It's a good
round word for it. Whether it will ever fit into American lingo is another
matter. Would make it confusing to say, "I've got a bum knee."

Both Brits and Southerners (I resist the temptation to make that Brits
and Grits) use the good crackly verb *reckon* to mean "think or assume,"
but my feeling is that Southerners use it more casually or semi-
resignedly—"Well, I reck'n I better get up from here and wash these

dishes"—and Brits more assertively: "I reckon a pint of bitter should do for any thirst."

➤ unacceptable

Bit of a bluff, surely. (Unless you're **Tupou IV, King Taufa'ahau** and you're in Tonga.) You say it when what you want to say is "If you do that one more time I swear to God I will . . ." Most things branded "unacceptable," by one would-be authority or another, get repeated, however disastrously, until the authority shifts its ground.

Donald Rumsfeld, when he was U.S. secretary of defense, to Congress, after Senator Hillary Clinton told him she didn't want to hear any more "rosy scenarios" regarding Iraq:

"My goodness. First of all, it's true, there is sectarian conflict in Iraq and there is a loss of life. And it's an unfortunate and tragic thing that's taking place. And it is true that there are people who are attempting to prevent that government from being successful. And they are the people who are blowing up buildings and killing innocent men, women and children and taking the heads off people on television. And the idea of their prevailing is unacceptable."

People in power tend to say something is unacceptable by way of setting that something up as (*a*) something that they have the power to accept or not, and (*b*) as something worse than what they are in fact willy-nilly accepting, or perpetuating, which is what needs to be addressed.

➤ unbeknownst

This must be the most archaic-seeming English word still commonly used and readily understood. *Beknown* has been obsolete for centuries, but this oldfangled extension from both ends of it (OED says the provenance of the *-st* is "unclear") is still fully functional, ***probably*** more so than its less elaborate synonym, *unbeknown*. Its comically fusty ring may have contributed to its longevity. "Unbeknownst to any but his most intimate friends, Edwin Luft has collected more than four thousand ceramic rabbits."

Actually, come to think of it, *unbeknown* (unbeknownst to WIII, judging from its joint definition of the two words) isn't interchangeable with *unbe-*

knownst, because *unbeknown* is an adjective ("Owing to circumstances un-beknown to any but his most intimate friends, Edwin Luft seldom leaves his trailer home"), whereas *unbeknownst* is a clause-modifying adverb, like *fortunately*. I wonder if you could get away with *beknownst*: "As must be beknownst to all but his most intimate friends, Edwin Luft is no one you want to spend an evening with." I was going to say that you'd think *unbe-knownst* would at least have lost its *k* by now, like *renowned*, till I looked up *renowned* and found that it never had a *k*: the *nown* part comes from the Latin *nomer*, to name. As you may know, *know* comes from the Old English *cnawan*, from the root *gno-*, whence also *can*, *cunning*, *notify*, *uncouth*, *cog-nizant*, *normal*, and **prothonotary**.

That *-st* is a curio in itself. It's not the same as the *-st* in *amongst* or *amidst* or the still-common-in-Britain *whilst*, nor as the *-st* in *first*, because—

But now I'm sounding like Edwin Luft on the various ways of doing a ceramic cottontail. If you're interested, check out all those *-st*'s in WIII. Because damn it, it *is* interesting. That *-st* may be **unique**.

An *amidist*, by the way, is a member of the Buddhist cult of Amitabha, which promises that the faithful will be reborn in paradise.

See **hopefully**.

➤ *understand*

Less arrogant than other languages' words that mean or have meant the same: the German *verstehen*, literally to stand in front of or on top of, and the Greek *epi-stasthai*, literally to stand on top of or over. But not as hum-ble as it might look: the prefix comes from a sense of *under* close to Ger-man *unter*, meaning not "beneath" but "between or among," as in "under these circumstances." Still, when someone says, convincingly, "I under-stand your predicament," it's nice to sense that in spirit he or she is under it with you, instead of on top of it looking down.

➤ *uneven*

A word of which hedgy reviewers are fond. Would you want to read a book that was even?

➤ *unique*

I have to be firm on this: *unique* is not to be modified. Adding **very** or **absolutely** is like putting a propeller on a rabbit to make him hop better. It won't work, and he won't be a rabbit anymore.

Would you say "very one-of-a-kind"? "Very sui generis"? (Maybe archly, "He's very 'one-of-a-kind,' don't you know.") Eighty percent of the AHD Usage Panel disagrees with AHD's laissez-faire Usage Note, which points out that *unique* is frequently used to mean *extraordinary* in "the language of advertising." Well, yes. People like to toss *unique* into a sentence because the perky *eek*, as in *chic*, adds phonic zing. But the word has *meaning*.

Heard on public radio: "Next we're going to look at different unique kinds of dessert." A unique *kind*? I guess. But *different* is heavily redundant.

➤ unreliable narrator

To some extent, **of course**, every narrator (from Latin *gnarus*, knowing) is. It is up to the reader to take this into account, as he or she will. And yet each of them, narrator and reader, must in some sense genuinely strive to be an **honest broker**.

> But once I start confessing the why-and-wherefore of my *behavior* (as one is expected to do in a book), I become so entertained by the personal drama of it all that everything I put down has a wonderful *ring* of truth; I feel myself growing from a particular person into a universal *design*—much as a musician might set out persistently to play the recorder and find himself always in the organ-loft. It is the *notes* that get the better of me: they have such a heavenly *sound* that I cannot think them false.
>
> —*Cards of Identity*, Nigel Dennis

➤ *unscribable*

Descriptive of something whose effect cannot be captured in writing. For instance, this joke:

Woman is auditioning. She sings, "You say potato, and I say potato. You say tomato and I say tomato. Potato, potato, tomato, tomato—let's call the whole thing off."

"O . . . kay. That will do, Ms. Goldstein."

"Gold*stein*!"

➤ *unto*

"Do unto others as you would have them do unto you" is a nice sentiment but an unreliable rule. People don't necessarily want or need to be done unto as you would have them do unto you. They want to be done unto as they want to be done unto. At least they think they do. At any rate it is no good saying, "At a time like this I would want to be left alone with my thoughts, so I left her alone with her thoughts, so what's the problem?," when in fact any fool could tell just from looking at her that she is exuding, without putting into so many words, the four words that make his blood run cold: "We need to talk."

It is too bad, though, that the word *unto* is archaic. If something is done *to* you, you are a victim, or at any rate an object. If something is done *for* you, you're obligated. *Unto* you sounds like a little bit of both. And in questions of injury (or perceived injury), it might soften, a bit, the taint of intentionality without avoiding the question.

"Why would you do that to me?"

"I didn't do it *to* you, I just . . ."

"Well, you did it *unto* me." There's an element there of *as far as I'm concerned. Unto* derives from *until*, which means *up to.* The *un-* in this case is an intensifier, as in *unloose*, not a negator, as in *unhinge*, and indeed it often pumps matters up a bit ("I say unto you"), but it's also iambic for rhythm's sake, and can be quite gentle in context: "Inasmuch as ye have done it unto one of the least of these, my brethren, ye have done it unto me." See **Goody Two-Shoes**.

➤ *upon*

My sister, Susan, teaching English to adults as a literacy volunteer, e-mailed me as follows:

One of our spelling words tonight was *upon*. Angelo, a very tattooed Hispanic youth who reads and spells pretty well, missed it because he said he never heard of that word before but he fishes a lot so he thought I said "a pond." Hard to argue with that reasoning.

Can you in fact think of good examples for the word *upon* for this audience other than "Once upon a time" which is in fact a bad example because they never heard the fairy tales before. Is *upon* archaic?

That got me thinking. If Angelo never heard fairy tales, he probably never heard *Showboat* ("Life upon the wicked stage ain't ever what a girl sup . . . *po*-ses") or a Shakespeare sonnet:

> If this be error and upon me proved,
> I never writ, nor no man ever loved.

(That sonnet snapper, incidentally, has always struck me as less than dispositive. We're expected to take the Will for the deed.)

When you get down to it, or *down on* it, *upon* is a literary word and seldom used anymore. Well, there's "The mob fell upon him and beat him silly," where "fell on" doesn't work. But that's dated too. People would generally say "jumped him" or something.

"Leapt upon the stage." I wonder if people say *leapt* much anymore. More likely would be "Jumped up on the stage." *Upon* may sound uppish or uppity. "'Pon my word!" "Happened upon a pod of hippopotami."

You do see "Burst upon the scene." "Summer—and deer ticks—will soon be upon us."

Upon has more bounce to it, rhythmically and sonically, than *on*. I wonder whether it has a future in rap. Hip-hoppers got to like plosives. See **P**.

➤ Urbandictionary.com

This valuable website specializes in cutting-edge slang terms that you aren't likely to find defined in print. Anybody in the world can submit an entry, and if it isn't rejected by the latitudinarian editors (you can volunteer to be one of those), it will appear on the site. There, anybody can vote for or against it by clicking on the appropriate thumb icon, up or down, and it will be ranked according to its approval/disapproval index to date. The myriad entries are alphabetical and browsable in various ways, so if you hear your children use a term that they picked up somewhere (in the gutter, say, or on Urbandictionary.com), you should be able to find it. Whether you will have the nerve, then, to discuss it with them is another matter. Many of the sexual practices defined on Urbandictionary.com are what I would latitudinarily call nasty. I like to think they are also largely notional on the part of young male definers. The definitions of political terms and figures are often scurrilous, but rationality tends to rise in the ratings—more so maybe than in actual political campaigns. The last time I looked both *liberal* and *conservative* were defined sensibly, if defensively, atop lots of stupid flaming. The entry on *America* is interesting in this regard.

My definition of *alligator arm*, by the way, has long reigned as number one.

➤ *Utopian*

The eponymous island of Sir Thomas More's *Utopia*, from the Greek *eu topos* (place where all is well) undercut with *ou topos* (no place), gave rise to this adjective for imagined ideal states. Plato's *Republic* was a Utopian book **avant la lettre**. Many Utopian schemes, novels, and short-lived communities have been floated over the years. (See **wh-** with regard to Samuel Butler's *Erewhon*.) Dystopian novels, such as *1984* and *A Clockwork Orange*, which conjure up the opposites of Utopias, tend to be more vivid, and Utopian visions work better as criticism of established orders than as practical models for earthly paradise. See Karl Marx on capitalism and communism, respectively.

More's Utopia abolished private property—no skin off the nose of a man with access to ecclesiastical property. It also practiced religious tolerance. When More came to ecclesiastical power in England, he persecuted heretics, and eventually he was hanged as one himself. His Utopia has at least two other bugs: slavery (only those who deserve to be enslaved or who volunteer to be) and "public lectures every morning before daybreak; at which none are obliged to appear [except] those who are marked out for literature."

At a reasonable hour in Chattanooga, William Henry Lewis, who writes award-winning short stories, spoke of his sense of place. He quoted an old teacher of his as saying, "Nothing happens nowhere." (See **double negative.**

This one *of course* amounts, intentionally and unimpeachably, to a positive, while gaining force from sounding folksily ungrammatical at first.)

At the same literary conference, I heard Wendell Berry—farmer, poet, novelist, and agrarian thinker—make a great speech about being local. He farms in the part of Kentucky where he grew up, and so do his son and his daughter. They raise food for consumption by their neighbors. Tall and calm at seventy-three, but inwardly concerned that he should be home attending to fifty-some-odd new lambs, Berry broke down the Civil War and the war in Iraq in terms of living where your roots are and dealing with people personally, not demographically. As I applauded heartily, I was also thinking, But these days, isn't it kind of Utopian?

See **artisanal**.

➤ *uvula*

From the Latin for "little grape," it's the little fleshy dangle in the back of your throat, an extension of the soft palate. I don't like to look at mine long enough to conclude whether "little grape" fits it. John Keats characterized a person who is prone to melancholy as he "whose strenuous tongue / Can burst Joy's grape against his palate fine." My uvula is not my idea of that grape.

The word itself, however, is so pleasing to the tongue, I'm surprised I've never run into it as someone's name, perhaps in a Flannery O'Connor story. Pronouncing *uvula* doesn't much involve the uvula, which really goes to work in the backwash of the French r sound. I wonder if French uvulae look different, from all the vibrating they do, in expressions like, for instance, *un rhume de poitrine* (a chest cold) or *avoir un chat dans la gorge* (to have a cat—we would say, uh, frog—in one's throat). In French the organ is either *uvule* or *luette*, also a nice name for someone in a story.

See **diaphragm; palate**.

v · V · v

A simple-looking letter, but the most complexly vibrant. It's our only labio-dental voiced spirant: *labio* for (lower) lip, *dental* for (upper) teeth, *voiced* for vocal-cord vibration, and *spirant* (or *fricative* would have done) for breath forced through a narrow passage. *V* gets *ev*-erything going.

You can form a *v* by holding up your first two fingers, spread, but different people can take that sign to mean "victory," "peace," the Boy Scout sign, or "up yours." On paper *V* is an abbreviation for *victory*, **verb**, *very*, *verse*, *versus*, *vide*, *volt*. *V* often contributes a forceful vibe: *vivid*, *vivacious*, *vim*, *vigor*, *vroom*, *va-va-voom*, *visceral*, *virulent*, *vehement*, *voluptuous*, *volatile*, *vinegar*, *vent*, *vital*, *virile*, *vulva*, *volcano*, *vortex*, *vitriol*, *violent*, *voodoo*, *revel*, *swerve*, *veer*, *very*, *viva!* Not to mention *Vo-do-de-o-do*.

Is it arbitrary that the bowed string instruments are *violin*, *viola*, *viola la gamba*, *violincello*? From the Italian *viola*, "probably of imitative origin," says AHD.

Okay, now I'm going to show you what is the most balanced word in English. I'm not going to put it into italics, because then it would be tipped. Okay, here it is: level. Balanced perfectly on the point of middle *v*.

Then let's consider this grouping: *lever*, *swivel*, *swivet*, *pivot*, *revolve*, *rivet*, *waver*, *shiver*, *hover*, *quiver*, *movie*. Various gatherings of energy around the vibrant balance-point *v*. Which is also, fittingly, the central feature of the human body's central feature, the navel.

Oh, and Elvis. It just now hit me that he is not only an anagram of *lives*, as everyone knows, but nearly one of *swivel*. "Elvis's swivel" is close enough to being a palindrome that it's bothersome. If it would go on ahead and be a palindrome, I could have closure. See **swive**.

➤ *valley*

From the **PIE** root *wel-²*, "to turn, roll; with derivatives referring to curved, enclosing objects," says AHD, and here we go:

Willow, *wallow*, *helix*, *whelk*, *walk*, *waltz*, *well*, *wale*, *vault*, *volume*, *involve*, *vulva*, *valve*.

You can see, in the strict visual sense, why *valley* would start with a *v* (and *mountains* with an *m*, and *tree* with a *t*, and maybe even—call me crazy—*fountain* with an *f*).

➤ *vegan*

In keeping with *veggie* (rhymes with *Reggie* and *wedgie*), this word ought surely to be pronounced vedjan. OAD does give that as a second pronunciation, but I've never heard anybody say it that way. Always veegan, with a hard *g*.

Veegan may sound greener, but vedjan sounds crunchier, if you ask me.

Vegetable comes from the Latin for "to enliven." *Vegetate* didn't mean to go stagnant until almost the nineteenth century.

Maybe vegans associate themselves with Vega, the star, whose name comes from the Arabic for "the falling (eagle)." Anybody ever eaten eagle?

➤ veracity

Is not a simple matter. Some people cause more misunderstanding by going around saying exactly what they think all the time, than others by being hypocritical.

> "Son," he [a salesman] said, "I'm not going to . . . tell you not to lie.
> I ain't going to tell you nothing impossible. All I'm going to tell you is
> this: don't lie when you don't have to. Else when you do have to,
> nobody'd believe you."
>
> —*The Violent Bear It Away*, Flannery O'Connor

➤ *verb*

From the Latin for "word." No one has a bad word for verbs. *Word* comes from the same root as *verb*: *wer-*, meaning "to speak." Which is a verb.

Buckminster Fuller said, "God is a verb." He—Fuller—wrote a book, *I Seem to Be a Verb*. The title comes from a longer statement in the book: "I know that I am not a category. I am not a thing—a noun. I seem to be a verb, an evolutionary process—an integral function of the universe."

Not to quibble, but *verb*, *process*, and *function* are nouns. If Fuller had said, "I seem to be a *think*, or a *do*, or a *write*," he would have sounded silly. It is true, however, that a sentence is predicated on the verb—can consist of a verb alone: "Charge!" "Look!" "Quit!"

The noun is the house, the adverbs and adjectives are the decor, and the goings-on are the verb. Granted, *goings-on* is a noun.

So let's not be so figurative. Consider these statements:

"If there's any comparison between the compassion and decency of the American people and the terrorist tactics of extremists, it's flawed logic" —President George W. Bush.

"We're human beings, with the blood of a million savage years on our hands. But we can stop it. We can admit that we're killers, but we won't kill today" —Captain James T. Kirk of *Star Trek*.

The former is based on faith and bluster, and focuses, softly, on nouns (and an adjective). The latter is based on evidence and resolve, and comes down to verbs. We might cite here Rob Corddry's justly celebrated *Daily Show* elucidation of the Bush administration's take on Abu Ghraib:

> Jon, there's no question what took place in that prison was horrible, but the Arab world has to realize that the U.S. shouldn't be judged on the actions of a . . . well, that we shouldn't be judged on actions. It's our *principles* that matter; our inspiring, abstract notions. Remember, Jon, just because torturing prisoners is something we *did* doesn't mean it's something we *would do*.

➤ *verbal*

Should mean "in words," but has become a synonym for *oral* (as in "verbal agreement"), no doubt because people think of *oral* only in connection with surgery and sex. Too bad.

➤ "Verbatim."

Every writer's answer, in her or his heart, to the question, "How would you like to be remembered?"

➤ *verbiage*

Never liked this word. Pejorative. See **language**.

➤ verse

Dorothy Parker said she developed her snappy prose style by writing verse. Not free verse, which is too often even flabbier than prose too often is, but strict metrical forms of verse.

Everyone should knock off a triolet once in a while.

SLIGHTLY IRREGULAR TRIOLET OCCASIONED
BY AN OFFICIAL EXPLANATION IN AN
AIRPORT OF CHICAGO

"We have to seize your toiletries
If liquids/gels exceed three ounces."
For *your* sake (your security's),
They *have* to seize your toiletries.
You didn't weigh your Crest and squeeze . . . ?
There! The keen-eyed sentry pounces.
He has to seize your toiletries
If liquids/gels exceed three ounces.

And see **sonnet**.

➢ *very*

This **adverb** doesn't add much and sometimes makes no sense. When Curt
Schilling, the pitcher, got his three thousandth strikeout in a game that
he lost, he told reporters, "It's very bittersweet." No. Something can be
very bitter or very sweet, but not very bittersweet. Nor very balanced nor
very nuanced. You can't wear your hat at a very rakish angle. And *very best*
is redundant.

The **adjective** is inflationary: "our very reason for being." Somebody
stick a pin in it.

➢ vowels

While my father was rattling **consonants** in the basement, my mother in
the kitchen would be doing her cooking, which made us go *ahhh*, and pro-
jecting her feelings, *ohhh*, *uhhh*, *oooh*: vowels. Had she been of different
ethnic stock, what a keener or an ululater she'd have been. As it was, she
sang old Methodist hymns about walking with Jesus, and came out with
unexpected words like *glory-osky* and *infidel*. And she would hoot or
squeal to let off steam, and she taught me to read pre-school, phonetically, and words have been peculiarly alive for me ever since.

We cannot live on consonants alone. "Playing 'bop' is like playing
Scrabble with all the vowels missing," said Duke Ellington.

They are *a e i o u*. They carry feeling and intent; the consonants (from
"to sound with") are the racks vowels are stretched upon, the poles they
are flown from, the cartons they are packaged in. My hat is off to consonants. But you can have a whole conversation without them:

"'ey!"
"Eeeee!"
"I . . ."
"Oh, you."

➢ voyeur

We are all televoyeurs now, and it doesn't become us. V. S. Pritchett wrote
of his work as a documentary reporter during World War II: "It is fascinat-

ing simply to see strange things, though I saw so many that each experience wiped out the one that preceded it. I was very conscious of being thinned away to the condition of voyeur."

The way people look at each other shapes the way they look to each other. When we look at someone without his or her being able to look back at us, it gives us an illusion of power. Movies and TV make that possible ad nauseam. We are looking at Jeanne Moreau, say, while she is looking at Jean-Paul Belmondo. What business do we have to be there?

➤ *vulva*

Same root (*wel-*[2]) as *waltz, willow, wallow, revolve, valley, helicopter, helix, vault, wallet, volume, evolve, valve.*

The vagina is the deeper organ (it means "sheath" in Latin), but the vulva, though it goes no further than the "vestibule of the vagina," as AHD puts it, *sounds* deeper, doesn't it? *The Vulva Monologues* would be, I don't know, sultrier, wouldn't it?

Not that it's any of my business.

You'd think this lip-poochy bilabial would be called *wa* or *wow*. Instead, it's *double-u*, which makes it the only English letter whose name contains neither the letter itself nor any of the letter's sounds. On top of that, the letter is formed not from two *u*'s (except in script), but from two *v*'s.

Well, there was no *w* in the Latin alphabet. Indeed, scholars tell us, by the time the English alphabet was in the process of formation, Romans had stopped using the sound of *w*. Old English wanted that sound, and where there's a will there's a way. Anglo-Saxon scribes tried two *u*'s side by side. Or, since *u* and *v* were pretty much interchangeable at the time, two *v*'s side by side.

That didn't fly. So scribes thought outside the box. They took a rune, which looked like a pointy *p* and was called *wen* or *wynn*, and made that the Anglo-Saxon *w*.

Okay, runes. They were ancient mystic symbols, a bit more letterlike than hieroglyphics, because they were not just pictorial but also sonic. The *wen* came from a set of them called *futhark*, after the sounds of the first six symbols. According to legend, the Norse god Woden discovered these runes by *sacrificing himself to himself*. That is more or less how he put it, apparently. Offered himself up to himself.

How is that for a concept? It's like cutting off your nose in homage to your face. But who else was he going to offer himself up to? He was the supreme god, who made earth and sky, and in whose name—or is it the rune's name?—we celebrate Wednesdays. Woden wounded himself with a spear and hanged himself from a windswept gallows for nine days, with nothing to eat or drink, until the runes came to him. (The *th* in *futhark* was another rune that the Anglo-Saxons adopted. They called it *thorn* and used it to represent the *th* sounds, soft and hard, for centuries. The *thorn* letter evolved into resembling, visually, a lowercase *y*, which is why we think there is such a thing as "ye olde giftshop.")

Back to *w*. In 1066 the Norman French took over England, and whether or not they were trying to get away from their Norwegian roots, having seen Paree, or whatever—they didn't go for the *wen*. As it happened, they had been using the old double-*u*, which had worked its way over to the Continent, where the Germans were pronouncing it *v* and the French were calling it, roughly, *doobla-vay* (as they do today) but giving it the *w* sound (if I have this right) and using it in proper names. One such name was *William*, the Conqueror, first Norman ruler of England. So even if the Normans had been into runes generally, you have to figure they weren't going to use a rune for that sound. So they replaced *wen* with two *v*'s that soon came to be linked as one letter.

Or something a lot like that. I believe there is some uncertainty on the part of scholars. I know there is some on my part, since for one thing *William* is usually translated into French as *Guillaume*, which I think has something to do with Welsh (Gwilym, you know?). At any rate *w* pronounced wuh in French today is confined to a few words picked up from English, like *whisky* (ignoring, *hélas*, the *h*) and *wattage*. In French the consonantal *w* sound is generally rendered by non-doublet vowel combinations, as in *oui*, which sounds like *we* because it's *oo-ee* run together.

Aren't we glad we don't call our alphabet *futhark*?

➢ *we*

When someone presumes to include you in a *we* you don't want to be part of, as in "We got ourselves into this," here is something you can say:

"Whaddya mean *we*? You got a frog in your pocket?"

➢ weatherese

In 1977 I covered a convention of professional TV weatherpersons— meteorologists—and discovered to my alarm that there was no general agreement as to which was cloudier: mostly sunny, or partly cloudy.

Both *meteorology* and *meteor* come from the Greek for "way up in the air."

➤ *weevil*

From *wee evil*? No, from the same root as *wave*. OED suggests the *wave* connection is to do with "moving about briskly." OED also gives us *weevily*, infested with weevils. A Mrs. C. Praed in 1889 wrote of throwing "a handful of weevily rice" to her hens.

Let us pause to consider that *hen* —like *cantata, chanteuse, cantor*, and *charm* (Latin *carmen*, song, poem)—comes from the root *kan-*, to sing. A hen that seems to be muttering to herself may be humming. Her song about weevily rice wouldn't be the blues, because to a hen the weevils are the best part. *Luck-luck-luck*, she might be singing. An envious hen is one who gets the lesser of two weevils.

Here's another great word from OED:

The verb *to weevle*, as in "The small boy weevles himself out from the boxes." Rare, though, it says. Too bad.

And from Roy Wilder Jr.'s *You All Spoken Here*: "*Hen waller jostle*: A lively movement in place, starting from the bottom and moving up. From the way a hen shakes all over in a dust bath."

➤ *weird*

Has been pretty much watered down into a vaguely **sonicky** (we hear a bit of *weeee-oooo*) substitute for *strange*, but the "weird sisters" of *Macbeth* were way beyond unconventional, and in Middle English *weird* meant "having power to control fate" (AHD). Not even the Hilton sisters qualify there, one hopes.

One of the strange things about *weird* is that it is an exception to the "*i* before *e*" rule (see **mnemonic**). Why can *weird* flout the rule and *wield* has to obey it? The influence of *weir*, or even of **eerie**? As far as I know (not **to my knowledge**), it's *uncanny* (which means, deep down in its root, unknowable).

➤ *well*

"The chicken tastes well" means the chicken is adept at tasting things, and I doubt a chicken's palate is all that discriminating. "Chicken tastes good" may sound inelegant to **some**, but it's correct, not to mention heartier.

"You're looking well" means "You're looking healthy." "You're looking good" means *mmmm*.

Wonder where the various sort of punctuational uses of *well* derive from. Perhaps the original was "Oh, well," meaning "Let's leave well enough alone." But how about "Well!" or "Well, well, well," or "Well, I'll be!" or just "Well, . . ."

Maybe all these *well*'s just well up. The **w** and *eh* sounds are contemplative, and the *l*'s get us rolling.

➢ *wh -*

In *which*, *when*, *where*, *whack*, I pronounce the *h* slightly, at least in my own throat. Dictionaries give hwich or (h)which, and so on, as the preferred pronunciation. But when I bring that *h* up to people, they give me blank looks. They think *whales* has the same sound as *Wales*. Come on, I say, at least you hear a wisp of breathy *h* in *wheeze! Whinney! Whoosh!* They begin to edge away. *Whiff?* I say. *Whisk? Whistle?*

To me there are two *why*'s, one as in "Why, bless my soul," pronounced wy, and the other as in "Why, baby, why?" pronounced hwy. Highly literate friends of mine don't hear the difference. I'll bet dogs do.

In Old English *why* was spelled *hwy* and *what*, *hwaet*. *Where* is from the Old English *hwaer*; *when* from the Old English *hwenne*; *whether* (which even I pronounce without the *h*) from the Old English *hwether*. (See **either**.) *Who*, *whose*, *whom* have lost the *w* sound, but kept the *h*. In Old English they were spelled *hwa*, *hwas*, *hwaem*.

Erewhon, Samuel Butler's **Utopian** novel, is said to be *nowhere* backwards, but it's not, quite—it's a little bit off in the middle of *nowhere*. There is, however, some sort of new-age business establishment in Chicago called (no capital) erehwon.

Surely you hear the *h*'s in *whisper*, *whistle*, *whinny*, *whine*, *whiff*, *whish*, *whoosh*, *whirl*, *whir*, and "It takes two hands to handle a Whopper." Chambers says the current spelling of *whisk* (see **egg**) appears first in 1577, but OED cites *whiske* in 1549, and *Quhiskis* (there's a spelling!) circa 1480.

Hmm. OED at *whisk* says, "The spelling with *wh*- was adopted as being . . ." Which is where it hit me that my obsession with *wh*- had led me to catch OED in an inconsistency: see **symbolic/presentive**.

And **arbitrary**.

➤ what-if history

I distrust anything that tries to establish what would have happened *if*—if Lee had or hadn't done something at Gettysburg, for instance, and the Civil War had gone the other way. The main thing history teaches us, as far as I can see, is that we don't know what happened. And now we're arguing about what would've if it hadn't?

➤ *whistle*

A cheerful sort of word (wet your whistle), but somehow not quite musical enough. Shouldn't there be an r in it, somehow? Little kid in my neighborhood when I was growing up couldn't whistle so he tried to verbalize a whistle noise when calling his dog, Lady: "Whirt, Lady, whirt."

German for "whistle" or "trick" is *Pfif*; for "tricky," *pfiffig*. Somehow *tricky* (see *K*) sounds a lot trickier than *pfiffig*. Germans aren't good at trickiness, perhaps, and maybe it's just as well.

➤ *whom*

Some would have had the Monotones in 1957 sing as follows:

> I wonder, wonder whom,
> Oom bi doo doo whom
>   [BOOM]
> Whom wrote the book of love?

That's because they weren't taught to diagram sentences. Today almost every reputable publication—certainly my daily bread, *The New York Times*—makes cringeworthy who/whom errors. Geoffrey K. Pullum on Language Log, online, says this about using *whom* when *who* is right:

> It's a desperately insecure clutching after a form that people no
> longer know where to use or how to control. *Whom* is like some
> strange object—a Krummhorn, a unicycle, a wax cylinder recorder—
> found in grandpa's attic: people don't want to throw it out, but
> neither do they know what to do with it. So they keep it around,
> sticking an m on the end of *who* every now and then when it seems
> like an important occasion. Columbus Day, for example, or when

trying to impress a grammarian or a maitre d'hotel (whom will be our waiter tonight?). Kiss *whom* goodbye. It is rarely heard in conversation now . . . This word is nearly dead. It has all but ceased to be . . . This is almost an ex-word.

Almost, but there's the rub. If we could dispense with it altogether, then okay. But we can't say "one of who," "both of who," "the rest of who," can we? I suppose in due time we can. But the distinction between *who* and *whom* is useful—makes the language more nimble—in the way that *I/me*, *he/him*, *she/her*, *we/us*, and *they/them* do, and if you have as much command of sentence structure as a mechanic has of nuts and bolts, you shouldn't have any trouble grasping *who/whom*.

If you're stuck as to whether to use *who* or *whom*, substitute *he* and *him*. (Or *she* and *her*.) Would you say, "I wonder whether him wrote the book of love"? No. Therefore, the pronoun is not the object of *wonder*, it is the subject of *wrote the book*. So it's *who*.

If you don't want to grasp the principle, then fall back on *that*: "The maniac that I was running from." Or leave out the pronoun: "The maniac I was running from." And if in doubt, go with *who*. "Ask not who the prophet hath foreseen" is incorrect, and misleading, but you could get away with it in conversation. "Ask not whom cares" is just dumb.

➤ Wilt: A Tall Tale

In 1974, when I was a staff writer for *Sports Illustrated*, I was dispatched to Bel Air, California, to cowrite a story with a giant. It would be Wilt Chamberlain's announcement, "as told to" me, that he was retiring as a basketball player. He had been a great one, maybe the greatest, most likely the strongest. Officially he was seven feet one inch tall and weighed 275 pounds, but he looked bigger. Starting with rather narrow ankles, he grew wider and wider as he went up, and none of him seemed to be fat.

Let me try to put him into perspective:

1. I am about six feet tall, roughly the same size as Peter Carry, an editor at *Sports Illustrated*. In pickup basketball we were about equally forceful on the floor, I would say, which is not saying much, but something.

2. Once Peter was interviewing Dave DeBusschere. DeBusschere was small to be such a great player himself—six feet six inches, 220 pounds. Peter mentioned that he'd always wondered what it was like under the basket in the NBA, all the bumping and straining for position. By way of a response, DeBusschere put the back of his hand against Peter's side and gave him a casual flick that flung him halfway across the room.

3. Once DeBusschere was quoted as saying how close to impossible it was, in the aforementioned jostling, to budge another great player, Bob Lanier, an inch—in part because Lanier stood six feet eleven inches, weighed 250 pounds, and had a tenacious spirit, but also because his feet, famously, were the biggest feet in basketball: size 22.

4. Once Lanier was so persistent in getting between Wilt and the backboard that Wilt lost patience. He grabbed Lanier by the hips, picked him straight up off the floor, feet and all, swung him around, and set him down out of Wilt's way.

5. Once Wilt said something to me as we stood side by side in an elevator, and when I turned to reply I noticed that the part of him that was at my eye level was his elbow. It appeared that there was as much of Wilt above my eye level as below it.

Some years later, Wilt added a dimension to his legend by estimating, in his second autobiography, *A View from Above*, that he had had sex with twenty thousand women. The editor of that book is my friend and some-time editor Peter Gethers. When he came to this figure in the manuscript, he called Wilt and said, "Uh, Wilt, we've been doing the math . . ." It worked out to about nine women a week from age fifteen to age fifty-five.

"Well," said Wilt, "there was this one birthday party . . ."

What strikes me as even more impressive is the idea of *breaking up with* twenty thousand women. The word-of-mouth as to his delicacy must have been pretty good. Another friend of mine had the temerity to ask Wilt how, exactly, he managed not to crush a sexual partner. "I pick her up, put her on the old pole, and spin her around," he said.

As a writing partner, he was no less accommodating. Some people are eloquent orally, but when you take down what they say, quite faithfully, and look at it in cold print, a great deal has been lost. Wilt, on the other hand, sounded like himself on the page: cogent, forthcoming, grammatical. All I had to do was ask him questions, take down his answers, and do some nipping, tucking, and reorganizing.

There was only one problem. This was not Wilt's first as-told-to experience, and he felt that the last one he had done for *Sports Illustrated* had misrepresented him in some regards, notably in the headline. He was doing this story on the strict condition that every word be subject to his approval.

He signed off on the body of the story without a quibble. But now we were sitting in his mountain aerie in Bel Air awaiting the headline. His home, I should mention, was appropriately large. Its ceilings were cathedralish, its views empyrean. Its decor included an element that I haven't seen in any other home: wolf muzzles. Wilt's decorator had acquired a considerable quantity of fur patches from the muzzles of wolves. I wish, in retrospect, that I had inquired into their provenance, but I didn't. Sewn together, they formed a herringbone pattern. Wilt had wolf-muzzle carpets and he had wolf-muzzle upholstery.

He also had several friends on hand, who were not as large as he was, but were large enough to be his friends, and they had taken it upon themselves to protect Wilt from being taken advantage of, as-told-to-wise, again. As we awaited the headline, they milled about, eyeing me narrowly from time to time. Back then, in the pre-computer and even pre-fax age, the transmission of journalistic copy was not instantaneous. Many's the wee hour I spent driving with my typewritten story to an all-night Western Union office, or reading out 2,500 words or so, with punctuation and spelling of unusual words, to a Western Union operator over the phone. By this time, technology had advanced to the point that you could carry around a big bulky "Mojo machine," as Hunter Thompson called it, that plugged into a phone outlet. You'd stick your typescript into it and verrrrry slowly, line by line, it would send a copy to *SI*'s offices in Manhattan.

In this case, it was very slowly bringing from those offices the headline that an editor had written. Wilt was calm, as usual, but his friends were pacing back and forth. The page finished appearing. I pulled it out of the machine. The main headline was MY IMPACT WILL BE EVERLASTING.

Of this, Wilt approved. He had said it, and it was commensurate with his stature. But when I looked at the subhead, I thought, Uh-oh.

A DOMINANT FORCE IN THE NBA, it said, IS RETIRING FROM THE GAME.

I handed it to Wilt. He read it aloud. His friends looked aghast.

"A dominant force?" Wilt asked me.

"Well . . . ," I said, "I think the operative words there are *dominant* and *force*. And you were certainly . . ."

"*A* dominant?" he said.

And his friends were walking around glaring at me and muttering, "*A* dominant? The man was *dominant*. Ain't no *a* to it."

"You perhaps prefer *the* dominant," I said to Wilt. And he nodded. One problem with that was, there were other dominant forces in the NBA. Another was that *The* would make that line too long to fit the space.

So I called the editor. Who had left.

Fortunately, *SI* had a great switchboard operator, Muriel. She was aware of her invaluability, and did not take any guff from anyone. Once *SI*'s imperious, hard-drinking French managing editor, Andre Laguerre, who had served with Charles de Gaulle during World War II, slammed his phone down. After a beat, it rang again. Andre's secretary picked up. She called in to Andre: "It's Muriel, for you," she said.

"*Andry*," said Muriel, "if *evuhry*body in the *build*ing h'*whanged* his receiver, I would have to have *brain surg*ery."

So Andry never whanged his receiver again.

What Muriel could do that made her position so secure was, she could somehow find anybody, wherever they were, and patch them into a conversation. This she did with the editor who had written the "A Dominant" subhead.

Unfortunately, she had found him in the HoHo, a Chinese restaurant and bar that had two features that appealed to *SI* editors. One, it was right next to the Time-Life Building, where *SI* was located. Two, every fourth drink was free. So it didn't hardly pay, when you think about it, not to have eight. And the editor was into about his sixth or seventh as I told him, "I'm here with Wilt, and we got the headlines, main one is fine, but the subhead, he doesn't like 'A Dominant.' He thinks '*The* Dominant' would . . ."

The editor answered me in a way that was all the more frustrating because it sounded sort of like human speech. "Thinguvit . . . Domin'm, a-domin'm . . ."

"I'm here *with* Wilt," I said, and he was looking way, way down at me as I sat on the couch, and there were guys walking around shaking their heads going, "Thing I don't see, you come into a man's *home*, and call him *a* dominant." And the wolf muzzles were bristling underneath me, and I couldn't get anything coherent out of the editor.

"I'm sorry, Wilt," I said. "You're going to have to talk to him."

I passed the phone way, way up to Wilt and he made his case. Invoked his contractual right. Somehow, he seemed to be having a conversation. Even . . .

"Yes, I'm aware what *dominant* and *force* mean. That's not the point. The point is . . . Well, yes, I know, but . . ."

To my astonishment, I heard Wilt being mollified. "All right. Okay," he said. He handed me the phone. The line was dead.

"Who the hell is *Muriel*?" he said.

➤ *win*

According to **Urbandictionary.com**: "with a very broad syntax of usage, generally indicating that something is great," or "succeeding at a task. 'You am *teh* win!'"

➤ *wonky*

Too bad that the word *wonk* has arisen (from no one knows where) to mean one who studies too much, because *wonky*, from the Old English *wancol*, unsteady, is such a good **sonicky** word for something slightly awry, as a cup that won't sit flat or a *wobbly* (also good and sonicky, from the same root as *weave*, *web*, *wave*, and *waffle*, and see *B*) table.

➤ *word*

"In the beginning was the Word," is how the Book of John begins. Well, it *would*, you may say, because John is a book. Today the pixel or the digit or something may have established primacy in the struggle against chaos.

But what do we say when somebody tells the truth, if we're cool?

Do we say, "Pixel"? "Pixel up, my brother," maybe?

No. "Word."

➤ words, dead-tailed

Henry David Thoreau spoke of *ornamentation* as "one of those words with a dead tail which architects very properly use to describe their flour-ishes." *Ornament* would have sufficed Thoreau, but he was no ornamenta-tor. Nor, it is safe to say, did he ever call himself—as do people who make comments on television—a *commentator*, who *commentates*. It's a shame that a commentator's output is called *commentary*, instead of *commenta-tion*, or *commentational* remarks, because then the way would be paved for *commentationalizer*.

➤ words, inadequacy of in certain contexts

Elizabeth Hardwick, in *The New York Review of Books*, refers to a memoir by Gennifer Flowers, *Sleeping with the President*:

> The author meets the often encountered measly aspect of words
> when hoping to describe sexual transport, but she makes her own
> strenuous effort in passage after passage, of which the following is
> the cleanest, we might say. "We continued to make love for several
> more hours, as Bill demonstrated more sexual libido than I have ever
> seen in a man. I'm not sure how many times he came, but he seemed
> to be inexhaustible. I remember thinking this is the kind of drive a
> man needs to become president of the United States."

You might think that Ms. Flowers, to quote Randy Newman, "shouldn't be thinking at all" in such a context. *Sexual libido* is redundant, two words where the second one would suffice (I almost wrote "amply suffice," which would have been the pot calling the kettle scorched), but who's counting?

The electrically prompt (see **adverb**) word here, *of course*, is Hardwick's adjective *measly*.

➤ words, naughty

Soon after his dictionary was published, Dr. Samuel Johnson paid a visit to Mrs. Brooke and Mrs. Digby, sisters, who commended him on his leaving out all naughty words.

"What! my dears!" Johnson exclaimed. "Then you have been looking for them?"

He did include *dung* ("the excrement of animals used to fatten ground"), *cuckold*, *bubby* ("a woman's breast"), *slut*, *prostitute* ("a public strumpet"), *piss*, *pessary* ("an oblong form of medicine, made to thrust up into the uterus upon some extraordinary occasions"), and *fart*, both noun ("wind from behind") and verb. He even gave examples of the last two from poetry, in the first case Suckling's:

> Love is the fart
> Of every heart;
> It pains a man when 'tis kept close;
> And others doth offend, when 'tis let loose.

In the second, Swift's:

> As when we a gun discharge,
> Although the bore be ne'er so large,
> Before the flame from muzzle burst,
> Just at the breech it flashes first;
> So from my lord his passion broke,
> He farted first, and then he spoke.

The sisters must have been looking for harder stuff.

➤ words, vis-à-vis life

V. S. Pritchett, in *Midnight Oil*, on his loquacious father:

> "You bore people. You go on too long," Mother would say from the
> sofa where she lay, longing for respite. The fact is that life had been so

totally translated into words for him that it had become meaningless. As a writer I am uncomfortably aware of the warning in this.

See *logocentric*.

➤ Wordsworth, William

De Quincey says that Wordsworth would grow impatient when anyone else spoke of mountains.

➤ *worthy enough*

No, no. Redundant. It's like "sufficiently satisfied," "more consummated"; it is watering down by piling on, rendering only notional the coin of the realm.

"Dollars to donuts." I daresay now there are donuts that cost more than a dollar apiece. Okay, that is economic inflation, which apparently we have to live with, though there's no gainsaying how destabilizing it is. But being unable to keep up with what dollars are worth isn't as treacherous as being unable to keep up with what words are worth.

"No one knows what's going on with all those numbers," said David Stockman, who was in charge of seeming confident of being able to keep up with those numbers, in the Reagan administration. What if we get to the point that no one knows what's going on with all those words?

Maybe we have. Got to that point. If so, I'm not ready to admit it. It's up to those of us who care about words to hang on to their intrinsics and their connections—connections to the world, and to our minds and fingers. We don't have to contribute to the inflation of words. We have to struggle to keep words from becoming *arbitrary*.

➤ *wring*

The *w* was pronounced in Anglo-Saxon. Now *wring* sounds no different from *ring*, but the *w* adds something. You wouldn't *wring* out the New Year, and you wouldn't *ring* out a rag. (Reggie Jackson, speaking of retirement, said he didn't want to "keep on wringing out the rag of ability.") Compare *wrestle*, *wrest*, *wretched*, and the sublimely uncomfortable *writhe*.

➤ **writing, when it isn't going smoothly, something to think about**

A blistering afternoon at a boat landing in the Florida panhandle, on the Gulf of Mexico. One man has backed an old corroded pickup truck bumper-deep into the water. His coworker, standing in a big flat cement-grey skiff full of nondescript, fadingly silvery little fish—shiners, generically—that they have dragnetted, begins to toss shovelfuls of the dead and dying fishlets into the truckbed. The first man sets the truck's brake, climbs into the back, grabs a rake, and starts leveling the load.

The fish-meal business. The shovel grates across the boat-bottom, smushed-shiner smears providing only intermittent lubrication, *grrrnk'f . . . grrrnk*, the sun beats down, the men are sweating, fish scales and guts smear their hands and arms and clothes and the work goes on.

The man with the shovel sees me watching and stops, and spits, and says in an equable tone:

"Only thing wrong with this kind of fishing, it's hard on a truck."

➤ **"written by" movie credit**

It's good for writers to get some appreciation. When movie actors feel free to improvise, complexities of character and story tend to give way. But:

You can't write a motion picture.

➤ *wrought*

Something imposing about this word. It has *rough* in it, **of course**, but that is of interest only to people (such as me) who wonder who put the *ugh* in *thoughtful*; who relish reading in the British press that one member of Parliament has called another a "malevolent vole"; who can't help seeing the five guys pushing fifty in the Royal Albert Hall:

> We're the five guys pushing fifty
> In the Royal Albert Hall:
> Roy and Al, the other Al,
> And Bert and Hal—and all
> Aligned in front of letter *L*,

> Which, you may recall
> From days of olden Rome has been
> A Roman noo-mer-all . . .

Foolishness. Not worthy of the word *wrought*, which is not the past tense of *wreak*, as is often assumed, but of *work*, in the sense of making something, forming something, bringing something about. (*Wreak*, which is related to *wrack*, *wreck*, and *wretch*, and which always means to bring about something negative, as in *wreak revenge*, overlaps with *wrought* in that you can say either *wreaked havoc* or *wrought havoc*.)

Here's a sentence I wrought with pleasure:

> How remarkable that *wrought*—the archaic but one might say revenant past tense not of *wreak*, as is often thought, but of *work*, in the sense "to work a miracle," or, I suppose, "to work a room" ("He did all the right drop-by's, wrought the right rooms")—contains *rough*.

"With pleasure," that is, until I sat back and tried to read it. Let me—no, no, I insist—be the first to concede that that sentence is overwrought. Too worked up. Not as in overcome by anxiety, but as in too elaborately de-signed. (Like overwrought iron.) I have had to dismantle the whole con-struction and start over.

Archaic though the word *wrought* is, it has stayed alive, in *overwrought* and in reference to the epochal message Samuel F. B. Morse sent, in 1844, over the electromagnetic telegraph that he had invented. Congress had at last come through with funds that had enabled him to lay a line between Wash-ington and Baltimore. Morse sat down in the U.S. Supreme Court chamber and, in the dot-dash Morse code he had devised, personally tapped out for the ages:

"Well, strip down and get relaxed."

No, I'm being foolish again. Morse would never have sent such a message.

That is an instant-message **e-mail**, which, as I write this, happens to be the big Washington news—bigger than Morse's inaugural message was when he sent it.

The "strip down" message is one that a congressman, as he was waiting for a vote to be called, sent to a teenage boy. So this, we might say, is what the miracle of electronic transmission has come down to, since that first brave new beginning. From that historic moment of high honor and no-ble promise, the nation has descended into man-boy cybersex. But before we indulge in **now-bashing**, let's take a closer look at back then.

Morse's virulent issues were more theological than sexual. So far as we know, his only brush with lechery was by way of exposé: a passionate anti-Catholic, he put out a book entitled *Confessions of a French Catholic Priest*, which purported to lay bare a Papist clergy driven by unnatural vows of celibacy into fornication, necrophilia, and cover-up dismemberment. Morse was at the time a widower well along into twenty-four years of am-bivalently courting, and either backing away from or being rejected by, various women half his age. To one of these he wrote: "The more I have thought of you friend C. the more I felt disposed to keep my thoughts locked up, for I am not so ignorant of myself as not to know that my too sensitive feelings were not always under the control of a judgment which ought to be mature from years." Eventually he would marry a pleasant woman thirty years his junior who was poor, deaf, pious, and reassuringly appreciative. They would have three children who would not turn out much better than the three from his first marriage, whom he had ne-glected while pursuing his dream of transporting thought through wire.

His father, Jedediah, had been the pre-eminent geographer of his day. Morse had expected to achieve equal prominence as a portrait painter, but when he was not chosen as one of the artists for the interior of the new U.S. Capitol, he had put all his chips on his telegraph idea. Now he was bigger than Jedediah had ever been.

The message Morse sent was, *of course*, "What hath God wrought."

From the Old Testament Book of Numbers. The children of Israel are wandering in the desert smiting every tribe that gets in their way. The king of Moab, not wanting to have to deal with the Israelites militarily, hires a Mesopotamian soothsayer named Balaam to put a curse on them. Balaam looks into the situation and decides that God wants him to bless the Israelites instead. He prophesies that Israel will "rise up as a great lion" and "drink the blood of the slain," to which the reaction will be, "What hath God wrought!"

Or, if you prefer the World English Bible's more contemporary trans-lation, "What has God done"—which sounds like it ought to be followed by "this time, for God's sake?"

Here, at any rate, was what:

For the first time (if you set aside smoke signals, aboriginal drums, Appalachian hollering, and semaphore), information could travel faster than people could hand-carry it. Could travel in fact at literally the speed of lightning. The media reaction, as we would say today, was rapturous. This providential new invention dispelled any fears that America had become too vast and populous to be held together. Dispersed families could now be constantly in touch: "This extraordinary discovery leaves . . . no elsewhere—it is all *here*." The end of all war was foreseen. In his excellent biography of Morse, Kenneth Silverman describes the consensus:

> Ultimately nations would be wired to each other, making the planet a neural map, what the *Christian Observer* called a "sensorium of communicated intelligence." Acting through the global cyborg, God's grand processes would realize His grand design of leading humanity toward salvation. As the *New York Herald* put it, "What a future!"

In the press now Morse was the Lightning Man. A congressman rose in the House to say: "His name is immortalized and will remain as long as time shall endure." "My praises," he told his brother Sidney, "ring from one end of the country to the other." He said he found himself exclaiming to *himself*, "What hath God wrought!"

Seventeen years later, the nation's North and South were engaged in a mutual bloodbath, of more than biblical proportions, and Morse was morose. He saw the Civil War as a "British aristocratic plot" designed to weaken American influence in the world. And although he was a Massachusetts native living in New York, he was also a devout defender of slavery. Lincoln's Emancipation Proclamation was to Morse "infamous, and ridiculous if it were not so wicked," an "abominable hallucination."

Morse's grounds were religious: "My fundamental axiom is the *degeneracy of man*." He denounced the religious liberals who had pushed Abolition—"the Christ rejecting humanitarian, the Bible spurning infidel, the pseudo merciful universalist, and the nothingarian, [who gave to] *freedom* & *liberty* an earthly, low, civil & political sense, as if an indiscriminate social & political liberty of every human being were the scope and end of man's redemption."

Some of the "self-evident truths" on which the Declaration of Independence based itself were "self-evident falsehoods," Morse argued. "*Slavery*, the subjection of one's will to the will of another, since the fall of man, is the rule, and not *liberty*." As for self-evidence, black people's features were visibly a debasement of "the human face divine."

Even after the war and in the North, these politics were by no means as "incorrect," as we say today, as today we might assume. Morse caught some *flak* for his pro-servility stance, but not as much as he did for accepting from the sultan of Turkey a gold brooch, studded with two hundred diamonds, which betokened his membership in that country's Order of Glory—"a Model of the Chiefs of the Nation of the Messiah," said the diploma. Legally, said carping voices in the press, this made him a pasha, a title which according to the U.S. Constitution should require him to forfeit U.S. citizenship.

But no one pressed him on the pasha thing. (He had impressed the sultan by running a telegraph wire from his palace to his harem and showing—by what message is not recorded—that it worked.) He received, and wore, decorations from many countries—even that of a Cavaliero Commandador of the Spanish Order of Isabella the Catholic. A statue of him was erected in New York's Central Park. His patents and his investment in Western Union had made him duly wealthy. His invention was acclaimed as "the greatest triumph of the human mind."

And yet Silverman's book—otherwise remarkably unjudgmental and even unsummational—is entitled *Lightning Man: The Accursed Life of Samuel F. B. Morse*.

The Lightning Man's "last four years," writes Silverman, "were a grim crescendo of unhappiness and abuse." He was still stewing over his failure to be accorded the eminence he felt he'd deserved as an artist, and when he tried to pick up the brush again after thirty years or so, he had lost his touch. His children, who had grown up either hapless or wild or both, were sources of grief to him (one, after killing a man, would become a cowboy in Buffalo Bill's Wild West show). But most of all, Morse was outraged and deeply depressed by the efforts of scoundrels and former colleagues to deny him full and sole credit for his invention. Whenever someone suggested even a friendly improvement, he would insist that he had already thought of that: "An arrangement for prolonging the *sound* of the *dash* in two ways, differing from yours, I put in operation back in 1844." Rhetorically God had wrought the telegraph, but Morse was dead set on going down as the man.

Silverman gives the last word on Morse's death to a former congressman named Smith who was by no means the model for *Mr. Smith Goes to Washington*. This Representative Smith had been instrumental in funding the telegraph project, but then he'd started going after chunks of the action. "Where I expected to find a *friend* I find a *FIEND*," Morse wrote. Since then Smith had done all he could to chip away at the Lightning Man's earthly immortality. Now, in a letter to another of Morse's detractors, Smith gloated: It was too bad the old man hadn't lasted longer, to face the latest charges they had brought against him, but they could console themselves in the belief that they had hastened his demise, by "overload[ing] his brain" with "strong visions" of "*receding glory*."

What a thing to say, about someone so freshly off to the big Glory. But Smith may have had Morse's number. Brought out his pedestal-philia, we might say, so that he died overwrought. There are all kinds of foolishness.

See **lightning**.

➤ *Wyoming*

I know the state is named for an Indian word meaning "large plains" (chosen for its sound rather than applicability to such a mountainous state), but doesn't it look like a gerund? There needs to be a verb. Wouldn't it be nice to read this news item:

> Now Wyomingians, if that is the word, can really enjoy their new state verb. Because now they know what it means. The verb, *to wyome*, was coined early this year by Jimson Gulley, a drive-time talk-show host on KWYO radio in Cheyenne. *Wyome* caught on to the point of spawning countless bumper stickers around the state saying, "Do You Wyome?" and "R U a Wyomer?" and "Wyomers Do It in Thin Air." But no one had quite *defined* the term until the results of KWYO's "What *Wyome* Means to Me" poetry contest were announced this week. Some of the more than 12,000 entries were not very wyological, like "When I wyome I lope like an antelope, / Because I can, like a cantaloupe," but twelve-year-old Bitsy Whitsell of Indian Fork struck what judges ruled was just the right note:

> You ask me why do I wyome?
> It means I love my state, my home.

x · **X** · x

Standing alone, it has more uses than the biggest Swiss army knife: a cross, a kiss, a sign of obscenity, an illiterate's signature, the spot where the treasure is. Times. *O*'s foe. A cancellation. Replacement for a letter in a word deemed unprintable. Wrong on the test. A drug whose full name is ecstasy. Christ. A vote. In cartoons, the eye of a person who's unconscious or drunk. An unknown or variable. Malcolm's surname. Ten.

Within a word, it's lively—a sound close to that of *kiss*, but further back in the throat, *eks*. Quicker, orally less complicated to pronounce than *sk*, which is surely why some people say "ax" for *ask*. "Ax me something" flows, "ask me" gets hung up on that *k*, you've got to let it go, *kuh*, and then move on. *Asked* is particularly clunky to pronounce, so people resort to "axt."

Doesn't the *x*—marking the spot—at the end of *fix* add to that word's intrinsic fixativity? If you were designing the English language from scratch, you wouldn't use the word *fumble*, say, to mean "place securely; make firm," would you? Nor would you designate *fumble* to mean *fit*, whose terminal letter fits it to a T.

➤ *x*

As in to x something out, it is the smallest unabbreviated verb in the English language. I can think of only two other single letters used as unabbreviated verbs. One is *k*, the baseball-scorecard symbol (of unknown origin) for a strikeout, used as a verb: Clemens k'd twelve. The other is *T*, meaning in basketball a technical foul, which becomes a verb when we say that a referee T'd someone up. Come to think of it, both of those sports terms tend to be used pretty exclusively in the past tense, which would make them, in practice, longer than one letter. At any rate both k and T are larger than a lowercase x, which is what is generally used in x-ing.

➢ *xyster*

Here's a Greek word that means what it (shudder) sounds like: a surgical instrument for scraping bones.

y · **Y** · y

Yes, ja, sí, oui, aye-aye, yay, I, my. What do all these words have in common? They are all affirmative. And they all either begin or end in the consonantal *y* sound. Spanish *si* or Italian *sí* flows into German *ja* as when we say, "Seeya later." And what goes on in your mouth as you make that *y* sound? Your lips are slightly parted and your tongue is cupped against your palate and working inward in exactly the way a nursing babe pulls on a nipple. If you are not in a relationship conducive to checking this out, just say *yum*, and try to remember.

    See *M*; *E*; *yeah*; *rhythm*.

➤ *y'all*

Not *ya'll*: that would be a contraction of *ya all*, or of *ya will*. This is a contraction of *you all*, therefore plural. People who grew up with this word face the Sisyphean task of correcting people who didn't and who insist that it is sometimes singular.

David Crystal, Honorary Professor of Linguistics at the University of Wales, Bangor, reports in his book *The Stories of English* that on his first visit to the United States, "I had my earliest face-to-face encounter with *y'all*." In Fort Worth, Texas, he entered a store that sold cowboy hats.

> The assistant greeted me with a *Howdy y'all* and a *What can I do for y'all*, and it was so unexpected that I actually looked round to see who else he was referring to . . . But I was the only one there. As I left, he said, *Y'all take care now*.
>
>   Outside I began listening seriously to the use of *y'all*. On the whole it did seem to be used when addressing more than one person, though sometimes the people were being viewed as a single body.

Let me say that I am often startled, myself, by British attempts to capture colloquial American speech. Malcolm Bradbury, in *Stepping Westward*, has a character say, "Now we all know that Harris boobed a bit in not making enough enquiries." Trevor Homer, in *The Book of Origins*, tells us that the astronaut Michael Collins is supposed to have said to Neil Armstrong, with regard to what his first words on the moon should be, "If you'd got any balls, Neil, you'd say, 'Oh my God, what is that thing?'"

Even if I were willing to stipulate that this "assistant" said what Crystal says he said, I wouldn't hold still for Crystal's leaping to this question:

> If *you* vs *y'all* doesn't convey a contrast of number (singular vs
> plural), then what does it convey? . . . A plausible suggestion is that
> *y'all* is "warmer," a sign of familiarity, friendliness, informality, and
> rapport, at least among young people. A 1970s study found it being
> commonly used by younger Virginians to convey this kind of
> warmth. However, many older people are still somewhat suspicious
> of it, and do not use it, perhaps associating it with past ethnic
> tensions, or finding it patronizing.

It may be that there was a fad of singular *y'all* among Virginian teenagers in the seventies, as the study Crystal cites—reported in *American Speech* in 1975—suggests. But that would hardly justify the generalization "if *you* vs *y'all* doesn't convey a contrast of number." A later comment in *American Speech* (where the singular *y'all* has been debated back and forth for thirty years now) seems right to me: "Arguments in support of putative singular *y'all* depend either on (1) data that is an artifact of the research situation or (2) a mistaken understanding of the pragmatics of the purported utterance."

Consider Crystal's concession that "sometimes the people were being viewed as a single body." Quite the opposite: when someone says to a waitress, "What do y'all have for dessert?" her single body is being viewed as representing several people—the ones who run the restaurant.

"As for my store assistant," writes Crystal, "I certainly felt he was being 'customer-friendly.'" Indeed. The one time in my life that I have been singularly addressed as "y'all" was on walking into a souvenir shop in New Orleans some years ago.

"*What?*" I inquired, looking around for the rest of me.

The person behind the counter shrugged. "The tourists like it," he said.

So if you're a salesman, especially one who, like this one, was from Ohio, go ahead and use singular *y'all*. But if you're a writer, interested in getting things right, or anyway credible, consider this comment by Mark Liberman on the Language Log website, September 18, 2005:

> In a "true-life tale" in today's NYT Magazine titled "Yoga, Y'all," Elizabeth Gilbert suggests that eastern spirituality . . . sounds faintly ridiculous, to people like her, when translated into a southern-states idiom . . .
>
> It's a good story, even if it demonstrates yet again that outlets like . . . the *New York Times* will revel in jokes at the expense of the southern U.S. that they'd never print if the target of ridicule were almost any other culture.
>
> However, I suspect that Ms. Gilbert invented many of the details . . . The first of her southern-fried quotations is, my language consultants tell me, regionally ungrammatical: "My new yoga teacher . . . bounded up to me, placed her nose an inch from mine and demanded, 'What's y'all's name?' with such friendly enthusiasm it made me wish I had more names."
>
> Cute. But all the American southerners I've ever asked about this tell me that they would never use *y'all* in reference to a single individual, no matter how many names he or she might have.

In *American Speech* in 1984, Gina Richardson of Georgetown University described an experiment she conducted, involving a series of tricky questionaires, that established to her satisfaction that "the traditional interpretation of *y'all* is indeed the valid one—*y'all* is an exclusively plural second person pronoun meaning 'more than one.'" It is true, she says, that she once heard an old friend of her father's greet her father as "y'all." The friend couldn't have been including her in the greeting, because she was entirely unexpected and hadn't yet entered the room. She might have sighed and concluded that, after all, there must be such a thing as a singular *y'all*.

But she didn't. She asked her father's friend what the deal was. He chuckled. Since her father's name was Elwood, the friend liked to tease him by invoking Elwood P. Dowd, the bibulous character, played by

Jimmy Stewart, who had an invisible rabbit friend named Harvey in the movie *Harvey*. The *y'all* was for Elwood and the rabbit.

➤ *yawp*

Walt Whitman boasted of his "barbaric yawp," and good for him. Now America has got itself backed into the corner of claiming to be defending *civilization*, of all things. Not our strong suit.

➤ *yeah*

You see this word spelled *ya*, or *yah*. You don't see it that way in the dictionary. Nor do you hear it that way, when a person who means it pronounces it. *Yeh*, maybe. But to get all the good out of it you have to say it, and spell it, *yeah*.

z · Z · z

The British call the letter *zed*, making it the only letter commonly spelled out into a more than one-letter word (*em* and *en* are printers' terms for spaces, and *queue* is not about the letter), except for *aitch*, a word which the British had to come up with because some of them—those of low aspiration, you might say—drop them.

There's an American dialect variation on *zed*: *izzard*. Rhymes with *blizzard*, *gizzard* (see **giblet**, in case you missed it along the way here), and *lizard*. None of these words has anything in common, etymologically, with any of the others. That's American English for you: more roots than a mangrove swamp.

In *King Lear*, the Earl of Kent tells Goneril's servant Oswald that he is "a knave; a rascal; an eater of broken meats; a base, proud, shallow, beggarly, three-suited, hundred-pound, filthy, worsted-stocking knave; a lily-livered, action-taking [settling quarrels by law instead of arms], whoreson, glass-gazing, superserviceable, finical rogue; one-trunk-inheriting slave; one that wouldst be a bawd, in way of good service, and art nothing but the composition of a knave, beggar, coward, pandar, and the son and heir of a mongrel bitch," and then "a whoreson cullionly barber-monger," and, finally, to top it all off, "Thou whoreson zed! Thou unnecessary letter!"

In Shakespeare's day, the letter z (the italic version of which is just **wonky** enough to be slightly unsettling) was often not included in dictionaries. People knew there was such a letter, going back to the Greeks, but the hard s could do its job, as indeed it does in words like—well, like *does*, but I was (and words like *was*) going to say *is*. Z had once been ejected from the Roman alphabet, perhaps by Appius Claudius, who is said to have hated it because when pronounced it reminded him of an old man hissing through bad teeth, but it had made its way back in. Shakespeare didn't use many words starting with *z*, but he used *zeal* thirty-three times. Did he spell it with an *s*? "What seal, what fury, hath inspired thee now?" "Honest Bardolph, whose seal burns in his nose?" We don't have his manuscripts, *of course*, but the First Folio, whose printer was Edward Blount, uses zeds. So much for the Earl of Kent.

There's *z*-juice in the buzz of bees and in the *bzzt* that a zap of electricity makes, at least in the movies—and when a mosquito flies into one of those bug-zappers, *though* I have always suspected that the audio on those is enhanced to make you think they're doing more than they are. Something like an electrical charge is carried by *z*'s in sparky, dynamic words mostly assumed to be imitative: *zap, zing, zoom, zip, zest, zowie, zigzag, zounds, sizzle, dazzle, snazzy, frizzy, fizz, jazz, whiz, grizzly, razzle-dazzle, razzmatazz, pizzazz, Shazam!* Also *enzyme* and a number of words, like *zymosis*, connected with fermentation. *Fizzle*, by the way, originally meant "fart"; it became more respectable by means of its connection to the sound of a firework fizzling out.

A visually juicy *Z* is the dash-slash-dash zigzag mark of Zorro, most memorably applied to the clothing of the **zaftig** Catherine Zeta-Jones in *The Mask of Zorro*. (Her Zeta, properly pronounced Zee-ta, is from one of her grandmothers, who was named for a ship. Her **hyphen** is used only professionally.)

Less often, *z* is connected with emptiness, or dead-endedness: *zero, zilch, zonked, zone out, zombie*. Then there's *zzzzz* as in snoring—but that is not the noise of snoring. It's the noise of a metaphor for snoring: "sawing logs." Since a *z* issues from the front of the mouth and a snore from back in the throat, the more **sonicky** cartoonese for snoring would be something on the order of *gggkk*, and in Japanese comics, as a matter of fact, people snore *g-g-g-g-g*. Better would be an extended *ch* as in German *ach*. The German for "to snore" is in fact *schnarchen*. German is made for snoring. *Accccchhhh-Pflug*. The French *ronfler* is too polite. (This may be the place to cite **Flaubert**'s observation in his *Dictionary of Accepted Ideas*: "It is clever raillery to say: 'Russian and Polish are not spoken, they are **sneeze**d.'" That's Jacques Barzun's translation into English, *of course*. Flaubert wrote: 'ÉTERNUER: *C'est une raillerie spirituelle de dire: le russe et le polonais ne se parlent pas, ça s'éternue.*" Only with *ça s'* does *éternue* evoke a wholehearted sneeze.)

➢ *zaftig*

Means plump in a good way; with a well-rounded figure; full-bodiedly curvy. But it comes from the Yiddish *zaftik*, juicy, succulent. Same root, way back, as in *sap*, the juice in a tree.

➢ *zany*

From Giovanni, a name of servants acting as clowns in commedia dell'arte.

➢ *zarf* or *zurf*

In old Turkey, a holder to keep your hand from being burned by a cup of hot coffee. It might be of filigreed silver or fragrant ebony wood or tortoiseshell or ivory, and sometimes it was studded with gems or coral. Today's equivalent is a sleeve of plastic or cardboard. The exotic *zarf* has some playful currency today (see **Urbandictionary.com**), but let us not ignore the savor of *sleeve*, from the same root as *slip*, as in "to slip on or slip into." And how about *cup*? A good, apt, orally pleasing word, it comes from an old family of hollow or round things, including *hip* and the German *Kopf*, head. We might like to connect *cup* to *cop*, for policeman (short for *copper*, a catcher), but now we're talking a separate etymological line, including *capture* and the verb *cop*, as in "cop a plea," "cop out," "cop a feel." Etymonline.com dates *cup* meaning "part of a bra that holds a breast" to 1938.

➢ *ze*

Put forward on **Urbandictionary.com**—and receiving mostly positive votes—as a "gender neutral" pronoun: "Ze is wearing such a cute shirt!" In opposition someone signing zeself "briggite" argues that *ze* means *the* in "a fake french accent." This opinion also receives mostly positive votes.
    See *he/she/his/her*.

➤ *zephyr*

The letter z was borne into Latin—whence it passed eventually into English—in a way that evokes Stephen Foster's dreamt-of Jeanie with the light brown hair.

That is to say, it was borne on a zephyr: the Romans added the Greek z to their alphabet after conquering Greece because they needed it to spell words borrowed from the Greek, for instance *zephyrus*, zephyr, from the Greek *zéphyros*, west wind. This is a good excuse to quote that great early English poem by Anonymous:

> Oh Western Wind, when wilt thou blow,
> The small rain down can rain?
> Christ! That my love were in my arms
> And I in my bed again.

(See my memoir *Be Sweet*, if I do say so myself, for a more extensive tribute to this poem.)

➤ *zero*

The Italians made this word end in *o*, as it should. Medieval Latin had it *zephirum*, from the Arabic *sifr*, nothing, whence our *cipher*. No dictionary makes any etymological connection between *zero* and **zephyr**, but it's something to think about, since a zephyr is so insubstantial.

➤ *zeugma*

Same root, *yeug-*, as *yoke* and *zygote*. It means applying a single word, especially a verb or adjective, in more than one sense to more than one noun.
Verb:
"With that, he stepped into a cowpie and the pages of history."
Adjective:
"Gimme a kiss."
"Your chance of that is as fat as your head."
Verb, again:
"When Teacher asked, 'Who can tell me what *solar plexus* means?,' nervous nerdy Erwin threw up his hand and his lunch."

➤ *zigzag*

From the French *ziczac* and German *zickzack*. I have to say, ours is better. Those *ck* or hard *c* sounds are hitches that hold too long; our *g* takes just long enough to evoke a change in direction that's marked but quick. So why did I fall back on those *k*'s, you may ask. Well, a *k* is generally crackly— for instance, *lickety-split*. But a *k* before a *z* requires a transition that is anatomically jerky for reasons that I will let you work out in the privacy of your own oral cavity.

➤ *zloty*

Seems like a funny word for a country's (Poland's) principal unit of currency, but it's Polish for "golden." The Dutch *guilder* is "golden" in that language. The Danish and Norwegian *øre*, the Swedish *öre*, and the Icelandic *eyrir* derive from *aurum*, the Latin for "gold." South Africa's *rand* comes from Witwatersrand, one of the world's richest gold mining areas. In Ghana, the *cedi*, which may come from a word for a small shell, is worth a hundred *pesewa*, from a word for "dark blue seed of a plant," which was once used as the smallest weight-measure of gold. Perhaps in a related vein, so to speak, Zambian money is the *kwacha*, equal to a hundred *ngwee*; those two words mean, respectively, "dawn" and "bright." And the Peruvian *sol* means "sun." On the other hand, the Botswanian *pula* means "rain." Or not on the other hand: people greet each other in Botswana with that word, which implies good fortune—in some countries, rain is rare as gold.

Less poetic is the etymology of the Greek *drachma*: from the verb for "to grasp."

➤ *zoology*

Pronounced zo-ology. Not zoo-ology. *Look at the letters*. Count the *o*'s.

➤ *zydeco*

From *les haricots*, the beans, pronounced with a thuddy sort of *r*: lay-za(*d*)-ico.

If music be the food of love . . . Or is it the love of food? Salsa is hot sauce, zydeco comes from beans, and jazz was invented (at least according to the man himself, Jelly Roll Morton) by a man named Jelly Roll. Rock groups have had food-associated names from Creem to Korn. Many people call an ocarina a sweet potato. The African "juba beat," one of the most essential riffs of rock 'n' roll, has been more popularly known as the hambone. How would we talk about jazz without the use of "chops," "cooking," "tasty," and "jam"? And if you don't think "jam" as in "jam session" has anything to do with food, you're forgetting Fats Waller's "Black Raspberry Jam," and his verbal asides thereto, like "Spread that jam around, yehhhhh."

➤ *Zyzzyva*

A class of **weevil**s. Last word in AHD. From the sound that that weevil characteristically makes.

So. Perhaps this is the place to quote **Flaubert**'s *Dictionary of Accepted Ideas* entry on **book**: "Always too long, regardless of subject."

Or Herman Melville to Nathaniel Hawthorne, after finishing *Moby-Dick*: "Am I not now at peace? Is not my supper good?"

Aah.

Acknowledgments

Of the many enablers of this book, the only ones uncredited in the text, I think, are the most important: my agent, Esther Newberg; my editor, Sarah Crichton; and the blasted/blessed copy editor and proofreader, Don McConnell and Karen Mugler, who picked nits that would have haunted me to the grave. I've always wanted to write a book like this, and thanks to them, I have.

Roy Blount Jr. grew up in Decatur, Georgia, attended Vanderbilt University and Harvard Graduate School, was a staff writer at *Sports Illustrated*, and has contributed to many publications, including *The New Yorker*, *The New York Times*, *The Atlantic Monthly*, and the *Oxford American*. He is a panelist on National Public Radio's *Wait, Wait . . . Don't Tell Me* and a member of *The American Heritage Dictionary*'s Usage Panel. He lives in western Massachusetts with his wife, the painter Joan Griswold.